The **Rough Guide** to

Naples & the Amalfi Coast

written and researched by

Martin Dunford

with additional contributions by

Jeffrey Kennedy and Katie Parla

www.roughguides.com

Contents

Cucina napoletana
colour section
following p.112

Theatrical Naples
colour section following
p.160

Colour maps following
p.272

Naples ▲ Mt Vesuvius

3

◄◄ Largo del Corpo di Nilo statue, Naples ◄ The Duomo, Amalfi

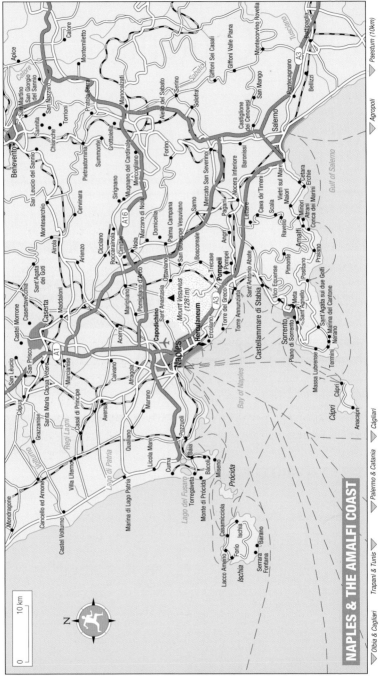

NAPLES & THE AMALFI COAST

0 — 10 km

Introduction to

Naples & the Amalfi Coast

Italy's third largest city after Rome and Milan, Naples couldn't be more different from its counterparts further north. Waves of invaders, from the Greeks to the Bourbons, have washed up here, making the city a unique hybrid: the ancient centre still bears the imprint of the Greeks and Romans, while a wealth of monumental Baroque buildings are the legacy of Spanish rule, and breezy seafront promenades give parts of the city a riviera-type feel. The city's prime vantage point in the Bay of Naples, within easy reach of an array of attractions, is a further draw: some of Europe's greatest archeological sites are scattered around the bay, not to mention the seismic wonders of Mount Vesuvius and the Campi Flegrei; Italy's most jaw-dropping stretch of coast snakes around Amalfi just a few miles south; and the fabled islands of the bay are so close that they're virtually suburbs of the city.

But it's the locals themselves that really set this region apart. All the pride and resentment of the Italian south, all the historical differences between the two wildly disparate halves of Italy, are sharply brought into focus here, particularly in Naples: both a lawless, petulant city that has its own way of doing things, and an intensely Catholic one, its streets punctuated by bright neon Madonnas cut into niches, and its miraculous cults regulating the lives of the people much as they have always done.

The Naples region comes with a lot of baggage; plenty of Italians have never been here, and swear that they never will. Internationally, too, its reputation isn't high, and has only worsened as the ongoing and well-publicized struggle against the mafia plumbs new depths. However, just two centuries ago Naples was one of the largest cities in Europe, and one of its greatest attractions, a must-visit for any self-respecting grand tourist. With Italian Unification, however, the power of the new capital, Rome, increased while that of Naples waned; it never recovered its earlier prosperity, and is still run down in many aspects.

▼ Vómero balcony, Naples

But with caution, and good information, Naples is no more dangerous than anywhere else in Italy: the city has undergone something of a renaissance in the last decade or so, and is a more accessible, more dynamic and above all an easier and more enjoyable place to visit than it used to be. Previously off-limits churches and palaces have opened their doors to the public, and the transport network around the city and the Bay of Naples is now better integrated, with extensions to the metro system in the pipeline, only held up by archeological digs. And all around the bay, the hotel and restaurant scene has kept pace, too, with boutique B&Bs and chic bars opening up, offering a nod to contemporary style without sacrificing local traditions.

Where to go

The diversity of attractions on offer in Naples and its region means that – time permitting – you can pack a lot into your holiday. With just a **weekend** to spare, Naples makes a great city-break option, giving you the right amount of time to cover the main sights, as well as wander enough of the atmospheric centro storico to get a feel for the place; if you have a **week** at your disposal, you could also take in some of the bay's famous archeological sights, as well as spend a couple of days island-hopping – or bypass the city altogether and take the dramatic coast road to the towns around Amalfi. Any **longer** than this and you can explore the city, coast and islands at your leisure – great public transport connections cut travelling time to a minimum.

If **Naples** is your base, head straight for the **centro storico** – a UNESCO world heritage site – whose dead-straight streets follow the grid of the ancient Greek and Roman settlements the city was founded on. This area is Naples' spiritual heart, home to an array of churches and palaces, and a street-level commerce that couldn't be further from the homogenized centres of many of Europe's major cities. The big museums and attractions are elsewhere, but if you experience only one thing in the city, it should be this.

Beyond the old centre, **Via Toledo** is the modern hub of Naples, a busy shopping street that leads up from a cluster of portside attractions – the **Palazzo Reale**, **Teatro di San Carlo** and **Castel Nuovo**, among others – to the **Museo Archeologico Nazionale**, which despite tragic neglect remains one of the great museums of Europe, home to the best of the region's ancient Roman finds. West of Via Toledo, the jungle of congested streets that make up the notorious **Quartieri Spagnoli** neighbourhood rubs shoulders with the elegant boulevards of **Chiaia**, a haven of designer shopping and high-end dining that is quite at odds with much of the rest of the city. Up above, reachable by funicular, **Vómero** is similarly well-heeled, a nineteenth-century residential quarter that boasts heart-stopping views and some of the city's most historic museums, most notably in the **Certosa di San Martino**. Northeast of here, on another of Naples' hills, **Capodimonte** harbours a former residence of the Neapolitan royals, now home to the excellent **Museo Nazionale di Capodimonte**, one of Italy's finest art collections.

The gardens of the Reggia di Caserta

But there's plenty to draw you out of the city too. To the south, the evocative remains of ancient **Pompeii** and **Herculaneum** need little introduction, but Roman ruins have been unearthed all along the coast, and the less famous remains of **Villa Oplontis** and **Stabiae** are also worth a visit. But there's more to this stretch of coast than relics: an ascent of **Vesuvius**, which dominates the coast south of the city, is an exhilarating experience, and you can access the gentler slopes of wooded **Monte Faito** by cable car. Beyond here, the sprawl of Naples peters out and you're into more obviously holiday territory, concluding with the resort town of **Sorrento** – an appealing mixture of earthiness and elegance.

To the west of Naples lie the fabled Phlegrean Fields or **Campi Flegrei**, so named for the volcanic activity that has been a feature of the region for centuries. The remarkable **Solfatara**, just outside the main town of Pozzuoli, is the most visible instance of this: an otherworldly landscape of bubbling mud and sulphurous fumaroles. Pozzuoli itself is home to a number of sights dating back to a time when it was the principal port of ancient Rome – remains which provide a taster of the ruined cities of **Báia** and **Cumae** beyond. North of Naples lie more ancient sites, principally in **Cápua** and in the provincial capital of **Benevento**, but the area's real draw is the vast royal palace at **Caserta**, an eighteenth-century pile which dominates the town.

The **Amalfi Coast** draws crowds of admiring visitors, and no wonder: its crags and cliffs, girdled by a spectacular coastal road, are as mind-blowing as you are given to expect. If you avoid the tourist hotspots, and travel outside the peak months of July and August, you'll find it bearably busy, and stunning coastal towns like **Amalfi**, **Ravello** and **Atrani** are some of the highlights of the entire region.

◄ House of the Small Fountain, Pompeii

The best of Naples

One of the real draws of Naples and its region is the incredible variety of attractions on offer along this short stretch of coast, from a wealth of art treasures to world-class cuisine, from chichi coastal resorts to a slumbering volcano. Below is our pick of the **best places to go for ...**

adventure Making the hike to the crater of Mount Vesuvius is an unmissable – and surprisingly manageable – experience. See p.122.

a big night out Naples' centro storico is the hub of the city's nightlife, with a lively mix of bohemian bars and chic cocktail lounges. See p.90.

a budget getaway Avoid the pricey coast and islands and your holiday budget will go a long way – Naples itself has plenty of inexpensive accommodation, and makes a good base for day-trips across the rest of the region. See p.45.

culture The impressive collections of the Museo Archeologico Nazionale and Museo di Capodimonte, plus the modern art museum, MADRE, not to mention the numerous churches crammed with Baroque art, make Naples the obvious base for a cultural break. See p.72, p.77 & p.57.

a family holiday Ischia's long, sandy beaches make the island the ideal choice for a break with the kids. See p.195.

getting back to nature Hike into the hinterland of the Sorrentine peninsula to escape the crowds and experience the beauty of the region in its most primal form. See p.132.

lazing on the beach Prócida has plenty of attractive beaches to choose from – and they're rarely overcrowded. See p.216.

miracles The blood of Naples' patron saint San Gennaro liquefies three times a year – to much local rejoicing. See p.56.

pampering The thermal spas of Ischia are perfect for easing away aches and pains. See p.195.

people-watching Long the preferred retreat of VIPs, from Roman emperors to modern-day superstars, Cápri has always provided plenty of opportunities for ogling. See p.185.

a romantic break The stupendous backdrop of the Amalfi Coast makes this the perfect romantic hideaway, not least the swanky hotels of hilltop Ravello. See p.161.

seaside fun Sorrento is the perfect coastal resort, with a lovely old town, good restaurants and appealing hotels at all prices – and its location is hard to beat too. See p.132.

a slap-up meal Naples is arguably Italy's greatest foodie location – not just the home of pizza, but great pasta, and freshly caught fish and seafood too. See p.86.

stepping back in time The towns of Pompeii and Herculaneum, both buried in the 79 AD eruption of Vesuvius, are a fascinating insight into the daily life of the ancient Romans. See p.117 & p.125.

a taste of the high life Five-star luxury is what Cápri does best, from its blow-the-budget hotels to its chic restaurants, frequented by a suitably glamorous clientele. See p.180.

The **islands** of the bay of Naples – Cápri, Ischia and Prócida – are a massive draw, and many people arrive at Naples' train station or port and ship right out again on the first ferry. Of the three islands, **Ischia** has perhaps the broadest appeal, much larger than its neighbours, and with an assortment of attractions that make it suitable for everything from a day-trip to a fortnight's holiday: climb to the top of its extinct volcano, relax in its healing spa waters, or just eat and laze the days away in one of its small-scale resorts. **Cápri** is smaller and more scenically spectacular, but it can be heaving in high season – and its high prices reflect its popularity. The dazzling landscape and sharp Mediterranean light make it

▲ Galleria Umberto I, Naples

truly special, however, and it would be a pity to come to Naples and not visit at least briefly – though it's best out of season or after the day-tripping hoards have gone home. Tiny **Prócida** is an alternative – largely unknown except to the locals, and out of season at least a sleepy haven of fishing villages and picturesque beaches.

When to go

Like the rest of southern Italy, Naples enjoys a mild Mediterranean **climate**, with warm summers and mild winters. The hottest months are June through to August, although temperatures are rarely uncomfortably high, and the islands and coast enjoy the benefit of a cooling breeze. The wettest period tends to be the autumn and early winter, when the region is prone to thunderstorms and downpours, particularly in October. January and February can be also be wet and cold, but conditions usually improve by March and April.

The **best times to visit** are warm and sunny May, June and September, also the months of the year when you're most likely to catch a festival

(see p.31). The soaring temperatures of August, and the fact that this is when the Italians take their annual holiday, make this the month to avoid, especially in the coastal resorts. To get the benefit of **off-season hotel rates**, it's worth considering a visit outside of these times: from April to mid-May and mid-September to October the prices are cheaper and the main centres are less busy.

Naples weather

The table shows average daytime temperatures and rainfall in Naples.

	Jan	Feb	Mar	Apr	May	Jun	Jul	Aug	Sep	Oct	Nov	Dec
Average daytime temperatures												
°C	8	9	12	14	18	22	25	26	22	18	13	8
°F	46	48	54	57	64	72	77	79	72	64	55	46
Rainfall (mm)												
	96	81	76	76	51	37	23	30	78	132	127	116

things not to miss

It's not possible to see everything that Naples and the Amalfi Coast have to offer in one trip – and we don't suggest you try. What follows is a selective taste of the region's highlights: great places to visit, outstanding buildings and spectacular scenery. They're arranged in colour-coded categories, which you can browse through to find the very best things to see and experience. All entries have a page reference to take you straight into the guide, where you can find out more.

01 Villa Cimbrone, Ravello Page **164** • The fabulous views from the belvedere here have graced a thousand postcards – but you still won't be disappointed.

02 **Monte Faito** Page **131** • The cable-car ride to the top of the mountain is spectacular, and its wooded heights offer plenty of opportunities for circular hikes, or even a trek to Positano on the other side of the peninsula.

04 **Sorrento** Page **132** • The Italian resort at its best, Sorrento is a lovely, elegant small town given over to the pursuit of pleasure.

03 **Museo di Capodimonte, Naples** Page **76** • Housed in a vast palace above Naples' city centre, this is one of the finest collections of Renaissance art in Italy.

06 Pizza, Naples Page 86 •

Where better to eat pizza than in the place where it was invented? Neapolitan-style pizza has a soft, thin base and simple toppings, baked quickly in a scorchingly hot oven.

05 Pompeii and Herculaneum

Pages **117** & **125** • Preserved by ash in the 79 AD eruption of Vesuvius, these two towns are a remarkable record of ancient Roman life: few other ancient sites come close.

08 Villa San Michele, Cápri Page 188 •

In contrast to Cápri's well-documented glamour, Axel Munthe's idyllic home surrounded by fragrant gardens reflects the island's simpler charms.

07 Duomo, Naples Page 55 •

Naples' cathedral is a real treasure trove, with Baroque art and excavations from the Greek and Roman eras, as well as the ornate San Gennaro chapel.

09 Centro storico, Naples Page
55 • There's nowhere like it – in Italy
or the world: wandering these ancient streets
and soaking up the atmosphere is an essential
Naples experience.

**10 Museo Archeologico,
Naples** Page 72 • Quite
simply, one of the world's greatest
collections of archeological artefacts
– and an opportunity to see items
unearthed at Pompeii and Herculaneum
up close.

11 Vesuvius Page 122 • Climbing to the summit of mainland Europe's only active
volcano is almost obligatory on a trip to the Bay of Naples.

12 La Mortella, Ischia Page **205** • This Mediterranean paradise, created from a volcanic stone quarry, makes a spectacular setting for concerts in memory of the gardens' founder, the English composer Sir William Walton.

13 Solfatara Page **105** • It's not every day you get the chance to walk inside the crater of a volcano: the bubbling Solfatara offer the rare opportunity to view geological phenomena up close.

14 Amalfi Page **154** • The whitewashed streets of the ancient maritime republic Amalfi, and its smaller neighbour, Atrani, are the most appealing places to stay on the Amalfi Coast.

15 Cappella Sansevero, Naples Page **63** • The Neapolitans' fascination with death is plain all over the city, from its roadside shrines to its catacombs, but this chapel holds the most chilling sight in a city of macabre attractions – as well as an array of ghostly sculptures.

Basics

Basics

Getting there

The easiest way to get to Naples from the UK and Ireland is to fly, and the city is now on the radar of some of the low-cost operators. From the US and Canada there are very few direct flights; most people fly via London or another European gateway and pick up a cheap flight on from there. An alternative is to fly direct to Rome and then take an onward flight or even a train – a journey of just an hour and a half from Rome by the fastest rail connections. There are no direct flights to Italy from Australia, New Zealand or South Africa, but plenty of airlines fly to Rome via Asian or European hubs.

Airfares depend on the **season**, with the highest being around Easter, from June to August, and from Christmas to New Year. Fares drop during the "shoulder" seasons – September to October and April to May – and you'll get the best prices during the November-to-March low season (excluding Christmas and New Year) and, generally, if you travel on weekdays.

Flights from the UK and Ireland

Naples isn't a major tourist destination, and although there are scheduled flights it's not nearly as well served as Milan, Rome or other large Italian cities. Because Sorrento and the Amalfi Coast are popular holiday destinations, a lot of carriers only operate services during the summer, which means that you can pay almost as much for flights out of season as you will at peak periods. Of the **full-service airlines**, British Airways flies twice a day from London to Naples, and bmi twice a week between April and October, currently Thursdays and Saturdays (Alitalia only fly via Rome). Among the **low-cost carriers**, easyJet flies from London Stansted, bmibaby runs services from London Heathrow, and the Italian carrier Air One from London City. Thomsonfly operate 1–3 flights per week from London Gatwick and Manchester, as well as one flight per week in high season from Bristol, Newcastle, Birmingham, the East Midlands and Glasgow. From **Ireland**, Aer Lingus operate summer flights direct from Dublin, and Thomsonfly one weekly from Belfast.

Fares depend, as ever, on how far in advance you book and the time of year, and the cheapest tickets come with restrictions: any changes incur additional fees, and tickets are rarely valid for longer than a month. Book far enough in advance with one of the low-cost airlines and you can pick up a ticket for £100–150 return including taxes, even in summer; book anything less than three weeks in advance and this can easily double. Scheduled airline fares, booked within a month of travel, will cost £100–150 out of season and £250–300 in summer.

Flights from the US and Canada

There are few direct options from **North America**. The Italian carrier Eurofly, part of the Meridiana group, flies direct between New York and Naples, but in general you'll get the widest choice of flights by flying to Rome and then taking either a connecting flight or a train. The troubled Italian flag-carrier, Alitalia, has most direct routes between the US and Rome, with daily flights from New York, Newark, Miami, Chicago, Boston and Miami. Among the national carriers, Continental flies from Newark, United from Washington DC, US Airways from Philadelphia and Delta from New York, while many European carriers fly to Italy (via their main hubs) from major US and Canadian cities – for example BA (via London), Lufthansa (via Frankfurt) and KLM (via Amsterdam).

The **fares** charged by each airline don't vary as much as you might think, and you'll often be basing your choice around flight timings, routes and gateway cities, ticket restrictions, and even the airline's reputation for comfort and service. It's quite a long flight

– around nine hours from New York, Boston and the eastern Canadian cities, twelve hours from Chicago, and fifteen hours from Los Angeles – so it's as well to ensure that you're comfortable and arrive at a reasonably sociable hour. The cheapest return fares to Rome or Naples start at around $1000, rising to around $2000 during high season.

From **Canada**, Air Canada and Alitalia operate direct flights from Toronto and Montréal to Rome; expect to pay around Can$1000–2000 return at most times of year.

Flights from Australia, New Zealand and South Africa

There are **no direct flights** to anywhere in Italy from Australia, New Zealand or South Africa, although plenty of airlines fly to Rome and Milan from Asian hubs. Return **fares** to Naples from the main cities in Australia go for around

Aus$1750 in low season and Aus$2500 in high season, and from New Zealand from around NZ$2000 during low season to around NZ$3000 in high season. From South Africa, reckon on paying at least ZAR7000–8000 return from Johannesburg or Cape Town.

Trains

Travelling **by train** to Italy isn't a particularly economical option, but you can at least break up your journey en route. The most direct route is to take the Eurostar from London to Paris, then the "Palatino" overnight sleeper from Paris to Rome (@www.artesia.eu); and you can reach Naples from Rome in just an hour and a half nowadays. Total journey time is around 24 hours, and if you book far enough in advance you can get a one-way ticket for a little over £100 in low season, though peak prices can be upwards of £250. Discounts for under-26s are sometimes

---

Six steps to a better kind of travel

At Rough Guides we are passionately committed to travel. We feel strongly that only through travelling do we truly come to understand the world we live in and the people we share it with – plus tourism has brought a great deal of benefit to developing economies around the world over the last few decades. But the extraordinary growth in tourism has also damaged some places irreparably, and of course climate change is exacerbated by most forms of transport, especially flying. This means that now more than ever it's important to travel thoughtfully and responsibly, with respect for the cultures you're visiting – not only to derive the most benefit from your trip but also in order to preserve the best bits of the planet for everyone to enjoy. At Rough Guides we feel there are six main areas in which you can make a difference:

• Consider what you're contributing to the local economy, and indeed how much the services you use do the same, whether it's through employing local workers and guides or sourcing locally grown produce and local services.

• Consider the environment on holiday as well as at home. Water is scarce in many developing destinations, and the biodiversity of local flora and fauna can be adversely affected by tourism. Patronise businesses that take account of this rather than those that trash the local environment for short-term gain.

• Give thought to how often you fly and what you can do to redress any harm that your trips create. Reduce the amount you travel by air; avoid short hops by air and more harmful night flights.

• Consider alternatives to flying, travelling instead by bus, train, boat and even by bike or on foot where possible. Take time to enjoy the journey itself as well as your final destination.

• Think about making all the trips you take "climate neutral" via a reputable carbon offset scheme. All Rough Guide flights are offset, and every year we donate money to a variety of charities devoted to combating the effects of climate change.

• Travel with a purpose, not just to tick off experiences. Consider spending longer in a place, and really getting to know it and its people – you'll find it much more rewarding than dashing from place to place.

available and advance booking is essential. If Italy is just one stop on a longer European trip you could invest in a **rail pass** – the Rail Europe website is a useful source of information.

Rail contacts

European Rail UK ☎ 020/7619 1083, 🖥 www .europeanrail.com.
Eurostar UK ☎ 0870/518 6186, 🖥 www.eurostar .com.
Rail Europe US ☎ 1-888/382-7245, Canada ☎ 1-800/361-7245, UK ☎ 0844/848 4064, Australia ☎ 03/9642 8644, SA ☎ 11/628 2319; 🖥 www.raileurope.com.
The Man in Seat 61 🖥 www.seat61.com.

Airlines, agents and operators

Online booking

A selection of good online booking websites is listed below.
🖥 **www.ebookers.com** (in UK), 🖥 www .ebookers.ie (in Ireland).
🖥 **www.expedia.co.uk** (in UK), 🖥 **www.expedia** .com (in US), 🖥 **www.expedia.ca** (in Canada).
🖥 **www.lastminute.com** (in UK).
🖥 **www.opodo.co.uk** (in UK).
🖥 **www.orbitz.com** (in US).
🖥 **www.travelocity.co.uk** (in UK), 🖥 www .travelocity.com (in US), 🖥 **www.travelocity.ca** (in Canada), 🖥 **www.travelocity.co.nz** (in New Zealand).
🖥 **www.travelonline.co.za** (in South Africa).
🖥 **www.zuji.com.au** (in Australia).

Airlines

Aer Lingus 🖥 www.aerlingus.com.
Air Canada 🖥 www.aircanada.com.
Air One 🖥 www.flyairone.com.
Alitalia 🖥 www.alitalia.com.
American Airlines 🖥 www.aa.com.
bmi 🖥 www.flybmi.com.
bmibaby 🖥 www.bmibaby.com.
British Airways 🖥 www.ba.com.
Continental Airlines 🖥 www.continental.com.
Delta 🖥 www.delta.com.
easyJet 🖥 www.easyjet.com.
Eurofly 🖥 www.euroflyusa.com.
KLM (Royal Dutch Airlines) 🖥 www.klm.com.
Lufthansa 🖥 www.lufthansa.com.
Meridiana 🖥 www.meridiana.it.
Thomsonfly 🖥 www.thomson.co.uk.

United Airlines 🖥 www.united.com.
US Airways 🖥 www.usair.com.

Discount flight agents

Flight Centre UK 🖥 www.flightcentre.co.uk, US 🖥 www.flightcenter.us, Australia 🖥 www .flightcentre.com.au, NZ 🖥 www.flightcentre.co.nz. Specializes in budget flights and holiday packages.
North South Travel UK 🖥 www.northsouthtravel .co.uk. Friendly, competitive travel agency, offering discounted fares worldwide. Profits are used to support projects in the developing world, especially the promotion of sustainable tourism.
STA Travel 🖥 www.statravel.com. Worldwide specialists in independent travel; also student IDs, travel insurance, car rental, rail passes and more. Good discounts for students and under-26s.
Trailfinders 🖥 www.trailfinders.com. One of the best-informed and most efficient agents for independent travellers.

Tour operators

UK

Alternative Travel Group 🖥 www.atg-oxford .co.uk. Inclusive 5-day walking holidays in the Amalfi Coast area.
Citalia 🖥 www.citalia.com. Long-established company offering city-break packages in three- and four-star hotels.
Italiatours 🖥 www.italiatours.co.uk. Package deals, city breaks and specialist Italian-cuisine tours. Also offers tailor-made itineraries and can book local events and tours.
Long Travel 🖥 www.long-travel.co.uk. Specialists in southern Italian holidays, with plenty of hotels and villas on their books.
Martin Randall Travel 🖥 www.martinrandall .com. Inclusive, small-group cultural tours, including a six-day Naples option, led by experts on art and history.
Nautilus Yachting 🖥 www.nautilus-yachting .co.uk. Yachting holidays, with boats available from Naples and Salerno and the services of a skipper if required.
Ramblers Worldwide Holidays 🖥 www .ramblersholidays.co.uk. One- and two-week walking holidays in the Sorrento peninsula, as well as a walking and sightseeing route through Campania and Basilicata.
Sunvil Holidays 🖥 www.sunvil.co.uk. Amalfi Coast hotel and villa holidays, with tailor-made fly-drive packages in three- to five-star hotels.

US and Canada

Adventure Center 🖥 www.adventurecenter.com. Week-long tours of Amalfi and the Bay of Naples.

The International Kitchen ⓦwww
.theinternationalkitchen.com. Four- and six-day
cookery courses in Amalfi and Praiano, as well as day
courses in the area.
Italian Connection Canada ⓦwww
.italian-connection.com. Walking tours in the Amalfi
Coast and islands, as well as cookery courses.
Italiatours ⓦ www.italiatours.com. Low-cost Italy
tour specialist with organized tours to Positano and
Sorrento.

Italy

Benvenuto ⓦwww.benvenutolimos.com. Local
Italy specialists with 60 years of experience and tours
of Naples, the Amalfi Coast, Salerno and Sorrento.
Capritime ⓦwww.capritime.com. Art, wine,
walking and boat tours on the island.

Australia

CIT ⓦwww.cittravel.com.au. Italian
specialists, with packages to the Amalfi Coast.

Arrival

Arriving in Naples is more painless than you might think – the train station is
central and the airport not far out of town. But it's worth knowing that the airport
is something of a hub for the region, and is well connected to Sorrento, Salerno
and the Amalfi Coast, as well as the city centre. The city's main train station is also
very well integrated to the public transport system not only across the city, but
also around the Bay of Naples and beyond.

By air

Naples' Capodichino **airport** (☏081.848.
88877, ⓦwww.gesac.it) is around 7km north
of the city centre. It is connected with Naples'
Piazza Garibaldi (the stop is in front of the
station at the McDonald's corner) by **bus** #3S
approximately every thirty minutes, and the
journey takes twenty to thirty minutes; buy
tickets (€1.10) from the *tabacchi* in the departures hall. There is also an official airport
bus, Alibus, also operated by ANM
(☏081.763.2177), which runs to Piazza
Garibaldi every twenty minutes between
6.30am and 11.30pm (6am–midnight in the
opposite direction); it isn't very much quicker
and is more expensive (€3), but it does have
the advantage of continuing to the Piazza del
Municipio and Stazione Marittima, from where
hydrofoils depart for the islands. **Taxis** tend to
take about as long as buses to reach the
centre, and cost €16–20.

Hourly buses to **Sorrento**, run by Curreri
Viaggi (ⓦwww.curreriviaggi.it), take an hour
and a half and cost €10 one way, while SITA
(ⓦwww.sitabus.it) operate four services daily
to **Salerno**, an hour away; tickets cost €7.

By train

By train, you're most likely to arrive at **Napoli
Centrale**, situated on the edge of the city
centre at one end of Piazza Garibaldi, at the
main hub of city and suburban transport
services; there's a **left luggage** office here
(open 24hr). Some trains also pull into
Stazione Mergellina, on the opposite side of
the city centre, which is connected with Piazza
Garibaldi by the underground Metropolitana.
For train enquiries phone ☏848.888.088,
check ⓦwww.trenitalia.com or go to the
information booths at Napoli Centrale (daily
7am–9pm) and be prepared to queue.

By bus

City, suburban and inter-city **buses** also stop
on Piazza Garibaldi, and the main companies
operate from here. CTP (☏081.700.1111,
ⓦwww.ctpn.it) run services to Caserta, and
SITA (☏081.552.2176, ⓦwww.sitabus.it) go
to Pompeii, Sorrento, Positano, Amalfi and
Salerno. You'll need to check the stops
carefully as they are not well signed and
subject to change.

Getting around

The only way to get around central Naples and stay sane is to walk. Driving can be a nightmare, and negotiating the narrow streets, hectic squares and racetrack boulevards on a scooter takes years of training. In any case, you'd miss a lot by not getting around on foot – Naples is the kind of place best appreciated from street level.

For longer journeys – and Naples is a big, spread-out city – there are a number of alternatives, both for the city itself and the bay as a whole; for travel beyond Naples, see p.24.

Naples transport

The city transport system is run by ANM, and their **buses** will get you pretty much everywhere, and although they are crowded and slow, they remain much the best way of making short hops across the city centre. The bus system is supplemented by the **Metropolitana** (℡800.568.866), a small-scale underground network that crosses the city centre. Trains depart about every eight minutes, stopping at four places between Piazza Garibaldi and Mergellina, running eventually out to Pozzuoli in about half an hour. New stations, complete with modern art installations – at Duomo, Piazza Municipio and Via Toledo – are in the process of being added to the network.

In addition, three **funiculars** scale the hill of the Vómero: one, the Funicolare di Chiaia, from Piazza Amedeo; another, the Funicolare Centrale, from the Augusteo station, just off the bottom end of Via Toledo; and a third, the Funicolare di Montesanto, from the station on Piazza Montesanto. A fourth, the Funicolare di Mergellina, runs up the hill above Mergellina from Via Mergellina but is currently closed.

Taxis

If you need to take a **taxi**, make sure the driver switches on the meter when you start (they often don't), or request a flat fare at the start of the journey – which you can do (there are published rates to key locations that taxi drivers have to adhere to if requested); otherwise fares start at €3 for the initial journey, €5.50 at night or at the weekend. Note that journeys to and from the airport incur an extra charge of €2.60. There are taxi ranks at the train station, on Piazza Dante, Piazza del Gesù and Piazza Trieste e Trento, among other places.

Tickets

Uniconapoli **tickets** for all ANM modes of transport cost a flat €1.10 for all journeys and forms of transport (valid 1hr 30min) and must be bought in advance from such places as *tabacchi*, newsstands, stations, or the transport booth on Piazza Garibaldi. An all-day ticket costs €3.10, or you can buy a three-day tourist ticket for €20, which also covers the Alibus to the airport and public transport on Cápri and Ischia.

City transport routes

Buses ℡800.639.525. **#R2**, Piazza Garibaldi–Corso Umberto I–Piazza Bovio–Via Depretis–Piazza Municipio–Via San Carlo–Piazza Trieste e Trento–Piazza Municipio–Via Medina–Via Sanfelice–Corso Umberto I–Piazza Garibaldi.
#R3, Mergellina Funicolare–Via Mergellina–Via Riviera di Chiaia–Piazza Municipio–Via Medina–Via Toledo–Piazza Municipio–Via San Carlo–Piazza Trieste e Trento–Piazza Municipio–Via Riviera di Chiaia–Mergellina Funicolare.
#R4, Via Cardarelli–Via Capodimonte–Piazza Dante–Via Depretis–Piazza Dante–Via Capodimonte–Via Cardarelli.
#E1, Piazza del Gesù–Via Mezzocannone–Via Santa Chiara–Via Duomo–Via dei Tribunali–Via Duomo–Corso Umberto I–Via Monteoliveto–Piazza del Gesù.
#CS, Via Brin–Piazza Garibaldi–Corso Umberto I–Via Duomo–Piazza Museo–Piazza Dante–Piazza Carità–Corso Umberto I–Piazza Garibaldi–Via Gianturco–Via Brin.

#140, Capo Posillipo–Via Mergellina–Piazza Vittoria–Via Riviera di Chiaia–Via Santa Lucia–Via Riviera di Chiaia–Via Mergellina–Capo Posillipo.

#401 (night bus), Piazza Garibaldi–Via Depretis–Piazza Municipio–Riviera di Chiaia–Viale Augusto–Via Diocleziano–Pozzuoli.

Metropolitana ☎ 800.568.866, @ www.metro .na.it. City centre stops include Piazza Garibaldi, Piazza Cavour, Montesanto, Piazza Amedeo, Vanvitelli, Mergellina, Museo, Dante – with stops at Duomo, Municipio and Toledo to come. Trains every 8min.

Funiculars ☎ 800.568.866. Funicolare Centrale, Piazza Augusteo–Piazza Fuga (daily 6.30am–10pm; every 10min). Funicolare di Montesanto, Montesanto FS–Via Morghen (daily 7am–1pm; every 10min). Funicolare di Chiaia, Parco Margherita–Via Cimarosa (daily 6.30am–10pm; every 12min). Funicolare di Mergellina closed at the time of writing.

Around the bay

For **trips around the bay** in either direction – or indeed to get from one side of the centre to another, there are three more rail systems. The **Circumvesuviana** runs from its own station on Corso Garibaldi, behind the main station of Napoli Centrale (and from Napoli Centrale itself), right round the Bay of Naples about every thirty minutes, stopping everywhere as far south as Sorrento, which it reaches in about an hour. In the opposite direction, the **Ferrovia Cumana** operates every ten minutes from its terminus in Piazza Montesanto west to Pozzuoli and Baia, as does the **Circumflegrea,** which takes a different route to the same terminus at **Torregevata**. Uniconapoli **tickets** (see p.23) are valid for all these suburban lines, though you will need to buy one that covers more zones than the basic ticket.

Bay transport routes

The website @ www.campaniatrasporti.it is a good place to plan your route, with details of all train and ferry services around the region.

Circumvesuviana ☎ 081.772.2444, @ www .vesuviana.it. A rail line running between Naples and Sorrento, with many stops around the southern part of the bay, including Ercolano and Pompeii, every 30min, from 5.09am to 10.42pm.

Circumflegrea and Ferrovia Cumana ☎ 800.001.616, @ www.cumana.it. These two lines connect Naples Montesanto to Fuorigrotta, Agnano, Bagnoli, Pozzuoli, Baia, Fusaro, Cumae and Torregáveta. Departures every 20min.

By ferry and hydrofoil

If you're doing any travelling at all around the Bay of Naples, sooner or later you're going to have to take a **ferry or hydrofoil**, and the good news is that the entire region is extremely accessible by sea, with plentiful connections both to the islands and all around the Bay and along the Amalfi Coast. The main operators to the islands are Alilauro, Caremar, Medmar and Snav, while the Metró del Mare service provides access from Naples around the Bay and along the Amalfi Coast. We've included details of all ferry and hydrofoil services in the relevant chapters, on p.148 and p.178, but bear in mind that the Naples daily newspaper, *Il Mattino*, carries timetables for most services.

By car, motorbike or scooter

Travelling **by car** in Naples is fairly challenging: the city centre is crazy and congested and the ring roads that surround it almost impenetrable. Bear in mind too that the **traffic** can be heavy on the main roads down towards Sorrento and along the Amalfi Coast, particularly during the holiday season.

Having said that, there's nothing like driving the Amalfi Coast road for a thrill, and renting a scooter or car either to get around Naples itself or some of the towns around can be a fun thing to do – though it's no place for a beginner. Reckon on paying around €300 per week in high season for a small hatchback, with unlimited mileage, if booked in advance. The major chains have offices in all the larger cities and at airports, train stations, and so on. You need to be over 21 to rent a car in Italy and will need a credit card to act as a deposit when picking up your vehicle.

Rules of the road are straightforward: drive on the right; at junctions, where there's any ambiguity, give precedence to vehicles coming from the right; observe the speed limits – 50kph in built-up areas, 110kph on dual carriage ways and 130kph on motorways (for camper vans, these limits are 50kph, 80kph and 100kph respectively); and don't drink and drive. Drivers need to have their dipped headlights on while using any road outside a built-up area.

Parking can be a problem pretty much everywhere, and attendants are especially active in tourist areas. Look for the **blue-zone** parking spaces which usually have a maximum stay of one or two hours; they cost around €0.70–1.50 per hour (pay at meters or buy scratch-cards from local tobacconists) but are sometimes free after 8pm and on Sundays. Much coveted **white-zone** spaces (white lines) are free; **yellow-zone** areas (yellow lines) are reserved for residents. On the Amalfi Coast you may want to check whether your hotel has parking, and what it charges; they usually use small enclosed garages, but these can cost up to €20 a day in the main resorts.

Although Italians are by no means the world's worst drivers, they don't win any safety prizes either. The secret is to make it very clear what you're going to do – and then do it. A particular danger for unaccustomed drivers is the large number of scooters that can appear suddenly from the blind spot or dash across junctions and red lights with alarming recklessness. Never leave anything visible in the car when you're not using it, including the radio. In Naples some rental agencies won't insure a car left anywhere except in a locked garage.

Car-rental agencies

Avis ⓦ www.avis.com.
Budget ⓦ www.budget.com.
Europcar ⓦ www.europcar.com.
Hertz ⓦ www.hertz.com.
National ⓦ www.nationaalcar.com.
SIXT ⓦ www.sixt.com.
Thrifty ⓦ www.thrifty.com.

Accommodation

Accommodation can be a major cost in certain parts of the region, such as the glitzy Amalfi Coast, where hotel prices can be off the scale. Naples itself has its fair share of pricey hotels but it's not a tourist centre and tends to be cheaper than many other Italian cities, and it's not hard to find decent mid-range options as well as really personable B&Bs and hostels.

In high season it is always a good idea to **book rooms in advance**, especially in the major resorts. The same applies during religious holidays (notably Easter), and anywhere where a festival is taking place. Most tourist offices carry full **lists of hotels** and other accommodation such as B&B and *agriturismo* options. They may be able to help you find a room at short notice, but few have dedicated accommodation services, and you're usually better off booking direct or through a hotel booking site like ⓦ www.venere.com. Always establish the full price of your room – including breakfast and other extras (tax and service charges are usually included) – before you accept it. It's often a good idea to call or email a day or so before arrival to **confirm your booking**. If you're going to arrive late in the evening, it's even worth another call that morning to reconfirm.

Hotels

Hotels – or *alberghi* – in Italy are **star-rated** from one to five; prices are officially registered for each room and must be posted at the hotel reception and in individual rooms (usually on the back of the door). The star system gives you an idea of what you can expect from a hotel, though it's essential to realize the system is based on an often eccentric set of criteria relating to facilities (say, a restaurant or an in-room TV) rather than notions of comfort, character or location. A three-star, for example, must have a phone in every room: if it hasn't, it remains a two-star, no matter how magnificent the rest of the hotel.

One-star hotels in tourist towns in high season tend to start at about €60 for a double room without private bath; **two-star** hotels cost upwards of €90 for an en-suite double; **three-star** places are rarely cheaper than €120. **Four-star** hotels are a marked step up: everything has more polish, and in rural four-stars you'll probably get a swimming pool; €150–200 is the typical range here (though some establishments are much pricier), while for a deluxe **five-star** (rare outside the major centres) you should expect to pay at least €250–300 a night, and at some of the really upscale places in Cápri or on the Amalfi Coast you can double that.

In the more popular centres, it's not unusual for hotels to impose a **minimum stay** of three nights in summer – usually July and August – or insist on you taking half-board where they have a restaurant. Note also that single rooms nearly always cost far more than half the price of a double, although kindlier hoteliers – if they have no singles available – may offer you a double room at the single rate: again, more likely outside high season.

Bed and breakfast

Legal restrictions used to make it very difficult for Italian home-owners to offer **bed and breakfast** accommodation, but in 2000 the law was relaxed and now there are hundreds of B&Bs in Campania. Prices at the lower end of the scale are comparable to one-star hotels, but one unexpected consequence of the change in the law has been the emergence of upscale B&Bs in noble *palazzi* and large private homes, and there are some

tremendous options in this category in Naples especially. Tourist offices and local websites often carry lists of B&Bs, and Ⓦwww.bed-and-breakfast.it is another useful resource. In addition to registered B&Bs you'll also find **"rooms for rent"** (*affitacamere*) advertised in some towns. These differ from B&Bs in that breakfast is not always offered, and they are not subject to the same regulations as official B&Bs; nearly all *affitacamere* are in the one-star price range.

Hostels and student accommodation

There are several excellent non-official **hostels** in Naples and some of the major resorts, but many hostels belong to the **Hostelling International (HI)** network and strictly speaking you need to be an HI member to stay at them. Many, however, allow you to join on the spot, or simply charge you a small supplement. Whether or not you're an HI member, you'll need to **book ahead** in the summer months. The most efficient way to book at hostels is using HI's own online booking system at Ⓦwww.hihostels.com.

Camping

There are plenty of **campsites** to choose from in the rural Campi Flegrei area, as well as some more upmarket options along the Amalfi Coast and on the islands. Prices in high season tend to start at €7–10 per person, plus €10–15 per pitch. If you're camping extensively, it's worth checking Italy's informative camping website, Ⓦwww.camping.it, for details of sites and booking facilities.

Agriturismo

An increasingly popular accommodation option is **agriturismo**, a scheme whereby farmers rent out converted barns and farm buildings. Usually these comprise a self-contained flat or building, though a few places just rent rooms on a bed-and-breakfast basis. This market has boomed in recent years, and while some rooms are still annexed to working farms or vineyards, many are simply smart, self-contained rural vacation properties. Attractions may include home-grown food, swimming pools and a range of activities from walking and riding to archery and mountain biking. Bear in mind though that many *agriturismi* have a **minimum-stay requirement** of one week in busy periods. Tourist offices keep lists of local properties, or you can search one of the growing number of *agriturismo* websites – there are hundreds of properties at Ⓦwww.agriturismo.com, Ⓦwww.agriturismo.net, Ⓦwww.agriitalia.it and Ⓦwww.agriturist.it.

Food and drink

You could be forgiven for coming to Naples just to eat. You're unlikely to be disappointed by the food anywhere in Italy, but Naples is something special, and the staples of its cuisine – most notably its world-famous pizza – contribute hugely to the reputation of Italian cuisine worldwide.

A basic introduction to eating out in the region is below, but there's a rundown on the best of Neapolitan cuisine in the *Cucina napoletana* colour insert, as well as a menu reader on pp.256–259.

Eating out

Restaurant meals are served in either a *trattoria* or a *ristorante*. Traditionally, a *trattoria* is a cheaper and more basic purveyor of homestyle cooking, while a *ristorante* is more upmarket, although the lines are pretty blurred these days. Other types of eating places include *spaghetterie*, bar-restaurants that serve basic pasta dishes and are often the hangout of the local youth, and o*sterie* – basically old-fashioned *trattorie* or pub-like places specializing in home cooking, though some upmarket places with pretensions to established antiquity borrow the name. It's hard to generalize with regard to **costs**, but in most mid-range places you'll pay €5–10 for a starter, and the same for a pasta dish, while the main fish or meat courses will normally set you back between €7 and €15.

Breakfast

Most Italians start their day in a bar, their **breakfast** (*colazione*) consisting of a coffee and a *cornetto* – a sweet croissant often filled with jam, custard or chocolate, which you usually help yourself to from the counter and eat standing at the bar. It will cost between €1 and €1.50. Breakfast in all but the best hotels is often a limp affair of watery coffee, bread and processed meats, and often you're better off just going to a bar.

No smoking

In January 2005 a law prohibiting smoking in restaurants and bars came into force across the country. Overnight, local neighbourhood bars became smoke-free zones; any establishment that wants to allow smoking has to follow very stringent rules in isolating a separate room – including doors and special air conditioning. Needless to say this is beyond the budget of most places and so the majority remain no-smoking throughout.

The menu and the bill

Traditionally, lunch (*pranzo*) and dinner (*cena*) start with the **antipasto** (literally "before the meal"), a course consisting of various cold cuts of meat, seafood and cold vegetable dishes. Some places offer self-service *antipasto* buffets. The next course, the **primo**, consists of a soup, risotto or pasta dish, and is followed by the **secondo** – the meat or fish course, usually served alone, except for perhaps a wedge of lemon or a garnish. Watch out when ordering fish, which will either be served whole or by weight – 250g is usually plenty for one person – or ask to have a look at the fish before it's cooked. Note that by law, any ingredients that have been frozen need to be marked (usually with an asterisk) on the menu, and you might decide that it's better to try the local fish rather than one flown in from the South Atlantic. Vegetables

There's a detailed **menu reader** of Italian terms on pp.256–258.

or salads – **contorni** – are ordered and served separately, and there often won't be much choice: potatoes will usually come as fries (*patate fritte*), while salads are either green (*verde*) or mixed (*mista*); vegetables (*verdure*) generally come very well boiled. Afterwards, you nearly always get a choice of fresh local fruit (*frutta*), ice cream (*gelato*) and a selection of **desserts** (*dolci*).

You will need quite an appetite to tackle all these courses and if your stomach – or wallet – isn't up to it, it's perfectly acceptable to have less. If you're not sure of the size of the portions, start with a pasta dish and ask to order the *secondo* afterwards. And don't feel shy about just having just an *antipasto* and a *primo*; they're probably the best way of trying local specialities anyway. If there's no menu, the verbal list of what's available can be bewildering; if you don't understand, just ask for what you want – if it's something simple they can usually rustle it up. Pretty much everywhere will have pasta with tomato sauce (*pomodoro*) – always a good standby for kids.

At the end of the meal ask for the **bill** (*il conto*), and bear in mind that almost everywhere you'll pay a **cover charge** (*coperto*) of €1–3 a head. In many *trattorie* the bill amounts to little more than an illegible scrap of paper; if you want to check it, ask for a **receipt** (*ricevuta*). In more expensive places, service (*servizio*) will often be added on top of the cover charge, generally about ten percent. If service isn't included then it's fine just to leave a few coins as a **tip** unless you're particularly pleased (or displeased) with the service.

Drinking

As in the rest of Italy, most Naples **bars** are functional places to come for a coffee in the morning or a quick snack during the day. It's cheapest to drink standing at the counter, in which case you pay first at the cash desk (*la cassa*), present your receipt (*scontrino*) and give your order. There's always a list of prices (*listino prezzi*) behind the bar and it's customary to leave a small coin on the counter as a tip for the barperson, although no one will object if you don't. If there's waiter service, just sit where you like, though bear in mind that to do this can cost up to twice as much as drinking at the bar,

especially if you sit outside (*fuori*) – the difference is shown on the price list as *tavola* (table) or *terrazzo* (any outside seating area).

An **osteria** can be a more congenial setting, often a traditional place where you can usually try local specialities with a glass of wine. Real enthusiasts of the grape should head for an **enoteca**, though many of these are more oriented towards selling wine by the case than by the glass. Naples has a lively after-dark scene, and many of its bars have live music or DJs. Some of these have taken to calling themselves **pubs**, with beer, particularly in its draught form, *alla spina*, an increasingly popular drink.

Coffee and tea

If pizza is Naples' most sacred food, then coffee is its liquid counterpart. It is consumed early and often and is almost always *espresso* or just *caffe*. An *espresso* will cost you €0.80–€1, a *cappuccino* about €1.30. Neapolitans are fiercely devoted to their favourite bar, even *barista*, and are chronically dissatisfied by coffee they consume outside the city limits. In Naples, coffee is taken either *amaro* (without sugar) or *zuccherato* (with sugar) and can be ordered *stretto* (extra short) or *lungo* (long). *Baristi* will begrudgingly make extra-long *café americano* when asked, but have been known to refuse making a *cappuccino* after noon. In the summertime, look for *caffè freddo* and *cappuccino freddo*, cold versions of old favourites. An *espresso* with a drop of hot milk is *caffè macchiato*; very milky coffee is *caffè latte* (ordering just a "*latte*" will get you a glass of milk); coffee with a shot of alcohol – and you can ask for just about anything – is *caffè corretto*.

Hot tea (*tè caldo*) comes with lemon (*con limone*) unless you ask for milk (*con latte*). Milk itself is drunk hot as often as cold, or you can ask for it with a dash of coffee (*latte macchiato*) and sometimes as a milkshake – *frappè* or *frullato*.

Soft drinks and water

Among the **soft drinks** (*analcolici*), there are a number of slightly fizzy, bitter home-grown drinks like Sanbittèr or Crodino, or the cola-like Chinotto, or try a **spremuta** or fresh fruit juice, squeezed at the bar. A crushed-ice granita is a great summer cooler, plus there's the usual range of fizzy drinks and concentrated juices. **Tap water** (*acqua dal rubinetto*) is quite drinkable, and you won't pay for a glass in a bar, though Italians prefer **mineral water** (*acqua minerale*) and drink more of it than any other country in Europe. It comes either still (*senza gas, liscia* or *naturale*) or sparkling (*con gas* or *frizzante*).

Beer and spirits

Beer (*birra*) is a lager-type brew which usually comes in one-third or two-third litre bottles, or on tap (*alla spina*) – measure for measure more expensive than the bottled variety. A small beer is a *piccola* (20cl or 25cl), a larger one (usually 40cl) a *media*. The cheapest and most common Italian brands are Moretti, Peroni and Dreher, all of which are very drinkable; if this is what you want, either state the brand name or ask for *birra nazionale* or *birra chiara* – otherwise you could end up with a more expensive imported beer.

All the usual **spirits** are on sale and known mostly by their generic names. There are also Italian brands of the main varieties: the best Italian brandies are Stock and Vecchia Romagna. A generous shot of these costs about €1.50, imported stuff much more. You'll also find **fortified wines** like Martini, Cinzano and Campari; ask for a Campari-soda and you'll get a ready-mixed version from a little bottle; lemon is *limone*, ice is *ghiaccio*. You might also try Cynar – believe it or not, an artichoke-based sherry often drunk as an aperitif with water.

There's also a daunting selection of **liqueurs**. Amaro is a bitter after-dinner drink

Ice cream

Italian **ice cream** (*gelato*) is deservedly famous, and a cone (*cono*) or "cup" (*coppa*) is an indispensable accessory to the evening *passeggiata*. Most bars have a fairly good selection, but for real choice go to a **gelateria** (we've listed our favourite places in the Guide), where the range is a tribute to Neapolitan imagination and flair for display. There's usually a veritable cornucopia of flavours (*gusti*) ranging from those regarded as the classics – like lemon (*limone*) and pistachio (*pistacchio*) – through staples including *stracciatella* (vanilla with chocolate chips), strawberry (*fragola*) and *fiordilatte* (similar to vanilla), to house specialities that might include cinnamon (*cannella*), chocolate with chilli pepper (*cioccolato con peperoncino*) or even pumpkin (*zucca*).

or *digestivo*, Amaretto much sweeter with a strong taste of almond; Sambuca a sticky-sweet aniseed concoction, traditionally served with a coffee bean in it and set on fire (though, increasingly, this is something put on to impress tourists). Another sweet alternative, from Sorrento, is *limoncello* or *limoncino*, a lemon-based liqueur traditionally drunk in a frozen vase-shaped glass. Strega is another drink you'll see behind every bar, yellow, herb-and-saffron based stuff in tall, elongated bottles: about as sweet as it looks but not unpleasant.

Wine

The volcanic slopes of Mount Vesuvius are among the most ancient wine-producing areas in Italy, but in spite of this the region doesn't have a great reputation for **wine**. The best choices among the Campanian whites are **Greco di Tufo, Fiano di Avellino** and **Falanghina** – all fruity yet dry alternatives. Ischia nowadays produces good white wine, notably **Biancolella**, while **Lacryma Christi**, from the slopes of Vesuvius, is available in red and white varieties and is enjoying a new-found popularity after years of being considered cheap plonk. Among the pure reds, there's the unusual but delicious **Gragnano**, a sparkling wine that's best served slightly chilled, and **Taurasi** – like the best wines of the region made from the local *aglianico* grape, which produces rich, elegant wines that can command high prices.

The media

Italy's decentralized press serves to emphasize the strength of regionalism in the country, and Naples is no exception, with strong local papers and supplements, although you may find yourself turning to foreign TV channels or papers if you want an international outlook on events.

Newspapers

Naples' daily **newspaper** is *Il Mattino* – like most Italian papers, not particularly comprehensible even if you speak Italian, but useful for local museum opening hours, ferry and train timetables and the like. Of the nationals, the posh paper is the right-of-centre *Corriere della Sera*, to which *La Repubblica* is the left-of-centre alternative, and both have Naples sections that are useful for listings whether or not you speak Italian. The tourist office publication, *Qui Napoli*, is also good for events information. The sports coverage in all these papers is relatively thin; if you want in-depth football reporting you need to try one of three national sports dailies – either the pink *Gazzetto dello Sport*, the Rome-based *Corriere dello Sport*, or *Tuttosport*. Finally, **English-language newspapers** are available the same day of publication, usually after lunch, at newsstands all over the region. *The International Herald Tribune*, available at most newsstands, is printed in Italy and includes an Italian news supplement.

Naples websites

Ⓦ**www.amalficoastweb**.com A useful resource for the towns along the coast, with accommodation suggestions and downloadable hiking maps.

Ⓦ**www.culturacampania.rai.it** A rundown of the region's cultural highlights, with details of upcoming events.

Ⓦ**www.inaples.it** The official tourist board site is a comprehensive source of information on Naples. You can also download the *Qui Napoli* booklet from here, which is handy for all sorts of information, from ferry schedules to events listings.

Ⓦ**www.napoli.com** Articles about the city, as well as cultural itineraries and listings.

Ⓦ**www.sorrentoinfo.com** A wealth of practical details on the town, including listings of hotels, restaurants and shops.

TV and radio

Italian **TV** has a justified reputation for ghastly quiz shows, mindless variety programmes and chat shows squeezed in between countless advertisements. There are three state-owned channels – Rai 1, 2 and 3 – along with the channels of Berlusconi's Mediaset empire – Italia 1, Rete 4, Canale 5 – and a seventh channel, Canale 7. Satellite television is fairly widely available, and some hotels will offer a mix of BBC World, CNN and French-, German- and Spanish-language news channels, as well as MTV and Eurosport.

Rai dominates Italian **radio** too, with three main stations. There are one or two decent local stations – Amore (105.8), Kiss Kiss Napoli (103), Radio Club 91 (91.0) – but on the whole the output is virtually undiluted Europop.

Check the following websites for details of the global frequencies of **world service** stations: BBC Ⓦwww.bbc.co.uk/worldservice; Radio Canada Ⓦwww.rcinet.ca; Voice of America Ⓦwww.voa.gov.

Festivals

Naples is a city that likes to enjoy itself, and the lively festivals and events that punctuate the year, both in the city and the surrounding area, can be worth organizing a visit around.

In Naples itself the biggest event is undoubtedly the festival of the city's patron saint **San Gennaro**, which takes place three times a year, but the more explosive **Santa Maria del Carmine** festival in July and the **Festa di Piedigrotta** in September also draw the crowds.

There's no shortage of music, theatre, or **cultural events** either, whether it's the Maggio dei Monumenti in May, the Napoli Teatro Festival in June or one of several film festivals that are held in Naples throughout the year, which offer pretty much the city's only opportunity to view English-language cinema. Outside Naples, Ravello's arts festival is gaining in stature as an annual event, and offers the chance to attend concerts in some unique settings, as does June's Vesuvian Villas festival, while inland Campania sees some fantastic *sagre* (food-based festivals) from September through to November (see box, p.224). Festivals are detailed in the relevant chapters of the Guide, along with other, smaller events, some of which you may just be lucky to stumble across on your trip.

Festival calendar

January

Naples (Jan 6) La Befana; the feast of Epiphany is celebrated in Naples with gifts for good children, and there's a market in Piazza del Plebiscito.

February

Naples Carnevale; celebrated every year in Naples and some of the towns around. There's no real parade, but everyone takes to the streets in costume, and at home people traditionally eat lasagne to mark the last meal before Lent.
Sorrento (Feb 14) Sant'Antonino; Sorrento celebrates its saint's day with a big parade and lots of fireworks.

March–April

Naples, Procida & Sorrento (Easter) During the Settimana Santa, solemn processions mark the lead-up to Easter, and are particularly resonant in some of the towns around the bay.
Naples (Sun in mid-April) Naples Marathon, Ⓦwww.napolimarathon.it. A full marathon, half-marathon or a 4km fun run, held annually in April.

May

Naples (first Sat in May) Festa di San Gennaro; festival for the city's patron saint, with crowds gathering in the cathedral to witness the liquefaction of San Gennaro's blood.
Naples (weekends in May) Maggio dei Monumenti; buildings and monuments that are usually kept closed open their doors, for exhibitions, concerts and readings, or just for visits.

June

Amalfi (first Sun in June, every four years) Regata delle Quattro Antiche Repubbliche Marinare; an ancient boat race between the cities of Venice, Genoa, Pisa and Amalfi, next hosted in Amalfi in 2009.
Naples (three weeks in June) Napoli Teatro Festival, Ⓦwww.teatrofestivalitalia.it; a new festival, showcasing Italian and foreign-language drama, song and dance in some fantastic venues around town.
Naples (ten days in June) Napoli Film Festival, Ⓦwww.napolifilmfestival.com; featuring shorts, feature-length films and documentaries in their original language.
Ravello (end June–Sept) Ravello Festival, Ⓦwww.ravellofestival.com; a festival of music, dance, literature and the visual arts, with big names coming to perform in great indoor and outdoor venues around the hill-town. Whatever you see, the settings are magical, and Oscar Niemeyer's landmark new auditorium is on the verge of completion.
Naples (June–Sept) Estate a Napoli; free outdoor concerts and events in atmospheric venues across the city.

31

July

Naples (July 16) Festa della Madonna del Carmine; the fireworks at this festival are among the city's best.

Naples (three days mid-July) Neapolis Festival, ⓦ www.neapolis.it; this three-day rock event held in the Arena Flegrea in Fuorigrotta is southern Italy's biggest, with an array of international as well as Italian names. Slated to be held in future at a renovated industrial park in Bagnoli.

Ischia (July 26) Festa di Sant'Anna; the island celebrates its saint's day with a parade of fishing boats and fireworks around the Castello Aragonese.

Vietri sul Mare (all month) Amalfi Coast Music and Arts Festival, ⓦ www.musicalstudies.com; chamber music and piano and vocal recitals in Vietri and other Amalfi Coast towns.

Ercolano, Portici (end July) Festa delle Ville Vesuviane; a long-running festival of classical music concerts hosted in the best of the Bourbon villas in the towns immediately south of Naples.

August

Pozzuoli (Aug 15) Ferragosto; August 15 is a national holiday in Italy, and celebrations are particularly serious in Pozzuoli where they climb a greased pole and there's a spectacular fireworks display.

September

Naples (early to mid-Sept) Festa di Piedigrotta, ⓦ www.festadipiedigrotta.it; one of the biggest events of the year, with a massive procession through the city centre from Mergellina, and ten days of special events.

Naples (Sept 19) Festa di San Gennaro; the second chance to witness the liquefaction of the blood of the city's patron saint.

Naples (two weeks mid-Sept) Pizzafest, ⓦ www.pizzafest.info; held for over ten years in the Mostra d'Oltremare showground in Fuorigrotta, this ten-day event is a celebration of Naples' most famous gift to the world, with food stalls, demonstrations and plenty of cheesy entertainment.

October

Naples (three days mid-Oct) Artecinema, ⓦ www.artecinema.com; a documentary film festival, with films in their original language.

November

Naples (five days mid-Nov) Independent Film Show, ⓦ www.em-arts.org; festival of experimental film, with screenings in the original language.

December

Naples (Dec 16) Festa di San Gennaro; the third and last San Gennaro event of the year.

Naples (all month) Natale; nowhere does Christmas cribs or *presepi* like the Neapolitans, and the city is appropriately festive during the month of December, but otherwise Christmas is a family affair, with a big – and traditionally meat-free – feast on Christmas Eve.

Naples (31 Dec) Capodanno; New Year is celebrated in style, with the festival of San Silvestro, which not only entails the throwing of old furniture out of windows but also traditional Italian food – *cotechino* sausage and lentils. Naples also hosts one of the country's best New Year firework displays, over the Castel dell'Ovo.

Travel essentials

Costs

Prices have risen considerably in Italy over the past decade, in particular accommodation costs, and although Naples is still cheaper than the cities of the north, the Amalfi Coast is conversely one of the most expensive areas in the country when it comes to food and accommodation. You'll pay more everywhere during the height of summer, although again in Naples itself prices are fairly stable even then.

Crime and safety

Naples is a big city with an even bigger reputation for petty **crime** – one that's not entirely without foundation but which also tends to be overplayed. With a bit of common sense, the city is for the most part no more dangerous than any other city of a million or so inhabitants.

There are some districts where it's wise to be cautious, or to avoid entirely late at night – areas around Piazza Garibaldi and Forcella, the Quartieri Spagnoli and La Sanità among them. Wherever you are, you should take the usual big-city **precautions**: walk with a purpose; try to avoid looking too much like a tourist; and plan your route in advance, so that you don't have to constantly resort to a map. If you own expensive jewellery or a flashy watch, think about leaving them in your hotel room; don't brandish expensive cameras, mobile phones or other desirable gadgetry in too ostentatious a way; and keep your bag close to your body with the strap in your hand in case of drive-by bag-snatchers (*scippatori*). Finally, don't let all this advice worry you

Emergency numbers

Police or any emergency service, including ambulance (Soccorso Pubblico di Emergenza) ☏113.
Carabinieri ☏112.
Ambulance (Ambulanza) ☏118.
Fire brigade (Vigili del Fuoco) ☏115.
Road assistance (Soccorso Stradale) ☏116.

unduly or stop you from enjoying Naples. If you're sensible, it's as safe as anywhere else in Italy.

To **report a crime**, you will need to make a *denuncia* (statement) at the police station. In Italy the **police** come in many forms, but the two most visible branches are the Carabinieri, with their military-style uniforms and white shoulder belts, who deal with general crime, public order and drug control, and the Polizia Statale, the other general crime-fighting force, who enjoy a fierce rivalry with the Carabinieri and are the ones who deal with thefts. Other branches of law enforcement are the Guardia di Finanza, responsible for investigating smuggling, tax evasion and other finance-related felonies; the Vigili Urbani, mainly concerned with directing traffic and issuing parking fines; and the Polizia Stradale, who patrol the motorways.

Electricity

The supply is 220V, though anything requiring 240V will work. Most plugs are two round pins: UK equipment will need an

Lost or stolen credit cards and traveller's cheques

American Express Credit cards ☏800.268.9824; traveller's cheques ☏800.914.912.
MasterCard Credit cards ☏800.870.866.
Thomas Cook Traveller's cheques ☏800.872.050.
Visa Credit cards ☏800.819.014; traveller's cheques ☏800.874.155.

adaptor, US equipment a 220-to-110 transformer as well.

Entry requirements

All EU citizens can enter Italy and stay as long as they like on production of a valid **passport**. Citizens of the United States, Canada, Australia and New Zealand also need a valid passport, but are limited to stays of three months. All other nationals should consult the relevant embassy about **visa requirements**. Legally, you're required to register with the police within three days of entering Italy, though if you're staying at a hotel this will be done for you.

Italian embassies and consulates abroad

Australia Embassy: 12 Grey St, Deakin, Canberra, ACT 2600 ☎02/6273 3333, ⊛www.ambcanberra .esteri.it. Consulates in Melbourne ☎03/9867 5744; Sydney ☎02/9392 7900; Adelaide ☎08/8337 0777; Brisbane ☎07/3299 8944; Perth ☎08/9322 4500.
Canada Embassy: 275 Slater St, Ottawa, ON, K1P 5H9 ☎613/232-2401, ⊛www.ambottawa .esteri.it. Consulates in Montréal ☎514/849-8351; Toronto ☎416/977-1566; Vancouver ☎604/684-7288; Edmonton ☎780/423 5176.
Ireland Embassy: 63–65 Northumberland Rd, Dublin 4 ☎01/660 1744, ⊛www.ambdublino .esteri.it.
New Zealand Embassy: 38 Grant Rd, Thorndon, Wellington ☎04/474 0591, ⊛www.ambwellington .esteri.it.
South Africa Embassy: 796 George Ave, 0083 Arcadia, Pretoria ☎012/423 0000, ⊛www .ambpretoria.esteri.it. Consulates in Johannesburg ☎011/728 1392; Cape Town ☎021/487 3903.
UK Consulate: 38 Eaton Place, London SW1X 8AN ☎020/7235 9371, ⊛www.conslondra.esteri .it. Consulates in Manchester ☎0161/236 9024; Edinburgh ☎0131/220 3695.
US Embassy: 3000 Whitehaven St NW, Washington DC 20008 ☎202/612-4400, ⊛www .ambwashingtondc.esteri.it. Consulates in cities nationwide, including Boston ☎617/722-9201; Chicago ☎312/467-1550; Detroit ☎313/963-8560; Los Angeles ☎310/826-6207; New York ☎212/737-9100; San Francisco ☎415/931-4924.

Foreign consulates in Italy

Australia Via Bosio 5, Rome ☎06.852.721.
Canada Via Carducci 29, Naples ☎081.401.338.

Ireland Piazza Campitelli 3, Rome ☎06.697.9121.
New Zealand Via Zara 28, Rome ☎06.441.7171.
South Africa Via Posillipo 46, Naples ☎081.552.5835.
UK Via dei Mille 40, Naples ☎081.423.8911.
US Piazza della Repubblica, Naples ☎081.583.8111.

Gay and lesbian travellers

Attitudes to gays and lesbians are fairly tolerant in Naples and especially the main resorts, although it's as well to be discreet in the smaller provincial towns and the old centre of Naples itself. The national gay organization Arcigay has a branch in Naples (Vico San Geronimo alle Monache 19, ☎081.552.8815), which can provide information on local events, while the website ⊛www.gay.it has a wealth of information on the scene in Italy. The age of consent in Italy is 18.

Health

As a member of the European Union, Italy has free reciprocal health agreements with other member states. **EU citizens** are entitled to free treatment within Italy's public health-care system on production of a European Health Insurance Card (EHIC), which you can obtain by picking up a form at the post office, calling ☎0845/606 2030, or applying online at ⊛www.dh.gov.uk. Allow up to 21 days for delivery. The EHIC is free of charge, valid for at least three years, and basically entitles you to the same treatment as an insured person in Italy. The Australian Medicare system also has a reciprocal health-care arrangement with Italy. Note, however, that this and the EHIC won't cover the full cost of major treatment (or dental treatment), and the high medical charges make travel insurance essential. You normally have to pay the full cost of emergency treatment upfront, and claim it back when you get home (minus a small excess); make sure you hang onto full doctors' reports, signed prescription details and all receipts to back up your claim.

In an **emergency**, go straight to the **Pronto Soccorso** (A&E) of the nearest hospital, or phone ☎113 and ask for *ospedale* or *ambulanza*.

A **pharmacist** (*farmacia*) is well qualified to give you advice on minor ailments and to dispense prescriptions; in Naples there are a number that are open outside normal hours (see p.97). If you need a **doctor** (*medico*) or a **dentist** (*dentista*), ask at your hotel or the local tourist office. Again, keep all receipts for insurance claims.

Insurance

Even though EU health-care privileges apply in Italy, you'd do well to take out an **insurance policy** before travelling to cover against theft, loss, illness or injury. A typical policy usually provides cover for the loss of baggage, tickets and – up to a certain limit – cash or cheques, as well as cancellation or curtailment of your journey. Many policies can be chopped and changed to exclude coverage you don't need – for example, sickness and accident benefits can often be excluded or included at will. If you do take out medical coverage, ascertain whether benefits will be paid as treatment proceeds or only after your return home, and whether there is a 24-hour medical emergency number. When securing baggage cover, make sure that the per-article limit – typically under £500 – will cover your most valuable possession. If you need to make a **claim**, you should keep receipts for medicines and medical treatment, and in the event you have anything stolen, you must obtain an official statement (*denuncia*) from the police.

Internet

Internet cafés are widespread in Naples, with a concentration around the station, though many of them are short-lived ventures. Reckon on paying around €2–5 for an hour online. It's increasingly common for hotels and even hostels to provide internet access, usually for free, and some cafés and bars have started to offer wi-fi too.

Mail

Post office **opening hours** are usually Monday to Friday 8.30am until 7.30pm, and on Saturday until 1pm. **Stamps** (*francobolli*) are sold in *tabacchi* and some gift shops, as well as post offices. The Italian postal system is one of the slowest in Europe, so if your letter is urgent make sure you send it *posta prioritaria*, which has varying rates according to weight and destination. Letters can be sent **poste restante** (general delivery) to any Italian post office by addressing them "*Fermo Posta*" followed by the name of the town. General information on Italian postal services is available on ☎803.160 or at Ⓦwww.poste.it.

Maps

The **maps** in this guide should be fine for most purposes, and nearly all tourist offices hand out free maps. The Campania tourist office produces an excellent series of maps to the whole region, including plans of all the major towns, cities and islands. Among commercial maps, the *Touring Club Italiano* map is probably the best stand-alone city plan of Naples available, and they do a decent map of the Bay of Naples too, while the Kompass map of the *Sorrentine Peninsula and Amalfi Coast* should be more than detailed enough for any trip.

Money

Italy's currency is the **euro** (€), which is split into 100 cents. There are seven euro notes – in denominations of 500, 200, 100, 50, 20, 10 and 5 euros, each a different colour and size – and eight different coin denominations, with 2 and 1 euros, then 50, 20, 10, 5, 2 and 1 cents. For the latest rates check Ⓦwww .xe.com.

Rough Guides travel insurance

Rough Guides has teamed up with Columbus Direct to offer you tailor-made **travel insurance**. Products include a low-cost **backpacker** option for long stays; a **short break** option for city getaways; a typical **holiday package** option; and others. There are also annual **multi-trip** policies for those who travel regularly. Different sports and activities (trekking, skiing, etc) can usually be included.

See our website (Ⓦwww.roughguides.com/shop) or call UK ☎0870/033 9988, Australia ☎1300/669 999, New Zealand ☎0800/559 911, or worldwide ☎+44 870/890 2843.

Banks usually offer the best rate of exchange; hours are normally Monday to Friday from 8.30am until 1.30pm, and from 2.30pm until 4pm. Outside banking hours, the larger hotels will change money or traveller's cheques, and there are plenty of exchange bureaux – normally open evenings and weekends too. Post offices will exchange American Express traveller's cheques and cash commission-free. The last resort should be any of the many Ufficio Cambio kiosks, almost always offering the worst rates (despite the "no commission" signs).

If you're travelling from the UK it's a good idea to have some cash on you when you arrive; otherwise you can withdraw euros using your **credit or debit card** in the local ATM machines (*bancomat*); there's usually a charge but you won't spend more getting money this way than any other. Travellers from elsewhere, or on longer stays, may prefer to use traveller's cheques; American Express and the Thomas Cook and Visa alternatives are widely accepted. Buying online in advance usually works out cheapest. Remember that all cash advances are treated as loans, with interest accruing daily from the date of withdrawal; there is often a transaction fee on top of this.

For **lost or stolen cards**, see p.33.

Opening hours and public holidays

Opening hours have become a bit more flexible, but much of the area still follows a traditional Italian routine, with most **shops and businesses** open Monday to Saturday from around 8am until 1pm, and then again from about 4pm until 7pm or 8pm, although many shops also close on Saturday afternoons and Monday mornings. Traditionally, everything except bars and restaurants closes on Sunday, though there's usually a *pasticceria* (pastry shop) open in the mornings and in general Sunday opening is becoming more common.

Most Naples **churches** open in the early morning, around 8am, and close around noon or 1pm, opening up again at 3–4pm and closing at around 7pm, but there are subtle variations and we've tried to give the most up-to-date times in the text. Sometimes a church or sight will be kept locked and if you're determined to take a look you have to ask for the key; we've given the details of custodians where they exist.

Most but not all **museums** are closed on Mondays, and you'll find that a number choose another day of the week to close. The opening times of **archeological sites** around the bay are more flexible: most are open every day, Sunday included, from 9am until one hour before sunset and thus different according to the time of year. In winter, times are drastically cut because of the darker evenings; 4pm is a common closing time.

In **August** most of Naples gets out of town, and many shops, bars and restaurants close, leaving the city to the tourists. On official **national holidays** everything closes down except bars and restaurants.

National holidays

January 1
January 6 (Epiphany)
Easter Monday (Pasquetta)
April 25 (Liberation Day)
May 1 (Labour Day)
June 2 (Day of the Republic)
August 15 (Ferragosto; Assumption)
November 1 (Ognissanti; All Saints Day)
December 8 (Immacolata; Immaculate Conception of the Blessed Virgin Mary)
December 25
December 26

Phones

You will hardly see an Italian without a **mobile phone** – or *telefonino* – clasped to their ear. If

Visiting churches and religious sites

The rules for visiting churches, cathedrals and religious buildings are much the same as they are all over the Mediterranean and are strictly enforced everywhere: **dress modestly**, which means no shorts (not even Bermuda-length ones) and covered shoulders for women, and try to avoid wandering around during a service.

Calling home from abroad

Note that the initial zero is omitted from the area code when dialling the UK, Ireland, Australia and New Zealand from abroad.

Australia international access code + 61.
New Zealand international access code + 64.
UK international access code + 44.
US and Canada international access code + 1.
Republic of Ireland international access code + 353.
South Africa international access code + 27.

you want to use your mobile phone in Italy, you are likely to be charged extra for incoming calls, as the people calling you will be paying the usual rate. If you want to retrieve messages while you're away, you might have to ask your provider for a new access code. If you have a GSM, dual- or tri-band phone which can be unlocked (check with your provider), it's worth considering investing in an Italian SIM card, which can be bought for about €10 from Italian providers TIM, Wind or Vodafone; ask for a "SIM *prepagato*". For further information about using your phone abroad contact your network or check out Ⓦwww.telecomsadvice .org.uk. Locally, any numbers that start with a 3 are mobile numbers and consequently more expensive to call.

Public telephones, run by Telecom Italia, come in various forms, but they usually have clear instructions in English. Coin-operated machines are increasingly hard to find and you will probably have to buy a **telephone card** (*carta* or *scheda telefonica*), available from *tabacchi* and newsstands in denominations of €5 and €10. You always need to dial the local code, regardless of where you are; all **telephone numbers** listed in this guide include the local codes – 081 for Naples and around, 089 for the Amalfi Coast. Numbers beginning ☏800 are free, ☏170 will get you through to an English-speaking operator, ☏176 to international directory enquiries.

Italian **phone tariffs** are expensive, especially if you're calling long-distance or internationally, and many people, even residents, use phone calling cards for **long-distance calls**. You can buy these from *tabacchi* for upwards of €5; common cards include the Columbus for calls to Western Europe and North America, the standard Scheda Telefonica Internazionale for the rest

of the world, and the Europa Card for calls to Europe, US and Canada only. To use one of these cards, you dial a central number and then enter a pin code given on the reverse of the card, before dialling the number you want to reach. Finally, you can make international reversed-charge or collect calls (*chiamata con addebito destinatario*) by dialling ☏170 and following the recorded instructions.

Time

Italy is on Central European Time – one hour ahead of Britain, six hours ahead of EST and eight hours ahead of PST in the US. It's also nine hours behind Perth, eleven hours behind Sydney, and one hour behind Cape Town and Johannesburg.

Tourist information

The **Italian State Tourist Board** (ENIT; Ⓦwww.enit.it) can be useful for maps and accommodation listings before you go – though you can usually pick up fuller information from tourist offices in Italy. Details of every town's tourist offices are given in the Guide.

Italian State Tourist Offices abroad

Australia Level 4, 46 Market St, Sydney, NSW 2000 ☏02/926 21666, Ⓦwww.italiantourism.com.au.
Canada 175 Bloor St East, Suite 907, South Tower, Toronto, ON M4W 3R8 ☏416/925-4882, Ⓦwww .italiantourism.com.
UK 1 Princes St, London W1B 2AY ☏0270/408 1254, Ⓦwww.italiantouristboard.co.uk.
US 630 Fifth Avenue, Suite 1565, New York, NY 10111 ☏212/245-5618; 12400 Wilshire Boulevard, Suite 550, Los Angeles, CA 90025 ☏310/820-1898; 500 North Michigan Ave, 506, Chicago, IL 60611 ☏312/644-0996; Ⓦwww .italiantourism.com.

Discount cards

You can cut the price of sightseeing by investing in the **Campania Artecard**, which gives free travel in Naples, on buses to Pozzuoli and Caserta, and on the Circumvesuviana, Circumflegrea and Cumana lines, plus free entry to several key sights, as well as large discounts on others. You can choose from a ticket that concentrates on city museums and sights of the Campi Flegrei (€16, valid for 3 days), another covering all the archeological sites of the bay (€30, valid 3 days), and others that are valid for longer, focus on different sights, or include sights but no transport. More information is available on ☏800.600.601 or at ⊛www.artecard.it.

Many state museums and archeological sites offer cut-price admission to **EU citizens**, with entrance often free to those under 18 and over 65, and a fifty-percent discount to those aged between 18 and 25. ISIC cards are not accepted at many sights because entry prices are based on age, rather than student status, so official ID such as a passport or driver's licence is best.

If you're planning to visit Herculaneum as well as Pompeii, it's worth knowing that there's a joint ticket that covers entry to both sights, plus the nearby Villa Oplontis, for €20 (valid three days); note, however, that these sites are also covered by the Campania Artecard (see above).

Travellers with disabilities

Facilities in Naples aren't geared towards travellers with disabilities, though progress is slowly being made to make accommodation, transport and public buildings more accessible. In Naples, cobbled streets, high kerbs, ad hoc parking and building works can make life difficult for those in wheelchairs and the partially sighted, while the steep hillsides of the Amalfi Coast in particular can present their own problems. On car-free Cápri, the lack of stairs makes getting around somewhat easier, though the slopes are very steep and the buses aren't wheelchair accessible. **Public transport** in general can be challenging, although some trains have disabled facilities; call ☏081.567.2991 in advance for assistance. You can ask at the local tourist office to give you a hand with finding adapted **accommodation**. The website ⊛www.turismoaccessibile.it is an excellent resource, with a wealth of useful information on everything from accessible hotels to wheelchair-friendly monuments and churches in Naples and the surrounding area.

Travelling with children

Children are adored in Italy and will be made a fuss of in the street, and welcomed and catered for in bars and restaurants. Hotels normally charge around thirty percent extra to put a bed or cot in your room, though kids pay less on trains and can generally expect discounts for museum entry: prices vary, but 11–18 year-olds are usually admitted at half price on production of some form of ID (although sometimes this applies only to EU citizens). Under-11s – or sometimes only under-6s – have free entry.

Supplies for **babies** and small children are pricey: nappies and milk formula can cost up to three times as much as in other parts of Europe. Discreet breastfeeding is widely accepted – even smiled on – but nappy changing facilities are few and far between. Branches of the children's clothes and accessories chain, Prenatal, have changing facilities and a feeding area, but otherwise you may find you have to be creative. High-chairs are unusual too, although establishments in areas that see a high volume of foreign visitors tend to be better equipped.

Guide

Guide

Naples

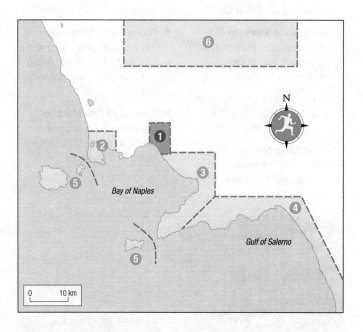

CHAPTER 1 # Highlights

* **The Duomo** The heart and soul of the city, home to the blood of San Gennaro and a host of other features besides. See p.55

* **San Lorenzo Maggiore** A beautiful Gothic church and the underground remnants of the city's ancient Roman marketplace. See p.58

* **Cappella Sansevero** The most macabre attraction in a city full of grotesque treasures. See p.63

* **Santa Chiara** The church and cloister here are one of the city's gems. See p.63

* **MADRE** Naples' superb modern art museum, with some great bespoke exhibits. See p.65

* **Museo Archeologico Nazionale** A fantastic archeological collection, home to the cream of the treasures from Pompeii and Herculaneum. See p.72

* **Museo Nazionale di Capodimonte** One of Italy's prime art collections. See p.76

* **Going to the football** Napoli are the pride of the city, and a visit to the Stadio San Paolo is a great Naples experience. See p.82

* **Certosa di San Martino** Some of the city's finest views, and one of its best museums. See p.84

▲ View from the Certosa di San Martino

Naples

The capital of the Campania region, and indeed of the whole Italian south, **NAPLES** is a city that comes laden with visitors' preconceptions. And it rarely disappoints: it is filthy, it is sprawling and overbearing, and it is most definitely like nowhere else in Italy – something the Neapolitans will be keener than anyone to tell you. Despite this, Naples has its own unique brand of charm, making it possible to endure the noise, harassment and disorder. Refreshingly lacking in tourist-ready gloss, the city is beautiful, but unassumingly so: down-at-heel churches are crammed with Baroque masterpieces, rustic *trattorie* serve up world-class cuisine, and a simple stroll through the centro storico yields no end of memorable vistas; a couple of days here and you're likely to be as staunch a defender of the place as its most devoted inhabitants.

Indeed, few cities on earth inspire such fierce loyalties, and yet Naples' great contradiction is that, with such impressive raw materials, it could reach far greater heights, and properly join the European tourist mainstream. But the city is more complex than that; ironically, its problems with organized crime and poverty are the very aspects which keep it the unique and culturally distinct place that it is – and neither the locals nor its increasing numbers of admiring visitors would have it any other way.

The **centro storico** is the heart of the city, a crowded, buzzing quarter, where Renaissance *palazzi* rise up above streets which hardly see any light. It's this part of town that rightly gets the most attention, with a dense concentration of sights, the legacy of the city's chequered history. It's quite different to anywhere else in Italy, indeed in Europe: less homogenized than other cities, and unique in its layout, which follows the grid of the ancient city underneath, with the palaces and churches of the French and Spanish eras grafted on top. There's always something to see in this part of town, and you could spend a couple of days happily wandering the streets here. But give time too to the modern neighbourhoods beyond: stretching up the city's hills and around the bay, these areas have an altogether different appeal, not to mention a handful of outstanding museums, and some amazing views from the most elevated points.

Some history

Naples was originally a Hellenistic city, founded by **Greek** settlers from the nearby colony of Cumae, who built a city on the mount of Pizzofalcone, Parthenope, and later moved down the hill to found a settlement they called **Neapolis** or "New City". It's this that forms the basis of modern-day Naples, which later became an important **Roman** settlement, at the heart of the resort area of the Bay of Naples during the Imperial era: the streets of the centro storico still follow the pattern of the old Greek and Roman streets.

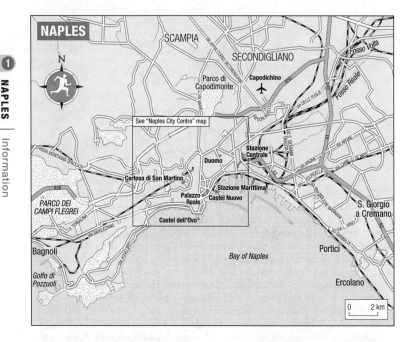

After falling into Byzantine hands several centuries after the fall of Rome, it was conquered by the **Normans** in the eleventh century, becoming part of the Kingdom of Sicily, which it remained for around eight hundred years, during which time – with the odd brief lapse – ownership of the city more or less alternated between the French and the Spanish. During medieval and early Renaissance times it was the capital of the dominions of the French **Angevin** dynasty, after which it fell under the sway of the **Aragonese** from Spain, who ruled until the mid-eighteenth century, developing it into one of the largest and most important cities in Europe. They were supplanted by the **Bourbons** from France, who founded the Kingdom of the Two Sicilies in 1734, and it became an important stop on any Grand Tour of Europe; and then at the turn of the nineteenth century the French Republicans under Napoleon briefly took over before it reverted to the Bourbons.

Naples only truly gained its independence as part of the Italian Unification in 1860, since when it has never regained its status as a major European capital. It was heavily bombed during World War II, after which the **Camorra** – active in the city for several centuries by then – gained a real foothold in the city, a position they have consolidated over recent years. For more on the history of Naples, see "Contexts", p.237.

Information

There are several **tourist offices** dotted around the city: one on Piazza del Gesù (Mon–Sat 9.30am–1.30pm & 2.30–6.30pm, Sun 9am–1.30pm; ☎081.551.2701), one opposite the Teatro San Carlo at Via San Carlo 9 (same hours; ☎081.402.394) and another in the Stazione Centrale (Mon–Sat 8am–8pm, Sun 9am–2pm;

☎081.268.779). Each of them give out free **city maps** as well as **transport maps**, which detail the many public transport options in and around the city (see below). It's also worth picking up an English-language copy of the monthly *Qui Napoli* (which can also be downloaded at ⓦ www.inaples.it), a useful source of information on the city, with events listings.

Accommodation

Perhaps the biggest change in Naples in recent years is its newly galvanized **hotel** industry. The palatial five-stars fronting the sea in Santa Lucia are still there, as are the faceless corporate options that dot the centre around Via Toledo and the port. A lot of places have been renovated, however, and new hotels have opened, not only giving the city a range of contemporary, boutique alternatives, but also lifting the general standard of accommodation to a new high.

If you've been travelling in the north of Italy, hotel **prices** in Naples may come as a pleasant surprise. The city is not a massive tourist draw on the scale of other Italian hotspots, and it is still possible to find bargains, particularly at weekends, when more business-oriented places often drop their prices. We've listed prices for double rooms in high season; most places include breakfast in the price.

If you can, try to **book in advance**, as the city's many decent B&Bs get booked up in high season (May–Sept). Naples' larger hotels often host business conferences, leaving them with few vacancies. The booking site ⓦ www.venere .com is a good last-minute option; you can also call them on ☎0845.602.7990 (Mon–Sat 8am–7pm). Or, if you arrive in Naples without a booking and can't find a room, any of the city's tourist offices (see p.44) distributes *Qui Napoli*, a free publication with an exhaustive list of hotels, B&Bs and hostels. Don't go with one of the touts hanging around the station: quite apart from the safety issues, they'll overcharge you.

Hotels and B&Bs

A good many of Naples' **budget** options are situated around **Piazza Garibaldi**, conveniently close to the train station, but a rather insalubrious and noisy district, and poorly placed for going out at night. Most people prefer to be based in the livelier, more atmospheric **centro storico**, where boutique hotels and small B&Bs run by young, artistic and enthusiastic Neapolitans are sprouting up everywhere – from the centre to the area around Via Toledo and into the **Quartieri Spagnoli** and **Montesanto**. There are also plenty of hotels clustered along the seafront of **Santa Lucia**, close by the Castel dell'Ovo, and in **Chiaia**, areas that should put any traveller wishing to take an evening *passeggiata* at ease. Most places here tend towards the high end; there are a few exceptions, but these tend to be small and fill quickly, so book in advance.

Piazza Garibaldi and around
See map, p.52.

Bella Capri Via Melisurgo 4 ☎081.552.9494, ⓦ www.bellacapri.it. Cheap rooms with views over the bay, and right by the port. The very welcoming staff can help you find bargains for island visits, too. They also run a hostel (see p.50). En-suite doubles cost €60–80 and there's ten-percent discount with this book.

Casanova Via Venezia 2 ☎081.268.287, ⓦ www .hotelcasanova.com. Perhaps the best of the budget options near the station, this creeper-clad hotel is quiet, run by an affable team, and has pleasant rooms (most of which are en suite) and a communal roof terrace. Doubles around €50.
Cavour Piazza Garibaldi 32 ☎081.283.122, ⓦ www.hotelcavournapoli.it. A stone's throw from the station, this is one of the area's more agreeable options, with ninety soberly decorated rooms, and

45

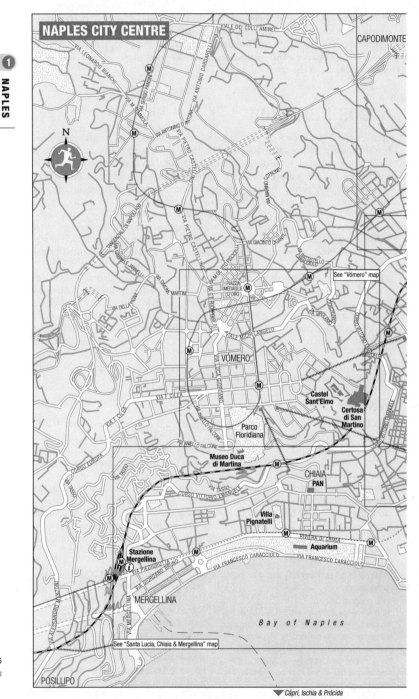

NAPLES CITY CENTRE

CAPODIMONTE

VIALE DEI COLLI AMINEI

VIA LEONARDO BIANCHI

VIA M. SERGIO PANSINI

VIA ANTONINO D'ANTONA

VIA ANTONIO CARDARELLI

VIA PIETRO CASTELLINO

VIA MARINO COTRONE

VIA GIACINTO GIGANTE

VIA BATTISTELLO CARACCIOLO

See "Vómero" map

VIA M. DE VITO PISCICELLI

VIA PIETRO CASTELLINO

TANGENZIALE DI NAPOLI E58

VIA GABRIELE JANNELLI

VIA SIMONE MARTINI

VIA DELLA

VIA G.B. RUOPPOLO

PIAZZA MEDAGLIE D'ORO

VIALE MICHELANGELO

VIA CILEA

VIA F. CILEA

VIA LUCA GIORDANO

VIA GIRTANI

VOMERO

CORSO VITTORIO EMANUELE

Castel Sant'Elmo

VIA ANIELLO FALCONE

Certosa di San Martino

Parco Floridiana

VIA ANIELLO FALCONE

CORSO EUROPA

VIA TASSO

Museo Duca di Martina

CHIAIA

PAN

VIA TASSO

CORSO VITTORIO EMANUELE

Villa Pignatelli

RIVIERA DI CHIAIA

VIA ALESSANDRO MANZONI

Stazione Mergellina

VIA PIEDIGROTTA

Aquarium

VIA FRANCESCO CARACCIOLO

VIA FRANCESCO CARACCIOLO

VIA GIORDANO BRUNO

MERGELLINA

VIA MERGELLINA

Bay of Naples

See "Santa Lucia, Chiaia & Mergellina" map

POSILLIPO

▼ Cápri, Ischia & Prócida

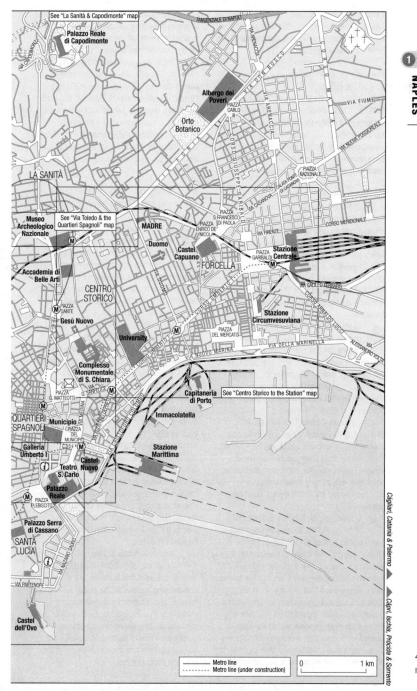

See "La Sanità & Capodimonte" map

Palazzo Reale
di Capodimonte

Albergo dei
Poveri

Orto
Botanico

PIAZZA
CARLO
III

VIA FIUME

VIA NUOVA POGGIOREALE

LA SANITÀ

PIAZZA
NAZIONALE

Museo
Archeologico
Nazionale

See "Via Toledo & the
Quartieri Spagnoli" map

MADRE

PIAZZA
S. FRANCESCO
DI PAOLA

PIAZZA
ENRICO DE
NICOLA

VIA FIRENZE

CORSO MERIDIONALE

Duomo

Stazione
Centrale

Accademia di
Belle Arti

Castel
Capuano

FORCELLA

PIAZZA
GARIBALDI

CENTRO
STORICO

VIA GADILEO FERRARIS

PIAZZA
DANTE

Gesù Nuovo

Stazione
Circumvesuviana

University

PIAZZA
DEL MERCATO

Complesso
Monumentale
di S. Chiara

VIA DELLA MARINELLA

PIAZZA
G. MATTEOTTI

VIA NUOVO MARINA

QUARTIERI
SPAGNOLI

Capitaneria
di Porto

See "Centro Storico to the Station" map

Municipio

PIAZZA
DEL
MUNICIPIO

Immacolatella

Galleria
Umberto I

Stazione
Marittima

Teatro
S. Carlo

Castel
Nuovo

Palazzo
Reale

PIAZZA
PLEBISCITO

Palazzo Serra
di Cassano

SANTA
LUCIA

VIA PARTENOPE

Castel
dell'Ovo

——— Metro line
········· Metro line (under construction)

0   1 km

attentive service. Some rooms have panoramic terraces. Special offers are often available on the website and there are discounts for extended stays. Parking available. Doubles €90–150.

Centro storico
See map, p.52.

Belle Arti Resort Via S. Maria di Costantinopoli 27 ☏081.557.1062, ⊛www.belleartiresort.com. Contemporary design meets historic elegance at this new boutique B&B near Piazza Bellini. Rooms are individually decorated with modern pieces and some have original seventeenth-century ceiling frescoes. Free internet access. Doubles cost €80–120.

Caravaggio Piazza Riario Sforza 157 ☏081.211.0066, ⊛www.caravaggiohotel.it. Right in the thick of things on the edge of Forcella, just around the corner from the Duomo, but quiet enough, on its own small square – which some of the nicer rooms in this elegant old *palazzo* overlook. The rooms are decent on the whole, if uninspired, but you do wonder what the hotel has done to get its fourth star. The official rate for a double is €190, but deals are often available.

Costantinopoli 104 Via S. Maria di Costantinopoli 104 ☏081.557.1035, ⊛www .costantinopoli104.it. A posh boutique hotel with its own small garden and swimming pool in a quiet building just off Piazza Bellini. The rooms and common areas are stylishly furnished with modern design elements. Ideally located for centro storico nightlife. Doubles from €220.

Des Artistes Via Duomo 61 ☏081.446.155, ⊛www.hoteldesartistesnaples.it. A comfortable place with simple rooms and young, friendly staff. Perks include a small bar and cheap internet service. Perfectly located 200m from the Duomo and within easy striking distance of the archeological museum and the centro storico. Good value doubles €55–100.

Donna Regina B&B Via L. Settembrini 80 ☏081.446.799, ⊛www.discovernaples .net. Located next to the MADRE and inside a former convent, this lovely and welcoming B&B is tastefully furnished with a mixture of family heirlooms and modern art. Each room is spacious and uniquely decorated; ask for the Mother Superior's chamber, home to a frescoed chapel. Doubles cost from around €100, and they also rent out small apartments around the city.

Duomo Via Duomo 228 ☏081.265.988, ⊛www .hotelduomonapoli.it. Newly and stylishly done up, but prices are still among the lowest in town. Most

rooms face onto a tranquil internal courtyard and all are en suite. Very welcoming, and in an ideal location for seeing all the major sights of the old centre. Doubles from around €70.

Tribù Via dei Tribunali 339 ☏081.454.793 or 338.409.173, ⊛www.tribunapoli.com. Behind the decrepit walls of the medieval Palazzo d'Angiò on Via dei Tribunali, two architects have created a peaceful artistic oasis of four rooms, each decorated with original ceramics, contemporary paintings and antiques. In fine weather, breakfast is served on an outdoor terrace in the *palazzo*'s courtyard. Doubles €80–120.

Via Toledo and the Quartieri Spagnoli
See map, p.67.

Il Convento Via Speranzella 137A ☏081.403.997, ⊛www.hotelilconvento.com. Occupying a good position in the Quartieri Spagnoli, this three-star has cosy rooms, furnished in a dark, old-fashioned style – and a couple, at the top, with their own private terraces. Doubles €80–180; deals are often available. Internet access is included.

Correra 241 Via Correra 241 ☏081.1956.2842, ⊛www.correra.it. Between Piazza Dante and the archeological museum, this three-star is decorated in primary colours, giving it a fresh, contemporary look. The rooms are a decent size, although the en-suite bathrooms are rather irritatingly up a separate staircase on a mezzanine level. There's a nice little roof garden, and internet access, though the breakfast is frugal, even by Naples standards. Doubles €75–120.

Palazzo Turchini Via Medina 21–22 ☏081.551.0606, ⊛www.palazzoturchini.it. Once home to an orphanage and a musical conservatory, the building sits on a busy street not far from the port and Piazza Municipio. Rooms are cosy with all mod cons, and there's a lovely roof terrace. Request a room that faces onto the internal garden for a tranquil night's sleep. Doubles €150–190.

San Francesco al Monte Corso Vittorio Emanuele 328 ☏081.423.9111, ⊛www .sanfrancescoalmonte.it. Occupying a commanding position on the slopes leading up to Vómero, this converted sixteenth-century monastery is an exceptional hotel, each of the 45 rooms beautifully decorated and offering panoramic views of the city. There is a pool, tranquil gardens and three restaurants in the grounds. Doubles €285.

La Sanità and Capodimonte

See map, p.74.

Villa Capodimonte Via Moiariello 66 ☏ 081.459.000, ⓦ www.villacapodimonte.it. Ideally sited for seeing the Palazzo Reale di Capodimonte, this recently opened modern option is very comfortable, and attractively located, surrounded by its own private park. Some rooms have views over the city's roofs to Vesuvius. Doubles €70–175.

Santa Lucia and Chiaia

See map, p.80.

Cappella Vecchia 11 Vico S. Maria a Cappella Vecchia 11 ☏ 081.240.5117, ⓦ www .cappellavecchia11.it. Just off Piazza dei Martiri in the heart of Chiaia, this B&B has six bright and comfortable en-suite rooms, each with free wi-fi. The young owners are very helpful and can help organize tours and excursions to the islands. Doubles €80–120.

Chiaja Hotel De Charme Via Chiaia 216 ☏ 081.415.555, ⓦ www.hotelchiaia.it. A lovely, quaint and very central hotel, with 21 rooms fashioned from an eighteenth-century patrician home – and with lots of antique furniture and old-world style to prove it. Doubles €100–165.

Chiatamone B&B Via Chiatamone 6 ☏ 081.060.8129, ⓦ www.hotelchiatamone.it. Located between Chiaia and Borgo Santa Lucia, this warm and welcoming family-run B&B has six spacious rooms with all mod cons and in a variety of configurations, including a mini apartment with small kitchen. Doubles from €110.

Excelsior Via Partenope 48 ☏ 081.764.0111, ⓦ www.excelsior.it. The *grande dame* of Naples hotels oozes sophistication and opulence from its wonderful waterfront location. Its grand rooms have views across the bay to Vesuvius and are well worth splashing out on, if only to say you've stayed in the same place as such luminaries as Maria Callas and Clark Gable. Doubles are €360, but check the website for offers.

Grand Hotel Parker's Corso Vittorio Emanuele 135 ☏ 081.761.2474, ⓦ www.grandhotelparkers .it. This upmarket and extremely comfortable hotel claims to be the oldest in Naples, and has hosted Oscar Wilde and Virginia Woolf, as well as King Vittorio Emanuele himself. The views from the dining room over the bay and east to Vesuvius are unparalleled; the drawback is that it is detached from the city's main sites so taxis or public transport are a must. Doubles €255–360.

Miramare Via N. Sauro 24 ☏ 081.764.7589, ⓦ www.hotelmiramare.com. This Art Nouveau gem is the less obvious – and cheaper – alternative to the giant and sometimes impersonal palaces on this stretch of the waterfront, with a more homely feel and a warmer welcome. Doubles are excellent value at €160–200, more for a sea view.

Palazzo Alabardieri Via Alabardieri 38 ☏ 081.415.278, ⓦ www.palazzoalabardieri .it. In the heart of Chiaia, this hotel is geared towards business travellers and discerning tourists looking for luxury and courteous service. The well-appointed rooms are decorated with parquet floors, marble and rich fabrics. Prices can vary from €160 for a double to upwards of €300.

Parteno B&B Via Partenope 1 ☏ 081.245.2095, ⓦ www.parteno.it. Seven individually designed and beautifully furnished rooms, all with balcony, in an eighteenth-century building on the waterfront near the Villa Comunale. Wonderful attention to detail by the owners distinguishes this place – including a great breakfast. Doubles €110–125.

Pinto-Storey Via Martucci 72 ☏ 081.681.260, ⓦ www.pintostorey.it. An evocative Art Nouveau building in a pleasant part of Chiaia, near Naples' most elegant shopping area and close to the Villa Comunale and the sea. Rooms are attractively furnished and many have views of the bay. Good value, with doubles from €130.

Rex Via Palepoli 12 ☏ 081.764.9389, ⓦ www.hotel-rex.it. In a striking Art Nouveau-style building designed by the renowned Italian architect Coppedè, this family-run hotel in Santa Lucia has some of the friendliest staff around. There's a large sitting room in the reception area frequented by the owner's family and friends, and the rooms are simple and tidy. Doubles €100.

Mergellina and Posillipo

See map, p.80.

Ausonia Via Caracciolo 11 ☏ 081.682.278, ⓦ www.hotelausonianapoli.com. A two-star decorated to give the impression you're on board a yacht, neatly placed in Mergellina, next to the stop for hydrofoils to the islands. Ask for one of the rooms with bay views. Doubles go for €120.

Mergellina Via G. Bruno 115 ☏ 081.248. 2142, ⓦ www.hotelmergellina.it. This homely budget option is situated just off Piazza Sannazzaro near Mergellina's port. Most of its spick-and-span rooms have balconies and all have free internet access. Excellent value, with doubles from around €110.

Hostels

Hostel Bella Capri Via Melisurgo 4
℡ 081.552.9494, ⓦ www.bellacapri.it; see map,
p.67. A brand new hostel, with four- or seven-bed
dorms, and adjoining bathrooms. There's free
internet and a large, light and airy breakfast room.
Right on the port, so perfect for accessing the
islands. No curfew. €20 per person in high season;
ten-percent discount with this book.

Hostel of the Sun Via Melisurgo 15
℡ 081.420.6393, ⓦ www.hostelnapoli.com; see
map, p.67. This clean, colourful hostel with kitchen
is probably the best and friendliest in Naples and
has a great position right next to the ferry dock for
the islands. It's well placed for going out too, and
there's no curfew: ask for Luca's nightlife suggestions. Dorm beds cost €20 per person and from
€45 per person in high season; breakfast included.
Ten-percent discount on hotel rooms with this
book.

Ostello Mergellina Salita della Grotta 23
℡ 081.761.2346, ⓦ www.ostellonapoli.com; see
map, p.80. This popular HI hostel has lovely
views of the bay, and is located not far from the
Mergellina metro station. There's a 12.30am
curfew, but ask for a double room (€40) and they
are more flexible. Breakfast included. There's
technically a three-day maximum stay in July &
Aug, but this is pretty flexible. Dorm beds €16.

Campsites

There are a number of **campsites** within a feasible distance of Naples. The closest
is the excellent and well-situated *Vulcano Solfatara* site in Pozzuoli at Via Solfatara
161 (℡ 081.526.2341, ⓦ www.solfatara.it; April–Nov), which has bungalows (from
€50 for two) as well as tent pitches. Take the Metropolitana to Pozzuoli and walk
ten minutes up the hill. When this campsite is closed, you're best off going to one
of the other sites around the bay – perhaps at Pompeii (see p.130), or, rather nicer,
Sorrento (see p.134), neither of which is more than an hour out from the city.

The City

Naples is a large, sprawling city, and although its centre is clear enough, focusing
on the centro storico and the shopping artery of Via Toledo, there are a number
of different neighbourhoods which you're likely to wander through. For
simplicity, we've divided it into **six main areas**. You're likely to arrive in the
area around **Piazza Garibaldi**, a scruffy, unenticing introduction to the city,
where the interest is more in the areas beyond the square – in Forcella and
down towards the port. West of here lies the ancient part of the city, or **centro
storico**, roughly corresponding to the Roman Neapolis and with the main
streets still following the path of the old Roman roads. This is much the liveliest
part of town, an open-air kasbah of hawking, yelling humanity that makes up
in energy what it lacks in grace. Buildings rise high on either side of the narrow,
crowded streets, cobwebbed with washing; there's little light, and not even
much sense of the rest of the city outside – certainly not of the proximity of
the sea. Naples' commercial and modern centre has **Via Toledo** as its spine,
from Piazza Trieste e Trento and the Palazzo Reale at its southern end to the
Museo Nazionale Archeologico at the top. North of here, **La Sanità and
Capodimonte** represent Naples at both its most poor and most grand, while
in the opposite direction the chic neighbourhoods of **Chiaia and Santa Lucia**
have a slower pace and a more upscale look all-round – a feel that continues to

some extent in the adjacent neighbourhoods of Mergellina and Posillipo. High above the city is **Vómero**, reachable by funciular and home to some of the city's most classic views of the bay and beyond.

Piazza Garibaldi and around

However you get to Naples, there's a good chance that you'll arrive in **Piazza Garibaldi**, a long, wide square crisscrossed by traffic lanes, that cuts into the city centre from the modern train station. It's the city's transport hub – most buses leave from here, as do the Metropolitana and Circumvesuviana lines – and one of its most hectic junctions; indeed it's Piazza Garibaldi, perhaps more than any other part of the city, that puts people off Naples, especially at the moment. The entire piazza is currently a vast construction site due to work on the new metro, and pedestrians are blocked by steel walls and challenged by traffic at every turn, especially when trying to reach the bus stops at the opposite side of the piazza. Of late, the area has also become a centre for the city's growing immigrant community, with a number of African restaurants and Moroccan grocery stores, and don't be surprised to hear Slavic accents too – many Ukrainians find their way here to work as housekeepers in the city.

Forcella

Off the northeastern corner of Piazza Garibaldi, the **Porta Capuana** is one of several relics from the Aragonese city walls, a sturdy defensive gate dating from 1490, delicately decorated on one side in Florentine Renaissance style. Next to it, the large domed church of **Santa Caterina a Formiello** is one of the city's most highly decorated Renaissance churches, while across the road, the much renovated **Castel Capuano**, with its decorative white plaster facade, was the residence of the Norman king William I, and later, under the Spanish, became a courthouse – which it still is.

Beyond Castel Capuano, Via dei Tribunali begins its long trek across the city centre, through the most easterly part of old Naples, the **Forcella** quarter, which spreads down from the Castel Capuano to Corso Umberto I, and is the main city-centre stronghold of the Camorra (Neapolitan mafia) and home to some of its most important families. It's always been one of the city's poorest areas, but it's also something of a vibrant open-air market, where sellers of knock-off CDs and sunglasses hawk their wares, alongside a vast quantity of food stalls – not to mention a couple of the city's best and most authentic pizzerias (see p.87).

Perhaps the most tangible manifestation of the district's ingrained poverty is the church of **Santissima Annunziata**, which lies on Via dell'Annunziata, one of the neighbourhood's busiest streets. The church was remodelled by Vanvitelli in the eighteenth century, and has a big, white wedding-cake of an interior. The real interest is next door, in a building that was once an orphanage, now a hospital. Through a little portico on the left, you can get a close look at the restored *ruota,* or wheel, in which unwanted babies used to be left for the church to look after. The space in the wheel is chillingly baby-sized, while a few displays in the next room summarize the work of the institution and include lists from the seventeenth century of babies who were left here – all named – in case you're in any doubt as to how much it was used in its heyday. Outside, you can see the window through which the babies would have been placed in the wheel, now bricked up and marked with the date – 27 June, 1875 – when they stopped taking them in.

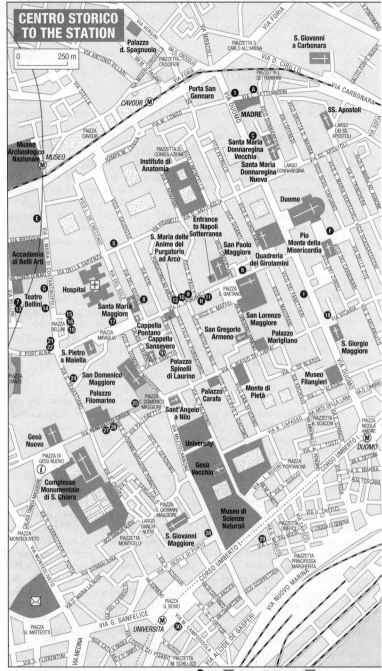

CENTRO STORICO
TO THE STATION

0 — 250 m

J (100m) ▼   Stazione Marittima (1km) ▼

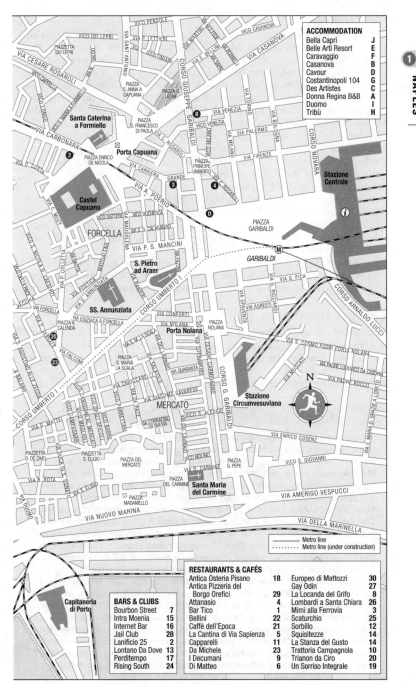

ACCOMMODATION

Bella Capri	J
Belle Arti Resort	E
Caravaggio	F
Casanova	B
Cavour	D
Costantinopoli 104	G
Des Artistes	C
Donna Regina B&B	A
Duomo	I
Tribù	H

BARS & CLUBS

Bourbon Street	7
Intra Moenia	15
Internet Bar	16
Jail Club	28
Lanificio 25	2
Lontano Da Dove	13
Perditempo	17
Rising South	24

RESTAURANTS & CAFÉS

Antica Osteria Pisano	18	Europeo di Mattozzi	30
Antica Pizzeria del		Gay Odin	27
Borgo Orefici	29	La Locanda del Grifo	8
Attanasio	4	Lombardi a Santa Chiara	26
Bar Tico	1	Mimi alla Ferrovia	3
Bellini	22	Scaturchio	25
Caffè dell'Epoca	21	Sorbillo	12
La Cantina di Via Sapienza	5	Squisitezze	14
Capparelli	11	La Stanza del Gusto	14
Da Michele	23	Trattoria Campagnola	10
I Decumani	9	Trianon da Ciro	20
Di Matteo	6	Un Sorriso Integrale	19

53

Mercato

Leading off the southwestern corner of Piazza Garibaldi, **Corso Garibaldi** runs down to the sea and the Mercato area, past the **Porta Nolana**, on the right, a solid Aragonese gateway that hosts a morning fish market in the surrounding streets, which are lined with a wonderful array of stalls piled high with wriggling displays of fish and seafood. Further down Corso Garibaldi, past the main Circumvesuviana rail terminal and off to the right, is the thirteenth-century church of **Santa Maria del Carmine**, on the corner of Piazza del Carmine. Landmarked by its distinctive curvaceous campanile, it is traditionally the church of the poor in Naples, particularly fishermen and mariners. Axel Munthe, the Swedish writer and resident of Cápri, used to sleep here after tending to victims of the 1884 cholera outbreak. It's a heavily decorated church, quite a contrast to the shabby square outside, and is known for the miraculous properties of a couple of objects inside: a wooden crucifix, hidden away in a wooden tabernacle below the arch of the transept, which dodged a cannonball during a siege in 1439 and has been revered ever since; and the Byzantine icon of the so-called *Madonna Bruna* or "Dark Madonna" behind the high altar, which is supposed to have saved the bell tower from a fire and is now celebrated every July 16 with a massive display of fireworks.

Just beyond Piazza del Carmine, the war-damaged **Piazza del Mercato** was for centuries home to the city's gallows, and is a bleak, dusty square even now. It's not an especially pleasant part of town, with nothing further to detain you.

Corso Umberto I

Dead-straight **Corso Umberto I**, also known as the *Rettifilo*, was built during the late nineteenth century not only as a traffic artery but also to separate the heart of the old city from the port during the cholera outbreak of the 1880s. The street spears through the old part of the city, a long, straight journey from the seedy gatherings of prostitutes and kerb-crawlers at its Piazza Garibaldi end, past many

The Port of Naples

Naples' **port** is in many ways the engine of the city, but it's a squalid and imperfect one; its quaysides and piers, yards and warehouses occupy nearly eleven kilometres of the waterfront. A mass of flyovers, decaying warehouses and factories stretch from the **Molo Beverello** passenger terminal to the merchant shipping docks further south, all the way down to the suburb of San Giovanni a Teduccio and beyond, littered with piles and piles of containers, mostly from China (Naples handles a huge percentage of the EU's trade with China – which in itself is a large percentage of the EU's trade overall). The port looks like a secure area, but it's not: according to the anti-Camorra author Roberto Saviano, well over half of all goods arriving in Naples are not inspected by customs, and most are prey to a series of mafia-sponsored scams that used to involve mainly cigarettes but now consist of more or less anything that will make money.

Most of the port was redeveloped in the late nineteenth century, when the main Via Cristoforo Colombo that leads alongside the waterfront was built. From a tourist's point of view there's nothing to see, and you wouldn't want to spend any of your time in Naples anywhere near here. But you may notice one building from an earlier time: the **Immacolatella**, on its own jetty about 200m past Molo Beverello, a former quarantine station which dates from 1740 and was the work of the painter and architect Domenico Vaccaro, who was also responsible for the much more visible cloister of Santa Chiara, and much else in Naples besides. The arch and fountain that used to stand alongside have been relocated to the Castel dell'Ovo (see p.78).

of the city's more mainstream shops, to Piazza Nicola Amore, from where Via Duomo heads up the hill to the right, dividing Forcella from the centro storico on its left-hand side. From Piazza Nicola Amore it continues past Naples' **University**, whose series of huge buildings dominates this part of town (see p.62), from where you can either cut through into the heart of the centro storico, or continue on to the symmetrical **Piazza Bovio** and its elegant seventeenth-century Fontana di Nettuno – and, beyond, the waterfront around the Castel Nuovo and Piazza Municipio, the city's modern centre.

The centro storico

The UNESCO-protected **centro storico** covers the area of the old Roman Neapolis, much of which is still unexcavated below the ground. Its two main streets are **Via dei Tribunali** and **Via San Biagio dei Librai** (the latter also known as Spaccanapoli): narrow thoroughfares, lined with old arcaded buildings, which lead due west on the path of the *decumanus maior* and *decumanus inferior* respectively of Roman times. Both streets are charged with atmosphere throughout the day, a maelstrom of hurrying pedestrians, revving cars and buzzing, dodging scooters. A third street, known as the **Anticaglia**, follows the *decumanus superior* across the top end of the ancient centre, and is quieter and with fewer sights as such, but still repays a wander.

Via del Duomo and around

Via del Duomo borders the centro storico to the east, a dead straight thoroughfare from the port and across Corso Umberto to Via Foria that was laid out after the 1880s cholera epidemic decimated this part of the city. A little way up on the right, the right aisle of the large church of **San Giorgio Maggiore** was demolished to make way for the street, which explains its somewhat lopsided appearance today. It doesn't look it, but it is one of Naples' oldest churches, as you'll see from the semicircular entrance, which was formerly the apse of an early Christian basilica and is the only part to have survived a mid-seventeenth-century earthquake – which probably qualifies San Giorgio as the city's most messed-about church. On the other side of Via Duomo, at no. 288, the rusticated **Palazzo Como** was built in the fifteenth century for a Florentine merchant and for years has housed the **Museo Filangieri**, a small collection of paintings and applied arts that has been closed for some time, and shows no sign of reopening; contact the tourist office for updates.

The Duomo

Tucked away unassumingly from the main street, Naples' **Duomo** (Mon–Sat 8.30am–12.30pm & 4.30–7pm, Sun 8.30am–1pm) is a Gothic building from the early thirteenth century (though with a late nineteenth-century neo-Gothic facade), dedicated to the patron saint of the city, **San Gennaro**. The church – and saint – are key reference points for Neapolitans: San Gennaro was martyred at Pozzuoli, just outside Naples, in 305 AD under the purges of Diocletian. Tradition has it that, when his body was transferred here, two phials of his dried blood liquefied in the bishop's hands, since which time the "miracle" has continued to repeat itself no fewer than three times a year: on the first Saturday in May (when a procession leads from the church of Santa Chiara to the cathedral) and on September 19 and December 16. There is still a great deal of superstition surrounding this event: San Gennaro is seen as the saviour and protector of Naples, and if the blood refuses to liquefy – which luckily is rare – disaster is supposed to befall the city, and many still wait with bated breath to see if the miracle has occurred. Interestingly, one of the few occasions in recent times that Gennaro's blood hasn't turned was in 1944, an event followed by Vesuvius' last eruption. The most recent times were in 1980, the year of the earthquake, and in 1988, the day after which Naples lost an important football match to their rivals, Milan. The miraculous liquefaction takes place during a special Mass in full view of the congregation (see box below), though the church authorities have yet to allow any close scientific examination of the blood. Whatever the truth, there's no question it's still a significant event in the Neapolitan calendar, and one of the more bizarre of the city's institutions.

Inside, the third chapel on the right is dedicated to San Gennaro. It's an eye-bogglingly ornate affair, practically a church in its own right, containing the precious phials of the saint's blood and his skull in a silver bust-reliquary from 1305 (stored behind the altar except for ceremonies). Further down the nave, there are paintings by seventeenth-century Neapolitan artists Luca Giordano and Francesco Solimena in the transepts, and some scraps of ancient fresco in the Gothic Minutolo chapel in the right transept, together with a large and gaudy funerary monument, while on the other side of the nave is a painting of *Our Lady of the Assumption* by Perugino and two altar doors by Vasari. Down below, the **crypt** of San Gennaro holds an altar dedicated to the saint – complete with bones – and a statue of a kneeling Cardinal Carafa, the crypt's founder.

Off the left-hand side of the nave, the basilica of **Santa Restituta** is actually a separate church, officially the oldest structure in Naples, erected by Constantine in 324 and supported by columns that were taken from a temple to Apollo on this site. Off to the right of the main altar, the **baptistry** (Mon–Sat 9am–12.30pm & 4.30–6pm, Sun 9am–1pm; €3) also contains relics from very early Christian times, including late fifth-century mosaics and a font believed to have been taken from a temple to Dionysus. The same ticket gives you entry to the **excavations** below the church (same hours), accessed from the

The miracle of San Gennaro

If you're in Naples at the right time (see p.55) it's possible to attend the service to witness the **liquefaction of San Gennaro's blood**, but you must be sure to arrive at the cathedral early. The Mass starts at 9am, and queues begin to form two hours before that; arrive much after 7am and there's a chance you won't get in. Once the line of Carabinieri have opened up the church everyone will make a dash for the front; for a good view of the proceedings you'll have to join them – and pushing and shoving is, incidentally, very much part of the procedure. The atmosphere in the church throughout the service is a boisterous one. The preliminary Mass goes on for some time, the chancel of the church ringed by armed policemen and flanked by a determined press corps, until a procession leads out of the saint's chapel holding the (still solid) phial of blood aloft, to much applause and neck-craning, and cries of "*Viva San Gennaro!*" After ten minutes or so of emotional imprecations the reliquary is taken down from its holder and inspected – at which point, hopefully, it is declared to tumultuous applause and cheering that the saint's blood is indeed now liquid, and the phial is shaken to prove the point. Afterwards the atmosphere is a festive one, stallholders setting up outside the church and the devout queuing up to kiss the phial containing the liquefied blood – a process that goes on for a week.

baptistry. Largely remains of a still earlier church, along with relics from the Roman and even the Greek ancient cities, the excavations cover a vast area. It's all a bit of a hotch-potch, but at least it's well laid out, with raised walkways and a clear route, and some things are easy to make out: remnants of Greek-era wall and road, Roman gutters and drainage systems, and mosaic floors from the fifth-century basilica. Finally, to the right of the cathedral there's the **Museo del Tesoro di San Gennaro** (Tues–Sat 9.30am–5pm, Sun 9.30am–2.30pm; €5), which contains an array of reliquaries, statuary and suchlike, and isn't really worth the entrance fee.

Via dei Tribunali and around

Via Duomo is crossed a little further up by Via dei Tribunali, one of the two main streets of old Naples, which leads straight through the heart of the old city to link to the modern centre around Via Toledo. It's richer in interest and sights than almost any other street in Naples, and you can spend many happy hours picking your way through its churches, palaces and underground caverns, stopping off for pizza at one of its numerous pizzerias before emerging at Piazza Bellini and strolling up to the archeological museum.

The Pio Monte della Misericordia

On the Forcella side of Via dei Tribunali you'll find the headquarters of **Pio Monte della Misericordia** (Thurs–Tues 9am–2.30pm; €5, or €10 joint ticket with MADRE and the Duomo's Museo del Tesoro), a still-functioning charity that was set up in the early seventeenth century to alleviate the plight of the poor. It's one of the artistic treasure houses of Naples; and most people come to see the charity's **chapel**. This beautiful octagonal structure houses not only Caravaggio's moving *Seven Acts of Mercy*, in pride of place over its high altar, but also a beautiful and emotional *Deposition* by the late seventeenth-century Neapolitan artist Luca Giordano – easy to miss as you come in – and Battistello Caracciolo's *The Freeing of St Peter* in the chapel next door. You can also visit the rooms of the organization's **picture gallery** upstairs, some of which are functioning offices and meeting rooms. The trustees of the charity still meet in the Sala del Governo at the far end, overlooked by four powerful paintings of Christ by Mattia Preti, and next door a little balcony looks down onto the church, and has Caravaggio-like paintings from the same era, notably the *Incredulity of St Thomas* by the Dutch painter Dirk van Baburen. The highlight of the other rooms is a rare self-portrait by Luca Giordano, showing the face of an arrogant and ill-tempered intellectual, glasses perched on his nose.

To Piazza San Gaetano

Via dei Tribunali continues past **Piazza Girolamini**, on which a plaque marks the house where, in 1668, Giambattista Vico was born. Vico was a late-Renaissance Neapolitan philosopher who advanced theories of cyclical history that were far ahead of their time and still echo through modern-day thinking: James Joyce's *Finnegan's Wake* was based on his writings. Vico lived all his life in this district and was buried in the church of **Girolamini**, which you can't visit but which also has a small picture gallery, the **Quadreria dei Girolamini** (Mon–Fri 9.30am–12.30pm; free), accessed off a rather overgrown cloister from Via Duomo 142, opposite the cathedral. Here, half a dozen dark and dusty rooms contain paintings of the Neapolitan school – mostly dark, brooding works, the best of which are Giuseppe Ribera's depictions of saints Paul, Andrew and Peter, and Guido Reni's *Flight into Egypt*, as well as paintings by Luca Giordano and Battistello Caracciolo in the last couple of rooms.

A little way down Via dei Tribunali, the streets open out a little at a spot which would have been the ancient agora or **forum** of the ancient Greek and Roman cities at **Piazza San Gaetano**, marked by the statue of the saint. On the right the basilica of **San Paolo Maggiore** stands on the site of a Roman temple that was rebuilt as a Christian basilica, its ancient roots manifest in a couple of Roman columns which help support the facade with its double staircase. The current church, dating from the seventeenth century, is a huge marbled structure with a wide central nave, decorated with some (sadly damaged) frescoes by Massimo Stanzione. There's little else of interest, apart from the sacristry to the right of the main altar, which is a confection of late seventeenth-century frescoes by Francesco Solimena, with the *Conversion of St Paul* depicted in typically melodramatic style.

San Lorenzo Maggiore

Almost opposite San Paolo Maggiore, at the top end of Via San Gregorio Armeno, the church of **San Lorenzo Maggiore** is a light, spacious Gothic structure, unspoiled by postwar additions and with a soaring Gothic ambulatory in its apse – unusual in Italy, even more so in Naples. It's a mainly thirteenth- and fourteenth-century building, though with a much later facade, built during the reign of the Angevin king Robert the Wise on the site of a Roman temple and market area – remains of which are in the cloisters. Evidence of its long and distinguished history is everywhere, from the fragments of mosaic floor under glass in the nave to scraps of medieval fresco and Renaissance funerary monuments. Certainly, it was at the centre of the golden age that Naples enjoyed under Robert, and the focus of its cultural activity. Petrarch stayed in the adjacent convent, and Boccaccio is said to have met the model for his Fiammetta – believed to be Robert's daughter – during Mass here in 1334.

You can also visit areas of the **convent**, a **museum** and – most interestingly – descend to the **excavations** beneath the church. The **museum** (Mon–Sat 10am–5pm, Sun 10am–1.30pm; €5), on several floors, has frescoes and statuary from the church, arrayed around a lovely painted small atrium, and on the top floor, a series of painted wooden figures from large-scale eighteenth-century *presepi* (see p.59). Off the courtyard of the **convent** are a few rooms from the old Angevin-era building, including the long, frescoed Sisto V room and the adjoining chapterhouse, its walls decorated with portraits of members of the religious orders based here in the late sixteenth century.

But the real draw are the **excavations**. Here you can explore the remains of the Roman forum as you walk along the old Roman pavement, passing a barrel-vaulted bakery, a laundry and an area of sloping stone banquettes, where it is thought that Romans reclined and debated the great issues of the day, kept warm by a fire beneath the stone. What was likely to have been the town's treasury shows a remarkable resemblance to a contemporary bank, with visitors having to negotiate a security-conscious double doorway before reaching the main area for business. The great tufa foundations of the Roman forum were built over the earlier Greek agora; a scale model shows how the latter was laid out, with the circular *tholos*, where some goods were sold, at its centre. It's a rare chance to see exactly how the layers of the city were built up over the centuries, and to get some idea of how Naples must have looked back in the fifth century BC.

Via San Gregorio Armeno

Via San Gregorio Armeno leads down to the other main axis of the old centre from here, Via San Biagio dei Librai, and is one of the old city's most picturesque streets, lined with places specializing in the making of **presepi** (Christmas cribs), a Neapolitan tradition that endures to this day, although the workshops along here turn them out more or less year-round. The often inventive creations now incorporate modern figures into the huge crib scenes, which can also contain water features, illuminated pizza ovens and tons of moss and bark. "Goodies" such as ex-mayor Antonio Bassolino are distinguished from such "baddies" as Silvio Berlusconi by their halos, while dear, departed saintly figures like Mother Theresa, Princess Diana and Gianni Versace are also commemorated.

On the right, the church of **San Gregorio Armeno** (Mon & Wed–Fri 9am–noon, Tues 9am–12.45pm, Sat & Sun 9am–12.30pm) is a sumptuous Baroque edifice with frescoes above the entrance by Luca Giordano, not to mention two stupendously ornate gilded organs, one on each side of the nave. It's also home to the relics of Santa Patrizia, another Neapolitan saint whose blood – like that of San Gennaro (see p.56) – liquefies on her saint's day (Aug 25), as well as every Tuesday morning. The saint's remains lie in a chapel on the right, while up above the south aisle you'll notice a series of grilles, through which the Benedictine nuns would view the services from the **Chiostro di San Gregorio Armeno** next door. You can sit in the cloister yourself by walking up the street to the convent entrance on the left (Mon–Sat 9.30am–noon, Sun 9.30am–1pm; free; you may have to ring the bell). It's a wonderfully peaceful haven from the noise outside, planted with limes and busy with nuns quietly going about their duties.

Napoli Sotterranea

Next door to the church of San Paolo is the entrance to **Napoli Sotterranea** (Mon–Wed & Fri tours at noon, 2pm & 4pm, Thurs noon, 2pm, 4pm & 9pm, Sat & Sun 10am, noon, 2pm, 4pm & 6pm; €9.30), whose ninety-minute underground **tours** explore what's left of the Greek city of Neapolis. The visit starts by exploring remnants of a Roman theatre – which is actually not far underground at all, and is accessed by way of an old one-room Neapolitan apartment or *basso* – artfully furnished as it would have been when they made the discovery forty years ago. You can see a couple of aisles of the theatre – though it's hard to get a sense of the whole – and it's incredibly well integrated with the buildings above. This is even more evident on Via Anticaglia itself, where two arches over the street are formed by the highest tier of the theatre, and the street curves slightly to follow its shape.

The other part of the tour takes in the **aqueducts** and cisterns that honeycomb the ground beneath the city, used from ancient times until the late nineteenth-century cholera outbreak, and then again as bomb shelters during World War II. The best bit is a candlelit squeeze through some narrow passage-ways to a couple of cisterns that have been refilled with water. For other tours of underground Naples, see p.69.

To Piazza Bellini

A little further down the street, at Via dei Tribunali 39, the skulls on the posts outside the church of **Santa Maria delle Anime del Purgatorio ad Arco** give you a clue that this is one of Naples' more morbid attractions: the site of a death cult that was outlawed in the 1960s by the Catholic authorities but still lives on in a semi-secret fashion in its downstairs **hypogeum** (Sat 10am–1pm,

Superstitious Naples

Naples must be one of the most **superstitious** places on earth – and, in some ways, the most cultish. For a start, there's the enduring belief that the liquefaction of the blood of a **saint** that died two thousand years ago will keep the city from harm (see box, p.56). But it doesn't stop there. There are other local saints that are believed to bring luck and succour to the afflicted – San Vicenzo in La Sanità, the madonnas of the Piedigrotta and Carmine churches, and modern-day saints like San Giuseppe Moscati who is remembered by a shrine in the Gesù Nuovo.

There's also an unhealthy fascination with **death**. Perhaps it's the presence of Vesuvius glowering on the horizon at every turn, but the notion of the end being just around the next corner is strong in Naples, and is manifest in the city's various death cults: shrines in the streets are regularly stocked with fresh flowers and votive offerings; people until recently used to "adopt" a skull in the city's underground cemeteries to cure illnesses; and in the church of **Santa Maria delle Anime del Purgatorio ad Arco** in the centro storico, Neapolitans still secretly make offerings to the dead, although the practice was banned by the church years ago.

Then there's the **lottery**, just a game of luck and numbers to some, but taken much more seriously in Naples, where an inbred belief in signs and omens, fortune and chance, is so strong – and where there are also so many people looking for a stroke of good fortune to pull them out of the gutter. The rules are different here, too, because the numbers have meanings, as determined by **La Smorfia**. This ancient Neapolitan book of dreams and their interpretations ascribes a number to just about anything you might dream about – for example, a pig would always be number 4, a nude woman 21, a hunchback 57, a bride 63, and so on; people who can interpret dreams and the Smorfia are in high demand.

Among countless Neapolitan legends is the **munaciello**, literally "little monk", a sprite who hovers around houses playing pranks on the inhabitants, leaving notes or moving things, breaking furniture, or whispering in the ears of people while they're asleep. These figures were originally associated with the tunnels and cisterns underneath Naples, from where they could gain access to people's houses and play tricks – any kind of disorder could be down to the *munaciello*. However, although you may notice their presence in your house, it's considered extremely bad luck to tell anyone about it.

Neapolitans also traditionally fear people with the *malocchio* or **"evil eye"** – folk who are perceived to have evil powers. Again, it's rooted in the city's obsession with fate and fortune, and naturally there are all sorts of ways of combating the bad luck or *jettatura* that the evil eye can cause. The leaves of various plants are said to be effective, and garlic of course; and historically men touching their genitals was supposed to avert misfortune. But the commonest and most effective way of dealing with the evil eye is to make the sign of horns by holding up your index and little finger and pointing at the ground, or to carry an amulet with the sign of horns – effective as long as they are red, pointed, twisted and given as a present: not hard to do given that they are sold as trinkets all over the city centre.

tours every 20min; €2). The church itself is nothing special, but the two dusty chapels down below hold tiled shrines to the anonymous dead who were worshipped here, revered as intermediaries between the earthly and divine, and given names that endeared the keepers of their graves to them. Some – to "Lucia" for example – are full of flowers and bones, and strewn with notes from well-wishers. It's a peculiar place: neglected, yet still very much in use.

Beyond the church, at Via dei Tribunali 362, the eighteenth-century **Palazzo Spinelli di Laurino** is worth a peek. The walls are studded with medallions depicting classical themes and the oval courtyard and monumental staircase tucked into the far corner are a great example of how rooted these grand old *palazzi* are in modern Neapolitan life: festooned with plants and satellite dishes, but with a real elegance beyond the chipped plaster and peeling paint.

Just past Palazzo Spinelli, on the right, the brick campanile of the church of **Santa Maria Maggiore alla Pietrasanta** stands out like a sore thumb. Naples' only surviving large-scale medieval monument, it dates from the eleventh century, and is actually a lot more interesting than the church itself just behind: little more than a large, domed shed put up in Cosimo Fanzago in 1653. There's another interesting feature just outside, the **Cappella Pontano**, a late fifteenth-century structure that looks like a Roman temple, commissioned by one Giovanni Pontano in 1492 as a funerary monument to his wife. Pontano was principal secretary to the Aragonese rulers of Naples, in particular Ferdinand I, and one of the most refined and accomplished men in Europe at the time. Renowned as a poet and humanist, he penned the Latin inscriptions that cover the walls.

The fourteenth-century church of **San Pietro a Maiella**, which anchors the end of Via dei Tribunali at Piazza Miraglia, seems oddly out of place, with a stone tower that has the feel of a French provincial church. Built as an Angevin church in the fourteenth century, it's a theme that's continued in the interior, which has been restored to its full Gothic splendour. High, bare stone arches give way to the building's only real decorative feature: a magnificent painted wooden ceiling that was the work of Matteo Preti in 1657. Attached to the church is a convent that houses the city's music school, home to a fabled library of books and music.

Follow the street past the church and turn right for **Piazza Bellini**, a rectangular open space which marks the end of the old city, and indeed always has: the ruins of the old Greco-Roman walls can still be seen at the bottom end of the square. It's a rare pocket of tranquillity in central Naples – a pleasant, leafy square lined with terraced cafés – making it a good spot for a coffee and a break from sightseeing.

Spaccanapoli

Running parallel to Via dei Tribunali, **Spaccanapoli** (literally, "Splitting Naples") cuts cleanly through the old city. It's a long street, and changes name several times: at the Via del Duomo end, it's **Via San Biagio dei Librai**, becoming **Via Benedetto Croce** at its western end, where it opens out at the large square of the Gesù Nuovo and the edge of old Naples.

To Sant'Angelo a Nilo

West from Via Duomo, **Via San Biagio dei Librai** leads past some impressive palaces. **Palazzo Carafa**, at no. 121, has a terracotta horse's head in the courtyard, a gift from Lorenzo de' Medici to embellish the new Carafa residence in 1471, while the rather grander **Palazzo Monte di Pietà** at no. 114, now owned by the Banco di Napoli, has a chapel with seventeenth-century frescoes by Corenzio. Off to the left, the sacristy has more frescoes, best of which are those by Bonito, painted a century later, representing the good deeds of the charity. Outside, the figures in the niches are by Pietro Bernini, father of the more famous Gianlorenzo, who sculpted half of Rome but never made it to Naples. There's a small display of paintings and sculpture in the rooms off the courtyard.

A little further on, **Largo del Corpo di Nilo** is home to a famous Roman statue of a reclining old man, thought to have been sculpted in Nero's time –

▲ Religious trinkets for sale on Via San Biagio dei Librai

a representation of the Nile that has a habit, it's claimed, of whispering to women as they walk by. Just beyond here, on **Piazzetta Nilo**, the little church of **Sant'Angelo a Nilo** (Mon–Sat 9am–1pm & 4.30–7pm, Sun 9.30am–1pm) is home to the city's earliest piece of Renaissance art: the funerary monument to Cardinal Rinaldo Brancaccio, who built the church adjacent to his palace and a hospital for the poor. It was commissioned by his executor Cosimo de' Medici, and made in Pisa in 1426 by Michelozzo and Donatello, and is a tall, columned affair, with an evocative, apparently very true-to-life figure of the cardinal supported by three caryatids and a delicate relief of the *Assumption* on the front by Donatello. Also worth a look is the *St Michael* on the high altar, a late sixteenth-century painting by another Tuscan artist, in this case Marco Pino, and a colourful and expressive piece of work.

The University and its museums
Off to the left of Via San Biagio is Naples' main **University** building, set between Via Paladino and Via Mezzocannone. The streets around here teem with students, and there's a lively buzz to the area. **Largo San Giovanni**, to the right of Via Mezzocannone, is a pleasant open space by Naples' standards – and you can wander through the university's courtyards from Via Paladino to Via Mezzocannone. The only real reason to visit is to see the four small collections that make up Naples' natural history museum – the **Centro Musei delle Scienze Naturali** – reached off the large courtyard at Via Mezzocannone 8 (Tues, Wed & Fri 9am–1.30pm, Mon & Thurs 9am–1.30pm & 3–5pm, Sat & Sun 9am–1pm; €2.50, or €4.50 for all four museums). These are of limited appeal, but you may want to stop off at the small zoological museum on the second floor, which has two large rooms of glass cases full of stuffed mammals, as well as various birds and molluscs. The small anthropological collection upstairs, focuses on reconstructions of human features, based on African models, as well as the inhabitants of ancient Herculaneum. Next door, there's a museum of mineralogy and a paleontology collection, with a skeleton of a large allosaurus.

Piazza San Domenico Maggiore

Further along Via San Biagio, **Piazza San Domenico Maggiore** is marked by the **Guglia di San Domenico** (1737), one of the whimsical Baroque obelisks that were originally put up after times of plague or disease, or to celebrate the Virgin. The partially fortified church of **San Domenico Maggiore** (daily 8.30am–noon & 4.30–7pm) flanks the northern side of the square, a long, high, originally Gothic building from 1289, though much recon- structed over the years. The frescoes in the Brancaccio chapel – second on the right – are its oldest feature, the work of Pietro Cavallini and dating back to the early fourteenth century. Their clear, bright colours depict the *Martyrdom of St John the Baptist* and a crucifixion scene with Dominican saints. Another chapel, further down on the same side, holds a miraculous painting of the Crucifixion which is said to have spoken to St Thomas Aquinas during his time at the adjacent monastery, while in the sacristy, off the right aisle, there are much later frescoes by Francesco Solimena, representing the *Triumph of the Dominicans*, and a small treasury (Sat 9.30am–noon & 4–7pm, Sun 9.30am–noon). However, the sacristy's real feature are the velvet-clad coffins of the Aragonese rulers of Naples stacked up on the balcony that runs all the way round – an odd sight, but an apt one, for it was the Spanish kings who made the San Domenico square and church the centre of their court in Naples.

The Cappella Sansevero

Branching off the top end of the square, Via de Sanctis leads off right to one of the city's odder monuments, the **Cappella Sansevero** (Mon & Tues–Sat 10am–6pm, Sun 10am–1.30pm; €6), the tomb-chapel of the di Sangro family, sculpted by Giuseppe Sammartino in the mid-eighteenth century. The decora- tion is extraordinary: the centrepiece a carving of a dead Christ, laid out flat and covered with a veil of stark and remarkable realism, not least because it was carved out of a single piece of marble. Even more accomplished is the veiled figure of *Modesty* on the left, and, on the right, its twin *Disillusionment*, in the form of a woeful figure struggling with the marble netting of his own disen- chantment. Look, too, at the effusive *Deposition* on the high altar and the memorial above the doorway, which shows one Cecco di Sangro climbing out of his tomb, sword in hand. The man responsible for the chapel, Prince Raimondo, was a well-known eighteenth-century alchemist, and **downstairs** are the results of some of his experiments: bodies of an upright man and woman, behind glass, their capillaries and most of their organs preserved by a mysterious liquid developed by the prince – who, incidentally, was excommu- nicated by the pope for such practices. Even now, the black entanglements make for a gruesome sight.

To Santa Chiara

The last stretch of Spaccanapoli is known as **Via Benedetto Croce**. The twentieth-century philosopher the street is named after spent much of his life in this neighbourhood, and used to live in the **Palazzo Filomarino** on the right, just before the campanile of the church of Santa Chiara. Croce died here in 1952, and the building is now given over to the library of the Italian histor- ical institute, which he founded (closed to the public).

Just past the *palazzo*, and the *Gay Odin* ice-cream parlour on the corner, the walls of the Santa Chiara convent mark the boundary of the Renaissance city. Here, the church of **Santa Chiara** (daily 8am–1pm & 4–7pm) is quite different from any other building in Naples. The Provencal-Gothic structure, built in 1328, was completely destroyed by Allied bombs during World War II, and on rebuilding was restored to its original bare Gothic austerity: quite refreshing after the excesses of most Neapolitan churches. There's not much to see **inside**, but the eighteenth-century majolica floor survived the bombing, as did the medieval tombs of the Angevin monarchs at the far end, which are very fine and include that of Robert the Anjou at the altar, sculpted in Florence in 1345, and showing the king both in full regalia and lying on his deathbed in a monk's habit. There are equally grand and finely sculpted monuments to Robert's son, Charles of Calabria, and Mary Valois, his second wife, while the so-called Clares' Choir behind has traces of frescoes once thought to have been by Giotto, although it is rarely open to non-worshipping tourists.

That's not it for Santa Chiara. The convent to the left of the church, established by Robert's wife, Sancia, has a **cloister** (Mon–Sat 9.30am–5.30pm, Sun 9.30am–2pm; €5) that is one of the gems of the city. A shady haven planted with neatly clipped box hedges, it's furnished with benches and low walls covered with colourful majolica tiles depicting bucolic scenes of life outside the convent walls – the work of Domenico Antonio Vaccaro. There's also a giant **presepe** or Christmas crib, to the right as you enter, and in the far corner a very well-organized **museum**, with a collection of pieces from the church before the bombing. The partially reconstructed frieze showing the Angevin kings is by Tino di Camaino, who sculpted many of the royal tombs, and the bits of stonework and statuary, and photos of the complex before and after the bombing, are all beautifully displayed. Outside, the excavated remains of a Roman bath complex – viewed by way of a series of raised walkways – provide yet more evidence of the ancient foundations on which Naples stands.

Gesù Nuovo

Just past Santa Chiara the street broadens out at **Piazza del Gesù Nuovo**, centring on the ornate **Guglia dell'Immacolata**, much larger than the San Domenico obelisk, and commissioned in 1743 by the Jesuits. On the right, the **Gesù Nuovo** church (daily 7am–1pm & 4–7.30pm) is distinctive for its lava-stone facade, originally part of a fifteenth-century palace which stood here, prickled with pyramids that give it an impregnable, prison-like air. The building was taken over by the Jesuit order in the 1580s and consecrated as a church at the turn of the seventeenth century.

The **interior** is as over-sized and over-decorated as most Jesuit churches, though its most interesting feature is perhaps a quieter one. The simple chapel on the far right, behind an altar dedicated to the Jesuit missionary St Francis Xavier, is dedicated to San Guiseppe Moscati, a local doctor who died in 1927 and was reputed to perform medical miracles – as you can see from the votive plaques, poems and scribbled thanks that cover the walls. There's also a re-creation of his consulting rooms, complete with desk, couch and the doctor's bed, and a display on his short life; he died in his late forties.

The rest of the church is rich in ornament and **paintings**, the most prominent being the large *Expulsion of Eliodoro from the Temple* (1725) by Francesco Solimena above the entrance, its composition reminiscent of Raphael's *School of Athens* in the Vatican. The frescoes of the apostles in the pendentives of the cupola are by Lanfranco, echoing his work in the Santi Apostoli church nearby (see p.66); the same artist decorated the rest of the dome but this collapsed in the 1688 earthquake, and the paintings with it. The altar in the left transept – dedicated to St Ignatius, founder of the Jesuit order – sports paintings and sculpture by the great Neapolitan Baroque artist Cosimo Fanzago. To the left of the main altar, the Cappella Ravaschiera holds around sixty wooden head reliquaries of Jesuit saints, all lined up as if for a performance – which seems appropriate, in this most theatrical of Neapolitan churches.

The Anticaglia

The third of the centro storico's Greco-Roman streets is the **decumanus superior**, which runs parallel to Via dei Tribunali a block further up Via Duomo. Formed of four streets –Via della Sapienza,Via Pisanelli,Via Anticaglia andVia dei Santi Apostoli – and known as the **Anticaglia**, it's the least busy and least visited of the old city's three main thoroughfares, but it does have a few low-key attractions of its own.

Santa Maria Donnaregina

Situated on its own peaceful square just off to the right of Via Duomo, the church of **Santa Maria Donnaregina Nuova** has been spendidly restored and converted to house the city's **Museo Diocesano** (Wed–Mon 9am–4.30pm, Sun 9am–2pm; €5).Two vast paintings of the *Miracles of Christ* by Luca Giordano face each other across the high altar, while the museum ranges around the sacristy and other rooms on the ground floor, as well as the upper galleries on either side. It's chock-full of dead Christs, martyred saints and all manner of gloom and gore by many of the better-known Neapolitan painters (Solimena, Vaccaro and Paolo de' Matteis, among others), but the exhibits are well displayed and the views of the church from the upper levels spectacular.

Take the alley up to the right of the church to reach its fourteenth-century counterpart, **Santa Maria Donnaregina Vecchia** (times vary according to exhibitions).The church was abandoned for the best part of two hundred years and now it too has been deconsecrated, a bare Gothic building that is officially part of the Naples modern art museum (see below) and given over to exhibitions. Whether or not there's anything interesting on, you may want to take a look, not only for the building itself but also to see the fourteenth-century marble tomb of Queen Mary of Hungary in the nave, supported by angels and studded with colourful mosaics, the work of the sculptor Tino di Camaino. Hopefully one day the upstairs nuns' gallery will be accessible too: it has a fantastic series of frescoes by Pietro Cavallini that you get tantalizing glimpses of from below.

MADRE

Steps from Donnaregina Nuova, the Museo d'Art Contemporanea Donnaregina – or **MADRE** for short – at Via Settembrini 79 (Mon & Wed–Fri 10am–9pm, Sat & Sun 10am–midnight; €7) is emblematic of Naples' rebirth as a creative city. Created in the Palazzo Donnaregina in 2005, it hosts temporary exhibitions on the ground and top floors and has a small permanent collection on its first and second floors, part of which is made up of works by some big-name contemporary artists specifically for the museum.The most prominent of these is the **mural** by Francesco Clemente, a NewYork-based Neapolitan artist who created the large fresco of Naples across the two floors on his return to the city for his first retrospective – a colourful work full of giant figures and riotous figurative detail.

On the **first floor** are works by Jeff Koons and Anish Kapoor, as well as a massive anchor – embodying the city's maritime roots – by Jannis Kounellis. The **second floor** gives a quick chronological rundown of some of the work of major figures of contemporary art, from Sixties artists Robert Rauschenberg and Carl Andre, right up to the work of Georges Baselitz, Damien Hirst's famous dot paintings, Gilbert and George's turd works and a few canvases by Anselm Kiefer. All in all, it's a nicely assembled collection, and there's a good café and bookstore too.

Santi Apostoli to San Giovanni a Carbonara

At the far end of the *decumanus superior*, the mid-fifteenth-century church of **Santi Apostoli**, on its own small square, is yet another tardis-like Naples structure that feels vast when you step inside. It's also a real treasure trove, principally for its mid-seventeenth-century frescoes by Giovanni Lanfranco, which fill the panels and pendentives of the ceiling with scenes of the martyrdom of the apostles: realistic, action-packed pieces with plenty to draw the eye. There's a great deal of neck-craning involved, however, and sadly the paintings are partially damaged and in need of restoration. Some of the other paintings in the church are in a similar state, though Lanfranco's depiction of the *Probatica pool* above the entrance is beautifully clear and bright.

The church of **San Giovanni a Carbonara**, which lies across Via Carbonara, marks the end of the *decumanus superior* and is something of a find in what is by any standards not Naples' most attractive quarter. Fronted by an elegant curving double staircase, the interior is notable for its Renaissance funerary monuments, none more monumental than the massive fourteenth-century memorial to Ladislas of Durazzo, son of the fourteenth-century king of Naples, Charles III, and his sister Joan II, which dominates the nave. It only just outdoes the monument in the round chapel behind, decorated with frescoes and majolica floor tiles from the 1440s, where Joan's lover Sergianni Caracciolo is remembered; the marbled magnificence of the Caracciolo di Vico chapel, off to the left, commemorates other members of the influential family.

Via Toledo and around

If you asked most people what they thought of as the centre of Naples, they'd say **Via Toledo**, sometimes known as Via Roma: the shop-lined modern thoroughfare that provides modern Naples' spine. Its southern end is anchored by Piazza Trieste e Trento, which in turn is edged by some of the city centre's most monumental buildings: the Palazzo Reale, Galleria Umberto I and the Castel Nuovo. From here, Via Toledo leads north in a dead-straight line, climbing the hill towards the **Museo Archeologico Nazionale** and separating the city into two very distinct parts. To its right, as far as Piazza del Gesù Nuovo, the streets and buildings are modern and spacious, centring on the unmistakable mass of the Fascist-era central **Post Office**, while to the left are two of the city's most densely populated and poorest neighbourhoods, the **Quartieri Spagnoli** and **Montesanto**.

Piazza del Municipio and the Castel Nuovo

Piazza del Municipio sits between the old city and the sea, a busy traffic junction that stretches from the ferry terminal up to the Palazzo Municipale, or city hall. It's a pleasant enough open space, but a mess at present, dominated as it is by the works underway to extend the city's metro. These in turn have been delayed due to the extent of archeological finds unearthed here, including Roman ships; this used to be the port of the ancient city. You can look down into the excavations from the walkways built to get pedestrians from one side to the other.

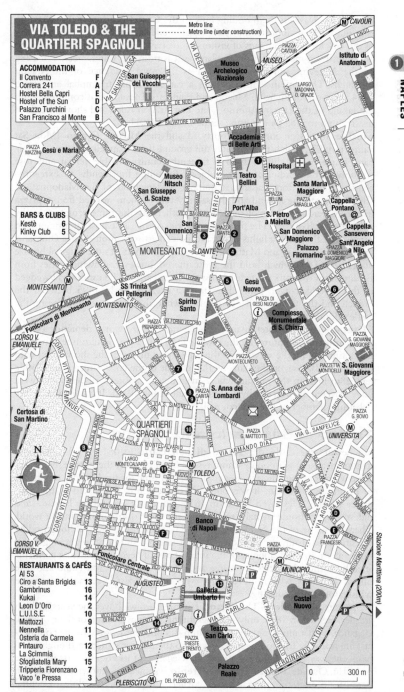

VIA TOLEDO & THE QUARTIERI SPAGNOLI

Metro line
Metro line (under construction)

ACCOMMODATION
Il Convento	F
Correra 241	A
Hostel Bella Capri	E
Hostel of the Sun	D
Palazzo Turchini	C
San Francisco al Monte	B

BARS & CLUBS
Kestè	6
Kinky Club	5

RESTAURANTS & CAFÉS
Al 53	4
Ciro a Santa Brigida	13
Gambrinus	16
Kukai	14
Leon D'Oro	2
L.U.I.S.E.	10
Mattozzi	9
Nennella	11
Osteria da Carmela	1
Pintauro	12
La Scimmia	8
Sfogliatella Mary	15
Tripperia Fiorenzano	7
Vaco 'e Pressa	3

Across the piazza is the brooding hulk of the **Castel Nuovo** or the "Maschio Angioino" (Angevin fortress), whose squat, crenellated turrets are the first view of the city for the thousands of visitors who arrive in Naples by cruise ship. It's as impressive a monument on dry land as it is from the water, erected in 1282 by the Angevins and later converted as the royal residence of the Aragon monarchs. The entrance incorporates a carved marble triumphal arch from 1454, the work of Pietro di Milano and Francesco Laurana, that commemorates the taking of the city by Alfonso I, the first Aragon ruler, and shows details of his triumph topped by a rousing statue of St Michael.

Inside, there's an imposing courtyard and the **Museo Civico** (Mon–Sat 9am–7pm; €5), which incorporates the ground-floor Cappella Palatina, a high, bare, single-naved church with a fifteenth-century marble portal and rose window and a handful of artistic objects, including fourteenth- to sixteenth-century frescoes from Caserta. A number of depictions of the Madonna and Child decorate the far end and the sacristy, one of them rescued from a piazza in the Materdei quarter of the city and others by the same sculptors as the triumphal arch outside. The first floor galleries of the castle host undistinguished canvases by the leading lights of the Neapolitan artistic canon – Luca Giordano, Francesco Solimena and Mattia de' Preti, among others. It's the original bronze doors from 1468 which hold the most interest, however, showing scenes from Ferdinand of Aragon's struggle against the local barons. The cannonball wedged in the lower left-hand panel dates from a naval battle in 1495 between the French and the Genoese that took place while the former were pillaging the castle's doors.

Upstairs there are later, mainly nineteenth-century works depicting Naples at the time, and sculptures by the prolific local Vincenzo Gemito (see also p.31). But ultimately it's the views from the top terrace that steal the show, along with the Sala dei Baroni, up the stairs on the left side of the courtyard: a huge Gothic hall, 28m high in the middle, whose magnificent umbrella-ribbed vaults were once covered in frescoes by Giotto – sadly long faded. It's still used as the debating chamber of the city council.

Teatro di San Carlo and around

Just beyond the castle, the **Teatro di San Carlo** (℡081.7972.331, 🅦www.teatrosancarlo.it) is an oddly unimpressive building from the outside, but it was the envy of Europe when it opened in 1737, in time for the birthday of Charles of Bourbon, for whom it was built (it's conveniently connected to the royal palace behind). Destroyed by fire in 1816 and rebuilt, it's still the largest – and oldest – opera house in Italy, and one of the most distinguished in the world. There's a statue of the Naples-born tenor Caruso in the foyer, although oddly the singer was badly received on his debut in 1900 and never again sang in his home town. To really appreciate the interior, you'll need to come to a performance here, though tickets are scarce and pricey (see p.94). You could also take one of the **tours**, which run regularly every day and cost €5 for a thirty-minute whisk around the building.

Opposite, the **Galleria Umberto I** has fared less well over the years, its high arcades, erected in 1887, only now beginning to recover some of their original elegance, with a much-needed restoration still underway. Some of the commercial life from Via Toledo is seeping back into the massive structure, though it still has some way to go before it attains the elegance of its counterparts in Rome or Milan. Outside, **Piazza Trieste e Trento** – sometimes known as Piazza San Ferdinando after the church on its corner – is probably as close to central

The Acquedotto Carmignano

The city's most elegant café, the *Gambrinus*, Via Chiaia 1, may seem an unlikely point of departure for a journey to underground Naples, but this is the place if you want to explore the **Acquedotto Carmignano**: a vast network of gullies and water cisterns, in use right up to the cholera epidemic of the 1880s. Hour-long **tours** leave from the café (Thurs 9pm, Sat 10am, noon & 6pm, Sun 10am, 11am, noon & 6pm; €10), but the visit actually begins at Vico Sant'Anna di Palazzo 40, in the Quartieri Spagnoli, where you descend 40m underground. Tours are mostly in Italian, but there's plenty to appreciate even if you can't follow the guide's narrative, such as graffiti from World War II, when the tunnels were used as bomb shelters, and any number of spooky caverns and passages. It's fun, too, to squeeze through some of the gaps in the rock, but be warned that some of the spaces you need to get through are very narrow indeed, and not for the claustrophobic.

Naples as you can get. Although more of a roundabout than a piazza, it's nevertheless a good place to watch the world go by while sipping a pricey drink on the terrace of the historic *Caffè Gambrinus*.

Piazza del Plebiscito

To the left of the *Caffè Gambrinus*, the expanse of **Piazza del Plebiscito** is a decent attempt to create a bit of civic grandeur, laid out in the early nineteenth century with a curve of columns modelled on Bernini's Piazza San Pietro in Rome, and spruced up over recent years. It's a favourite place to stroll in the evening, and hosts summertime installations by renowned contemporary artists, although the colonnades are still graffitied and run-down in places. Flanked by the buildings of the Naples prefecture on each side, and with the Palazzo Reale on the left, is the church of **San Francesco di Paola** (Mon–Sat 8.30am–noon & 3.30–7pm), a monumental building from 1836 that was modelled on the Pantheon. Inside, it's a rather chilling structure, with an enormous dome that dwarfs even the Neoclassical features of its interior, let alone its hapless congregation.

The Palazzo Reale

The **Palazzo Reale** (Thurs–Tues 9am–7.30pm; €4) forms the fourth side of Piazza del Plebiscito, and is a vast and very grand affair, hogging all the best views of the sea from this part of town. That said, it's a bland, derivative building for the most part, and even a bit of a fake: it was thrown up hurriedly in 1602 to accommodate Philip III on a visit here and was never actually occupied by a monarch long-term. Indeed, it's more of a monument to monarchies than monarchs, with the various dynasties that ruled Naples by proxy for so long represented in the niches of the facade, from Roger the Norman to Vittorio Emanuele II, taking in, among others, Alfonso I and a slightly comic Murat on the way.

The palace's **first-floor rooms** are decorated with Baroque excess: gilded furniture, trompe-l'oeil ceilings, overbearing tapestries, impressive French Empire pieces and scores of seventeenth- and eighteenth-century paintings, including works by Guercino, Carracci and Titian, as well as Flemish old masters. The grand, white marble double staircase, which sweeps up one side of the palace's central courtyard, is probably the finest in a city not short of sweeping staircases, and at the top on the right is one of the gems of the palace – the private **theatre**, which is refreshingly restrained after the rest of the palace.

▲ San Francesco di Paola

Numerous rooms and antechambers follow: the throne room has a ceiling studded with gilded figures representing different parts of the Kingdom of Two Sicilies in 1818, as well as a rather shabby gilded throne; the Great Captain's Room has ceiling frescoes by the Neapolitan master Battistello Caracciolo, depicting the conquest of the kingdom of Naples in 1502 by the Spanish; and the Flemish Room, so named for its collection of Dutch art, includes a painting by one of Rembrandt's most gifted pupils, Nicolas Maes.

Rooms 14–19 hold the cream of the palace's art collection, including large-scale works by Luca Giordano, Andrea Vaccaro and various followers of Caravaggio, Mattia de' Preti and the Dutch painter Gerrit van Honthorst among them. The **Hercules Room** or Ballroom, at the end, is suitably vast, although its name comes from the fact that the archeological museum's *Farnese Hercules* used to reside here. Finally there's the **chapel**, whose *presepe* (Christmas crib) is one of the city's largest, filled with mainly eighteenth-century figures – 210 in all.

The Quartieri Spagnoli

Scaling the footslopes of Vómero to the west of Via Toledo are some of the city's narrowest and most crowded streets. The grid of alleys was laid out to house Spanish troops during the seventeenth century, hence the name: the **Quartieri Spagnoli**. In some ways it's an enticing area, in that it's what you expect of Naples, with the buildings so close together as to barely admit any sunlight. But it's a poor, densely populated part of town too, home to the Camorra and the notorious Neapolitan *bassi* – one-room windowless dwellings that open directly onto the street – and one you might want to avoid wandering too deeply into at night.

To Sant'Anna dei Lombardi

On the other side of Via Toledo from the Quartieri Spagnoli, immediately east of **Piazza Carità**, the streets are modern and less obviously appealing. The main focus is the busy junction of **Piazza Matteotti**, which is surrounded by some brutalist yet elegant modern architecture, and anchored by the broad sweep of the **Post Office** building – a huge and stylish homage to the art of delivering the post on time (ironic in any part of Italy, where the postal system is considered a joke). Built in the 1930s, up close it's a bit worse for wear, but it is at least elegantly echoed by the resoundingly Modernist police headquarters across the square.

Behind the post office you're on the edge of the old part of the city. Walking up Via Monteoliveto from here takes you to the little square that is home both to the Carabinieri and the church of **Sant'Anna dei Lombardi** (Tues–Sat 8.30am–12.30pm). Rebuilt after wartime bombing, it holds some of the city's finest Renaissance art, including a sacristy painted in the mid-sixteenth century by Vasari with allegorical frescoes showing *Religion*, *Faith* and *Eternity* on the three Gothic vaults of the long room. Next door is a rather startling group of eight almost life-sized figures mourning the dead Christ by Guido Mazzoni (the faces are said to be portraits), from 1492. Don't miss the two works by the fifteenth-century sculptor Antonio Rossellino in the chapel to the left of the entrance: a nativity scene from 1475 and the tomb of Mary of Aragon, daughter of Ferdinand I. A beautiful *Annunciation* by Benedetto di Maiano lies in the chapel on the right.

Montesanto and the Museo Nitsch

Off Via Toledo to the west, just beyond Piazza Carità, is the atmospheric district of **Montesanto**, with its appealing main drag, Via Pignasecca, leading to lively Piazza Pignasecca and the Montesanto funicular station. It's as vibrant a part of Naples as you'll find, with any number of food stalls, tripe joints and grocery stores, particularly around Piazza Pignasecca.

The area harbours just one sight, in the recently opened **Museo Nitsch** at Vico Lungo Pontecorvo 29/d (Mon & Wed–Sun 9am–7pm; €6.50), occupying a fantastic position in a former electricity substation, tucked away in the heights of Montesanto, with a terrace overlooking its densely packed rooftops, and offering perfect views of a glowering Vesuvius. Part of local art impresario Guiseppe Morra's Foundation, the museum itself is a somewhat bizarre collection of the works of the Austrian performance artist Hermann Nitsch, who specializes in large-scale events in which naked men and women are "crucified" with dead sheep parts and entrails draped around their bodies, usually witnessed by crowds of devotees. There are photos and videos – complete with soundtrack – along with exhibits of the tools of his trade: bloodstained cloths, surgical instruments and liturgical garments. Though the display makes disquieting viewing, and certainly won't be to everyone's taste, it's somehow thoroughly Neapolitan in its theatrical shockability, and strangely doesn't seem out of place here at all.

Piazza Dante and around

Nearby **Piazza Dante**, designed by Luigi Vanvitelli during the eighteenth century, cuts an elegant semicircle around a graffitied statue of the poet. Cross the square and cut through the seventeenth-century **Port'Alba** for the very appealing **Piazza Bellini** (see p.61) and the old city, or push straight on up the street to the archeological museum, housed in a grandiose, late sixteenth-century army barracks on the corner of Piazza Cavour. On the way, you may want to stop off at the **Accademia di Belle Arti** (Mon–Thurs 10am–2pm, Fri 2–6pm; €5) – the city's art school, and a very grand one too, with a small gallery of paintings and sculptures on its second floor. There are a few pre-nineteenth-century paintings, among them a *St Catherine* by Mattia de' Preti, but otherwise it's mainly work from the nineteenth century and beyond: busts, of Verdi among others, by local sculptor Vincenzo Gemito (whose work you may have also seen in the Villa Pignatelli); paintings by the important nineteenth-century Neapolitan artist Domenico Morelli, who was president of the academy for the last two years of his life, along with work by his more Impressionistic student Antonio Mancini. There's also a section representing the 1960s right up to the present day, with a final room of contemporary artworks and multimedia pieces.

The Museo Archeologico Nazionale

Naples isn't really a city of museums – there's more than enough to observe on the streets – and most displays of interest are kept in the city's churches and palaces. The unmissable **Museo Archeologico Nazionale** (Wed–Mon 9am–7.30pm; €6.50; bus #C40 or the Metropolitana from Piazza Garibaldi) is an exception, home to the Farnese collection of antiquities from Lazio and Campania and the best of the finds from the nearby Roman sites of Pompeii and Herculaneum. Despite the pedigree of the exhibits, however, the museum is at best tatty and at worst in a state of complete disarray, with endless reorganizations. Because of this, locations of exhibits are liable to change, and departments may close at short notice. The core collection of paintings and mosaics are generally on display, however – and these are truly one of the city's highlights.

The ground and mezzanine floors

The **ground floor** of the museum concentrates on sculpture from the **Farnese collection**, displayed at its best in the mighty Great Hall, which holds imperial-era figures like the *Farnese Bull* and *Farnese Hercules* from the Baths of Caracalla in Rome. The former is the largest piece of classical sculpture ever found, the latter a colossal statue whose statue are a modern replacement. There are also portrait busts of various Roman emperors and VIPs – a statue of Hadrian's boyfriend Antinous, a reclining woman, perhaps Agrippina, a huge bust of Vespasian with the top sliced off, as well as busts of Caracalla, Domitian, Commodus and others. Don't miss Ephesian Artemis, an alabaster and bronze statue with rows of bulls' scrota embellishing the goddess's chest, and bees, mini-beasts and sphinxes adorning her lower half.

Halfway up the double staircase, the **mezzanine floor** holds the museum's collection of **mosaics** – remarkably preserved works, giving a superb insight into Roman customs, beliefs and humour. The fascinating collection includes images of fish, crustacea, a wonderful scene of wildlife on the banks of the Nile, a cheeky cat and quail with still life beneath, masks, skulls and simple abstract decoration – all from the House of the Faun in Pompeii. Highlights include a realistic *Battle Scene* (no. 10020), which perhaps shows Alexander the Great, *Three Musicians with Dwarf* (no. 9985), an urbane *Meeting of the Platonic Academy* (no. 124545), and a marvellously captured scene from a comedy, *The Consultation of the Fattucchiera* (no. 9987), with a soothsayer giving a dour and doomy prediction. Also worth looking out for are the lovely *Head of a Woman* (no. 124666) and *Antifrite and Poseidon* (no. 10007), from the house of the same name in Herculaneum.

At the far end of the mosaic rooms is the intriguing **Gabinetto Segreto** (Secret Room), containing erotic material – paintings and sculpture mainly – taken from the brothels, baths, houses and taverns of Pompeii and Hercula-neum. The objects in the collection weren't always segregated in this way; it was the shocked Duke of Calabria who, having taken his wife and daughter to view the museum, decided that the offending objects should be removed from the gaze of ladies. From then until the time of Garibaldi they were kept under lock and key, disappearing again from public view in the twentieth century for long periods. The artefacts, from languidly sensual wall paintings to preposterously phallic lamps, bear testimony to Roman licentiousness, although the phallus was often used as a kind of lucky charm rather than as a sexual symbol – cheerfully hung outside taverns and bakeries to ward off the evil eye. There's a group of paintings displaying a variety of sexual positions, and a lot of erotic mythological art, making this an admirably serious and smut-free collection, though it's hard to repress a giggle at the sculpture of a headless man whose toga is failing to mask an erection, or the graphic but elegantly executed marble of Pan "seducing" a goat.

Also on the mezzanine are displays of **money and commercial artefacts** – mainly Roman but going right up to the Bourbons. There are examples of very early Roman and Hellenistic currency, and later Roman coinage – a gold coin with an image of Augustus, several large hoards from Pompeii, including golden Republican and Imperial coins from the Porta di Sarno, as well as an amazing studded chest, sets of scales from Minturno and even stamps for receipts.

The first floor

Upstairs, the enormous **Salone della Meridiana** holds a sparse but fine assortment of Roman figures, notably a wonderfully strained Atlas and a demure Venus adjusting her sandal – Roman replicas of Greek originals. Beyond here, a series of rooms holds **finds from the Campanian cities** – everyday items like bronze cooking pots and wine jugs, glass bottles and vases, silver, ceramics, even foodstuffs (petrified cakes, figs, fruit and nuts), together with a 1:100 model of Pompeii in cork. Further rooms show Campanian **wall paintings**, lifted from the villas of Pompeii and Herculaneum and other sites around the bay, and amazingly rich in colour and invention. It's worth devoting time to this section, which includes works from the Sacrarium – part of Pompeii's Egyptian temple of Isis, the most celebrated mystery cult of antiquity – the discovery of which gave a major boost to Egyptomania at the end of the eighteenth century. In the next series of rooms, some of the smallest and most easily missed works are among the most exquisite. Among those to look out for are a paternal *Achilles and Chirone* (no. 9109); the *Sacrifice of Iphiginia* (no. 9112) in the next room, one of the best preserved of all the murals; the dignified *Dido abandoned by Aeneas and the Personification of Africa* (no. 8998); and the series of frescoes telling the story of the Trojan horse. Look out too for the group of four small allegorical pictures, including a depiction of a woman gathering flowers entitled *Allegoria della Primavera* (no. 8834) – a fluid, Impressionistic work capturing both the gentleness of spring and the graceful beauty of the woman; a snapshot-like portrait of a young man and woman, *The Baker Terentius and his Wife* (no. 9058); and a nearby *Perseus and Andromeda* (no. 8995).

On the other side of the first floor, there are finds from one particular house, the **Villa dei Papiri** in Herculaneum, containing mainly sculptures in bronze. The *Hermes at Rest* in the centre of the second room is perhaps the most arresting item, overcome with exhaustion, but around are other adept statues – of athletes, suffused with movement; a languid *Resting Satyr*; the convincingly woozy *Drunken Silenus*; and, in the final room, portrait busts of soldiers and various local bigwigs.

La Sanità and Capodimonte

The archeological museum sits just outside the old centre of Naples, from where the busy nineteenth-century triangle of **Piazza Cavour** stretches off to the left as you come out, and the arterial Via Foria beyond, which heads off towards the airport. Off to the left, five-minutes' walk from the museum, the **Orto Botanico** or Botanic Gardens (Mon–Fri 9am–2pm, by appointment only; ☎081.449.759), founded in 1777 by Ferdinand IV, is a detour worth making if you're interested in such things, a small oasis of lush vegetation that feels quite at odds with the location. Alongside it is the enormous facade – actually only one fifth of the size originally planned – of the **Albergo dei Poveri**, a workhouse built in 1751, that has been empty for

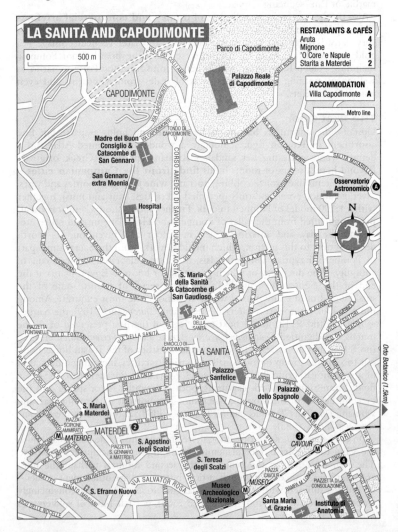

years and forms a vast, oddly derelict landmark along the top side of Piazza Carlo III.

North of the archeological museum, the workaday district of **La Sanità** and, further north still, verdant **Capodimonte** are worth the trip, not least for the sumptuous **Palazzo Reale di Capodimonte**, the area's key sight.

La Sanità

Before you reach the botanical gardens, opposite the Porta San Gennaro into the old city, you can delve into the old quarter of **La Sanità**, whose name literally means "health" due to its position outside the walls of the old city. Though one of the city's poorer neighbourhoods, it's also full of Neapolitan folklore, the birthplace of the revered Italian comic actor Totò – worth a wander for its street-level commerce, sometimes more reminiscent of downtown Mumbai than Italy. **Via dei Vergini** leads through the heart of the district, passing the **Palazzo dello Spagnuolo** at no. 13 – a gem of a building built in 1738 by the Neapolitan Baroque architect Ferdinando Sanfelice which has a fantastic and almost unique series of staircases that double back on each other at the rear of the building's courtyard. Until recently it was the headquarters of the influential Morra foundation (see p.71), and is subsequently in a good state of repair – unlike the decrepit and slightly older **Palazzo Sanfelice** a little further up at no. 6, which ironically was the architect's own home.

Follow Via dei Vergini to the Dominican church of **Santa Maria della Sanità** on the piazza of the same name, a scrubby little square, right by the bridge that connects the city centre to Capodimonte. Built in the early seventeenth century, its design was based loosely on Bramante's for St Peter's in Rome, and it's certainly a grand building inside, although its most appealing features are on a smaller scale. Look out for a couple of paintings by the ubiquitous Luca Giordano: the *Virgin with Hyacinth and Rose* on the left as you go in, and a painting of San Vincenzo on the right. The latter is a venerated piece; in fact the church is sometimes known as San Vincenzo for the esteem in which the saint is held. Perhaps of most interest are the **Catacombe di San Gaudioso** beneath the church (daily guided tours at 9.30am, 10.15am, 11am, 11.45am & 12.30pm; €5), an early Christian burial ground that like so much of Naples is an intriguing mix of different eras. The entrance is immediately beneath the high altar, where a Byzantine fresco of San Gaudioso, a bishop from Africa who came to Naples in the fifth century, gives way to frescoes and fragments of mosaics of the same period, along with shelves that were used to bury the dead, one of which was supposedly the last resting-place of the saint himself. But this is not just an early Christian burial place; the Dominicans ended their days here too, in seated niches where they would dessicate and then be buried elsewhere. There's also a series of tombs for the great and the good of the Dominican order, and it was another tradition that their skulls be removed and set in the wall above a skeletal painting while their body rested behind. Oddly, you can find more fifth-century frescoes mixed up in all this, and tours end in a barrel-vaulted room that was a Roman cistern.

Capodimonte

Right by the church of Santa Maria della Sanita, elevators link La Sanità with Corso Amedeo up above, the main road to **Capodimonte**, and from here it's about a ten-minute walk to another burial site, the **Catacombe di San Gennaro** at Via Capodimonte 13 (Tues–Sat tours hourly 9am–noon & 2–3pm, Sun 9am–noon; €5; bus #R4 from Via Toledo, or #178 from the Archeological

Museum), next door to the huge Madre del Buon Consiglio church, halfway up the hill to Capodimonte. Bigger and more open than the San Gaudioso catacombs, this site is best known for being the final resting-place of San Gennaro, whose body was brought here in the fifth century. It's a Christian burial ground, where the wealthy were placed in chapels on shelves and the poor were dumped on the ground – a class system it's easy to discern even now. There are some early frescoes of San Gennaro and saints Peter and Paul in some of the niches, as well as earlier red Pompeian-style ceiling frescoes next to a Byzantine Christ. Nearby, you can look down to the next level at Gennaro's supposed tomb, and a mosaic of the bishop that brought him here.

The Palazzo Reale di Capodimonte

At the top of the hill, the **Palazzo Reale di Capodimonte** with its adjoining **park** was the royal residence of the Bourbon King Charles III,

▲ The Palazzo Reale di Capodimonte

built in 1738 and now housing the superb **Museo Nazionale di Capodimonte** (Thurs–Tues 8.30am–7.30pm; €7.50). Perhaps the best collection of art in Italy after the Uffizi gallery in Florence, you could easily spend an entire day here, taking in the many important works by Campanian and international artists, as well as curious *objets d'art* and fine pieces of Capodimonte porcelain.

The three-storey museum is organized not chronologically, but by collection, built up by the Borgia, Farnese and Bourbon rulers of the city, who amassed some superb **Renaissance and Flemish** works. On the **first floor** are fine portraits of the Farnese pope, Paul III, by Titian, and, in the Borgia collection, an elegant *Madonna and Child with Angels* by Botticelli, as well as Lippi's soft, sensitive *Annunciation*, and other works by Renaissance masters: Bellini's impressively coloured and composed *Transfiguration*; Giulio Romano's dark and powerful *Madonna of the Cat*; and Marcello Venusti's small-scale 1549 copy of Michelangelo's *Last Judgement* – probably the only chance you'll get to see the painting this close up. It's not just Italian work either: there's El Greco's flashy but atmospheric *Soflon*, a couple of Brueghels – *The Misanthrope* and *The Parable of the Blind* – and two triptychs by Joos van Cleve. Look out also for Titian's lascivious *Danaë* and a Masaccio *Crucifixion*.

Head for the **second floor** for some outstanding Italian paintings from the fourteenth and fifteenth centuries, of which the most famous is the *St Louis of Anjou* by Simone Martini, a fascinating Gothic painting glowing with gold leaf. An overt work of propaganda, it depicts an enthroned Louis crowning Robert of Anjou and thereby legitimizing his rule. Elsewhere there are paintings that used to hang in Naples' churches: Niccolò Colantonio's *St Jerome in his Study* was painted for the altar of San Lorenzo Maggiore, and the delicate *Annunciation* by Titian used to hang in San Domenico Maggiore. The long series of rooms finishes off in fine style with one of Caravaggio's best known works, *The Flagellation*. Beyond are a number of paintings by the artists of the Neapolitan Baroque – Ribera, Giordano, Stanzione – while upstairs is a smattering of **twentieth-century works**, of which the most notable is a painting of an erupting Vesuvius by Andy Warhol.

If you have time to spare, take a walk around the **royal apartments** on the first floor, smaller and more downbeat than those at Caserta but in many ways more enjoyable, not least because you can walk freely through the rooms. High spots are the airy, mirrored ballroom, lined with portraits of various Bourbon monarchs and other European despots; an eccentric room entirely decorated with porcelain, sprouting three-dimensional Chinese scenes, monkeys, fruit and flowers; and a series of rooms of beautifully decorated plates.

Santa Lucia to Posillipo

The neighbourhoods to the southwest of Via Toledo, stretching around the bay towards Posillipo, are the city's most salubrious. Indeed anyone strolling from the station at Piazza Garibaldi, through Forcella and the old parts of town, might think they'd reached a different city by the time they reached the elegant storefronts of **Chiaia** and the pavement cafés around Piazza dei Martiri. The upscale feel continues around the statuesque hotels of **Santa Lucia** and along the wide boulevards that connect this part of town to the port at **Mergellina** and to **Posillipo** just beyond, in parts of which you might almost fancy you had reached the Amalfi Coast itself.

Monte Echia

The hill that rises up above the heart of the city at the bottom of Via Toledo, **Monte Echia** was the birthplace of Naples, where Greek settlers founded a place they called Parthenope. Later, when it outgrew its location, it became Paleopolis or "old city" – as opposed to Neapolis or "new city", which was built at the bottom of the hill and gave Naples its name, while the original settlement took on a more gentrified air over the years. In the seventeenth and eighteenth centuries it was considered to be one of the classier parts of town, and even today it – and the **Pizzofalcone** neighbourhood here – retains a slightly separate feel, due partly to the fact that it's tucked out of the way on the hill.

Although there are no major sights in this part of town, reaching the Castel dell'Ovo and waterfront hotels by way of Pizzofalcone and Monte Echia makes a pleasant **walk**. Behind the church of San Franscesco di Paola (see p.69), off Via Chiaia, it's a five-minute stroll up Via Serra to **Santa Maria degli Angeli**, a large church with an enormous dome, before turning left down Via Monte di Dio, past the **Palazzo Serra di Cassano** on the left, and making a right to the military academy that tops the hill here and its attached church, the **Nunziatella**. This Baroque jewellery-box of a church was built by Ferdinando Sanfelice in 1700 and is decorated with paintings by Francesco di Mura. Retrace your steps back across the main road to Via Egiziaca di Pizzofalcone, where there's another church, **Santa Maria Egiziaca di Pizzofalcone**, the creation of Cosimo Fanzago in 1651, whose lovely proportions and octagonal shape show the church of San Franceso immediately below just how it's done with domes; two works by Paolo de' Matteis face each other across the main altars. Follow the road around the edge of the military academy to a small **park**, where you can rest up and take in one of the best views of the city, before descending down a zigzagging road to the Santa Lucia quarter immediately below. Following this route without stopping would take 20–30 minutes, or a very pleasant hour or so if you take in the sights on the way.

Santa Lucia and the Castel dell'Ovo

Just south of Piazza del Plebiscito, the road curves around towards the sea and the **Santa Lucia** district, home to most of the city's poshest hotels on the streets around the seafront Via Partenope, and one or two decent restaurants. Its main artery, **Via Santa Lucia**, leads off to the right, beneath the hill of Monte Echia (see box above), while down on the waterfront the sculptural **Fontana dell'Immacolatella** was the work of Pietro Bernini and used to stand outside the seventeenth-century Immacolatella quarantine building in the old container port (see p.54). Beyond it, the grey mass of the **Castel dell'Ovo** or "egg-castle" (Mon–Sat 9am–6pm, Sun 9am–2pm; free) takes its name from the whimsical legend that it was built over an egg placed here by Virgil in Roman times: it is believed that if the egg breaks, Naples will fall. Actually the islet on which it stands was developed in ancient times, then in the fifth century by a community of monks; the citadel itself was built by the Hohenstaufen king Frederick II and extended by the Angevins. It's had various functions over the years, and has been greatly modified. **Inside**, it's just a series of terraces and empty echoing halls, sometimes used for temporary exhibitions. But the **views** you get from its battlements are among the best in town: the 360-degree panorama over the entire bay and back over Naples itself is quite a sight. Come as late in the day as possible, clamber about on the cannons, take in the views as the sun sets over Posillipo, and then go for a drink or dinner at the quayside restaurants of the **Borgo Marinaro** below. Cheesy, but the perfect end to a day in Naples.

Chiaia

The **Chiaia** neighbourhood displays a sense of order and classical elegance that is quite absent from the rest of the city, its buildings well preserved, its residents noticeably more affluent – although parts of the district, especially that which spreads up the hill towards Vómero, are as maze-like and atmospheric as anywhere in the city. **Via Chiaia** leads west from Piazza Trieste e Trento into a quite different Naples from the congested *vicoli* of the centro storico or Quartieri Spagnoli, lined with the city's fanciest shops and bending round to the elegant circle of **Piazza dei Martiri** – named after the nineteenth-century revolutionary martyrs commemorated by the column in its centre. It's fringed by a couple of pleasant cafés to take the weight off, and from here you can get a taste of the neighbourhood by following Via G. Filangieri, which turns into Via dei Mille as far as **PAN**, or the Palazzo delle Arti di Napoli, at Via dei Mille 60 (Mon–Sat 9.30am–7.30pm; €5). Occupying the enormous Palazzo Rocella, this is an exhibition space for contemporary art, along with an arthouse cinema and bookshop. Drop down from here to Via Santa Teresa a Chiaia, which turns into Via Piscielli, and follow this as far as the church of **Santa Maria in Portico** – a walk that gives a sense both of Chiaia's upscale commercialism and its authentic neighbourhood charm. The church of Santa Maria is in itself nothing special, but you may want to look in for the giant *presepe* (Christmas crib) in its sacristy, just to the left of the altar – an unsettling ensemble of almost life-sized figures in seventeenth-century costume.

▲ The Castel dell'Ovo

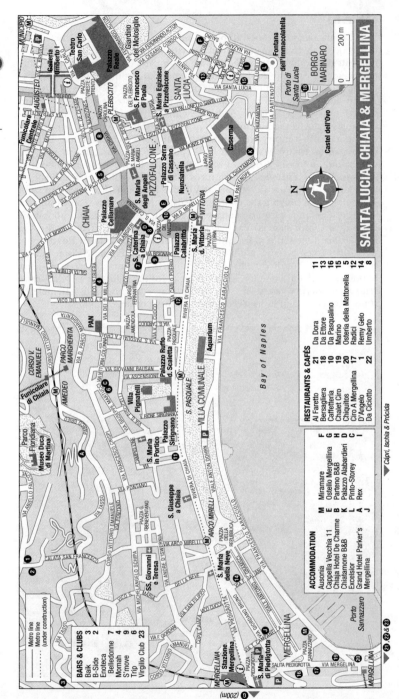

SANTA LUCIA, CHIAIA & MERGELLINA

Bay of Naples

Càpri, Ischia & Pròcida

BARS & CLUBS

Baïk	3
B-Side	2
Enoteca Belledonne	7
Momah	4
S'move	9
Trip	6
Virgilio Club	23

ACCOMMODATION

Ausonia	M	Miramare	M	
Cappella Vecchia 11	E	Ostello Mergellina	E	
Chiaia Hotel De Charme	B	Parteno B&B	B	
Chiatamone B&B	K	Palazzo Alabardieri	K	
Excelsior	L	Pinto-Storey	L	
Grand Hotel Parker's	A	Rex	A	
Mergellina	J		J	

RESTAURANTS & CAFÉS

Al Faretto	21	Da Dora	11
Bersagliera	18	Da Ettore	13
Caffetteria	10	Da Pasqualino	16
Chalet Ciro	19	Marino	15
Chiquitos	20	Osteria della Mattonella	5
Ciro A Mergellina	17	Radici	12
D'Angelo	1	Remy Gelo	14
Da Ciciotto	22	Umberto	8

Metro line
Metro line (under construction)

Villa Comunale and around

From Piazza dei Martiri, you can stroll down to the waterfront and **Villa Comunale**, Naples' most central city park, richly adorned with classical sculpture. The park offers the best position from which to appreciate the city as a port and seafront city, the views stretching right around the bay from the long lizard of its northern side to the distinctive silhouette of Vesuvius in the east, behind the cranes and far-off apartment blocks of the sprawling industrial suburbs. The road that skirts the park, **Via Caracciolo**, is named after the Neapolitan sea captain, Francesco Caracciolo, who was executed by the British after defecting to the French cause in 1799, and it makes for a relaxed walk around the bay to Mergellina, particularly in the early evening when the lights of the city enhance the views. On the way you might want to take in the Mediterranean marine life at the century-old but newly restored **Aquarium** (March–Oct Tues–Sat 9am–6pm, Sun 9.30am–7.30pm; Nov–Feb Tues–Sat 9am–5pm, Sun 9am–2pm; €1.50). It comprises just one large room, lined with tanks filled with impressive giant turtles, eels and rays, as well as a couple of artificial rock pools.

Villa Pignatelli

Across the other side of the Riviera di Chiaia from the aquarium, the gardens of the **Villa Pignatelli** (Wed–Mon 8.30am–1.30pm; €2) are a peaceful alter-native to the Villa Comunale, and the early nineteenth-century house itself, now a museum, is kept in much the same way as when it was the home of a prominent Naples family and a nineteenth-century meeting place for the city's elite. Built by Sir Ferdinand Acton in 1826, by the standards of some of Naples' palaces, it's a rather modest affair: Palladian in style but with a grand Doric-columned portico, with half a dozen rooms on the ground floor, still decorated as they would have been in Acton's time. He only lived here until 1841, when the villa was bought by the Rothschilds and later the Pignatelli-Cortes family – descendants of the notorious Spanish conquistador, as evidenced by the bust of him in the ballroom, rescued from his pillaged funerary monument in Mexico City. The ballroom is a grand open space, divided between areas for the dancers and musicians, and the rest of the ground floor is equally sumptuous, from the central "red room", added by the Rothschilds, to the "green room" with its collection of Meissen and Capodimonte porcelain, and the dining room and library on either side. Upstairs, off the elegant circular vestibule, there's a small collection of artworks: pride of place goes to Guercino's arresting depiction of St George and a collection of sculptures of street urchins and old men by the nineteenth-century Neapolitan artist Vincenzo Gemito. There's also a room of local landscapes, notably a depiction of the "village" of Chiaia in 1700, by the Dutch painter Gaspar van Wittel.

Mergellina and Piedigrotta

Via Caracciolo stretches around the bay for just over a kilometre, at the far end of which lie the harbour and main square – **Piazza Sannazzaro** – of the **Mergellina** district, a pleasant seaside neighbourhood that's a departure point for hydrofoils to the bay's islands. There's not a lot to see here, but it's worth wandering down to the "*porticciolo*" for an ogle at the yachts and an ice cream or pastry at one of the chalets in the waterfront park. Or stroll in the other direction to look in on the little church of **Santa Maria in Piedigrotta** next door to the train station. The church butts up against the cliff and grotto

Football in Naples

The district of **Fuorigrotta**, literally "beyond the grotto", the other side of the Mergellina hill, is not really of interest unless you're going to a football match, since it's home to SSC Napoli's **San Paolo** stadium. Football is something of a religion in Naples, although support is not as fanatical as it used to be since the club's bankruptcy and subsequent relegation from the national *serie* A to C1 status. However, they've recently been rescued by the movie mogul Aurelio De Laurentiis and have made it back – and are thriving – in the top flight.

To get to the ground, take the Cumana railway from Montesanto to Mostra and the stadium is right in front of you. Tickets, available from the offices facing you as you approach, or from the club's outlets in town, cost from €18 for seats in the end stands or "*curve*", up to €60 in the side or "*tribuna*" stands.

(see below), from which it – and the district – takes its name (literally "foot of the grotto"). Originally from the 1350s, and rebuilt in the sixteenth century, the church is mainly of interest for the Madonna that sits on the altar and is carried through the streets every September 8 in one of the city's most popular festivals.

Immediately behind the church, in the **Parco Vergiliano** (daily 9am–6.30pm), a path leads to a monument to Giacomo Leopardi, the doomed nineteenth-century Italian Romantic poet, who died in Naples of cholera at the ripe old age of 39, but is generally considered one of the lions of nineteenth-century Italian literature. From here, the path leads up to the entrance to a first century BC tunnel that was built to connect Neapolis with Puteoli (modern-day Pozzuoli); it's said to be nearly a kilometre long but you can't go inside and instead have to make do with the medieval frescoes that decorate its entrance. The park takes its name from the fact that it was once thought that the poet Virgil was buried here, in the stone beehive to its side, and although there's no truth in this, the setting is lovely, and it's worth climbing up the steep steps to the right of the tunnel entrance for a closer look at Virgil's supposed last resting-place.

Posillipo

Posillipo is an upmarket suburb of swanky villas and deep pockets but little of appeal to tourists, though you may want to come out here to eat, either in Posillipo itself or in the seaside village of **Marechiaro**, reachable by taking bus #140 from Via Santa Lucia and then changing to bus #23. There's also the dense and lovely **Parco Virgiliano**, also reachable on bus #140, and, just beyond, another, recently excavated Roman tunnel, the **Grotta di Seiano**, on Salita Coroglio (Mon–Sat tours at 9.30am, 10.30am & 11.15am but only sporadically open; free). The tunnel links the Mergellina side of the hill to the Roman **Villa Pausilypon** on the other side, once the home of one Vedius Pollio, a freed slave who built his villa and tunnel together for the convenient access it gave him to the city. The villa itself has been pillaged mercilessly over the years, and there's not much of it left, but you can still make out a small amphitheatre, the remains of a temple and a small shrine. The site itself, at the end of the promontory, is magnificent, while down below you can see the cove of **La Gaiola** with its small beach, reachable by a steep path.

Vómero

Like Chiaia below and Mergellina to the west, **VÓMERO** – the district
topping the hill immediately above the old city – is one of Naples' relatively
modern additions: a light, airy and peaceful quarter connected most directly
with the teeming morass below by funicular railway. It's a large area but mostly
residential, and you're unlikely to want to stray far beyond the streets that fan
out from each of the three funicular stations, centring on the grand symmetry
of **Piazza Vanvitelli**, fringed by cafés and the location of a vibrant summer-
evening *passeggiata*.

Castel Sant'Elmo

Five-minutes' walk from the Morghen funicular station, the **Castel Sant'Elmo**
(Thurs–Tues 9am–6.30pm; €3) occupies Naples' highest point and is an
impressive fortification, a fourteenth-century structure once used for incar-
cerating political prisoners and now lording it grandly over the streets below.
Its six-pointed star layout was cleverly designed to defend its position,
requiring fewer men and arms than a conventional citadel, and it remained an
important fortress right up to Bourbon times, when it was used to imprison
dissidents against the regime, and then again as a military prison after Unification. Nowadays it houses libraries and archives and hosts exhibitions, concerts
and antiques fairs, as well as boasting some of the very best views of Naples.
You can usually go in for the views if there's nothing on, but if you're heading
for Certosa San Martino just beyond there's no need, as this affords an even
better panorama.

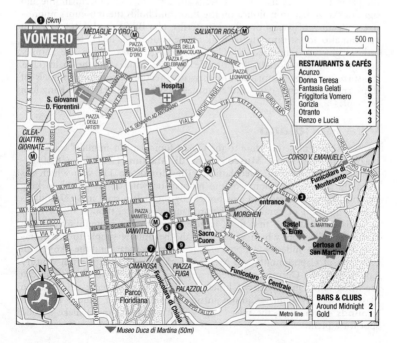

Certosa di San Martino

The fourteenth-century monastic complex of the **Certosa e Museo di San Martino** (Thurs–Tues 8.30am–7.30pm; €6) is one of Naples' prime historical attractions, with a wealth of plunder from the city and beyond, though unfortunately with very little information in English. Founded by Charles of Calabria, the son of Robert of Anjou, in 1325, and renovated and restored over successive centuries, it's a sprawling complex, and one, along with the Castel Sant'Elmo, that you're somehow always aware of wherever you are in Naples. Indeed, the views from its cunningly constructed terraced gardens are worth the entrance fee alone – short of climbing Vesuvius, as good a vista of the entire Bay of Naples as you'll get – but there is much to see in the rest of the museum too.

The monastic **church** occupies the first courtyard, a highly decorated affair with a colourful pavement and works by some of the greats of Neapolitan painting. On the ceiling are frescoes by Giovanni Lanfranco depicting Christ in Glory with Saints; above the high altar, you can see an *Adoration of the Shepherds* by Guido Reni; and the chapels that fringe the small nave are decorated by Domenico Vaccaro, Massimo Stanzione, Battistelo Carraciolo and Cosimo Fanzago, among others. Have a look too in the rooms off the high altar, where there is a sacristy lined with wood-inlay cupboards and, beyond, a series of frescoes recording the *Triumph of Judith* by Luca Giordano.

In the **museum** proper, there are more paintings by the Neapolitan masters as well as two sculptures by Pietro Bernini – *San Martino on Horseback* and a *Virgin and Child* – and paintings by Stanzione in the former apartments of the prior. The library has frescoed walls and ceilings, and a meridian line and signs of the zodiac in majolica on the floor, and holds the museum's impressive collection of *presepi* or Christmas cribs. The Baroque **cloister** – which you can also access through the back of the church – is lovely too, though a little neglected, renovated by Cosimo Fanzago who added the monks' cemetery in the corner, identifiable by the skulls on the balustrade. It's surrounded by historical and maritime sections displaying models of ships, and documents, coins and costumes recording the era of the Kingdom of Naples.

Villa Floridiana

Vómero's third museum, close to the Chiaia funicular ten-minutes' walk from Piazza Vanvitelli, is the **Museo Duca di Martina** (Wed–Mon 8.30am–1.30pm; €2.50), set in the Neoclassical **Villa Floridiana**. The villa, which was formerly the summer home of the morganatic wife of the Bourbon king Ferdinand, Lucia Migliaccio, was bought by the Italian state in 1927 and has been a museum of ceramics and porcelain ever since, though it's of fairly specialist interest. The first floor is given over to the museum's European porcelain collection, which varies from the beautifully simple to the outrageously kitsch – hideous teapots, ceramic asparagus spears and the like – with examples of Capodimonte and Meissen work, as well as eighteenth-century English, French, German and Viennese pieces. On the lower floors you can see Ming- and Qing-dynasty Chinese porcelain, Japanese pieces and Murano glass, as well as some exquisite inlaid ivory boxes and panels. The lush **grounds** surrounding the villa (daily 9am–1hr before sunset) make a good spot for a picnic.

Eating

Nowhere else in Italy is food so much part of the culture as it is in Naples. The city bursts with *pasticcerie*, pizzerias, markets, cafés, restaurants and *friggitorie* (fried-food vendors), and nearly every aspect of social life involves food in some way; even the city's famous nativity scenes feature markets, fishmongers and people eating heaped plates of spaghetti. Neapolitan cuisine consists of simple dishes cooked with fresh, seasonal ingredients (see the *Cucina napoletana* colour section for more on regional specialities), each a testament to the 2600 years of conquest that have moulded the city's culture.

Snacks, cakes and ice cream

Cheap, affordable **snacks** are a Neapolitan staple. Most bars sell food – pastries in the morning or all day and sandwiches or light meals in the afternoon, and Neapolitans take their desserts and coffee seriously and consume them often. Throughout the city, it is still possible to find places that roast their own coffee beans, make their own pastries on the premises, and even manufacture their own ice cream. This painstaking dedication to tradition produces some stellar results – and, arguably, contributes to obesity rates that are well above the national norms. Finally, the city's great **friggitorie**, selling pizza by the slice and all manner of deep-fried treats, make a tempting option for snacky lunches.

Piazza Garibaldi and around

Attanasio Vico Ferrovia 2/4, off Via Milano; see map, p.52. This bakery, tucked away on a backstreet near the train station, specializes in delectable *sfogliatelle* – both types, either *frolla* (with shortbread crust) or *riccia* (with a shell-shaped crunchy crust), both served warm, fresh from the oven.

Centro storico

See map, p.52.

Bar Tico Via del Duomo 27. Just a short walk from the Duomo, this bar does excellent coffee made from their own artisanal roast. However, while their *espresso* and *cappuccino* are delicious, they are really known for their transcendent *caffè brasiliano* (*espresso* with milk foam, sugar and cocoa).

Caffè dell'Epoca Via Santa Maria di Costantinopoli 82. Excellent coffee and an assortment of pastries and snacks with a few tables outside, offering a front-row seat for the chic bohemian scene in the adjacent Piazza Bellini.

Capparelli Via dei Tribunali 324–327. Opposite San Paolo Maggiore, this small *pasticceria* serves hot, flaky *cornetti* and *sfogliatelle* to take away. For a few extra euros, grab a table and an espresso at their bar next door.

Gay Odin Via Benedetto Croce 61. One of several locations (there are two on Via Toledo alone), the

Spaccanapoli branch of this long-established *chocolatier* also sells decadent ice cream.

Scaturchio Piazza San Domenico. This elegant old Naples standard has been serving coffee and pastries in the heart of Spaccanapoli for decades. Elbow your way to the counter or grab a table in the shade of the Church of San Domenico. There's another branch right by the Montesanto funicular station.

Via Toledo and the Quartieri Spagnoli

See map, p.67.

Gambrinus Via Chiaia 1–2. The oldest and best known of Neapolitan cafés, founded in 1861. Not cheap, but its aura of chandeliered gentility and outside seating on Piazza Trieste e Trento makes it worth at least one visit. Pastries, cakes and snacks are available daily from early morning until after midnight.

La Scimmia Piazza Carità 4. One of two locations (the other is in Piazzetta del Nilo in Spaccanapoli), this *gelateria* serves a wide selection of ice creams, though their traditional flavours like chocolate and *stracciatella* (chocolate chip) are by far the best. Specialites include bon-bons and chocolate-covered banana ice cream on a stick.

L.U.I.S.E. Via Toledo 266. This centrally located *tavola calda* is a good lunch stop, serving a wide selection of home-made savoury snacks and hot meals including *timballo di pasta* (baked pasta) and *peperoni imbottiti* (stuffed peppers) at low prices. One of several locations (Piazza dei Martiri is another).

Pintauro Via Toledo 275. A famous *pasticceria* near Galleria Umberto I whose founder is credited with inventing the *sfogliatella* in 1818. They are known also for their *caprese* (chocolate and almond cake).

Sfogliatella Mary Galleria Umberto I 66. Delicious *sfogliatella* pastries. Queue up with the locals to get your sugar fix at the Via Toledo entrance to the Galleria Umberto shopping complex.

Vaco 'e Pressa Piazza Dante 84. True to its name ("I'm in a hurry"), this *friggitoria* on Via Toledo sells cheap, delicious Neapolitan street food like *zeppole* (fried doughballs) and *arancini* (rice balls) to a hungry university crowd.

La Sanità and Capodimonte
See map, p.74.

Aruta Via Porta San Gennaro 34. This industrious *pasticceria* turns out thousands of pastries a day for the neighbourhood's bars and restaurants. They sell a small sampling of treats like tasty *biscotti di mandorla* (almond paste cookies), and intoxicating *babà* at a counter in the front, but be sure to peek into the back where all the magic happens.

Mignone Piazza Cavour 146. A stone's throw from the Museo Archeologico, this pastry shop turns out some of Naples' best *sfogliatelle frolle*, made fresh on site and displayed with other local treats behind a glass case. They also have a vast assortment of cakes and cookies.

Santa Lucia and Chiaia

Caffetteria Piazza dei Martiri 30; see map, p.80. This elegant Chiaia institution is a fine place both for a leisurely early-morning coffee and an evening aperitif, with good coffee, tables outside on the square and tasty cakes and snacks.

Mergellina and Posillipo
See map, p.80.

Chalet Ciro Via Caracciolo 1–2. Right by the Mergellina port, *Ciro* is a Neapolitan institution known for its *babà* (spongy dough soaked in rum and syrup) and *bignè di San Giuseppe* (cream-filled pastries made around Carnival time). Its marathon opening hours (6.30am–2am) make it a dependable early-morning or after dinner pit-stop for sweets or ice cream.

Chiquitos Via Posillipo 1. A great *frullati* place, with fruit shakes for around €3, right on the water-front at Mergellina, where the buses stop.

Remy Gelo Via F. Galiani 29a. Near the Mergellina hydrofoil terminal, this place does superb ice creams and *granite*. Their speciality is *remygnon*, miniature portions of *gelato* covered in chocolate.

Vómero
See map, p.83.

Fantasia Gelati Piazza Vanvitelli 22. Set in Vómero's busiest square, this *gelateria* serves home-made ice cream in some unique flavours – try the "Benevento" (dark chocolate, almond and nougat) – and an assortment of *frutta farcita* (frozen fruit stuffed with ice cream). There are four other locations, including one at Via Toledo 381.

Friggitoria Vomero Via Cimarosa 44. A fried-food snack bar opposite two of Vómero's funicular stations. Their deep-fried aubergines and potato croquettes are surprisingly light.

Otranto Via Scarlatti 78. Simply delicious *sorbetto* and *gelato artigianale* just off Piazza Vanvitelli. Flavours change with the season and the ingredients are of the highest quality. The lemon sorbet is especially good.

Restaurants and pizzerias

As Naples is not primarily a tourist-geared city, most restaurants are family-run places frequented by locals and as such generally serve good, traditional Neapolitan food at very reasonable prices. You can eat well pretty much everywhere, but inevitably certain districts do certain things best: the **centro storico** and **Quartieri Spagnoli** are still home to many simple places that serve a limited menu of daily specials based on what is fresh in the market; **Chiaia** and **Vómero** host more formal restaurants that serve a greater selection of regional specialities; for pricey fish meals with a view, there's the Borgo Marinaro in **Santa Lucia** and **Posillipo**.

Piazza Garibaldi and around

See map, p.52.

Antica Pizzeria del Borgo Orefici Via Luigi Palmieri 13 ⊤081.552.0996. A couple of tables inside, and a little terrace outside, at which you can enjoy great pizza to the sounds of the thundering Corso Umberto traffic. The very large pizzas more than make up for the lack of ambience, starting at €3 and stopping at €5.50 for the delicious *salsiccia e friarielli* (sausage and bitter greens).

Da Michele Via Cesare Sersale 1–3 ⊤081.553.9204. Tucked away off Corso Umberto I in the Forcella district, this is the most determinedly traditional of all the Naples pizzerias, offering just two varieties (allegedly the only two worth eating) – *marinara* and *margherita* – for about €3. Don't be surprised if you are shuttled to a communal table and seated with strangers; and don't arrive late, as they sometimes run out of dough and the neighbourhood can be a bit offputting after dark. Closed Sun.

Europeo di Mattozzi Via Marchese Campodisola 4–10 ⊤081.552.1323. Alfonso Mattozzi acts as the consummate host, creating a warm and familial dining experience for his dedicated patrons at this restaurant not far from the waterfront. Local dishes like *alici fritti* (fried anchovies) and *pasta e patate con provola* (pasta and potatoes with provolone cheese) dominate, and the home-made *babà* is not to be missed. Around €40 for a full meal excluding wine. Closed Sun & Mon–Tues for dinner.

Mimì alla Ferrovia Via A. d'Aragona 21 ⊤081.570.6883. A real old-fashioned, bustling restaurant, and something of a haven in the none-too-desirable streets off Piazza Garibaldi, serving traditional Neapolitan food at reasonable prices – pasta dishes for €6, mains for €10. Closed Sun & 2 weeks Aug.

Trianon da Ciro Via P. Colletta 42–46 ⊤081.553.9426. In spite of its large size, you are bound to encounter a queue at *Trianon*, across the street from the historic theatre of the same name, in the Forcella district – but the magnificent pizzas are worth the wait. They serve all the classics from around €4.

Centro storico

See map, p.52.

Antica Osteria Pisano Piazza Crocelle ai Mannesi 1–4 ⊤081.554.8325. A small and very traditional *trattoria* with a reasonably priced menu of well-loved local standards – a few pasta dishes, mainly with fish and seafood, and a short menu of meaty mains for €5–8. Closed Sun & Aug.

Bellini Via Santa Maria di Costantinopoli 80 ⊤081.459.774. Full of old-world charm, this historic establishment has a great convivial outside terrace screened by foliage. The service is formal and entertaining, provided by cummerbunded, and occasionally cranky, waiters. Neapolitans come for the house speciality, *linguine al cartoccio* (pasta with seafood baked in paper; €12.50), but pizzas and other local specialities are also on offer. At lunch, a small *friggitoria* on the terrace sells *pizzette* to take away. Closed Sun evening.

La Cantina di Via Sapienza Via Sapienza 40–41 ⊤081.459.078. Proprietor Gaetano's no-nonsense food and service draws a busy lunch crowd from the nearby hospital and university. *La Cantina* dishes up hearty home-cooked classics like *polpette fritte* (fried meatballs) for €5 and a staggering array of seasonal vegetable side dishes like *caponata* (sweet-and-sour aubergine) and *peperoni fritti* (fried peppers) for €2. Full meals for €10–12. Closed dinner & Sun.

I Decumani Via dei Tribunali 58–61 ⊤081.557.1309. This is one of several excellent pizzerias along this stretch and is commonly recognized as one of Naples' best. Freshly remodelled and warmly tiled, *I Decumani* has come a long way since it was a hole-in-the-wall *frigittoria* (still active next door). The *fritti misti* are a must, as are the huge, delicious pizzas, which average €4. It's one of the few places in the centro storico open on Sun too. Closed Mon.

Di Matteo Via dei Tribunali 94 ⊤081.294.203. The crowded *friggitoria* outside announces this terrific and well-located pizzeria – one of the best and most famous in the city. For table service, walk in and take a left, then head upstairs with authority and ask for a table. The spartan decor may be reminiscent of a hospital cafeteria, but the enormous pizzas, from €3.50, more than make up for it. *Pizzette*, *arancini* and other cheap Neapolitan street food (€1 each) to take away are sold at the entrance. Closed Sun.

La Locanda del Grifo Via del Giudice 14 ⊤081.442.0815. With tables on a ramshackle square just off Via dei Tribunali, this place has a short menu of just half a dozen pasta dishes and 6–8 mains – mainly fish – plus pizzas from €3. Great location, good food and excellent value.

Lombardi a Santa Chiara Via B. Croce 59 ⊤081.456.220. Located on Spaccanapoli near the church of Santa Chiara, this well-respected ristorante-pizzeria is known for its pizzas, though there is a moderately priced menu of Neapolitan dishes on offer as well – it's reasonably basic, but with its upstairs room perhaps a little less so than some of the other centro storico pizzerias. Closed Sun.

Sorbillo Via dei Tribunali 32 ☎081.446.643. *Sorbillo* has a die-hard cult following that snubs the family's new pizza joint (also called *Sorbillo*) on the same block in favour of the original. In business since 1935, the family, composed of 21 siblings, is committed to using the highest quality ingredients – the best mozzarella from nearby Agerola, sweet Vesuvian tomatoes and fine olive oil – a novel idea in the pizza business. Pizzas from €3. Closed Sun.

Un Sorriso Integrale Vico S. Pietro Majella 6 ☎081.455.026. A long-established vegetarian restaurant in the courtyard of a *palazzo* just off the bohemian Piazza Bellini. This is an excellent budget option serving cheap and delicious organic meals like *melanzane alla parmigiana* (aubergine in a tomato and parmesan sauce) on paper-covered tables. A plentiful six-dish tasting menu costs €9 and full meals can be had for €12–15. There is a small organic food shop attached to the dining room. Closed Sun.

Squisitezze Via Santa Maria di Costantinopoli 100 ☎081.401.578. A new arrival, this self-described "cheesebar" serves typical *formaggi* and *salumi* from Campania, in an ultra-modern setting. A five-cheese tasting costs €12 and can be paired with one of the ten wines by the glass on offer. Light meals are served too, or head upstairs to *La Stanza del Gusto* (see below) for full service. Closed Sat lunch & Sun.

La Stanza del Gusto Via Santa Maria di Costanti-nopoli 100 ☎081.401.578. Chef Mario Avallone was one of Naples' first culinary innovators, opening *La Stanza* in Chiaia in 1996. Now at its new location in the centro storico, he continues his dedication to creative, seasonal dishes like *tonno del coniglio* (marinated, shredded rabbit), using only local and sustainable ingredients. There's just one room, so book ahead. Tasting menus start at €35. Closed Sat lunch & Mon.

Trattoria Campagnola Piazza Nilo 22 ☎081.551.4930. A pleasant place to sit and watch the centro storico go by, while tucking into *Campagnola*'s short menu of tasty pasta dishes and simple main courses. Cheap and very cheerful. Closed Sun.

Via Toledo and the Quartieri Spagnoli

See map, p.67.

Al 53 Piazza Dante 53 ☎081.549.9372. Like Via Toledo, Piazza Dante can be a bit of a desert at night, so this place is quite a haven, brightly lit and furnished in simple style, and serving well-priced, uncomplicated food – pasta dishes for €5, mains for €6–8. Closed Tues.

Ciro a Santa Brigida Via Santa Brigida 71 ☎081.552.4072. This stalwart of the central Naples restaurant scene is looking a bit tatty these days, and the service can vary from slapdash to fawning. But the food is great: try the pasta in a Neapolitan meat sauce, rich with melting meat and onions – or one of the seafood pastas or fish mains. Closed Sun.

Kukai Via C. de Cesare 55 ☎081.411.905. This stylish sushi bar is about as far away from Neapolitan ambience – and cuisine – as you can get. Simple and delectable sushi, sashimi, soups and noodles will satisfy any diner in need of a break from pizza and pasta. Meals from €20. *Kukai Nano*, next door at no. 52, has a lunch buffet for €8. *Kukai* open daily; *Kukai Nano* closed Sun & Mon.

Leon D'Oro Piazza Dante 48 ☎081.549.9404. On the eastern side of the wide-open Piazza Dante, *Leon D'Oro* has been going strong since the 1950s. They serve great pizzas and pastas from €5 and their vast plates of seasonal vegetable and meat *antipasti* are a meal in themselves. Closed Sun dinner & Mon.

Mattozzi Piazza Carità 2 ☎081.552.4322. In business since 1890, this pizzeria just off Via Toledo is one of Naples' oldest. The "Mattozzi" house special comes with mozzarella, cherry tomatoes, ham, mushrooms and rocket, and there's also a selection of Neapolitan pasta, meat and fish specialities.

Nennella Vico Lungo Teatro Nuovo 103–105. Born as a cheap cafeteria, *Nennella* still serves up authentic Neapolitan cuisine like *pasta e fagioli* (soup with pasta and beans) and sautéed *friarielli* (local chicory-like greens). The very basic decor has changed little since the cafeteria days, but this only adds to the charm. There are queues at lunchtime – get there before the 1.30pm rush. A full meal will cost €10–12. Closed Sun.

Osteria da Carmela Via Conte di Ruovo 11/12 ☎081.549.9738. Bang next door to the Teatro Bellini, this is just one room, serving variations on traditional Neapolitan cuisine – great fish, excellent *antipasti*, and tasty pasta and meat too, in an intimate and friendly environment. Quite a find. Closed Sun.

Tripperia Fiorenzano Via Pignasecca 14. Not for the faint of heart, but this is genuine Neapolitan cuisine. This takeaway-cum-*osteria* with strips of tripe hanging at the entrance serves Neapolitan classics like *o' muss* (pig muzzle with a squeeze of lemon) and *trippa al pomodoro* (tripe in tomato sauce) at a handful of tables. Closed Sun.

La Sanità and Capodimonte

See map, p.74.

'O Core 'e Napule Via M. Pagano 48–50/Via Misericordiella 23/24 ℡ 081.292.566. A short walk from the Museo Archeologico, this restaurant serves up delicious pizzas, pastas and fish. A speciality is the *tronchetto*, a folded pizza filled with mozzarella and ricotta baked to perfection and draped with *prosciutto*, tomatoes, mozzarella and rocket. There is a shaded patio outside for summer dining.

Starita a Materdei Via Materdei 27–28 ℡ 081.557.3682. The Starita family has been serving pizza and *fritti* in the Materdei neighbourhood, uphill from the Museo Archeologico, since 1901, and along the way have created unique classics like the *montarana*: pizza dough that is deep-fried before being garnished with tomato and cheese then baked (around €5). For dessert, try the *angioletti*, deep-fried dough slathered in Nutella. Closed Sun.

Santa Lucia and Chiaia

See map, p.80.

Bersagliera Borgo Marinaro 10–11 ℡ 081.764.6016. Fine food, especially seafood, in an elegant setting, though inevitably you pay for the location, right next to the Castel dell'Ovo with views of Vesuvius, and for the "*O Sole Mio*" minstrels who wander between the tables outside. The house special is *tagliatelle alla bersagliera* (pasta with squid, shrimp, clams, mussels and cherry tomatoes); the home-made desserts are delicious. Closed Tues.

Da Dora Via Palasciano 30 ℡ 081.680.519. Dining here is a bit like eating in the badly lit kitchen of an eccentric Neapolitan grandmother with a penchant for marine kitsch. The menu is exclusively fish, prepared simply and thoughtfully to a discerning clientele. Specialities include *crudi* (raw shellfish and fish *carpaccio*) seasoned with olive oil and pepper, and *linguine alla Dora* (with shrimp, mussels, clams and langostines). Full meals from €55 without wine. Closed Sun & Aug.

D'Angelo Via A. Falcone 203 ℡ 081.578.9772. A somewhat formal establishment, with the feel of a banqueting hall teetering above the city. The dining rooms and panoramic terrace offer spectacular views over Naples and the bay to Vesuvius. Dishes like *paccheri con rana pescatrice* (ring-shaped pasta with monkfish) use the freshest of local ingredients. Book. Closed Mon & Tues.

Da Ettore Via Santa Lucia 56 ℡ 081.764.0498. In the heart of Borgo Santa Lucia, this casual and lively neighbourhood restaurant is famous for its *pagnotielli* – *calzoni* stuffed with mozzarella, ham

and mushrooms, for €7, and there is a wide selection of pizza and pasta dishes. Good quality and value in a neighbourhood not known for either. Closed Sun.

Marino Via S. Lucia 118 ℡ 081.764.0280. A warm and welcoming family-style place in Santa Lucia with good pizzas and reliable Neapolitan dishes like *scialatielli* (long home-made pasta) with aubergine, tomato and mozzarella for €6. Great value, and one of the area's few really worthwhile restaurants. Closed Mon.

Osteria della Mattonella Via Nicotera 13 ℡ 081.416.541. Uphill from Piazza del Plebescito, this family-run Chiaia institution covered in wall-to-wall majolica (*mattonella* means tile) oozes with old-fashioned charm. The offerings are simple and rustic, like the *maccheroni alla genovese* (pasta with meat and onions) for €6. Closed Sun dinner.

Radici Riviera di Chiaia 268 ℡ 081.248.1100. In spite of its snooty clientele and fashionable setting, this new addition to Chiaia's culinary scene is true to the roots of Neapolitan cuisine, but transcends them to create elegant, creative, delicious dishes. The menu changes regularly, and the wine list is extensive. Expect to pay €45 for a full meal, excluding wine. Closed Mon–Fri at lunch & Sun.

Umberto Via Alabardieri 30 ℡ 081.418.555. For more than ninety years *Umberto* has been serving marvellous food to the well-heeled Chiaia district. Divided into a simple pizzeria and a more upscale restaurant, both offer a combination of traditional and innovative choices, including gluten-free dishes. Pizza from €6, spaghetti with clams €9.50. Closed Mon.

Mergellina and Posillipo

See map, p.80.

Al Faretto Via Marechiaro 127 ℡ 081.575.0407. Very atmospheric, romantic and smart, and offering both pizza and fish, this Posillipo restaurant provides sweeping views over the bay from its airy dining room. Though pizza is on offer, most come for the exceptionally fresh local fish served with great style. In summer, phone ahead to reserve a place on the outdoor veranda, suspended over the sea. Full fish meals from €45, excluding wine. Closed Mon.

Ciro A Mergellina Via Mergellina 18–21 ℡ 081.681.780. Not to be confused with the pastry shop of the same name nearby, this popular ristorante-pizzeria is known for its huge *antipasto della casa* – mozzarella, fried vegetables, aubergine in parmesan, seafood salad, and *polipetti affogati* (octopus in tomato sauce) – but save room for a classic pizza or fish dish. Crowded at weekends, so best to call ahead. Closed Mon.

Da Ciciotto Calata Ponticello a Marechiaro 32 ℡081.575.1165. Reservations are essential at this small Posillipo *trattoria*, with tables outside overlooking the bay. The place might have a rustic feel, but the food is anything but: specialities are *carpaccio di pesce crudo* and raw shellfish. A full meal excluding wine will cost from €45. To get here, follow Via Marechiaro to the end, where it opens out onto a small piazza. Take the steps off the far end that lead down to the sea and turn right at the bottom of the first flight.

Da Pasqualino Piazza Sannazzaro 79 ℡081.681.524. In the business of serving local fish dishes since 1898, this old-school Mergellina ristorante-pizzeria does great and affordable seafood and pizzas. A plate of mussels in broth costs €5, and pizzas made in a wood-burning stove start at €3.50. There is an outdoor patio for summer dining. Closed Tues.

Vómero

See map, p.83.

Acunzo Via D. Cimarosa 60–62 ℡081.578.5362. Opened by the Acunzo family in 1936, and owned by Michele and Caterina since 1964, this low-key *trattoria* has a bustling atmosphere and friendly staff and is upmarket Vómero's best pizza joint.

Locals crowd into its spartan interior for the wonderful pizza, available in more than forty varieties, best enjoyed after a plentiful serving of *fritti*. Closed Sun.

Donna Teresa Via Kerbaker 58 ℡081.556.7070. One of the few vestiges of simple dining left in Vómero. Business folk flock here at lunchtime when looking for a home-cooked meal like *sartù di riso* (rice baked with vegetables and meat) or *polpette al sugo* (meatballs in tomato sauce). Little English is spoken so come armed with a dictionary. Expect to pay €12–15 for a full meal. Closed Sun.

Gorizia Via Bernini 29 ℡081.578.2248. Not far from the Centrale and Chiaia funicular stops, *Gorizia* offers a full menu, but follow the lead set by the locals and skip it in favour of some of Vómero's most respectable pizza (though inferior to nearby *Acunzo*), served in a casual and unpretentious setting. There are outdoor tables too. Closed Mon.

Renzo e Lucia Via T. Angelini 33 ℡081.578.0874. Just beneath Castel Sant'Elmo, this place has a formal air, reflected in the spacious dining room and elegant gardens and terraces. The restaurant holds a prime position in Vómero, affording amazing views over Naples and the bay. A full meal will cost around €35, excluding wine. Closed Mon.

Nightlife and entertainment

Neapolitan **nightlife** is largely concentrated in two neighbourhoods: the centro storico and the Chiaia district. The old part of the city centre is crammed with bars appealing to budget-conscious students and a chic bohemian crowd – there are a half-dozen decent choices in or near Piazza Bellini alone – and many have outdoor seating that spills into the city's piazzas and alleyways. The same area also has a number of pubs, especially on Via Paladino and Via Mezzocannone near the university, with cheap cocktails and music – electronica, reggae and rock – till late. Bear in mind that things don't really get going until at least 10pm, and most places are closed in the hot **summer months**, when everyone congregates in the open air in Piazza del Gesù Nuovo and Piazza San Domenico Maggiore, or the gay-friendly cafés on Piazza Bellini instead. Chiaia is home to a young professional crowd that prefers the upscale district's see-and-be-seen lounge bars. The district also harbours a few good wine bars and pubs, which tend to put on an "*aperitivo* hour", opening around 5.30/6pm for an after-work happy-hour buffet.

Later on, the action moves to the city's **clubs** (see p.91) and **live music venues** (see p.92).

For nightlife **listings**, pick up *Zero* (ⓦwww.zero.eu), or *Urban*, free monthly publications available in bars, or for big events see ⓦwww.angelsoflove.it, Italy's answer to the Ministry of Sound.

Neapolitan sounds

Trends in Neapolitan music (see also the *Theatrical Naples* colour section) have been influenced in the modern age by the city's strange, harsh dialect, and to some extent by the American jazz and swing that were introduced by the US military in World War II, bringing an international flavour to traditional Neapolitan songs. The 1970s saw one of Italy's most concentrated musical movements in the urban blues scene of **Pino Daniele** and music which developed around the **Alfa Romeo factory** out at Pomigliano d'Arco, which had a radical reputation at the time, and now plays host to an annual jazz festival. **Rap** and **hip-hop** exploded onto the scene in the 1990s, a fusion of traditional Neapolitan sounds and African and American influences, with groups such as Almamegretta, Bisca and 99 Posse using their music to comment on the state of Naples and Italian society in general. More recently, Spaccanapoli, an offshoot of the workers' groups at Pomigliano, had a hit album, *Aneme Perze* ("Lost Souls"), combining serious social critique, modern dance music and age-old Neapolitan forms. The Fonoteca music store (see p.97) is a good place to pick up the latest releases.

Bars, pubs and wine bars

Baik Via A. Falcone 372; see map, p.80. A mainstay of Naples nightlife, this chilled-out lounge bar's *aperitivo* buffet heaves with ethnic food to match its exotic decor. Outside, a leafy patio is perfect for summer drinks. Extensive wine list. Daily 6pm–midnight. Closed Aug.

B-Side Via A. Falcone 275 ☎333.596.8162; see map, p.80. A cool and unpretentious pub with a popular *aperitivo* buffet, good cocktails, temporary art exhibitions and nightly DJ sets. Tues–Sun 6pm–1am. Closed Aug.

Enoteca Belledonne Vico Belledonne a Chiaia 18 ☎081.403.162; see map, p.80. This *enoteca* attracts a discerning Chiaia crowd with its convivial atmosphere, Italian wines and selection of cheeses and *salumi*. Wines are chosen by the glass or bottle – there are hundreds on display in glass cases. Daily 6pm–2am. Closed Aug.

Intra Moenia Piazza Bellini 70 ☎081.290.988; see map, p.52. A left-leaning "literary café" and one of several trendy haunts on Piazza Bellini, where tables spread across the square. Open all day and into the night, this is a lovely place to sit and read under the wisteria on a sunny day or get a drink on a balmy night. There are light meals and ice cream too, as well as internet access. Daily 10am–2am.

Internet Bar Piazza Bellini 74; see map, p.52. Originating as an internet café, this is *Intra Moenia*'s less expensive neighbour. Neapolitan actors and artists gather under its parasols in the summer, and the bar is a venue for cultural events

such as poetry readings and photography exhibitions. Daily 6pm–3am.

Lontano Da Dove Via Bellini 3 ☎081.549.4304; see map, p.52. A bookstore, tearoom and literary café all rolled into one, with live performances of mostly jazz and blues, held three nights a week. Mon, Tues & Thurs 10.30am–1pm & 5–8pm; Wed, Fri & Sat 10.30am–1pm & 5pm–1.30am. Closed July & Aug.

Perditempo Via San Pietro a Maiella 8 ☎081.444.958, ⓦwww.perditempo.org; see map, p.52. Browse through new and used books, CDs and LPs at this new arrival near Piazza Bellini. The well-stocked bar serves beer and cocktails and draws an arty and intellectual crowd, and often hosts book presentations, live music and DJs too; check the website for details. Mon–Sat 5.30pm–2am. Closed Aug.

S'move Vico dei Sospiri 10 ☎081.764.5813, ⓦwww.smove-lab.net; see map, p.80. Evening festivities at this self-described "musicfoodbar" get started with a generous *aperitivo* buffet at 7pm. Later, a smart Chiaia clientele arrive for acid jazz, techno and funk. Mon–Sat 11am–3am, Sun 7pm–3am.

Trip Via Martucci 64 ☎081.195.68.994, ⓦwww.cra.na.it; see map, p.80. Located in Chiaia near Piazza Amadeo, and dripping in 1950s kitsch, *Trip* is a café by day and a cocktail bar at night, hosting a wide range of cultural events, art exhibitions and lectures for the intellectually curious. Light meals are served and there is a Saturday brunch too. Mon–Sat 11am–3pm & 6pm–midnight. Closed Aug.

Clubs

The city has plenty of **clubs**, both large and small. Owing to licensing laws, some nightclubs require a *tesserino* or membership card to gain entry, which costs from €10 and can be bought at the door. Others charge a flat cover charge, generally from €15 to €35, which includes the price of a drink. Things get going around midnight or 1am, but it's worth remembering that in July and August most clubs close for the summer and move out to towns around the bay, such as Posillipo, Bácoli, Fusaro and Pozzuoli.

Arenile Via Corroglio 14b ☎081.570.6035, ⓦwww.arenilereload.com. White cabanas line the volcanic sand beach, pool and gardens of this ultra-hip *stabilimento* (beach club) in Bagnoli. After dark, the hip-hop, latin and house beats take over and the clubbers dance on the sand until the early hours. Bus #C9 from Piazzale Tecchio. June–Sept daily 9am–4am.

Gold Via Sgambati 47; see map, p.83. Also known as "ex-Madison Street", its previous moniker, this huge, upmarket club on the outskirts of Vómero has themed events and visiting DJs. In addition to its two bars, there's a restaurant on the third floor. Entrance around €20. Fri–Sun 10pm–4.30am. Closed June–Sept.

Jail Club Via Sedile di Porto 65 ☎347.170.3585, ⓦwww.jailclub.it; see map, p.52. One of the city's newer, larger clubs, popular with students. The music is usually DJ-led, but there are also live shows, often featuring local death-metal bands. Entrance around €5.

Momah Via Vito Fornari 15 ☎081.422.334, ⓦwww.momah.it; see map, p.80. Descend the stairs near the corner of Via dei Mille in the posh Chiaia district, and immerse yourself in *Momah*, a small and exclusive club where house, techno and trance attract Naples' beautiful people. Thurs–Sun 10pm–4am. Closed June to mid-Sept.

Rising South Via S. Sebastiano 19 ☎335.879.428, ⓦwww.risingrepublic.com; see map, p.52. The coolest club in the centro storico, with a velvet Baroque interior and great cocktails (try the refreshing Cucumber Slumber). You'll need to be on the list Thurs, Fri and Sat, so call in advance. Tues is "Erasmus party" night, aimed at foreign exchange students, Wed reggae and Thurs–Sat electrolounge and guest DJs. Tues–Sun 10pm–3am. Closed mid-May to Sept.

Virgilio Club Via Lucrezio Caro 6 ☎081.575.5261, ⓦwww.virgilioclub.it. High up in the Parco Virgiliano on the slopes of Posillipo, this fun club gets jam-packed on summer nights when they open a leafy terrace overlooking the bay. Entrance from €20. June to mid-Oct Wed–Sun 10pm–4am; rest of year opening variable.

Live music

The centro storico's **live music venues** host mostly local and Italian bands, although the jazz clubs do pull a wider European playlist. For big names, try the Napoli Jazz Festival (ⓦwww.napolijazzfestival.it) during the first two weeks of August. Big international pop and rock artists usually bypass Naples, though once a year in July the Neapolis Rock Festival (ⓦwww.neapolis.it) draws important acts – and huge crowds – to the Mostra d'Oltremare convention centre in Fuorigrotta.

Around Midnight Via Bonito 32A ☎081.742.3278, ⓦwww.aroundmidnight.it; see map, p.83. A popular jazz club in Vómero that intermittently dips a toe into blues. There are live performances every night, mostly by Italian musicians, although the occasional international star graces the stage. Light meals are also served. Tues–Sun 8pm–1am. Closed July & Aug.

Cinema

Most **films** shown in Italy – whether on TV or the big screen – are dubbed. If a film is being shown in its original language, the letters V.O. (short for *versione originale*) will be written beside the listing, but this is an extremely rare occurrence in Naples. For film times, check the Naples city section of a daily newspaper, which usually lists cinemas by area. In general, cinemas are open from around 4pm, with the last showing at 10pm or 10.30pm. Expect an abrupt intermission halfway into the film, usually inserted at an inopportune moment in the film's narrative. **Tickets** range from €5 to €8. See also pp.31–32 for details of annual **film festivals**, which may offer the only opportunity to view any English-language cinema in the original language.

Bourbon Street Via Bellini 52–53
℡ 338.825.3756, ⓦ www.bourbonstreetjazzclub.
com; see map, p.52. A premier venue for Italian
and international jazz acts, bringing a slice of
American jazz culture to the heart of Naples' centro
storico. Even the walls are authentic – the bricks
were imported from New Orleans. Tues–Sun 9pm–
3am. Closed June–Aug.
Kestè Largo S. Giovanni Maggiore Pignatelli
℡ 081.551.3984, ⓦ www.keste.it; see map, p.67.
Bar, café, gallery and live music venue opposite the
university. Go early for the *aperitivo* buffet and
stay for the band or DJ set. Tues 7.30am–8pm,
Wed–Fri 7.30am–2.30am, Sat & Sun 9pm–2.30am.
Closed Aug.

Kinky Bar Via Cisterna dell'Olio 21
℡ 335.547.7299, ⓦ www.kinkyjam.com; see map,
p.67. Contrary to what the name suggests, this
popular centro storico bar is Naples' prime venue
for reggae, rocksteady, dancehall and ska, with DJs
and live acts from Europe and the Caribbean.
There's also a 200-strong cocktail list. Tues–Sun
9pm–4am. Closed mid-June to mid-Sept.
Lanificio 25 Piazza E. De Nicola 46
℡ 081.658.2915; see map, p.52. Beside the Porta
Capuana, this former nineteenth-century wool
factory has been transformed into a venue for experimental music and contemporary performance art.
The stark interior hosts pianists, DJs and artists from
around the world.

Classical music, opera and theatre

For more highbrow **culture** there's the legendary **Teatro di San Carlo** (see p.94), an opulent venue given over to classical concerts, opera, and ballet. You'll find tickets hard to come by, however, as they are mostly sold on subscription, but if you do manage to get hold of one, dress up. Teatro Bellini puts on theat-rical performances by important playwrights, but in Italian only. Smaller and more casual venues offer a variety of entertainment ranging from traditional Neapolitan comedies (Teatro Trianon) to experimental theatre (Nuovo Teatro Nuovo). Naples' Nuova Orchestra Alessandro Scarlatti (℡ 081.410.175, ⓦ www .nuovaorchestrascarlatti.it; tickets from €10), the city's renowned travelling symphony orchestra, performs at the Auditorium RAI on Viale Marconi 7 and other venues around town.

▲ Teatro di San Carlo

Tickets for live performances

Each theatre has its own box office that sells **tickets** during normal business hours and right before performances. Otherwise, tickets can also be purchased at the following outlets:

Box Office Galleria Umberto I 17 ☏081.551.9188, ⊛www.boxofficenapoli.it; Mon–Fri 9.30am–1.30pm & 3.30–7pm, Sat 9.30am–1.30pm.

Concerteria Feltrinelli bookstore, Piazza dei Martiri/Via Santa Caterina a Chiaia 23 ☏081.764.2111, ⊛www.concerteria.it; Mon 4.30–8pm, Tues–Sat 10am–1.30pm & 4.30–8pm.

Promos Guida bookstore, Via Merliani 118–120, Vómero ☏081.556.4726, ⊛www .promosnapoli.it. Another branch is at the Guida bookstore at Port'Alba (☏081.442.0814); Mon 4–7.30pm, Tues–Sat 10.30am–1.30pm & 4–7.30pm.

Tkt Point Corso Vittorio Emanuele 55 ☏081.529.4939, ⊛www.tktpoint.it; Mon–Sat 9am–1pm & 4–8pm, Sun 10am–1pm.

Nuovo Teatro Nuovo Via Montecalvario 16 ☏081.497.6267, ⊛www.nuovoteatronuovo.it. A venue for creative and experimental theatre in the heart of the Quartieri Spagnoli. Tickets €10.

Teatro Augusteo Piazzetta Duca d'Aosta 263 ☏081.414.243, ⊛www.teatroaugusteo.it. Just off Via Toledo, this theatre hosts a wide range of performances including nineteenth-century Neapolitan folk music and world music. Tickets from €25.

Teatro Bellini Via Conte di Ruvo 14 ☏081.549.1266, ⊛www.teatrobellini.it. This nineteenth-century theatre, elegantly decked out in red velvet and gold, hosts theatrical performances of the works of Goethe, Svevo, Wilde and Shakespeare (in Italian), as well as occasional classic Neapolitan works (in dialect). Tickets from €12.

Teatro Palapartenope Via Barbagallo 115 ☏081.570.0008, ⊛www.palapartenope.it. The 6000-seat Palapartenope in Fuorigrotta hosts theatrical performances, festivals, events and concerts of all musical genres. Their more intimate Casa della Musica-Federico I (⊛www .casadellamusicanapoli.it), part of the same complex, puts on similar events. Tickets from €15.

Teatro di San Carlo Via di San Carlo 98F ☏081.797.2331, ⊛www.teatrosancarlo.it. Classical concerts, operas and ballets by Europe's best conductors and companies in this sumptuous historic opera house adjacent to the Palazzo Reale. Tickets from €25, but hard to get.

Teatro Sancarluccio Via San Pasquale a Chiaia 49 ☏081.405.5000, ⊛www.teatrosancarluccio .com. Performances at this Chiaia theatre include chamber music, perfomance art and cabaret – and they host a Baroque music festival in late Sept. Tickets from €15.

Teatro Stabile di Napoli Piazza Municipio 1 ☏081.551.0336, ⊛www.teatrostabilenapoli.it. Three theatres in one: the eighteenth-century Mercadante and Ridotto are both in Piazza Municipio, while nearby is Eduardo De Filippo's San Ferdinando, featuring the best of Italian touring theatre companies. Tickets from €15.

Teatro Trianon Piazza Calenda 9 ☏081.225.8285, ⊛www.teatrotrianon.it. In the heart of Forcella, this refurbished cinema has been transformed into a venue for traditional Neapolitan theatre and song. Tickets from €10.

Shopping

The character of Neapolitan neighborhoods is often defined by the **shops** that are found there. It would be hard to imagine the **centro storico** without its industrious Via San Gregorio Armeno, the epicentre of nativity-scene production, where handmade wood and terracotta figures are crafted by local artisans. The centro storico is also the place for books and prints, especially around Port'Alba off Piazza Dante, while nearby on Via Santa Maria di Costantinopoli are a plethora of antique dealers, art restorers and carpenters. The entire length of **Via Toledo** from Piazza Dante to Piazza del Plebescito is dominated by mainstream and chain stores, while designer boutiques and antiques stores populate **Chiaia**, amplifying the district's upmarket feel.

In general, shops are **open** Monday afternoons from 4pm to 8pm, and Tuesday to Saturday from 10am to 2pm and from 4pm to 8pm. Sundays in Naples are dedicated to long lunches and football games and, with the exception of a few places in the centro storico, shops are closed all day.

Antiques

Antichità Ciro Guarracino Via V. Gaetani 26 ☏081.764.6912. Not far from Piazza dei Martiri in Chiaia, this third-generation antiques dealer sells furniture, *objets d'art* and paintings from the Baroque era through to the early twentieth century. Mon 4–8pm, Tues–Sat 10am–2pm & 4–8pm.
Maurizio Brandi Antiquariato Via D. Morelli 9–11 ☏081.764.3882. Maurizio Brandi offers a stellar selection of antiques near Piazza dei Martiri in Chiaia. He specializes in furniture but has a fine collection of ceramics, porcelain and silver as well. Mon 4–8pm, Tues–Sat 10am–2pm & 4–8pm.

Art, crafts and gifts

Aleph Design Via dei Tribunali 309–339 ☏081.454.793 & 338.409.9173, ⊛www .alephdesign.info. Alessandra D'Aniello's handcrafted terracotta ceramics are inspired by Naples, its landscape and textures. The showroom is in the historic Palazzo d'Angiò and you can watch her work in her atelier nearby on Via S. Paolo 11. Open daily by appointment.
Di Virgilio Via San Gregorio Armeno 18 ☏081.549.1642. Craftsmen have been producing handcrafted terracotta figures here for three gener-ations, ranging from the traditional holy family to surreal pop-culture figures such as Barack Obama and Diego Maradona. Daily 9am–8pm.
Maestranze Napoletane Via Conte di Ruvo 7–8 ☏081.544.8836, ⊛www.maestranzenapoletane .com. Near Piazza Bellini, this is one of the few places left in the city where you can still see the once ubiquitous art of marble intarsia. The studio specializes in marble-inlaid furniture and art pieces. Mon 4–8pm, Tues–Sat 10am–2pm & 4–8pm.
Napolimania Via Toledo 312–313 ☏081.414.120. A one-stop-shop for all things Neapolitan, where the assortment of Naples-inspired souvenirs, gadgets and bizarre novelties is endless. Good if you're stuck for a present or souvenir. Daily 10am–2pm & 4–8pm.
La Smorfia Via Anticaglia 23 ☏081.293.812, ⊛www.laboratorialasmorfia.it. Young artisan Fabio Paolella employs eighteenth-century traditions when creating his handmade terracotta Nativity figurines for his centro storico shop. A trained art

restorer, he also repairs and sells antique Nativity characters and church decorations. Mon 4–8pm, Tues–Sat 10am–1.30pm & 4–8pm.

Books

Colonnese Via S. Pietro a Maiella 32–33 ☏081.459.858, ⊛www.colonnese.it. Just off Piazza Bellini, this publishing house and bookshop sells a vast array of new, used and out-of-print books and specializes in eighteenth- and nineteenth-century Neapolitan literature and books on the city's language and culture. Mon–Fri 9am–1.30pm & 4–7.30pm, Sat 9am–1.30pm.
Feltrinelli Via S. Caterina a Chiaia 23 ☏081.240.5411, ⊛www.lafeltrinelli.it. A busy three-storey bookstore with a selection of English guidebooks, fiction and magazines. There is a café for lingering, and the Concerteria box office is handy for concert or theatre tickets. A second location is on Via S. Tommaso D'Aquino 70–76. Mon–Thurs 10am–9pm, Fri 10am–10pm, Sat 10am–11pm & Sun 10am–2pm & 4–10pm.
Lontano Da Dove Via Bellini 3 ☏081.549.4304. A bookstore, tearoom and literary café by day and a pub/jazz club in the evenings. It is a lovely place to leaf through a book over coffee while seeing the centro storico sights. Mon, Tues & Thurs 10.30am–1pm & 5–8pm; Wed, Fri & Sat 10.30am–1pm & 5pm–1.30am. Closed July & Aug.

Clothes, shoes and accessories

Barbaro Galleria Umberto I ☏081.411.284, ⊛www.barbaronapoli.it. This stylish store has several branches within the Galleria Umberto I, specializing in sleek and expensive pieces by Italy's top designers, for men, women and the home. Mon–Sat 10am–8pm, Sun 10am–2pm.
Livio de Simone Piazza Santa Maria degli Angeli 11 ☏081.764.3827. Livio began designing bright, colourful, handprinted clothing for women in the 1960s, and his "Neapolitan batik" tradition is now continued by his daughter at a boutique in Chiaia. Mon 4–8pm, Tues–Sat 10am–1.30pm & 4–8pm.
Marinella Riviera di Chiaia 287 ☏081.245.1182, ⊛www.marinellanapoli.it. This atelier has been making fine silk ties in original prints for a discerning Chiaia crowd and foreign heads of state since 1914. They sell shoes and other formal

Markets

You can find everything from food and clothing at budget prices to rare works of art and antiques at Naples' morning **markets**, generally open Mon–Sat 8am–2pm. Each has its own character and is worth a browse, if only to see how they operate as one of the pillars of Neapolitan social and commercial life.

Mercato di Forcella Between Piazza Garibaldi and Umberto I. Everything, legal and otherwise. Daily 9am–noon.

Mercato dei Fiori Piazza Municipio beneath Castel Nuovo. Flower market. Daily at dawn.

Mercato dei Vergini Piazza dei Miracoli and around. Food and clothing. Daily 8am–2pm.

Mercato della Pignasecca Via Pignasecca and around. Food, clothing and kitchenware. Daily 8am–1.30pm.

Mercato di Porta Nolana Via San Cosmo, near Piazza Garibaldi. Fresh fish. Daily 7am–1.30pm.

Fiera Antiquaria Napoletana Villa Comunale, Chiaia. Antiques market. Last two Sundays of the month 8am–2pm.

Mercato di Antignano Piazza Antignano, Vómero. Clothes, shoes, accessories and homeware. Mon–Sat 7am–3pm.

accessories as well. Mon–Sat 7am–1.30pm & 4–8pm.

Mario Valentino Via Calabritto 10 ☎081.764.4262, ⊛www.mariovalentino.it. This Chiaia institution, once a favourite of Sophia Loren, Jackie Kennedy and Ava Gardner, produces custom-made shoes and ready-to-wear clothing and accessories for women. Mon 4–7.30pm, Tues–Sat 10am–1.30pm & 4–7.30pm.

Portolano Via Chiaia 140–141 ☎081.418.354, ⊛www.marioportolano.it. At this small shop in Chiaia, the Portolano family make hand-crafted custom and ready-to-wear leather gloves that are known for their elegance, style and quality. Mon–Sat 9.30am–1.30pm & 4–7pm.

Talarico Vico Due Porte a Toledo 4B ☎081.401.979, ⊛www.mariotalarico.it. Delicately worked umbrellas in chestnut, bamboo and horn, made in the Quartieri Spagnoli since 1860. Prices start at around €70. Mon–Sat 6.30am–8pm.

Tramontano Via Chiaia 142–3 ☎081.414.837, ⊛www.tramontano.it. Located in Vómero near Piazza Vanvitelli, this shop has been producing handmade leather handbags, luggage and accessories since 1865. There's a second location at Via Luca Giordano 25b. Mon–Sat 10am–1.30pm & 4–8pm, also Sun 10am–1.30pm Oct–June.

Department stores

Coin Via Scarlatti 86–100 ☎081.578.0111, ⊛www.coin.it. Large by Italian standards, this deparment store in Vómero is a step up from UPIM

and sells name-brand clothing, handbags, underwear and cosmetics. Mon–Fri 10am–10pm, Sat 10am–8.30pm, Sun 10am–2pm & 4.30–8.30pm.

UPIM Via dei Mille 59 ☎081.417.520, ⊛www .upim.it. Chiaia's moderately priced department store sells clothing basics, housewares and cosmetics. There is another location on Via A. Doria 40 in Fuorigrotta. Daily 9am–8.30pm.

Food and wine

Arfè Via Santa Teresa a Chiaia 45 ☎081.411.822, ⊛www.arfe.it. A posh delicatessen in Chiaia offering the highest quality cheeses, cured meats, olive oils, pâtés, vinegars and other celebrated products from Campania and across Italy. Look out for the local *capocolla* from Agerola and the fresh *mozzarella di bufala*.

Enoteca Belledonne Vico Belledonne a Chiaia 18 ☎081.403.162, ⊛www.enotecabelledonne.com. Choose from hundreds of labels at this Chiaia *enoteca* (wine bar) that doubles as a wine shop. There is an ample supply of prestigious Campanian wines, including many small Italian producers. Daily 6pm–2am. Closed Aug.

Gay Odin Via Toledo 214 ☎081.400.063, ⊛www .gayodin.it. Originally from Piedmont, Italy's chocolate capital, this family has been whipping up artisan chocolates and handmade confections for Neapolitans since 1922. Look for their signature *foresta*: milk chocolate moulded to resemble a tree branch. Eight other locations in Naples, including one nearby at Via Toledo 427, and another at Via

Benedetto Croce 61. Mon–Sat 9.30am–8pm, Sun 10am–2pm.

Limonè Piazza San Gaetano 72 ☎ 081.299.429, ⓦ www.limoncellodinapoli.it. Limoncello, the potent liqueur and nearby Sorrento's most famous export, is the focus of this shop, which also sells lemon-infused grappa and sweets, and a range of other liqueurs like *crema di melone*. Mon–Wed 4–8pm, Thurs–Sun 10am–2pm & 4–8pm.

Mexico Piazza Dante 86 ☎ 081.549.9330. Located in Piazza Dante, and famous for its rich and aromatic *espresso*, Mexico sells its own special blends of slow roasted beans to coffee aficionados seeking to re-create *caffè napoletano* at home. There is also a fine selection of coffee-based confectionery. Mon–Sat 7.30am–8pm.

Timpani e Tempura Vico della Quercia 17 ☎ 081.551.2280. This deli and *tavola calda* near Piazza del Gesù specializes in classic Neapolitan dishes and *fritti* and sells a well-chosen selection of cheeses, *salumi* and Campanian wines. They will pack your purchases for travel and deliver to your hotel. Mon–Sat 10am–8pm, Sun 9.30am–2pm.

Jewellery

Brinkmann Piazza Municipio 21 ☎ 081.552.0555, ⓦ www.brinkmann.it. Founded in 1900 by a German jeweller, the Brinkmann family continues the century-long tradition of making and repairing high-quality watches and designing elegant jewellery. Second location at Via dei Mille 72 in Chiaia. Mon 3.30–7.30pm, Tues–Sat 10am–1.30pm & 3.30–7.30pm.

Caso Piazza San Domenico Maggiore 16 ☎ 081.551.6733, ⓦ www.caso.it. In the heart of Spaccanapoli, Caso sells exquisite grand tour- and *belle époque*-era jewellery, including delicately carved corals and cameos and rare micromosaics inspired by works uncovered in Pompeii. Mon 4.30–7.30pm, Tues–Fri 9.30am–1.30pm & 4.30–7.30pm, Sat 9.30am–1.30pm.

De Paola Via A. Caccavello 67 ☎ 081.578.2910. On a quiet street near Castel Sant'Elmo, De Paola sells stunning antique and contemporary cameos in shell, coral and agate, as well as attractive coral jewellery. Mon–Sat 9am–8pm, Sun 9am–1.30pm.

Music

Fonoteca Via Morghen 31C ☎ 081.551.2842, ⓦ www.fonoteca.net. A bar and music store in Vómero that sells records and CDs of all genres, ranging from Neapolitan folk to hip-hop in dialect. Mon–Wed 10am–1am, Thurs–Sat 10am–2pm, Sun 6pm–1.30am.

Perditempo Via San Pietro a Maiella 8 ☎ 081.444.958, ⓦ www.perditempo.org. Browse through a large collection of new and used CDs and LPs in the basement of this bar and live music venue near Piazza Bellini. They sell books as well. Mon–Sat 5.30pm–2am. Closed Aug.

Listings

Airlines Alitalia ☎ 06:2222; BA ☎ 199.712.266; easyJet ☎ 848.887.766.

Car rental Avis ☎ 081.751.6052; Europcar ☎ 081.780.5643; Hertz ☎ 081.780.2971; Maggiore ☎ 199.151.120, Sixt ☎ 191.100.666.

Consulates Canada, Via Carducci 29 ☎ 081.401.338; UK, Via dei Mille 40 ☎ 081.423.8911; US, Piazza della Repubblica 2 ☎ 081.583.8111.

Exchange Outside normal banking hours you can change money and traveller's cheques at the booth inside Stazione Centrale (daily 8am–7.30pm).

Hospital To call an ambulance, dial ☎ 118; hospital numbers include ☎ 081.747.1111 and 081.220.5797, or go to the Guardia Medica Perma-nente in the Palazzo Municipio, open 24hr.

Internet Internet Point at Via de Sanctis 27, just around the corner from Piazza San Domenico, which charges €1.50 an hour.

Laundry Bolle Blu, Corso Novara 62–64, just up from the Stazione Centrale (Mon–Sat 8.30am–8pm).

Pharmacies The pharmacy at Napoli Centrale is open 24hr and there's a list of those open at night in the newspaper *Il Mattino* or posted on pharmacy doors.

Police ☎ 112 or 113; you can speak to an operator in English. The main police station (*questura*) is at Via Medina 5 (☎ 081.794.1111); you can also report crimes at the small police station in the Stazione Centrale. To report the theft of a car call ☎ 081.794.1435.

Post office The main post office is in the enormous building on Piazza Matteotti, just off Via Toledo (Mon–Sat 8.15am–7.20pm).

Taxis ☎ 081.202.020, ☎ 081.570.7070, ☎ 081.551.5151, ☎ 081.556.4444.

Tours CitySightseeing Napoli operate a hop-on-hop-off service taking in the sights on

Kids' Naples

Make no mistake – Naples is a great place to visit with **kids**. Its culture of extremes, the diversity of its attractions, not just in the city itself but in the surrounding area, and the sheer buzz of its streets, are more than enough to keep children of all ages entertained. The following is a list of favourite children's attractions:

Catacombs see p.75. The subterranean chambers of the dead hold an irresistible fascination.

Castel dell'Ovo see p.78. About as close to a classic castle experience as it's possible to get – with a great location and lots of passageways and levels to chase about on.

Aquarium see p.81. Fish and sea creatures never fail, and there's a petting pool for the really small.

Edenlandia Viale Kennedy 76 ☏081.239.4090, ⓦ www.edenlandia.it (see website for opening hours; €2.50). Naples' big out-of-town amusement park is a useful stand-by when all else fails.

Herculaneum and Pompeii see p.117 & p.125. Where could be better for a fun-yet-educational day out than these fascinating ancient Roman sites?

Vesuvius see p.122. The chance of scaling a real-life active volcano is not to be passed up.

Via San Gregorio Armeno see p.59. Children love the little figures and inventive crib scenes that they make and sell on this street.

Città della Scienza Via Coroglio 57/104 ☏081.242.0024, ⓦ www.cittadellascienza.it (Tues–Sat 9am–5pm, Sun 10am–7pm; €7). A real hands-on museum experience for slightly older children with enquiring minds.

Napoli Sotterranea and the Acquedotto Carmignano see p.59 & p.69. It's grown-up sightseeing, but it also involves squeezing through narrow underground passages with a candle – great for imaginative kids.

Parco Vergiliano see p.82. A little way out of town, but probably the city's best open space, with a playground and shady spots for picnics.

---

several routes around town between May and Sept; tickets cost €22 and are valid for 24hr. Tours leave from just in front of the Castel Nuovo.

Travel agents CTS, Via Mezzocannone 25 (☏081.552.7975), for discount tickets, budget flights and so on. You could also try Wasteels, Stazione Centrale (☏081.201.071).

The Campi Flegrei

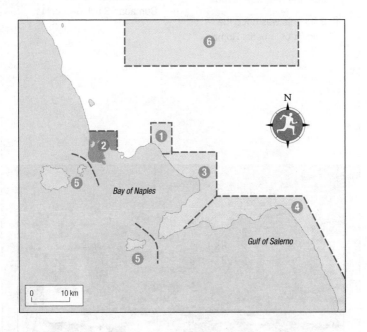

CHAPTER 2 # Highlights

✳ **The Solfatara** A seething, semi-active volcano that's perhaps top of Pozzuoli's must-see sights. **See p.105**

✳ **Pozzuoli restaurants** The town's portside establishments are a great place to sample seafood fresh from the bay. **See p.106**

✳ **Báia** This was once the chicest of imperial Roman resorts, now with heaps of monumental ruins and a fine archeological museum to show for it. **See p.107**

✳ **Cumae** The earliest Greek settlement on the Italian mainland was home to the enigmatic and profoundly influential oracle, the Cumaean Sibyl. **See p.111**

▲ The harbour at Pozzuoli

The Campi Flegrei

The area around Naples is one of the most geologically unstable in the world. Vesuvius is only the best known of the many and varied examples of seismic activity in the province, the most concentrated instances – volcanic craters, hot springs, fumaroles – being west of the city in the region known as the **Campi Flegrei** (Fiery Fields), from the Greek *phlegraean*, "burning". These are the Phlegraean Fields of classical times, a mysterious area by turns mythologized by Homer and Virgil as the entrance to Hades and the Forum of Vulcan, the god of fire, and eulogized as the Elysian Fields for the sheer gorgeousness of its landscape, which in those days was prime real estate for the movers and shakers of Roman society, as well as the site of several of the Greco-Roman world's most mystical holy places. These days the mystery of old requires some determination to imagine. As is the case all around the bay, the creeping presence of Naples dominates pretty much everywhere, in the form of unsightly, mostly illegal construction. Suburban blight masks much of the extraordinary natural beauty, and the legendary volcanic activity is now mostly extinct, or at least dormant for the time being. Having said that, parts of the area are still picturesque, while others retain some of the doomy, mythic associations that drew the ancients here in the first place, and there are substantial and fascinating remains of their presence.

Pozzuoli is the first place to head for, home to an array of different sights, and worth visiting especially at weekends, when the fish restaurants are in full swing and you can visit its Rione Terra excavations. Pozzuoli is also a departure point for the islands of Ischia and Prócida (see Chapter 5), and it's also easy to reach the ancient sites at **Báia** and **Cumae** from here – neither of which you will want to miss if you're spending any time at all in the area. Just outside Báia, the regional **archeological museum** is also worth a look – but if you need some respite from dusty relics, head for the beaches at **Bácoli**.

Festivals

In addition to the celebrations associated with the blood of San Gennaro (see p.56) – the main one here being on September 19 – Pozzuoli also goes in for a significant Ferragosto event (the Assumption, Aug 15). At the port, youths compete in the Gara del Palo, which involves balancing on a long, soapy wooden pole out over the water to try to snag a banner. Most end up taking a dive, of course. In Bácoli, a feast worth showing up for is the Sagra delle Cozze (Mussels Festival), on or around July 26, when boatloads of the black, shimmering shellfish are boisterously consumed.

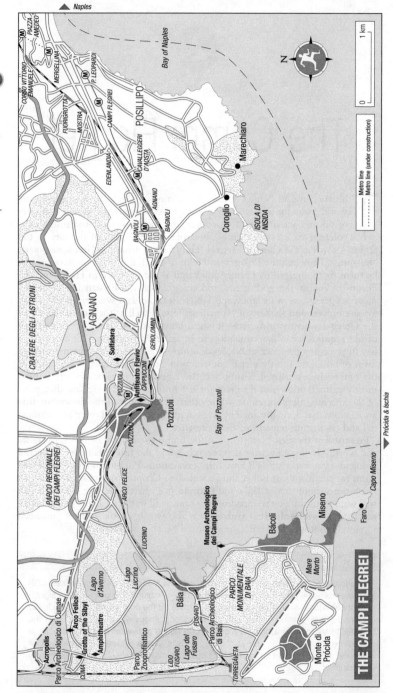

THE CAMPI FLEGREI

Pozzuoli

The first town that can really be considered free of Naples' direct sprawl is **POZZUOLI**, which sits 14km to the west on a stout promontory jutting out from the slender crescent of volcanic hills behind. For several centuries it was the main port of the Roman Empire, where all the grain from Egypt arrived, until Emperor Trajan expanded the port of Ostia, at the mouth of the Tiber. The name derives from the Latin original *Puteoli*, meaning "little wells", probably a reference to the many thermal springs that have been a feature of the area for all of recorded history. The town was also the source of the all-important pink *pozzolana* volcanic sand employed when the Romans invented the first concrete. The original cement that holds together Roman buildings, both here and throughout the ancient world, has withstood the elements for some 2000 years and counting (the most stunning example being the vast cast-concrete dome of Rome's Pantheon).

Despite achieving a measure of contemporary glamour as the home town of screen goddess Sophia Loren – for whose seventieth birthday celebrations in 2004 the city fathers managed a quick but fairly effective civic facelift – modern Pozzuoli is an ordinary little place, nothing special but friendly and likeable enough, and of use to most visitors merely for its **ferry connections** to the islands of Prócida and Ischia. However, although you wouldn't necessarily want to stay here for the place itself, there are a few sights of archeological importance, plus it makes a good base from which to take in the rest of the Campi Flegrei.

Arrival, information and accommodation

You can **get to** Pozzuoli from Naples on the Metropolitana, or on the Ferrovia Cumana line from Montesanto station; both take about twenty minutes. Buses #152 and SEPSA M1 also run direct from Piazza Garibaldi. The Metropolitana/ FS station is situated above the main part of Pozzuoli, off Via Solfatara, ten-minutes' walk from the port, and so is better if you're just going to see the Solfatara; the Cumana station is in the centre of town, not far from the Temple of Serapis, so makes more sense if you're visiting the town only.

There's a **tourist office** a little east of the port at Piazza Matteotti 1a (Mon–Sat 9am–3.30pm; ☏081.526.6639, ⓦwww.infocampiflegrei.it). **Accommodation** options include the *Hotel Solfatara*, Via Solfatara 163 (☏081.526.2666, ⓦwww .hotelsolfatara.it; doubles €60), conveniently situated on the corner of the street that leads to the volcano, right at the bus stop. It's a pleasant, modern place, with handsome, well-appointed guestrooms, good views of the bay, and a sunny, wood-beamed restaurant specializing in fresh fish daily. Alternatively, if you feel inclined

---

Pozzuoli on the move

Pozzuoli has suffered more than most of the towns around here from the area's **volcanic activity**, and subsidence is still a major – and carefully monitored – problem. Almost all of the ancient town is now under water – as with other significant parts of the Campi Flegrei – because of a phenomenon called bradyseism (from the Greek words for "slow" and "movement"), a rare, large-scale rippling effect of volcanic activity deep under the earth's crust, which results in perpetual "slow earthquakes", causing continual rising and lowering of the land. Parts of the place have been slowly rising for the last five hundred years or so, while others are gradually sinking – in some spots up to 2cm a year.

POZZUOLI

Bus Station (500m) (800m)

Solfatara, Santuario di San Gennaro & Vulcano Solfatara Campsite (1km)

POZZUOLI M

RESTAURANTS
Il Capitano 1
Don Antonio 2

Temple of Serapis

Anfiteatro Flavio

FS Rail Line

Pozzuoli

Porto

Villa Comunale

Villa Avelino

PISCINA LUSCIANO

RIONE ORTODONICO

Cumana Rail Line

Rione Terra Entrance

RIONE TERRA

CORSO UMBERTO I

(600m)

N

Metro line   0   100 m

ACCOMMODATION
Solfatara A
Terme Puteolana B

to take the cure, try the *Hotel Terme Puteolana* at Corso Umberto I 195, a little way east of the port next to the Gerolomini Metro/Cumana stop, right on the sea (☎081.526.1303; doubles €75), Pozzuoli's classic spa establishment. Rooms are spacious, and therapeutic services offered include thermal baths and mud wallows. For **camping**, consider the excellent and beautifully landscaped *Vulcano Solfatara* site at the entrance to the Solfatara itself (☎081.526.7413; ⓦwww.solfatara.it; April–Oct). As well as tent pitches, there are double bungalows (€50), a large swimming pool, a grocery store and a snack bar/restaurant with terrace seating and a good-value set menu.

The Town

Pozzuoli has a number of well-preserved relics of the Romans' liking for the place. Just beyond the Cumana station, between Via Roma and Via Sacchini, east of the port, the so-called **Temple of Serapis** sits enclosed within a small park, often flooded in winter, and thus often closed, but easy enough to see in its entirety from outside. Its name derives from the unearthing here of a statue of the Pluto-esque Egyptian god, *Serapis Enthroned* (now in Naples' Museo Archeologico Nazionale), but in fact the structure has since proved to be not a temple but a richly embellished produce market from the first to the third centuries AD, one of the largest known that has been excavated. It's pretty decrepit, but you can still make out the shape of the buildings: most of the shops were arranged around the perimeter portico and courtyard, while the temple-like circular central structure, the *tholos*, was where fish was sold. At the northern end, occupying a large apse, was a *sacellum* (shrine) dedicated to the worship of the imperial family and of the market's divine protectors – among them Serapis, since many Alexandrians resided here – so, at least in part, the place did serve as a temple. Notice that the shrine's three (of four original) freestanding columns of *cipollino* marble are eaten away halfway up by stone-boring molluscs, from when the structure lay mostly under water for hundreds of years, providing yet another example of how the elevation of this unquiet land ceaselessly shifts.

On the other side of the port, the **Rione Terra** (Sat & Sun 9am–6pm; ☎081.741.0067 or toll-free ☎848.800.288; €3) booking required provides the chance for a slightly more accessible look at Pozzuoli's Roman past – an extensive if sometimes erratically open excavation, accessible by way of an entrance just above the tourist office off Via Marconi. The name originated in the Middle Ages, when what was the ancient acropolis of the Greek town and the heart of the Roman port, some two square kilometres in all, served as the citadel (*terra* in the local dialect). You have to go on a tour, which takes you through a set of ancient Roman streets, lined with structures that are considered to have been apartments (*insulae*), taverns (*tabernae*), millers-bakers (*pistrina*), warehouses (*horrea*), brothels (*ganea*) and other establishments, as well as tunnels and the remains of the majestic Corinthian-columned *Capitolium*, itself founded on an earlier Greek temple. There are also several extant frescoes and mosaics, and some textbook examples of *opus reticulatum* walls, the distinctive diamond pattern achieved by pushing pyramid-shaped blocks of tufa into wet concrete – a type of construction used only from the first century BC until the second century AD, after which regular horizontal brick construction became the norm.

Probably the best of Pozzuoli's Roman sights, however, is the **Anfiteatro Flavio**, on Via Antifeatro just north of the centre (Mon & Wed–Sun 9am–1hr before sunset; €4 combined ticket with Cumae and the Parco Archeologico in Báia), which was at one time the third largest in Italy, after the Colosseum and the amphitheatre at Cápua (see p.227), holding some 20,000 spectators. It was begun under Nero and completed by Vespasian, and it's still reasonably intact, though visitors are not allowed in the seating area. The subterranean chambers for gladiators and wild beasts are in especially good shape, and lying around is an abundance of beautifully carved architectural fragments – perhaps the most intriguing aspect of the place – retrieved from various shrines and other structures that were associated with the vast entertainment venue.

The Solfatara and Santuario di San Gennaro

Just north of the Anfiteatro Flavio, ten-minutes' walk up the hill from the Metropolitana/FS station (bus #152 and the SEPSA M1 stop outside), you can smell the **Solfatara** (daily: April–Sept 8.30am–7pm; Oct–March 8.30am–5.30pm; €5.50) well before you see it: the exposed crater of a semi-extinct volcano, into which you can walk – further tangible evidence of the seismic plight of the area. The volcano hasn't erupted for a couple of thousand years at least – in fact, it was a major tourist attraction in Roman times, too; what you walk out onto is actually the plug or cap of cooled-off magma that for the moment blocks the cone. Not surprisingly, it's a weird, lunar sort of landscape: fetid vapours rise from the strangely discoloured rocks and the grey-yellow ground is hot to the touch (and sounds hollow underfoot), emitting eerily silent jets or fumaroles that leave the air pungent with the odour of sulphur. No wonder the ancients thought the entrance to Hades was located nearby. Look for guides lighting paper torches near the fumes, which seems to cause the air itself to ignite into billows of thick smoke all around – a favourite trick, caused by the condensation of sulphur in the vicinity. In the nineteenth century some of these fumaroles were covered with brick, creating a nearly unbearable heat (90°C) in a sauna-like box in which you can crouch if you can bear it, while elsewhere bubbling, grey, gloopy mud is fenced off – though it might make an excellent mineral bath in theory. Locals, in fact, still swear by the salutary effects of the rotten-egg ambience the place emits, inevitably recommending that anyone with a respiratory ailment come here and breathe deeply of the brimstone stench for an hour or so.

A three-minute walk further up the hill on the right is the sixteenth-century **Santuario di San Gennaro** (daily 9am–1pm & 4.30–7pm; free), built on the supposed site of the final martyrdom of Naples' patron saint, under the merciless Diocletian; some accounts say Gennaro first faced wild beasts in the amphitheatre, which he somehow survived, only to be executed anyway. There's an engraved stone niche here, kept behind glass in a chapel off to the right, stained with splashes of the saint's blood (he was beheaded) that reputedly glows at the same time that his blood liquefies in Naples, which it does three times a year (see box, p.56).

Eating and drinking

One of the best times to visit Pozzuoli is on a Sunday, when the whole town turns out for the morning fish market, afterwards eating lunch in one of several waterfront **restaurants**: *Il Capitano*, at Lungomare C. Colombo 10 (☏081.526.2283), is decent, and does a good *zuppa di pesce* for around €20, or, if you can do without the outside tables and views, there's the unpretentious ☘ *Don Antonio* (☏081.526.7941; closed Mon), which specializes in excellent fresh fish and seafood and does great *fritti misti* and seafood pasta dishes at very reasonable prices; it's up narrow Via Magazzini off the old port – follow the quayside round the ferry dock and it's on the left, just past the *Toscano gelateria*.

Local lore

The distance across the gulf from Bácoli to Pozzuoli was the subject of two stories in classical times, one legendary, the other factual. The first concerns the proverbial **"boy on a dolphin"**, a favourite subject of Greco-Roman poets and artists. According to Pliny and other ancient sources, the tale was true: Simon, a boy from Báia, befriended one of the gregarious sea mammals and received regular lifts from it across to school at Pozzuoli and back. After several years, the boy died of an illness, and the grieving dolphin beached itself and soon followed suit.

The other account, a historically recorded event, took place in 39 AD, when the emperor **Caligula** decided to fulfil a prophecy uttered, according to conflicting reports, either by Thrasyllus, a celebrated mathematician, or by Trasullus, an astrologer from Rhodes. The pronouncement went to the effect that Caligula "would no more be emperor of Rome than he would be able to drive his chariot across the Bay of Baiae". So, slyly rising to the challenge, he simply lined up the entire Roman fleet, over four hundred boats, and laid planks on them all the way across the water. Roman gossipmonger Suetonius gives a lurid portrayal of the ceremony that accompanied the madman's feat, complete with drunken revelries, orgies and blasé cruelties.

This part of the Campi Flegrei is also the torrid setting for yet another ancient saga, the wonderfully salacious **Satyricon** by Petronius — a depiction of the excesses of ancient life that accords perfectly with the scathing assessments of Cicero, Seneca and other outraged critics of Rome's decadent ways.

Báia

The next town, 7km along from Pozzuoli, is **BÁIA**, an uninspiring port town with a set of imperial-era Roman ruins piled up on the hill above. The name is said to derive from that of one of Ulysses' companions, who died here. Ancient Baiae was one of the bay's most favoured spots in Roman times, a trendy resort where all the most fashionable and powerful of Rome's patricians had villas: the Emperor Hadrian died here in 138 AD, and Nero was rumoured to have had his mother Agrippina murdered nearby. You can get here by SEPSA **bus** from Pozzuoli, or by taking the Cumana rail line to Lucrino and a shuttle bus from there.

The Parco Archeologico

The port area of Báia is nice enough in a workaday way, but the real draw are the extensive remains of an important Roman palace of the first century BC to the fourth century AD with its enormous baths (not temples as was once thought), leaving you in no doubt of the town's demographics in ancient times – preening imperial fatcats and phalanxes of hapless slaves. Steps lead up from the main street to the entrance to the **Parco Archeologico** (closed at time of writing but usually open Tues–Sun 9am–1hr before sunset; €4 combined ticket with Anfiteatro Flavio and Cumae), where you can explore the excavations, which are structured across some seven terraced levels and enjoy an evocative setting. Follow the steps down from the entrance level to the first terrace of the palace: the so-called Rooms of Venus in the southern sector contain patches of Roman stuccowork, depicting birds and mythical creatures, and a statue of Mercury, beheaded by vandals. In the centre, where the *Aphrodite Sonsandra* sculpture was found (now in Naples' Museo Archeologico Nazionale), are the remains of a theatre that was later converted into a fountain, as well as an open space – thought to be a *piscina* (pool) – with a pretty garden portico on one side. Perhaps the most impressive structure is to the east, the misnamed Temple of Mercury, actually part of the palace's gigantic baths complex, the circular domed form (late first century BC) echoed by later monuments, including the Pantheon in Rome. To the north, the so-called Temple of Diana, also part of a baths complex, has marble reliefs and a large octagonal chamber.

The Museo Archeologico

Most of the finds from Báia and around have found their way into the **Museo Archeologico dei Campi Flegrei** (Tues–Sun 9am–3.45pm; same ticket as Parco Archeologico), housed in part of the town's mammoth fifteenth-century Aragonese castle – an unexciting fifteen-minute walk up the hill towards Bácoli (or you could take the Torregáveta bus from Lucrino, getting off at the castle and then walking back for the ruins). Among the finds on display here is a *sacellum* – a shrine dedicated to the imperial cult – from the forum of ancient Misenum on Capo Miseno, rebuilt here on the ground floor, with columns, a sculpted pediment and twin idols of emperors Vespasian and Titus as nude athletes, slightly odd with their middle-aged heads on the bodies of young, muscular men, as well as a unique equestrian bronze, in which the horse is rearing. The most complete part is the bronze emperor, who is depicted as Domitian, although his face was subsequently replaced with that of Nerva. There's also a *nymphaeum* or monumental fountain, partially reconstructed on the upper floor, found underwater off a nearby cape and including sculptures of Ulysses and stalwart Baio (from the story of the Cyclops), two winsome figures of Dionysus and others of various imperial figures – a model shows you how it would have looked.

In another part of the museum, one of the most unusual exhibits is that of ancient plaster casts (*gessi*) – literally hundreds of fragments: a face here, a foot or hand there. These were actual casts of the original classical Greek bronzes of such works as the *Apollo Belvedere*, the *Tyrannicides* and the *Amazons of Ephesus*, and were used as models by marble sculptors in ancient Baiae, to supply all the grand villas with sufficient decoration. Also noteworthy are an elegant standing *Persephone* and the exquisite Parian marble head of *Athena Lemnia*, which was found in the Rione Terra of Pozzuoli and is one of only two copies known of the celebrated fifth-century BC work by Phidias. Finally, the castle terrace gives wonderful views back over the bay to Báia, Pozzuoli and beyond.

▲ View over Baia from the Museo Archeologico

Watery archeology

Glass-bottomed boat tours are a good way of exploring the ruined substructures of the now totally submerged villas and the Portus Julius facilities along Báia's coastline – the work again of relentless bradyseism (see box, p.103). How much you can actually make out depends a great deal on the state of the water on the day you make the trip, but you will at least be able to discern walls and floor-plans, plus a few columns, and with a little luck some mosaic pavements. Tours are organized by BaiaSommersa (℡349.497.4183, ⓦwww.baiasommersa.it) and leave daily except Mondays at 10am, noon and 3pm; they cost €10 per person, and you must book a place in advance. For diving enthusiasts, it's worth knowing that BaiaSommersa also runs guided dives of the same sites.

Practicalities

If you're wondering what the hedonistic high-life in Báia might have been like, a tempting taste is on offer at some of its **hotels and restaurants**. *Il Gabbiano* (℡081.868.7969, ⓦwww.ilgabbianohotel.com; €90–170) at Via Giulia Temporini 99, towards Lago Lucrino, is plush and panoramic, with a superb restaurant and deluxe guestrooms, offering views from its lofty perch over the Campi Flegrei and the entire bay. The restaurant features a garden terrace seating with more stunning views; the speciality is fresh fish. If you'd like to try a spa alternative, there's the *Villa Luisa* at the other end of Lago Lucrino, Via Tripergola 50 (℡081.804.2870, ⓦwww.villaluisaresort.it), which offers a full range of therapeutic services using thermal waters at the ancient baths known as the *Stufe di Nerone* (ⓦwww.termestufedinerone.it; doubles around €100). The rooms are very comfortable, with balcony views, and the hotel stands in close proximity to the lake. The **pizzeria** *Il Tucano* (℡081.854.5046; closed Mon), right in the port of Báia at Via Molo di Baia 40, does a huge variety of good-value juicy Neapolitan-style pizzas and sells them by the metre.

Bácoli, Misenum and Capo Miseno

Immediately below Báia's castle, **BÁCOLI** (ancient Bauli, a name associated with one of the Twelve Labours of Hercules, the muscle-bound demigod also credited with single-handedly creating nearby Lago Lucrino) isn't an especially attractive town, but it has several significant ruins from ancient times, the first of which is the **Sepulchre of Agrippina** (daily 9am–1hr before sunset; free; call ℡081.523.4368 if site is not open), off the Via Spiaggia di Bácoli, actually a small theatre (*odeon*) which was transformed into a *nymphaeum* (fountain) at some point. The name derives from the belief that it was here that Nero had his mother assassinated and interred in a large mausoleum.

A short walk further along, on Via Cento Camerelle, lie the so-called **Cento Camerelle**, or "one hundred small rooms" (daily 9am–1hr before sunset; ℡081.855.3284; free) – in reality two large, complex cisterns carved largely out of a tufa cliff, with passageways between them, built to service the many villas along here, most of which remain unexcavated.

A few streets away, the **Piscina Mirabilis** – "marvellous pool" (daily 9am–1hr before sunset; ℡081.523.3199, ring the bell for the custodian at Via Piscina Mirabilis 9 if not open) – is the next remnant of note, built out on a promontory that commands the ancient military port of Misenum: a massive and elegantly arched reservoir with forty-eight pilasters, providing for the needs of the fleet. The tank – some 70m long, 15m high and 26m wide – was fed by the Serino aqueduct, also built by Augustus.

The reservoir served the nearby imperial port of **Misenum** – the name is said to derive either from that of another companion of Ulysses or from Aeneas's trumpeter – which involved cutting a canal through to allow access to the inland basin. Nowadays silting has isolated the water here from the open sea, and it is now known as Lago Miseno or the Mare Morto (Dead Sea), but in the first century AD under Augustus this was a major naval base. Not much of this has been excavated either, but there are a few ruins – of a small amphitheatre and shrine – mixed in with the housing that surrounds the lake.

Finally, don't miss the view from the top of **Capo Miseno** itself, the lofty outcrop at the very tip of the Phlegraean Peninsula. Its commanding position, controlling both the Gulf of Pozzuoli and the Prócida Channel, made it a perfect strategic location. Today, there's an important lighthouse at its summit, and from here you can take in the nearby islands of Prócida and Ischia and the expanse of the entire Bay of Naples.

Practicalities

In Bácoli, the rustic, family-run **restaurant**, *Osteria–Pizzeria "da Caliendo"* (℡081.523.4721, ⊛www.sibilla.net/caliendo; closed Tues) at Via Miseno 17, right by the shore of the Mare Morto, specializes, besides pizza, in fresh seafood *antipasti* and pasta dishes. If you decide to **stay**, the *Hotel Club Cala Moresca* down on Capo Miseno itself, at Via del Faro 44 (℡081.523.5595, ⊛www .calamoresca.it; doubles from €150), is a nice option, with lovely views of Prócida and Ischia from its hilltop garden setting, a good restaurant, a pool and private access to the sea. Friendly, family-run *Villa Iorio*, Via Vincenzo Scotto 73, Monte di Prócida (℡081.868.1249, ⊛www.guesthousenapoli.com; two-night minimum; closed Nov), offers stupendous views all the way to Cápri and pleasant **self-catering** mini-apartments, some with terraces, for upwards of €80; it's a kilometre – or a five-minute bus ride – from the sea.

Lago del Fusaro, Torregáveta and around

A ten-minute walk inland from Báia (take the road from the entrance to the ruins), the Ferrovia Cumana skirts around the bottom of **Lago del Fusaro** – actually a lagoon rather than a real lake. Though densely populated in former times, the entire area became a royal hunting preserve in the eighteenth century, which explains the little Rococo jewel-box of a building set out in the lake on a tiny islet, a couple of minutes from the Cumana station. The **Casino Reale** (under restoration at time of writing but usually open Sun 10am–1pm; €1) was built as a royal hunting and fishing lodge, and is now an elegant octagonal folly, the work of Carlo Vanvitelli, the son of the king's favourite architect, who was also responsible for the English Garden at the palace in Caserta (see p.223). Over the years, guests here have included Sir William Hamilton, Mozart, Rossini, a tsar or two and many other crowned heads of state, whose portraits are displayed in the gallery of famous visitors. Only a few traces of the once-lavish interior adornment remain, however – a few modest frescoes, some chandeliers and furniture – the vagaries of political

Beaches

The best of the area's **beaches** are at Bácoli, to one side of Capo Miseno, just outside of the gulf and southwest of the so-called Mare Morto, on the **Miliscola Lido**. There are some nice *scoglie* (rocky coves and reefs) to explore, and beach services are provided by a number of establishments lined up along the seashore. Be warned, however: the limited sandy area gets packed during high season, not only with sun-worshippers but also with rows and rows of lounge chairs and big, stripy umbrellas – for which you'll pay the usual charges.

upheaval having seen off the rest. Most unfortunately, a massive fresco cycle that Goethe deemed the best work of art in Naples was destroyed during the Neapolitan Revolt of 1799, and the once-renowned azure floor of the main salon suffered a similar fate towards the end of World War II.

Following the king's predilection, Lago del Fusaro remains a popular spot for fishing, as the locals lined up along the concrete pier of the dull little village of **TORREGÁVETA** beyond testify. Torregáveta is the meeting point of the Cumana and Circumflegrea lines, and also where you go to take a bus to Cumae.

Cumae

About 6km up the coast from Torregáveta, the eighth-century BC town of **CUMAE**, lying in ruins since the ninth century AD, was the first Greek colony on the Italian mainland, a source of settlers for other colonies (Naples

▲ The Grotto of the Sibyl

– Neapolis – was originally settled by Greeks from Cumae) and a vital centre of Hellenistic civilization. It was home to an important soothsaying priestess of Apollo, the so-called **Cumaean Sibyl**, from whom Tarquinius purchased the Sibylline Books (see box below), which became the guiding inspiration for the Republic.

The site

The **site** (daily 9am–1hr before sunset; €4 combined ticket with Anfiteatro Flavio and Báia), a short walk from the bus or Circumflegrea stop, is spread over a large area and not at all comprehensively excavated. Still, the only part you're likely to want to see forms a tight nucleus close to the entrance. The best-known feature is the **Grotto of the Sibyl**, discovered only in 1932, and considered by some to be the long-sought temple seat of one of the most famous of all ancient oracles (though wet-blankets say the structure served some military purpose). The entrance is a 131-metre-long, downright spooky gallery (*dromos*) excavated out of a solid mass of volcanic tufa – trapezoidal and vaguely anthropomorphic in shape, reminiscent of many Creto–Mycenaean tomb corridors – penetrating deep under the side of the acropolis, which stands high above. Strips of light enter from a series of tall slits in the western, seaward wall, creating a striking visual rhythm of dark and light that can be hypnotic as you walk along. At the end of the passageway, from the dim obscurity of an alcove with stone benches, the Sibyl would dispense her cryptic prognostications, allegedly in perfectly metrical verse.

Ancient Roman prophecies

The tale of the acquisition of the **Sibylline Books** by Lucius Tarquinius Superbus, or Tarquinius Priscus, the semi-legendary last king of Rome, is one of the most enduring of Roman myths. Around the time of the founding of the city of Rome, an old woman arrived in the city and offered nine books of prophecies to King Tarquinius. Because she was demanding an extortionate sum, the King refused to pay up. The woman then burned three and offered the remaining six to Tarquinius at the same price, which he again declined. She then burned three more and repeated her offer. Tarquinius finally relented and bought the last three at the original steep price, and the woman – afterwards held to be none other than the Cumaean Sibyl – promptly vanished. The books, which were believed to contain unparalleled wisdom within their pages, were kept thereafter in the Temple of Jupiter on Rome's Capitoline Hill, to be consulted in times of crisis.

The **Cumaean Sibyl** features most famously in Virgil's *Aeneid*, book VI, when Aeneas, princely demigod, offspring of Venus and heroic refugee from defeated Troy, came to Cumae to consult the Sibyl – an event elaborated in lines from Virgil, now posted on either side of the entrance to the grotto. The seeress is said to have conducted him on a bracing tour of the Underworld, the opening to which was considered to be nearby, where the spirit of his father transmitted to him visions of founding the "New Troy" further to the north, and of naming it Rome. It is certain that Virgil, Augustan Rome's official epic poet and propagandist, largely fabricated his *Aeneid*, conflating an incongruous range of earlier sagas into a new tale calculated to provide the proud Latins with a high-flown pedigree (most pointedly for the Julian line, who were treated as direct descendants of Aeneas and therefore of Venus) and with an exalted foundation myth. Thus their city's imperial inclination towards world conquest would be divinely mandated and magically linked to the supreme glories of Homeric Greece.

Cucina napoletana

The most famous elements of the Italian diet – pasta, pizza and pastries – are the staples of Neapolitan cuisine. But it's not all home-grown: restaurant menus here read like a veritable history of foreign occupation. The Greeks brought olive trees and grapevines; the Romans imported grains used to make bread; and Arab traders promoted citrus and aubergine cultivation and introduced durum wheat, used as the basis for countless varieties of pasta. And the locals have the Spanish to thank for another staple of cucina napoletana: the humble tomato, a key ingredient in the venerable pizza marinara.

Scamorza cheese for sale ▲

Neapolitan scarola ▼

Traditional spaghetti alle vongole ▼

Vegetables and cheese

This traditionally poor cuisine based on fresh produce featured little meat until the mid-twentieth century. Typical *contorni* (vegetable dishes) include bitter, leafy greens like *scarola* and *friarielli*, served sautéed in oil and garlic; *zucchine alla scapece* (sweet-and-sour courgettes); and *caponata* (a cooked vegetable salad made with aubergine, tomato and capers). Local cheeses such as cow's-milk *scamorza* and the softer mozzarella *di bufala*, made with buffalo milk, are widely available (the regions to the north and east of Naples are important mozzarella-producing areas).

Pasta and main courses

Pasta is often served with just a simple sauce of fresh tomatoes and basil, and laced with garlic; in Neapolitan sauces, garlic, onion and parmesan are rarely combined. Aubergines and courgettes turn up endlessly in sauces, as does the tomato-and-mozzarella pairing – particularly good as gnocchi *alla sorrentina*. You should also try the classic *pasta alla genovese* (with slow-cooked meat and onions). Of the seafood pastas, clams combine with garlic and oil for superb spaghetti *alle vongole*; mussels are often prepared as *zuppa di cozze* (with hot pepper sauce and croutons); and fresh squid and octopus are ubiquitous. The baked dishes *sartù di riso* (rice timbale) and *gattò di patate* (mashed-potato cake with diced ham and cheese) are common *trattoria* lunch options. Meat specialities include *braciole* (meat rolls stuffed with breadcrumbs, pine nuts and raisins) and *polpette* (meatballs) cooked in a rich tomato sauce; among the fish mains are *polipetti affogati* (literally, "drowned octopus"), sautéed in white wine, and *fritto misto* – small fish from the bay served deep-fried, bones and all.

Pizza

Naples' most affordable food is also its most sacred; a local saying goes "you can insult my mother but never my pizza-maker". Crusty pizza baked rapidly in a searingly hot wood-fired oven and doused in olive oil is a speciality of the city-centre pizzerias – though great pizza is readily available all over the region. The archetypal Neapolitan pizza is the *marinara* – not, as you might think, anything to do with seafood, but topped with just tomato, garlic and basil, no cheese. The simplest toppings tend to be the best – *margherita* (with tomatoes and cheese), or perhaps *salsiccia e friarelli* (with sausage and local bitter greens).

Best for …

▶▶ **Foodie souvenirs** Try Naples' Arfè for gourmet preserves and cheeses and Enoteca Belledonne for Campanian wines (see p.96). Buy locally produced *limoncello* in Sorrento.

▶▶ **Ice cream** The *gelato* at Naples' *Remy Gelo* is second to none (see p.86).

▶▶ **Picnics** Naples' lively Piazza Pignasecca (see p.96) is an enjoyable place to try food shopping, Neapolitan style.

▶▶ **Pizza** It's not hard to come by excellent pizza in Naples – but old-timer *Di Matteo* (see p.87) is consistently great.

▶▶ **Seafood** Pozzuoli's Sunday morning fish market (see p.106) is a good time for a visit – head to one of the local restaurants for a seafood feast.

▶▶ **Sweets** *Andrea Pansa* in Amalfi (see p.159) sells delectable candied sweets and pastries.

▶▶ **Traditional delicacies** Rural Campania holds no end of food festivals, dedicated to everything from porcini mushrooms to prickly pears (see p.224).

▲ Fresh produce for sale in Spaccanapoli, Naples

▼ Ready for the pizza oven

Neapolitan arancini ▲

A typical pasticceria ▼

Sfogliatelle fresh from the oven ▼

Street food

A plethora of food stalls or **friggitorie** sell delectable fried snacks; the Neapolitan classics below are perfect for lunch on the run.

▶▶ *arancini* large, breaded rice balls filled with meat or mozzarella
▶▶ *crocchè* potato croquettes
▶▶ *fiorilli* courgette flowers in batter
▶▶ *pizzette* bite-sized pizzas
▶▶ *panzarotti* ravioli parcels
▶▶ *panini napoletani* pizza dough stuffed with ham, cheese and mortadella, folded into quarters and wrapped in paper to take away
▶▶ *scagliuozze* fried polenta
▶▶ *sciurilli* fried courgette flowers

Pastries and desserts

Neapolitans take their desserts very seriously, and the pastries and *gelato* served here are often *artigianale* or *di produzione propria* (homemade). Queues are commonplace at the top *pasticcerie*, particularly on Sundays, when locals take home fancy parcels of cakes to round off their slap-up lunch. Perhaps the best known of the region's celebrated pastries are sfogliatelle, ricotta-filled sweets made in two forms – "*riccia*" (shell-shaped with a crunchy, flaky crust) and "*frolla*" (flat and round with a shortbread crust). Another civic symbol is *babà*, a brioche soaked in a sugary rum syrup, sometimes split open and stuffed with cream. *Torta caprese*, a chocolate and hazelnut cake dusted with powdered sugar, makes a delicious accompaniment to Naples' world-class coffee. If you happen to be in the area during March, look out for *zeppole di San Giuseppe*, deep-fried doughnuts stuffed with custard, made in the weeks preceding and following the saint's day on March 19.

But some of the best of Cumae is still to come. Climb up the steps to the right of the cave entrance and follow the winding **Via Sacra** past a constructed belvedere on the left and the fairly scanty ruins of a temple on the right of an archaic fifth-century Greek **temple of Apollo** overlain by Roman modifications and then by a sixth-century Christian basilica. At the highest point you'll find the remains, mostly just the base and one arch, of a **temple of Zeus**, which has experienced similar accretions over nearly a thousand years. Colossal marble cult statues and other artefacts found here, such as Egyptian statuary from a temple of Isis and eighth-century BC Greek tomb furnishings, are now preserved in Naples' Museo Archeologico Nazionale. Still, apart from the antique vestiges, the **views** here are one of the best reasons to come: from the far side of the Acropolis, look away south across the Lago del Fusaro to the bottom corner of the peninsula's coast; and clamber down to the other side of the temple to take in the curving shore north up to the Gulf of Gaeta.

Arco Felice and the Lago d'Averno

There are more ancient traces inland, most notably the **Arco Felice**, a grandiose triumphal gate about 2km east of Cumae. Standing some 20m high, it marks a point where the Romans cut through a mountain in order to connect Via Domitiana from Cumae to Puteoli. Just 1km from the arch, on the eastern shore of **Lago d'Averno**, there's also the ruined shell of a second-century hall that was originally as big as Rome's Pantheon, and like it, domed. The structure is commonly called the **Temple of Apollo**, though it was actually most likely part of an important baths complex. The lake itself is the Lake Avernus of antiquity, a volcanic crater that the Greeks believed – and Homer and, later, Virgil wrote – was the **entrance to Hades**: sacrifices were regularly made here to the chthonic deities that lurked beneath the murky surface, and birds flying over were said to suffocate instantly from the noxious miasma given off by the lake's infernal waters. Indeed the name may derive from a Greek word meaning "without birds". Despite such beliefs and the deeply rooted sanctity of the spot, it was here that Agrippa constructed a military harbour, the Portus Iulius, in 37 BC, joining it to Lago Lucrino by a canal, and, in turn, joining that lake by a canal to the open sea. The military installations on Avernus were also linked by tunnels to the port of Cumae, thus completing the strategic scheme. However, when Augustus later had Agrippa build the military port at Capo Misenum, sacred Avernus reverted to its tranquil, if gloomy, inviolability.

Today the lake is still quiet, in fact thoroughly tamed, with a paved promenade part-way around it; and the surrounding hills are no longer as thickly forested as in ancient times (they were logged long ago by Agrippa). It's a good place to stroll idly and contemplate the crumbling glories of bygone epochs, although there's not really any other reason to come here – the water of the nearby sea is much more enticing for a swim, and there are more pristine local sites for a hike (see box, p.114).

Practicalities

If you want to stay in the Cumae area, there's an all-purpose and very attractive tourist complex close by, the *Averno Damiani*, Via Montenuovo Licola Patria 85 (℡081.804.2666, ⓦwww.averno.it), offering a **hotel** with double rooms for €95, independent bungalows for €105 for two people and a **campsite**; amenities include a large restaurant, a club, a thermal spa and tennis courts.

Nature reserves

There are two **nature reserves** in the Campi Flegrei: the craters of **Monte Nuovo** and **Astroni**, both of them extinct volcanoes that have been taken over by rampant vegetation. The former is Europe's newest mountain and one of its smallest volcanoes, which sprang up on 29–30 September 1538, when violent seismic activity buried the village of Tripergole and sent all the Puteolani fleeing to Naples. It's now a verdant cone in the midst of white houses and has been declared an **Oasi Natural-istica** (Mon–Fri 9am–1hr before sunset, Sat & Sun 9am–1pm; ☎081.804.1462; free). Located at the Pozzuoli end of Lago Lucrino, it's 140m high, with a switchback path up to the rim and then more pathways down into the steep-sided crater. Most of the interior is also thickly forested and makes a fine spot for a picnic.

   Le Cratere degli Astroni is a World Wildlife Fund Nature Reserve, 3km northwest of Pozzuoli on Via Agnano agli Astroni (daily 9.30am–2pm, guided tours 10am, 11am, noon & 1pm; ☎081.588.3720; €5; take bus C14 from the Cumana stop of Pianura or from Bagnoli, bus P6 from Pozzuoli; or bus C2 from Naples arrives within 2km of the entrance). The volcano is much the older of the two, having arisen some 4000 years ago, and the Romans are known to have had a thermal spa here, though no traces have yet been discovered and the springs vanished after the nearby eruptions of 1538. Since the reserve was established in 1987, flora and fauna have made an impressive advance, and Astroni is an especially rich site for birdwatchers. The oval caldera is 2km by 1.6km wide, circumscribing small mountains of up to 255m in height, a large lake on the southern side, near the entrance, and two small ponds towards the centre. There's a good dirt road (the old royal hunt road), which affords an approximately two-hour circuit around the central Colle dell'Imperatrice, and there are several sixteenth-century towers too — lookouts for what was once the royal hunting preserve – although the paths around the rim of the crater itself are open only for scientific research.

Otherwise, there's the nearby *Santa Marta*, Via Licola Patria 28, Arco Felice (☎081.804.2404, ⓦ www.santamartahotel.com; doubles €78–88), a simple, modern, comfortable **hotel** featuring a good restaurant with terrace seating, just 100m from the sea.

South of Naples

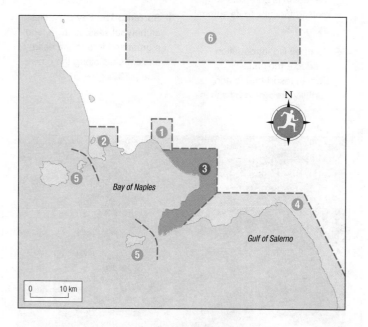

CHAPTER 3

Highlights

✳ **Herculaneum** The quieter and arguably easier to discern alternative to Pompeii. See p.117

✳ **Vesuvius** Mainland Europe's only active volcano, visible from just about everywhere in the Bay of Naples; no trip to the region is complete without making the hike to its summit. See p.122

✳ **Pompeii** No introduction needed – the ancient Roman resort buried and partially preserved by ash in Vesuvius's 79 AD eruption, and one of the greatest ancient sites you'll ever visit. See p.125

✳ **Monte Faito** The cable-car ride up from Castellammare is fantastic, and the views at the top well worth the trip. See p.131

✳ **Sorrento** The Bay of Naples' archetypal seaside town, and a great antidote to the nearby ancient sites along the coast. See p.132

▲ Pompeii

South of Naples

T he coast **south of Naples** is perhaps the least attractive stretch of the Bay, the Circumvesuviana train edging out through derelict industrial buildings and dense housing that squeezes ever closer to the track. You're on the train for around twenty minutes before you begin to feel anything like free of the city, and even then the settlement is almost entirely unbroken, the train tracks and main *autostrada* south picking their way through a dense grid of apartment blocks and market gardens which stretch all the way down to the sea. Behind, Vesuvius glowers over it all, suburban sprawl peppering its slopes like a rash. Most people come here for the ancient sights of **Herculaneum** and **Pompeii**, or to scale **Vesuvius**, all easy day-trips from Naples – or they skip the lot for the resort town of **Sorrento**. The latter is definitely worth spending some time in: it's a really enjoyable town, the first place that feels truly separate from the suburbs of Naples, and it can also make a good base for seeing some of the best of the Amalfi Coast, as well as a clutch of appealing towns and villages nearby.

Herculaneum

The first real point of any interest on the coast south of Naples is the town of **Ercolano**, the modern offshoot of the ancient site of **HERCULANEUM**, which was destroyed by the eruption of Vesuvius on August 24, 79 AD. There's not much to the new town, but the site is smaller and somewhat quieter than Pompeii and a little closer to Naples and Vesuvius, making it not only an attractive alternative, but also a little simpler if you want to scale Vesuvius and see one of the ancient sites on the same day.

The site

Situated at the seaward end of Ercolano's main street, a ten-minute walk from the Circumvesuviana station, the site of **Herculaneum** (daily: March–Sept 8.30am–7.30pm; Oct–Feb 8.30am–6pm; €11 or combined ticket with Pompeii and the Villa Oplontis, valid three days, €20) was discovered in 1709, when a well-digger accidentally struck the stage of the buried theatre. Excavations were undertaken throughout the eighteenth and nineteenth centuries, during which period much of the marble and bronze from the site was carted off to Naples to decorate the city's palaces, and it wasn't until 1927 that digging and preservation began in earnest. Herculaneum was a residential town, much smaller than Pompeii, and as such it makes a more manageable site, less architecturally

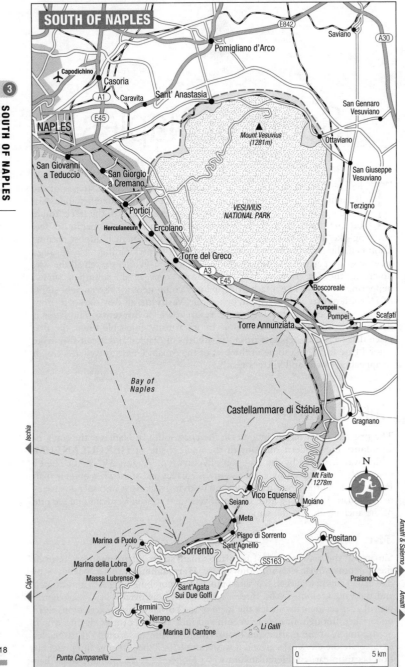

impressive, but better preserved and more easily taken in on a single visit. Archeologists held for a long time that unlike in Pompeii, on the other side of the volcano, most of the inhabitants of Herculaneum managed to escape. However, recent discoveries of entangled skeletons found at what was the shoreline of the town suggest otherwise, and it's now believed that most of the population was buried by huge avalanches of volcanic mud, which later hardened into the tufa-type rock that preserved much of the town. In early 2000 the remains of another 48 people were found; they were carrying coins, which suggests they were attempting to flee the disaster.

Cardo III
Because Herculaneum wasn't a commercial town, there was no central open space or forum, just streets of villas and shops in a grid based on three very straight main thoroughfares. Start your tour just inside the entrance at the bottom end of Cardo III, where you'll see one of the largest properties of the ancient town, the **Hotel**, though it's also one of the most incomplete and you can only really get a true impression of its size from the rectangle of stumpy columns that made up its atrium. Across the street, the **House of the Argus** is more complete, a very grand building judging by its once-impressive courtyard. Further up on the right, there's the **House of the Skeleton**, with its mosaic-covered *nymphaeum*, and a **thermopolium** or café on the corner, with a well-preserved counter still with its sunken jars. The most interesting house on Cardo III is a little way up on the right, however – the **Hall of the Augustals** – basically a temple dedicated to the worship of the cult of the Emperor Augustus. It's one of the site's most impressive large rooms, with four giant columns holding up the blackened remains of the wooden frame of the house and everything focusing on the wall paintings that face each other in the apse-like space on the right. The frescoes are from the first century AD, and show on one side Hercules with Juno and Minerva, and on the other Hercules with an Etruscan god.

Cardo IV
Backtrack to where Cardo III joins the Decumanus Inferior and you'll see the large **Thermae** or bath complex stretching across to Cardo IV. There are two entrances to the baths: one just off the atrium on Cardo V and the other on Cardo IV. The first entrance takes you into the domed frigidarium of the men's section, decorated with a floor mosaic of dolphins, and with a caldarium containing a plunge bath and a scallop-shell apse. Still intact are the benches where bathers sat and the wooden, partitioned shelves for clothing. On Cardo IV is the entrance to the women's section, which has a well-preserved black-and-white mosaic of Triton and sea creatures, and original glass shards in its window. Across Cardo IV there's the **Samnite House**, which has an attractive atrium, with a graceful loggia all the way round and a hole in the roof decorated with animal spouts. Three doors down, the **House of Neptune and Amphitrite** holds sparklingly preserved and richly ornamental wall mosaics featuring the gods on one wall, hunting dogs and deer on a vibrant blue background on another. Adjacent is the **House of the Beautiful Courtyard**, so called for its central atrium, which unusually has steps up one side with a balcony at the top. It also has a perfectly preserved mosaic floor, beyond which another room displays skeletons of bodies under glass still lying in the positions in which they fell.

From here you can stroll back down to the seaward end of Cardo IV, where the **House of the Wooden Partition** still has its original partition doors (now

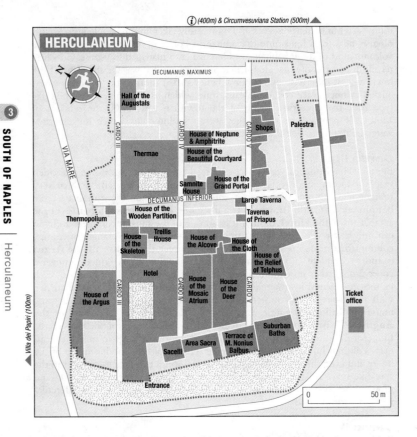

under glass) – evidence that it was the home of a poorer class of person than many of the buildings here. The next-door **Trellis House** was a plebeian boarding house, originally divided into separate apartments, and with an upper-storey balcony overhanging the streetfront that was built using so-called *opus craticium*, a building method that used poor-quality material held together by wooden frames – making it ironic that this very well-preserved example should still be standing. At the bottom end of Cardo IV stands the **House of the Alcove**, where you can follow a perfectly preserved mosaic-paved passage right round to the back of the house, while beyond, the **House of the Mosaic Atrium** was a grand villa in its day and retains its mosaic-laid courtyard, corrugated by the force of the tufa; sadly it's often closed.

Cardo V

Turning right at the top of Cardo IV takes you around to Cardo V and most of the rest of the town's **shops**, which include a baker's, complete with ovens and grinding mills, a weaver's, with loom and bones, and a dyer's, with a huge pot for dyes. Behind the shops on the left you can see the **Palestra**, where public games were held, and accessible by way of a monumental gateway halfway down, beyond which there's a large colonnade and an apsidal hall, along with a terrace of rooms up above, giving an impression of just how large a structure this was. Back on Cardo V, opposite the entrance to the Palestra, the **House of the**

Grand Portal, on the corner of the Decumanus Inferior, is so called for its doorway with Corinthian columns, still very much intact. Opposite here, the Large Taverna has a well-preserved counter, while another shop, on the right, the Taverna of Priapus, has a faint but still suggestive painting above the counter. Next door to this is the House of the Cloth with its blackened original steps (behind glass), while next door the House of the Deer was another luxury villa, its two storeys built around a central courtyard and containing corridors decorated with richly coloured still lifes. It would have occupied one of the most sought-after locations in town, with a central sitting room leading to a terrace with what would have been a commanding sea view. Opposite, the House of the Relief of Telephus is the second-largest villa in Herculaneum, the home, it's thought, of one M. Nonius Balbus, proconsul of Crete and an associate of Augustus himself, and discovered with a collection of sculptures that includes the relief you can see on the wall, showing Telephus, the son of Hercules.

From here, the end of Cardo V, the path descends under a covered passageway down to the so-called Suburban Baths on the left: one of the most impressive – and intact – structures in Herculaneum, complete with extremely well-preserved stuccowork and a pretty much intact set of baths; it also has a complete original Roman door, the only one in Herculaneum that wasn't charred by fire. If you find it open, its damp mustiness makes it certainly the most evocative stop on a tour of the site. Next door, the Terrace of M. Nonius Balbus is so called for the funerary altar in the centre, which

The Villas of Portici and Ercolano

It wasn't only during Roman times that Ercolano was considered a desirable place to live. In fact the town and its neighbours only really took on their present unprepossessing appearance during the last half-century, and in the late eighteenth century and into the nineteenth century they were home to some of the most chichi residences on the bay – indeed, unbelievable as it might seem now, this stretch was once known as the Miglio d'Oro or "Golden Mile". Many of the villas that were built here during that time are still standing (there are 122 in all) and some are occasionally open to the public, while others are used for conferences,exhibitions and concerts, and a few venues host an arts festival in June; for more details go to ⓦwww .villevesuviane.net.

The Reggia di Portici, in nearby Portici – best accessed on the main train line to Salerno – is probably the most sumptuous of all the villas, designed by Ferdinando Fuga and Luigi Vanvitelli in the late eighteenth century and now home to the agriculture faculty of Naples' university. It was originally used to house the best of the finds from Herculaneum, and although these days there's not a great deal to see inside, it's open from Monday to Friday during office hours, and behind it there's a botanical garden occupying the former royal hunting grounds that is open at weekends too.

In Ercolano the Villa Campolieto (Tues–Sun 10am–1pm), within walking distance of the Herculaneum ruins, is another creation of the Vanvitelli family (Luigi and his son Carlo), built between 1763 and 1773, and has a few rooms open to the public – though the reason most people come here is for the concerts and plays that are held during the summer.

Finally, the Villa Favorita, also in Ercolano and easily reached on foot (Tues–Sun 10am–1pm), was built in the 1760s by Ferdinando Fuga and is perhaps the most pleasant of all the villas to visit because of its park, which stretches down to the waterfront, though most of the main building, and the outbuildings in the park, are used for conferences.

remembers the good deeds and great works of the proconsul, while beyond, the two temples – the **Sacellum of Venus** and **Sacellum of the Four Gods** – are decorated respectively with a marble altar and reliefs of Minerva, Neptune, Mercury and Vulcan.

The Villa dei Papiri

Situated just to the north of the main site, the **Villa dei Papiri** is the best-known of all the Herculaneum villas, the home of Julius Caesar's father-in-law, Lucius Calpurnius Piso, a learned man who was an enemy of Cicero and a consul of the Republic before his son-in-law. His villa supposedly stretched for more than 200m along what would have been the waterfront here, and was by far the most luxurious residence in the vicinity, built on several levels and housing a vast library of around two thousand scrolls as well as a large collection of sculptures, some of which you can see in Naples' Museo Archeologico Nazionale. What was left of the (carbonized) scrolls is archived at the museum too. They have been excavating the villa for longer than anyone can remember, and even now only a section of it has been opened to the public, partly owing to conservation issues. At the time of writing it was closed, but it is sometimes open to groups of up to 25 people (Sat & Sun 9am–noon); visit Ⓦ www .arethusa.net for the current picture.

Mount Vesuvius

Since its first eruption in 79 AD, when it buried the towns and inhabitants of Pompeii and Herculaneum, **Mount Vesuvius** (daily: Jan & Feb, Nov & Dec 9am–3pm; March & Oct 9am–4pm; April & May, June & Sept 9am–5pm; July & Aug 9am–6pm; €6.50) has dominated the lives of those who live on the Bay of Naples, its brooding bulk forming a stately backdrop to the ever-growing settlements that group around its lower slopes. There have been more than a hundred **eruptions** over the years (see box opposite), and the people who live here still fear the reawakening of the volcano, and with good cause – scientists calculate it should erupt every thirty years or so, and it hasn't since 1944. It's carefully monitored, of course, and there is apparently no reason to expect any movement for some time. But the subsidence in towns like Ercolano is a continuing reminder of the instability of the area, one of southern Italy's most densely populated.

There are several ways of **getting to Vesuvius**, or at least the car park and huddle of souvenir shops and cafés which sit just above the greenery among the bare cinders of the main summit and crater. You can drive here, and pay for parking. Or there are roughly hourly **buses from Pompeii** – the CS station and Piazza Anfiteatro – between 8.05am and 3.35pm; the journey takes just over an hour and the last bus back is at 4.40pm. Tickets cost €9 return. Two of the buses go **via Ercolano** CS station, leaving there at 8.25am and 12.45pm; tickets from there cost €7.60. You can also hire minibus taxis from Ercolano CS station, which charge €15 per person and wait while you see the crater – but you have to wait until they're full at both ends. There are two **bus services** daily **from Naples**' Piazza Garibaldi (*Hotel Terminus*) – at 9.25am and 10.40am, taking an hour and a half and returning at 12.30pm and 2pm respectively.

Making the **ascent** to the crater from the car park takes twenty to thirty minutes depending on how fit you are. It's a medium-to-strenuous stroll across reddened, barren gravel and rock along a marked-out path that nowadays is roped off to minimize the chance of stumbling and falling down the sheer drop

Vesuvius: will she blow?

The only active volcano in mainland Europe, Mount Vesuvius dominates the Bay of Naples from almost wherever you stand, a huge and menacing presence that overlooks the most densely populated volcanic region in the world. The crater and summit have changed with almost every eruption, and it's likely that the profile of Vesuvius you're looking at now is nothing like the one the ancients would have seen. It's almost the classic volcano shape, but not quite, owing to the fact that its main summit and caldera – Monte Somma – was blown off in an earlier eruption and is now separated from the current summit by a five-kilometre-wide valley. The main summit today is 1281m high, and the crater 650m wide and 230m deep, and it's this that you can visit – a bare, cindery expanse from which it's possible to see the calcified lava flows of the previous eruptions, but below which the fertile soil is lushly forested and intensively cultivated with vines and market gardens.

Vesuvius has had plenty of **eruptions** over the years, most famously in 79 AD, when it buried Pompeii and Herculaneum and most of the towns around with hot ash (not lava), and most recently in 1944, when part of the rim of the crater was blown away and the nearby towns of San Sebastiano and Massa di Somma were destroyed – an event memorably described by Norman Lewis in his war memoir *Naples'44*. In between those two events there have been many other violent eruptions – among them one in 472 AD, when ash from the volcano could be seen as far away as Constantinople, and another in 1036, when lava flows were seen for the first time. In the Middle Ages the volcano was largely dormant until a massive eruption in 1631 which killed three thousand people, since when there has been an eruption at least four times each century. The first eruption of the twentieth century, in 1906, sent more lava down the mountain than ever before – after which Vesuvius was 100m shorter. Everything has been quiet since 1944, which, chillingly, is the longest period of dormancy in its history; indeed, most experts agree that not only is Vesuvius well overdue another eruption, but because of the way volcanoes work, when it does blow it may well be the most violent eruption for some time – not much comfort to the million or so people who live in its potential danger zone.

It's nothing new that the slopes of Vesuvius are heavily populated: the volcano's flanks have always drawn settlement thanks to their fertile soil and mild climate – a lushness that is particularly evident as you make your way up to the top. The mountain has been monitored closely since the first observatory was built on its slopes in 1841, and the authorities remain as alert as ever. There is a detailed evacuation plan, which assumes two weeks' notice of a major eruption, and which would be capable of shifting half a million out of the biggest danger zone, where they could be in the way of pyroclastic flows of lava. Nonetheless, Vesuvius is prone to sudden, extremely intense eruptions, and if this happens the chances of a mass evacuation of its very densely populated slopes are remote in the extreme. The authorities are trying to discourage construction on the volcano – hence the rather derelict nature of many of the buildings near the top – and have even offered financial incentives to people to move away; and the mountain is also protected within its own national park (Ⓦwww.parconazionaledelvesuvio.it). For the moment the volcano is quiet – but looking at its history and the massively developed straggle from Naples that encircles it, you can't help feeling that it is a very large accident waiting to happen.

to the right. At the top is a deep, wide, jagged ashtray of red rock swirled over by midges and emitting the odd plume of smoke, though since the last eruption effectively sealed up the main crevice this is much less evident than it once was. There's also a small kiosk selling drinks and trinkets, and the path continues halfway around the crater so you can get a view from the other side – a further fifteen minutes or so on foot.

Villa Oplontis and Boscoreale

Ten minutes or so beyond Ercolano on the Circumvesuviana line, the suburb of **Torre Annunziata** is no more appealing than any of the other towns around here at first sight, and it seems almost perverse that it's home to one of the best-preserved Roma villas around these parts, the **VILLA OPLONTIS** (daily: April–Oct 8.30am–7.30pm; Nov–March 8.30am–5pm; €5.50, includes Boscoreale and Stabiae, or €20, includes Pompeii and Herculaneum as well), part of a known complex of patrician Roman buildings here that have yet to be excavated. The site is just a short walk from the Circumvesuviana station; there's precious little reason to deviate from this route, and it's unlikely you will be tempted in any case. The upside of the villa's location, of course, is that you're more than likely to have it almost to yourself.

Also a victim of the 79 AD eruption, the villa is hardly an essential sight given the proximity of Herculaneum and Pompeii, and parts of it have been under restoration for a fair while. But it would have been a sumptuous residence in its day (it's now thought to have belonged to Poppea, the second wife of Nero) and is remarkable for the scale and elegance of its architecture, wall paintings and gardens. From the vast atrium, adorned with intricate architectural paintings of columns and shields, the vista extends right through the house, to the colonnaded portico surrounding it and the restored, formal gardens bordered with box hedges. Like villas of today, this one also had its own sun terrace and swimming pool, and bones discovered under the lawn suggest that a goat kept the grass in check. Inside, some of the highlights include the frescoed **salone** or sitting room on the right side, where frescoes show peacocks and theatrical masks, and there are panelled Roman doors that were calcified by the lava. Adjacent is the bright-red and tawny-yellow **caldarium** in the villa's baths complex, where a pastoral painting portrays Hercules, draped in lion skin, in the garden of the Hesperides, while above him, astride a seahorse, sits a sultry Nereid; in the other direction is a frescoed

▲ Amphorae, Villa Oplontis

triclinium or dining room and the villa's **kitchens** just behind. Strolling through the villa from here takes you through various courtyards and inner gardens, a small one with a fountain, facing what would have been the villa's main entrance hall or **atrium** (the building faced the sea), followed by a small **peristyle** with a fountain, edged by servants' quarters, and a larger **peristyle** fringed with columns that served as a peaceful internal garden. Close by, the **latrines** show the easy genius of Roman plumbing, while a frescoed **corridor** leads to the **swimming pool**, a huge affair some 60m long, deliberately tilted towards the sea to allow successful drainage. Along one side are a series of rooms frescoed with images of nature that were either small internal gardens or **viridariums**, or just **sitting rooms** frescoed with foliage to relax and restore their patrician occupants.

Boscoreale

The **Antiquarium of Boscoreale**, reached by taking the Circumvesuviana two stops from Torre Annunziata (daily: April–Oct 8.30am–7.30pm; Nov–March 8.30am–5pm; €5.50, includes Villa Oplontis and Stabiae), is the second minor ancient site in the area, a small archeological museum in a modern, purpose-built structure that houses finds from a group of nearby villas, also buried in the 79 AD eruption. Unlike the villas at other sites, these were rustic farmhouses rather than upscale holiday homes, and most of the finds here reflect that – pots, agricultural tools and the like. The excavations of one of the nearby farmhouses, the **Villa Regina**, which specialized in vines and the production of wine, are also open to the public. You can view rooms that would have been used for grape-pressing, a wine cellar and barn, and even see the calcified tracks from a cart that was found in the vicinity.

Pompeii

The best-known Roman town to be destroyed by Vesuvius – **POMPEII** – was a much larger affair than Herculaneum and one of Campania's most important commercial centres in its day. After a spell as a Greek colony, Pompeii came under the sway of the Romans in 200 BC, later functioning as both a moneyed resort for wealthy patricians and a trading town that exported wine and fish products, notably its own brand of fish sauce. A severe earthquake destroyed much of the city in 63 AD, and the eruption of Vesuvius sixteen years later only served to exacerbate what was already a desperate situation.

The site

The **site** of Pompeii (daily: April–Oct 8.30am–7.30pm, last entry 6pm; Nov–March 8.30am–5pm, last entry 3.30pm; €11; combined ticket with Herculaneum and Villa Oplontis, valid three days, €20; ⓦ www.pompeisites.org) covers a wide area, and seeing it properly takes half a day at the very least; really you should devote most of a day to it and take plenty of breaks – unlike Herculaneum there's little shade, and the distances involved are quite large: comfortable shoes are a must. There is a **bar-restaurant** on site for when you really flag – although the best thing to do is to bring lots of supplies, including a picnic lunch, with you.

All of this makes Pompeii sound a bit of a chore – which it certainly isn't. But there is a lot to see, and you should be reasonably selective: many of the streets aren't lined by much more than foundations, and after a while one ruin

Vesuvius had been spouting smoke and ash for several days before the eruption and in fact most of Pompeii had already been evacuated when disaster struck: out of a total population of 20,000 it's thought that only 2000 actually perished, asphyxiated by the toxic fumes of the volcanic debris, their homes buried in several metres of volcanic ash and pumice. **Pliny**, the Roman naturalist, was one of the casualties – he died at nearby Stabiae (now Castellammare) of a heart attack. His nephew, Pliny the Younger, described the full horror of the scene in two vivid letters to the historian Tacitus, who was compiling a history of the disaster, writing that the sky turned dark like "a room when it is shut up, and the lamp put out".

In effect the eruption froze the way of life in Pompeii as it stood at the time – a way of life that subsequent excavations have revealed in precise and remarkable detail; indeed Pompeii has probably yielded more information about the ordinary life of Roman citizens during the imperial era than any other site: its social conventions, class structure, domestic arrangements and its (very high) standard of living. Some of the buildings are even covered with ancient graffiti, either referring to contemporary political events or simply to the romantic entanglements of the inhabitants; and the full horror of their way of death is apparent in plaster casts made from the shapes their bodies left in the volcanic ash – with faces tortured with agony, or shielding themselves from the dust and ashes.

The first parts of the town were discovered in 1600, but it wasn't until 1748 that **excavations** began, continuing more or less without interruption – after 1860 under the auspices of the Italian government – until the present day. Indeed, exciting discoveries are still being made, and a flood of new funds is being used to excavate a further twenty hectares of the site; it is hoped to resolve whether or not the survivors attempted, in vain, to resettle Pompeii after the eruption. A privately funded excavation some years ago revealed a covered heated swimming pool, whose erotic wall paintings have been deemed by the Vatican to be unsuitable for children. And, in a further development, a luxury "hotel" complex was uncovered in 2000 during the widening of a motorway, slabs of stacked cut marble suggesting it was still under construction when Vesuvius erupted.

Bear in mind that most of the best mosaics and murals (from Herculaneum too) are in Naples' Museo Archeologico Nazionale, and that as you can only see a small proportion of the finds *in situ*, visits are best supplemented by an additional one to the museum.

begins to look much like another. Again, vandalism, lack of money and the usual inertia that afflicts many Italian archeological sites mean that often, the most interesting structures are kept locked and only opened when a large group forms or a tip is handed over to one of the custodians; others are only open at set times, so you might want to coordinate your visit accordingly. It's worth studying the site map, which you'll find at every entrance – pins on the map indicate which areas are currently closed, as the site is in continuous restoration. To be sure of seeing as much as possible you could take a tour, although one of the pleasures of Pompeii is to escape the hordes and absorb the strangely still quality of the town, which, despite the large number of visitors, it is quite possible to do.

As regards a **route**, there are two main entrances to Pompeii: Porta Marina, right by the Pompeii-Scavi-Villa dei Misteri CS station, and Piazza Anfiteatro, on the other side of the site in modern Pompei. You can take either, but given its proximity to the station where you'll most likely arrive, the Porta Marina makes most sense as a starting-point and is the way we've written our account – from west to east, with a side trip to the **Villa dei Misteri** at the end.

The western sector

After you've entered the site from the western, Pompeii-Villa dei Misteri side, through the Porta Marina, the first real feature of significance is the **Forum**, a long, slim open space surrounded by the ruins of what would have been some of the town's most important official buildings – a basilica, temples and a market hall. The rectangle of huge column slabs on the right of the site entrance mark the **Basilica**, a courtroom basically, where the judges would sit at the far, still-columned end, in front of the only bit of wall that survives. At the opposite end of the Forum, steps lead up what would have been a **Temple of Jupiter**, on the left of which are literally hundreds of amphorae recovered from the site, along with some examples of the calcified bodies for which Pompeii is famous. Walking north from here takes you towards some of the town's more luxurious houses. The **House of Pansa** is a large villa around two courtyards, the second of which has most of its columns intact. Turn left out of here and you reach the **House of the Tragic Poet**, named for its mosaics of a theatrical production and a poet inside, though the "Cave Canem" (Beware of the Dog) mosaic by the main entrance is more eye-catching; it also has a pretty courtyard and some painting fragments, accessible by way of an entrance on the side street. Next door, there's the **Thermopolium Caupona**, a café-restaurant where you would have taken what you wanted from the counter and eaten it at tables in the back. Further along the same street the residents of the **House of the Faun**, the largest house in Pompeii, had a friendlier "*Ave*" (Welcome) mosaic outside their house, beckoning you in to view the atrium and the copy of a tiny, bronze, dancing faun (the original is in Naples) that gives the villa its name, not to mention the extensive garden behind. This is where the damaged mosaic of Alexander the Great in battle, now in Naples' Museo Archeologico Nazionale, was found.

On the street behind, the **House of the Dioscuri** is another grand place, with a large atrium, where many more of the paintings now in Naples were unearthed. Further down the same street, the **House of the Vettii** (undergoing restoration at the time of writing) is one of the most delightful houses in Pompeii and one of the best maintained, a merchant villa ranged around a lovely central peristyle that gives a good impression of the domestic environment of the city's upper middle classes. The first room on the right off the peristyle holds the best of Pompeii's murals actually viewable on site: the one on the left shows the young Hercules struggling with serpents; another, in the corner, depicts Ixion tied to a wheel after offending Zeus, while a third shows Dirce being dragged to her death by the bull set on her by the sons of Antiope. There are more paintings beyond here, through the villa's kitchen in a small room that's normally kept locked – erotic works showing various techniques of lovemaking (Greek-style, woman on top; Roman-style, man on top) together with an absurdly potent-looking statue of Priapus from which women were supposed to drink to be fertile; phallic symbols were also, it's reckoned, believed to ward off the evil eye. Along the street from here, the **House of the Golden Cupids** (also under restoration at the time of writing), holds a wall painting of Jason, just about the depart on his quest to find the golden fleece, as well as a pleasant garden.

The eastern sector

Cross over to the other side of the site for the so-called **new excavations**, which began in 1911 and actually uncovered some of the town's most important quarters, stretching along and beyond the main **Via dell'Abbondanza**. On the corner of Via dell'Abbondanza, the **Stabian Baths** is Pompeii's oldest

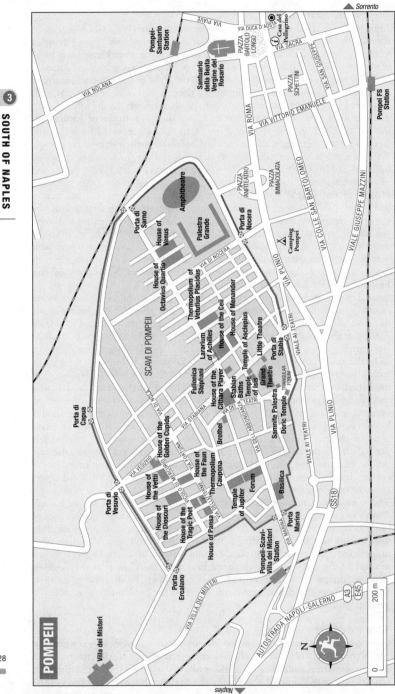

POMPEII

Naples

Sorrento

Villa dei Misteri

Pompei-Santuario Station

VIA PIAVE
VIA DUCA D'AOSTA
Casa del Pellegrino
PIAZZA BARTOLO LONGO
VIA SACRA

Santuario della Beata Vergine del Rosario

VIA NOLANA

PIAZZA SCHETTINI

VIA SAN GIUSEPPE

Pompei FS Station

VIA ROMA
VIA VITTORIO EMANUELE

VIALE GIUSEPPE MAZZINI

Porta di Sarno

House of Venus

Amphitheatre

Palestra Grande

PIAZZA ANFITEATRO
PIAZZA IMMACULATA

Porta di Nocera

Camping Pompei

VIA COLLE SAN BARTOLOMEO

SCAVI DI POMPEII

House of Octavius Quartio

VIA DI NOCERA

Thermopolium of Vetutius Placidus

House of the Ceil

House of Menander

Lararium of Achilles

Temple of Asclepius

Little Theatre

Porta di Stabia

VIA PLINIO

Porta di Capua

Fullonica Stephani

House of the Cithara Player

Temple of Isis

Grand Theatre

TRIANGULAR FORUM

VIALE AI TEATRI

VIA STABIANA

Stabian Baths

VIA DELL'ABBONDANZA

Sammite Palestra

Doric Temple

VIALE AI TEATRI

House of the Golden Cupids

Brothel

VIA DEI TEATRI

Porta di Vesuvio

House of the Vettii

House of the Faun

Thermopolium Caupona

Temple of Jupiter

Forum

Basilica

VIA PLINIO

House of the Dioscuri

House of the Tragic Poet

House of Pansa

VIA MARINA

Porta Marina

SS18

Porta Ercalano

Pompeii-Scavi-Villa dei Misteri Station

VIA VILLA DEI MISTERI

Villa dei Misteri

AUTOSTRADA NAPOLI-SALERNO

A3 E45

200 m

0

N

baths complex, with a still partially arcaded courtyard and various other bath interiors, all remarkably intact (though it, too, has been under restoration for a while). Just behind the baths, and perhaps appropriately situated down a small side street, is the town's principal **brothel** – very much a purpose-built structure, with small cubicles complete with beds, all still intact. Above the doorways, on the walls, are the remains of paintings depicting various sexual positions, and a Priapus with three phalluses – an opportunity for the tour guides to really get into their stride.

Back in front of the baths, take Via dei Teatri south off Via dell'Abbondanza to a relatively peaceful part of the site, where a columned portico gives way to the **Triangular Forum**, which opens out to the steps of a very ruined **Doric Temple**, originally from the sixth century BC, and beyond that to what would have been a lovely circular temple around an ancient well – a good place to have your picnic. Immediately below the Triangular Forum is the small, grassy, column-fringed square of the **Samnite Palestra** – a refectory and meeting-place for spectators from the nearby **Grand Theatre**, which is very well preserved and still used for performances. Walk around to the far side of the Grand Theatre, down the steps and up again, and you're in front of the **Little Theatre** – a smaller, more intimate venue also still used for summer performances and with a better-kept corridor behind the stage space.

On the corner, beyond this complex of buildings, there's a small **Temple of Asclepius**, with a short flight of steps leading up to a central podium, and a slightly more intact **Temple of Isis** next door. Follow the road east from here and you're in front of the **House of the Ceii**, on the left, where there's a painting of a hunting scene showing wild boar and other animals in the room behind the main courtyard. Opposite, the **House of Menander** is often closed, but if you can get in you'll see one of the most complete of Pompeii's large villas, with wonderful paintings, one of which depicts the dramatist from which the house takes is name, others showing scenes from the Trojan War around a room with a mosaic of the Nile. Thought to have belonged to the family of Nero's wife Poppea, the villa had its own bath complex too, decorated with floor mosaics depicting sea creatures and servants offering toiletries and bath oils.

Walk up from here to rejoin Via dell'Abbondanza, where the **Lararium of Achilles** has a niche with a delicate relief depicting scenes from the Trojan War – tiny figures, showing Achilles and Hector doing battle; like so much else here, it's amazing they have survived. Next door, the **Fullonica Stephani** is a well-preserved laundry, with a large tiered tub for washing, while the **House of the Cithara Player**, a few steps back in towards Porta Marina, is a vast complex on several levels with a number of leafy courtyards that for some reason are often devoid of other visitors – and you could spend quite a while poking around here. Further east, past the well-preserved shop counter and mural of the **Thermopolium of Vetutius Placidus**, stop off at the **House of Octavius Quartio**, a gracious villa fronted by great bronze doors. Paintings of Narcissus gazing rapt at his reflection and Pyramus and Thisbe frame a water cascade in the back, where once water flowed down a channel and into the villa's lovely garden, which has been replanted with vines and shrubs. Next door, the **House of Venus in a Shell** is equally of interest; it has a pretty courtyard with one of the site's best-preserved paintings on its back wall, showing Venus reclining in a giant floating clam shell surrounded by cupids, as well as little architectural studies around the main courtyard.

Make a right turn from here to the **Amphitheatre**, one of Italy's most intact and accessible, and also its oldest, dating from 80 BC. It once had room for a crowd of some 12,000 – well over half the town's population. Next door, the

Palestra is a vast parade ground that was used by Pompeii's youth for sport and exercise – still with its square of swimming pool in the centre. It must have been in use when the eruption struck Pompeii, since its southeast corner was found littered with the skeletons of young men trying to flee the disaster.

The Villa dei Misteri

One last sight you shouldn't miss at Pompeii is the **Villa dei Misteri**, a suburban mansion that is probably the best preserved of all Pompeii's palatial houses. Located half a kilometre from the Pompeii-Villa dei Misteri station, or just outside the Porto Ercolano exit from the site, it's an originally third-century BC structure with a warren of rooms and courtyards that derives its name from a series of paintings in one of its larger chambers: depictions of the initiation rites of a young woman into the Dionysiac Mysteries, an outlawed cult of the early imperial era. Not much is known about the cult itself, but the paintings are marvellously clear, remarkable for the surety of their execution and the brightness of their tones and colours. They follow an obvious narrative, starting with the left-hand wall and continuing around the room with a series of freeze-frames showing sacrifice, flagellation, dancing and other rituals, all under the serene gaze of the mistress of the house.

Practicalities

To reach Pompeii **from Naples**, take the Circumvesuviana to Pompeii-Villa dei Misteri, a 35-minute journey, which leaves you right outside the western, Porta Marina entrance to the site. You can also take the roughly hourly mainline train (direction Salerno) to the main Pompei FS station, on the south side of the fairly characterless modern town; this is only a better bet if you want to enter the site from the opposite side or you are staying in modern Pompei. At the main station, ignore the taxi drivers offering to take you to the entrance for a large fee – it only takes around ten minutes to walk. Head away from the station towards the tall belltower, turning left at the main square to follow the signs to "Pompeii Scavi". After around 200m you come to the eastern entrance, just off Piazza Antifeatro, the site itself screened by an avenue of trees.

 Most people visit Pompeii on day-trips from Naples and Sorrento, but in case you want to make the town an overnight stop, there are plenty of **hotels** and an excellent **youth hostel**, *Casa del Pellegrino*, Via Duca d'Aosta 4 (℡081.850.8644; dorms €14–16.50), situated in the centre of modern Pompei, ten-minutes' walk from the Piazza Antifeatro entrance. There are also a couple of handy **campsites** including *Camping Pompei* at Via Plinio 113, south of the main entrance (℡081.862.2882, ⓦwww.campingpompei.com), which has double bungalows (around €45), as well as tent pitches. Modern Pompei's **tourist office** at Via Sacra 1, just off the main square (Mon–Sat 9am–6pm; ℡081.850.7255), has maps of the site, town plans and details of accommodation.

Castellammare di Stabia and around

By the time you reach **CASTELLAMMARE DI STABIA**, a few kilometres further around the bay, the urban shadow of Naples has started to lift a little, though the cranes and containers of its portside areas don't make you any more likely to want to stop. There are, however, one or two reasons to jump off the Circumvesuviana: a third minor and relatively unvisited ancient site, **Stabiae**, and the cable-car trip to nearby **Monte Faito**, which is not only a spectacular if short journey, but also leaves you well placed to hike across the peninsula to the Amalfi Coast in a matter of hours.

Stabiae

The best-known attraction of Castellammare itself is the site of **STABIAE** – or strictly speaking the **Villa San Marco** and a group of associated villas (daily: April–Oct 8.30am–7.30pm; Nov–March 8.30am–5pm; €5.50, includes Boscoreale and Villa Oplontis), which you can reach by taking bus #1 from the Cirumvesuviana station – the ruins are quite a walk away, up behind the main part of Castellammare.

Stabiae was a seaside resort in 79 AD, and a wealthy one at that, before being buried like everything else under Vesuvius's hot ash – the most famous victim was the Roman historian Pliny the Elder, who set out from the naval port of Misenum across the bay to better observe the eruption, and just managed to make it here, only to expire like everyone else. The site was in fact discovered and excavated earlier than Pompeii, in the mid-eighteenth century, but it soon lost out to the larger and more alluring digs nearby and fell into relative obscurity. Although there's not much you can visit, what you can see leaves you in no doubt as to the sort of people who would have lived in Stabiae. Of the villas, the Villa San Marco is the largest, and has its own private baths, as well as a series of courtyards complete with frescoes and mosaics that are the match of any of those in Pompeii or Herculaneum; the nearby Villa Arianna also has its fair share of decorative detail, although its most impressive aspect is the spacious internal courtyard.

Monte Faito

Castellammare's other main attraction is somewhat more accessible: the **funivia** or cable car up to the top of **MONTE FAITO** (1100m; daily every 20–30min: mid-June to Aug 7.25am–7.15pm; Sept to mid-June 9.35am–4.25pm; €6.71 return, children €2.58, July & Aug & Sun €7.23). The *funivia* is right next to the Circumvesuviana station, and the journey takes just eight minutes, but even so it's not for those of a delicate disposition, giving as it does increasingly stupendous views of the bay and of the deepening gulf between you and the tree-filled hillside below. At the top, there are a couple of bars selling drinks and sandwiches, and if you really can't face the trip down it's comforting to know that several roads meet here and there's a Circumvesuviana bus stop nearby.

Paths leads off in two main directions: if you're feeling lazy you can take the one off to the right (west), which in a short while descends to Piazzale dei Capi and the *Sant'Angelo* hotel (☎081.879.3042, ⓦwww.santangelofaito.it; doubles €50), walkable in about fifteen minutes or so. You can have a drink or eat lunch in the hotel's panoramic restaurant, which has views right up the coast to Sorrento and across the peninsula to the Bay of Salerno. Outside of high season at least, a more peaceful or airy spot you couldn't hope to find.

Walking in the opposite direction from the *funivia* station, it's more of a hike to the **Santuario San Michele**, at 1278m the second-highest spot on the mountain. The sanctuary is a small chapel built on the site of a tenth-century original, and the walk there takes around ninety minutes; taxis go there too, for €10 a head, and the panorama over the bay once you're there is magnificent – though the route taxis take is inevitably less spectacular than the path. Beyond the sanctuary, a path climbs steeply up to Monte Faito's highest point at 1444m, **Monte San Michele**, where the view takes in everything on both sides of the peninsula from Naples to Salerno. This leg takes about another hour, and you'll know when you're more than halfway there when you pass the **Sorgente dell'Acqua Santa** spring, which has gushed forth in its little grotto ever since St Michael blessed it with his sword.

Walking from the *funivia* station to Monte Faito's summit at Monte San Michele and back is a good day's hike, stopping for a picnic on the way. But if you're feeling particularly energetic, and are suitably prepared, you could trace your steps back a short way from the summit and pick up the main path all the way to **Monte Pertuso** or **Santa Maria al Castello**, each a signposted two-hour walk away up above the Amalfi Coast, and from there down to **Positano** – a further hour or so's descent.

Vico Equense

The small resort town of **Vico Equense** marks the end of Naples' urban sprawl and the beginning of the brighter, lighter, more pleasure-driven delights of the Sorrentine peninsula. In the main part of town, the excellent *Da Gigino Pizza al Metro*, Via Nicotera 15 (℡081.879.8309), the self-proclaimed "university of pizza", is Vico's most significant attraction: a giant restaurant and buzzing takeaway that not only does fantastic pizza but has a full restaurant menu too – right down to a tub of live lobsters by the cash desk. People come from as far away as Naples (no slouch itself when it comes to pizza restaurants) to sample its pizza, which is sold by the metre. It's not easy to find: walk out of the harbour, turn first left and then right at the top and it's on the right after about 50m.

The great pizza notwithstanding, you wouldn't want to spend your entire holiday in Vico Equense, but down at the bottom of a winding road there are a couple of stretches of sandy **beach** here to keep you occupied.

Sorrento

Topping the rocky cliffs close to the end of its peninsula, 25km south of Pompeii, the last town of significance on this side of the bay, **SORRENTO** is solely and unashamedly a resort, its inspired location and mild climate drawing foreigners from all over Europe for close on two hundred years. Ibsen wrote part of *Peer Gynt* in Sorrento, Wagner and Nietzsche had a well-publicized row here, and Maxim Gorky lived for over a decade in the town. Nowadays it's strictly package-tour territory, but really none the worse for it, with little of the brashness of its Spanish and Greek equivalents but all of their vigour, a bright, lively place that retains its southern Italian roots. It's not hard to find decent and affordable restaurants, or, if you know where to look, reasonably priced accommodation, and there's really no better place outside Naples itself from which to explore the rugged peninsula (even parts of the Amalfi Coast) and the islands of the bay.

Arrival and information

Sorrento's **train station** is located in the centre of town, five-minutes' walk from the main Piazza Tasso along busy Corso Italia; the **bus station** is just in front. There's a **tourist office** in the large yellow Circolo dei Forestieri building at Via Luigi de Maio 35, just off Piazza Sant'Antonino (Mon–Sat 8.45am–6.15pm; ℡081.807.4033, Ⓦwww.sorrentotourism.com), which has free maps and bus and ferry timetables, and information about excursions.

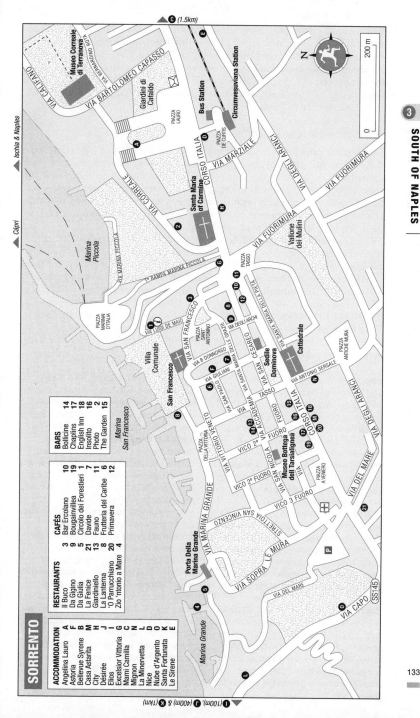

SORRENTO

ACCOMMODATION

Angelina Lauro	A
Astoria	F
Bellevue Syrene	B
Casa Astarita	M
City	H
Désirée	J
Elios	I
Excelsior Vittoria	G
Mami Camilla	C
Mignon	L
La Minervetta	N
Nice	D
Nube d'Argento	O
Santa Fortunata	K
Le Sirene	E

RESTAURANTS

Il Buco	3
Da Gigino	9
Da Giulia	5
La Fenice	21
Giardiniello	13
La Lanterna	8
'O Parrucchiano	20
Zi' 'ntonio a Mare	4

CAFÉS

Bar Ercolano	10
Bougainvillea	9
Circolo dei Forestieri	1
Davide	7
Fauno	11
Frutteria del Caribe	6
Primavera	12

BARS

Bollicine	14
Chaplins	17
English Inn	18
Insolito	16
Photo	2
The Garden	15

0 _____ 200 m

You can walk pretty much everywhere in Sorrento, but if you want a bit of easy orientation, it's worth taking one of the **mini train tours** that leave every 35 minutes from Piazza Tasso (daily 9am–midnight; €6 adults, €3 children); tours last about half an hour. You can rent **scooters** at Jolly Service & Rent, just off the eastern end of Corso Italia at Via degli Aranci 180 (℡081.877.3450), and at the other end of town at Corso Italia 3 (℡081.878.2403, ⓦwww.jollyservice .eu). Rates start at €27 a day, €150 a week.

Accommodation

Sorrento has more **hotel** beds than anywhere else in the Bay of Naples, and you should have no problem finding somewhere to stay, though you'd be well advised to book ahead at any time of year to secure the best options. There are some truly splendid places to splurge, both in Sorrento itself and in next-door Sant'Agnello – grand places with fantastic views and venerable histories, as well as a cool boutique alternative, but there are decent budget options too, both in the town itself and on the road out to Massa Lubrense.

There's a private **youth hostel**, *Le Sirene*, at Via degli Aranci 160 (℡081.807.2925, ⓦwww.hostellesirene.com; dorm beds €20–25, doubles from €45, including breakfast), which is a bit spartan but decent enough. To get there from the train station, turn right on the main road and Via degli Aranci is 200m down on the left. The closest of the **campsites** is the scenic *Nube d'Argento*, right on the other side of the town centre, 100m from the end of Corso Italia at Via del Capo 21 (℡081.878.1344, ⓦwww.nubedargento.com). If that's full, try the slightly cheaper *Santa Fortunata*, just over a kilometre further on at Via del Capo 41 (℡081.807.3579, ⓦwww.santafortunata.com; April–Oct), which has a private beach and superb sea views, as well as bungalows and cabins for around €70.

Hotels

Astoria Via Santa Maria delle Grazie 24 ℡081.807.4030, ⓦwww.hotel astoriasorrento.com. It's unusual to find a hotel right in the heart of old Sorrento, and this place, which opened in 2008, is quite special, with reasonably sized doubles that have been nicely furnished and come equipped with TV, telephone and a/c for just €80. You couldn't be more central if you tried, and at this price, it's a bargain.

Bellevue Syrene Piazza della Vittoria 5 ℡081.878.1024, ⓦwww.bellevue.it. This lovely nineteenth-century hotel, built on the remains of a Roman villa, boasts glorious views and has lifts down to the bathing facilities below, free to hotel guests. Most of the rooms have been recently renovated and are very spacious, varying from €200 for a courtyard view to €300 for a sea view in high season; deals are often available.

Casa Astarita Corso Italia 69 ℡081.877.3991, ⓦwww.casastarita.com. More of a *pensione* than a hotel, this cosy, friendly place has six nice rooms overlooking the street, all with bathroom, flat-screen TVs and fridges, and charges around €100 a night, including internet access. A couple of the rooms have space for an extra bed, in which case the price is €120.

City Corso Italia 221 ℡081.877.2210, ⓦwww .sorrentocity.com. A relatively small hotel, with only twelve rooms, and reasonable enough, with all facilities, but only really worth considering if you need something handy for the station, as there are nicer places for the same price elsewhere in Sorrento. Doubles €115.

Désirée Via Capo 31/B ℡081.878.1563, ⓦwww .desireehotelsorrento.com. About 700m from the end of Corso Italia, this family-run hotel has rather uninspiringly furnished doubles with balconies overlooking the sea, for around €95 a night (triples and quads also available) – though they vary a bit in size. Prices include parking and access to the stony beach below. There's a roof terrace too.

Elios Via Capo 33 ℡081.878.1812, ⓦwww .hotelelios.it. This very friendly one-star enjoys a good location next door to the slightly sprucer *Desirée*, and its fourteen rooms, most with sea views, go for €80, though Rough Guide readers get a €5 discount. The rooms are nothing special, but they enjoy lovely views. Prices don't include breakfast other than coffee, but there's a kitchen for rustling up your own which you can enjoy on the large seaward-facing terrace.

Excelsior Vittoria Piazza Tasso 34 ℡081.807.1044, ⓦwww.exvitt.it. This fabulously grand hotel has been owned by the same family since 1834, and its grand entrance is right in the centre of town. It's set in a lovely formal garden with a lemon and orange grove and has a large pool; the lift from the swish terrace bar plunges straight down to the seafront; and the service is immaculate yet friendly. The rooms are gorgeous, and you can choose from a garden-view double from €370 to one with a sea view for €450.

Mami Camilla Cocomella 4 ☏ 081.878.2067, ⓦwww.mamicamilla.com. A hotel and cookery school rolled into one, with a great family atmosphere and, as you'd expect, great food. You can do one-off classes, or come for anything between one and four weeks, and attend more intensive and structured courses – prices range from around €300 for twelve hours' tuition in a week to four weeks of solid teaching for around €1700. If you don't want to sign up for a course, ordinary doubles go for €60.

Mignon Via Sersale 9 ☏ 081.807.3824, ⓦwww .sorrentohotelmignon.com. A two-star with well-appointed rooms, either with balconies, or, if you're lucky enough to get a room at the back overlooking the garden, with a shared terrace. Rooms come with satellite TV, a/c and free internet access; doubles €100.

La Minervetta Via Capo 25 ☏081.877.4455, ⓦwww.laminervetta.com. Sorrento's only real boutique hotel is something special, with just twelve rooms, perched on the cliff overlooking Marina Grande. Rooms have been decorated with careful attention to detail by the architect son of the original owner, and there's a lovely lounge terrace overlooking the sea, and below that a plunge pool. Sorrento's best option if you want to splurge: prices range from €300 to €400.

Nice Corso Italia 257 ☏ 081.878.1650, ⓦwww .hotelnice.it. This couldn't be more convenient for the station, and it's a friendly place, with 29 rooms, most of them good-sized, if blandly furnished, doubles for €70–90. The front rooms can be a bit noisy; the back ones are more peaceful and overlook an orange and lemon grove.

The Town

There's nothing special in the way of sights in Sorrento itself, but it's pleasant to wander through the streets that make up its **old town**, most of which are pedestrianized. **Via San Cesareo** forms a backbone to the small grid of streets lined with shops selling tourist gear and *limoncello*, but it's an atmospheric old quarter full of life and bustle. The arched **Sedile Dominova**, a seventeenth-century loggia that was once the meeting-place of local nobles and is now used as a veteran's club, forms a kind of historical focal point, at the junction of Via San Cesareo and Via Giuliani, and from here you can stroll down to the shady gardens of the **Villa Comunale**, whose terrace has lovely views out to sea. Off to the right, peek into the small thirteenth-century cloister of the church of **San Francesco**, planted with vines and bright bougainvillea – a peaceful escape from the bustle of the rest of Sorrento.

At the northern edge of the old town, Sorrento's main artery is **Corso Italia**, which is pedestrianized every evening after 7pm for the lively *passeggiata*. Midway down, **Piazza Tasso** is the effective centre of town, built astride the gorge that cuts through Sorrento; it was named after the wayward sixteenth-century Italian poet to whom the town was home and has a statue of him in the far corner. A little way down Corso Italia, on the left, Sorrento's **Cattedrale** has been much rebuilt, and the real challenge of its gaudy interior is how to tell the fake marble from the real. The bishop's throne, on the main aisle, is certainly real, dating from the late sixteenth century, and the intarsio scenes on the back of the choir stalls (an inlaid wood technique specific to the town that endures mainly for tourists) add a genuine Sorrentine touch.

The Museo Bottega della Tarsialignea

There's more intarsio work on display in the nearby **Museo Bottega della Tarsialignea** at Via San Nicola 28 (June–Sept Tues–Sun 10am–1pm & 4–7.30pm; Oct–May Tues–Sun 10am–1pm & 3–6.30pm; €8). Appropriately housed in an ancient mansion in the artisanal quarter of the old town, it's a

▲ A view of the bay from Sorrento

shrine to Sorrento's craft speciality of inland woodwork – cheap and pretty awful examples of which you see all over town. Don't let the tourist tat put you off: the ground floor here has some clever and stylish examples of contemporary local intarsio work (it's for sale, but not at all cheap), while upstairs is the work of Sorrento's late-nineteenth-century intarsio greats – Luigi Gargiulio, Michele Grandville and Giuseppe Gargiulio – beautiful if sometimes overwrought pieces that inevitably upstage the touristy stuff, much of which, ironically, is produced in the workshops of this neighbourhood. Elsewhere in the museum are displays of the tools needed to make intarsio pieces, and information in English in each room, as well as townscapes and models of Sorrento in the nineteenth century, when it became a stop on the Grand Tour, and the tourist boom really began.

The Museo Correale di Terranova

The local **Museo Correale di Terranova**, housed in the airy former palace of a family of local counts at the far end of Via Correale (Wed–Mon 9am–2pm; €6), might kill an hour or so. It has lovely views over the bay and next door's orange and lemon groves, which gradually emerge as you climb its grand staircase, and a tranquil garden at the back. It holds various Roman finds – busts, sarcophagi, inscriptions – including an announcement by Vespasian after the 79 AD earthquake, and various domestic bits and pieces. There are also examples of local intarsio work, the highlight of which is a fantastic seventeenth-century ebony and ivory inlaid comic strip of Tasso's *Gerusalemme Liberata* – along with a lot of badly lit paintings by local artists upstairs, best of which by far is the late eighteenth-century roulette game, *Il Biri Bisso*, painted on wood by one Francesco Celebrano, and local scenes of fisherfolk, ruins and landscapes by relocated Dutch and Flemish artists, who were clearly more inspired here than at home.

Nearby, the **Giardini di Cafaldo**, at Via Correale 27 (daily: April–Sept 9am–9pm; Oct–March 9am–6.30pm), is a nice place to unwind, an orange and lemon grove cut through with paths where you can taste and buy delicious home-produced liqueurs at a small outdoor café.

The beaches

Strange as it may seem, Sorrento isn't particularly well provided with **beaches**, and in the town itself you either have to make do with the small strips of sand of the **Marina San Francesco** lido, right below the Villa Comunale gardens and accessible by a lift or steps, or the rocks and tiny, crowded strip of sand at Sorrento's pleasant fishing harbour at **Marina Grande**, fifteen-minutes' walk or a short bus ride (roughly every 30min) west of Piazza Tasso. Both places cost around €3 a head for the day, plus charges for parasol (€2) and chair rental (€4), although there is a small patch of sand, immediately right of the lift exit at Marina San Francesco, that is free. There are several ways to get down to Marina Grande on foot: the nicest either follow the city walls from the end of Via San Nicola or the road that edges past the *Hotel Bellevue Syrene*, off the Villa Comunale; both end up at the same flights of steps that lead down to the east end of Marina Grande's bay, just above the *Da Giulia* restaurant. There's also a small, stony **beach** below the *Tonnarella* and *Désirée* hotels, a few hundred metres out of town to the west, though this charges €3.50 entrance, plus the usual costs for parasol and beds, and it gets quite shady in the afternoon – far better in the morning. If you don't fancy the crowds in Sorrento, you can always try the beaches further west or east; see p.139 and p.141.

Eating and drinking

Sorrento has no shortage of **restaurants**, and most of them are at least reasonable, although inevitably in a town so devoted to tourism you can come across places where the service is slow and the food not up to scratch. The places below are some of the better offerings.

The town also has a lively after-dark scene, kicking off with the *passeggiata* along the Corso. There are plenty of decent spots for a **drink** around town, from down-to-earth pubs to swanky lounge bars (see p.138).

Cafés and gelaterie

Bar Ercolano Piazza Tasso 28. The friendlier and less self-important of the two main bars on Piazza Tasso – with not such good views of the parading crowds, but a lot shadier when it's hot. A good place to start the day with a pastry.

Bougainvillea Corso Italia 16. This always busy and convivial joint has one of old Sorrento's widest choices of ice cream flavours – around eighty at the last count – and a garden to enjoy them in.

Circolo dei Forestieri Via Luigi di Maio 35. Used by foreigners rather than locals, who miss out on its fancy, old-world charm, decently priced if basic food and wonderful views. A good place to bring kids who are bored with pizza and pasta – they do burgers and suchlike – or for a pre-dinner aperitif.

Picnic food

There's a Standa supermarket on Corso Italia, just around the corner from the bus and train station, and a decent *salumeria* at the other end of Corso Italia, past the *English Inn*, plus another supermarket, Conad, just beyond the end of Corso Italia, on the left as you leave town on Via Capo.

Davide Via Giuliani 41. A decent, long-established, family-owned and -run *gelateria* right in the centre of Sorrento.

Fauno Piazza Tasso 13/15. *The* place to watch the crowds drift by during the evening *passeggiata* – if you can bear the thinly disguised contempt the waiters have for the tourist hordes. Food includes the usual pasta dishes, burgers and omelettes.

Frutteria del Caribe Via Giuliani 56/A. This place is *frullati* (smoothie) heaven; plus they do crushed-ice *granite* and all sorts of other good things, including crepes.

Primavera Corso Italia 142. There's a great choice of flavours at this veteran *gelateria*, just off Piazza Tasso. Check out the photos of the famous and infamous who have stopped by for a quick *cono*.

Restaurants

Il Buco Rampa Marina Piccola 11, Piazza Sant'Antonino ☎081.878.2354. Housed in the wine cellar of a former monastery, this is Sorrento at its gastronomic best, with a real variety of *antipasti* and *primi* that focus on local ingredients and a *secondi* menu that is mainly fish-based. You can order à la carte and pay around €18 for a pasta dish, €25 for a main course, or choose from set menus that start at €50 for three courses. Closed Wed.

Da Gigino Via degli Archi 15 ☎081.878.1927. A great, no-nonsense choice, with excellent pizzas and good pasta and main courses; pizza from €7. Closed Tues except in Aug.

Da Giulia Via Marina Grande 67 ☎081.807.2720. With a menu as short as the menus in the upper town are long, this restaurant serves simple food in perhaps Sorrento's best location – on the waterfront of Marine Grande. It's very good for pasta dishes, with half a dozen great seafood and tomato-based *primi*, and the same number of principally fishy *secondi*. No credit cards.

La Fenice Via degli Aranci 11 ☎081.878.1652. Just outside the immediate centre, and as such as popular with locals as with tourists. It's always busy, and does good fish, served in a covered patio full of plants. Mains go for around €18. Closed Mon.

Giardiniello Via Accademia 7 ☎081.878.4616. Just off Corso Italia, this pizzeria-ristorante with a small garden specializes in fish, shellfish and barbecued meats, and is a touch cheaper than the other places in the centre of town; try the *gnocchi alla sorrentina* at €5. Closed Thurs.

La Lanterna Via San Cesareo 23 ☎081.878.1355. Down a dead end off Via San Cesareo, just off Piazza Tasso, this has long been one of the better restaurants in the centre of town, with tables outside and consistently good food – it does great fish, but much else besides. It's moderately priced, and there's also a *Lanterna Due*, around the corner on Via Santa Maria delle Grazie. Closed Wed.

'O Parrucchiano Corso Italia 67 ☎081.878.1321. More of a conservatory than a restaurant, this vast place is very popular with locals and tour groups alike, and the food is decent and good value; try the *cannelloni con la ricotta*. Closed Wed.

Zio 'ntonio a Mare Via Marina Grande 44 ☎081.807.3033. Down on one of the jetties at Marina Grande, this is one of Sorrrento's more upscale choices for fish and seafood, with a fine seafood *antipasti* table, served on a covered terrace.

Bars and pubs

Bollicine Via Accademia 7. In the heart of the old town, this is a small, wood-panelled wine bar with a wide range of good Campanian wines.

Chaplins Corso Italia 18. Almost opposite the *English Inn*, a friendly place with regular live football and rugby.

English Inn Corso Italia 55. Capacious English-style pub which serves pub food and has an outside dance floor.

The Garden Corso Italia 50/52. A wine shop and wine bar with a few outside tables that is a great place to take the weight off. It has beer on tap too; you can get the usual wine-bar fare (cheeses, salads and panini for lunch), and there's a restaurant attached (entrance around the corner).

Insolito Corso Italia 31. A defiantly cool DJ bar, all-white and trendy, open all day until late.

Photo Via Correale 19/21. Just beyond Piazza Tasso, this place has a restaurant on one side with a menu of light starters and international mains, and a trendy bar on the other, with photo exhibitions and a canopied garden. It's surprisingly inexpensive, though its studied boutiquey ambience means you could be pretty much anywhere.

Listings

Bookshops In the centre of town, Libreria Tasso, Via San Cesareo 96, has Sorrento's best selection of English-language books. Capsa, just around the corner from the station at Corso Italia 249, also has Italian and some English books and CDs.

Kids There's a small children's playground halfway down on Via Califano on the right, just past the Museo Correale, where kids can play while their parents chill out at its handy café-bar. Children might also like the mini train rides around the town centre – see p.134.

Scooter rental You can rent scooters at Jolly Service & Rent, just off the eastern end of Corso Italia at Via degli Aranci 180 (☎081 877 3450),

and at the other end of town at Corso Italia 3 (☎081.878.2403, ⍟www.jollyservice.eu). Rates start at €27 a day, €150 a week. Guarracino, Via Sant'Antonino 19 (☎081.878.1728), just off the piazza of the same name, rents bikes.

Watersports Sorrento Diving Center, Via Marina Piccola 63 (☎081.877.4812, ⍟www.sorrentodiving center.it) organizes dives for beginners and qualified divers on Punta Campanella (see p.141).

East of Sorrento

Back around the bay **to the east**, Sorrento's ribbon of settlement blends almost invisibly into a number of other coastal villages. Their small and densely populated centres are skirted by the main coast road, which is all many Sorrento-bound travellers see of them. There are, however, one or two things that might draw you here from Sorrento, not least some marginally better beaches.

The first is **SANT'AGNELLO**, centred on the main Piazza Matteotti on the coast road, where you'll find the train station – five-minutes' walk from the sea at **Punta San Francesco**. Here the **Marinella** beach has a nice strip of dark-grey sand that is reachable by lift from the promenade above (daily: June–Sept 7am–10pm; Oct–May 9am–7pm; €5 plus a small charge for the lift and the usual extras for umbrellas and sunbeds). There's a **café** with a terrace on the promenade and a couple of **hotels** – the plush *Corallo* (☎081.807.3355, ⍟www.hotel corallosorrento.com; doubles €240), overlooking the sheer drop below, and the friendly *Mediterraneo* (☎081.878 1352, ⍟www.mediterraneosorrento.com; doubles €130–200) sitting just across the main road.

The next town along, **PIANO DI SORRENTO** has an explanade overlooking the **Marina di Cassano** far below, where a workaday harbour has a short stretch of dark-grey sandy beach at each end, reachable by a zig-zag road, and overlooked by the pleasantly breezy, modern *Klein Wien* **hotel** (☎081.532.1825, ⍟www.kleinwien.it; doubles €280). At the western end of the esplanade, the **Museo Georges Vallet** (Tues–Sun 9am–7pm; free) makes the most of its excellent location by hosting weddings, concerts and other functions in its lush gardens and sumptuous terraces. It also hosts a small archeological museum, displaying mostly finds from the Sorrentine peninsula, including some beautiful marble reliefs from the Massa Lubrense villa, as well as a scale model of the Villa Romana Pollio at Capo di Sorrento, among whose ruins you may have swum, and showing clearly how the original building would have incorporated the rock swimming pool there.

Finally there's **META**, only worth visiting for **Alimuri beach**, which consists of two decent-sized stretches of grey sand on a small spit that sticks out from the high-sided cliffs of the bay. A lift can deliver you there from the road above, or you can drive down to a small car park.

Southwest of Sorrento

The main coast road – **Via del Capo** – climbs out of Sorrento to head southwest towards **Massa Lubrense**, the small administrative centre and market town for most of the villages at this end of the Sorrentine peninsula. Five minutes on the bus or twenty minutes on foot from Sorrento's centre, there are a couple of prime swimming spots. The first is the **Ruderi Villa Romana Pollio**, ten-minutes' walk from the bus stop at Capo di Sorrento on the main road (itself about 1.5km from town), where the ruins of a Roman villa lie on and around the seashore rocks, "Regina Giovanna", which are fairly flat and swathed with walkways; there's also a lovely enclosed seawater pool. The other is reachable by strolling 100m further along the main road and taking a path off to the right just before the *Hotel Dania*, which shortcuts in ten minutes or so to the **Marina di Puolo**, a short stretch of mainly sandy beach lined with fishing boats and a handful of trattorias that is perhaps the nicest place to swim just outside Sorrento. You can also reach this by car by taking a turn-off a few hundred metres beyond the path that winds down to the beach – there are (paid) parking spaces just above the beach and you walk the rest of the way. Of several **trattorias** here, the *San Rafael* is one of the best, a full-service restaurant with an outside terrace and a small snack bar that does great pizzas.

Massa Lubrense and Marina della Lobra

About 3km beyond Marina di Puolo, **MASSA LUBRENSE** is a pleasant enough market town perched above the sea, but with nothing much in the way of sights. It's the main centre of the local area, and a good place to stay if you're after something quieter, poised between Sorrento itself and the smaller resorts on the south coast of the peninsula and also well placed for some great walking in the hills hereabouts. The *La Primavera* **hotel**, at Via IV Novembre 3 (℡081.808.9556, ⊛www.laprimavera.biz; doubles €95), is a decent, if relatively frill-less, option with a good restaurant. For **food**, just off Massa Lubrense's main drag, *Il Tritone*, Via Massa Turro 2/A (℡081.808.9046), does seafood pasta dishes and excellent pizzas, though its garden is a little lacking in atmosphere – quite an achievement on such a beautiful stretch of coast.

A few kilometres below Massa Lubrense, **MARINA DELLA LOBRA** is a quiet harbour with a pleasant waterfront **restaurant** in *Funicolì Funicolá*, and an attractive **accommodation** option in *Agrimar*, on the left as you descend into the village at Via Vincenzo Maggio 40 (℡081.808.9682) – a friendly place with a collection of rustic chalets with en-suite bathrooms. There's a lovely garden and terrace with views over the sea and the harbour below, and occasional evenings of Neapolitan music – all for €40 per person per night.

Termini and Nerano

Less than five kilometres south of Massa Lubrense, **TERMINI** is an airy, cheerful place with an almost too perfectly framed view of Cápri from its main square, and an appealing boutique **hotel** in the form of *Relais Blu*, Via Roncato 60 (℡081.878.9552, ⊛www.relaisblu.com; closed Nov to mid-March; doubles €260–400), whose eleven large rooms and suites are beautifully furnished in a cool marine style; there's an excellent **restaurant**, too. Beyond Termini the road descends to **NERANO**, where there are another couple of good **accommodation** choices: *Olga's Residence*, Piazza Nerano 3 (℡081.808.1013, ⊛www.olgasresidence.com), an apartment hotel with a pleasant garden and swimming pool overlooking the bay below, and apartments ranging in price from around €800 a week out of season to €1100–1300 in season, and *Casale Villarena*, at Via Cantone 3 (℡081.808.1779, ⊛www.casalevillarena.com), a small and secluded complex of self-catering apartments set within a well-maintained garden that go for €600–1200 out of season, €1200–2000 a week in season, though daily rates are also available out of season (from €105–130 per night for a two-person apartment). Down below Nerano, almost in Marina del Cantone, there's also the *Nettuno Villaggio* **campsite** (℡081.808.1051, ⓦwww.villaggionettuno.it), which as well as tent pitches has bungalows for €80–135 a night, and four apartments in a Saracen tower for €145–195 a night. It also has a diving centre that runs trips out to the choice spots of Punta Campanella (see below).

Marina del Cantone

Down below Nerano, stretched languidly around the beautiful **Bay of Ieranto**, **MARINA DEL CANTONE** has a strip of pebbly beach lined with parasols and sunbeds in front of several bar-restaurants. There's a spot in the middle where you can just throw down your towel; otherwise it costs the usual €10 or so for a couple of beds and sunshade. Once you've tired of the sun and sea, you could take a boat excursion to Cápri or rent a boat for around €100 a day from one of a couple of local operators. You can take these around the headland to the right to the **Punta Campanella**, a protected reserve that is a great place to snorkel and dive – though if you want to do the latter then you'll need to contact the diving outfit at the *Nettuno Villaggio* (see above).

Marina del Cantone is an unusually good place for foodies, with no fewer than three gourmet **restaurants**, so you're spoilt for choice if you want to skip the beach and just come here to eat. At one end, *Lo Scoglio* (℡081.808.1026) has its own landing stage giving access to the visiting celebs from Cápri who come here to sample the restaurant's great fish dishes and renowned *spaghetti alle zucchine* in its glassed-in jetty. Right on the beach, the *Taverna del Capitano* has a similarly fancy restaurant, with *primi* and mains going for €25–30 and very attentive service in a starchy atmosphere quite at odds with the beach just outside. You can also **stay** here – rooms with balconies and sea views cost around €110 (℡081.808.1028, ⓦwww .tavernadelcapitano.it). A more spartan option is *La Certosa*, a little further along (℡081.808.1209; doubles around €70), whose *Pappone* restaurant downstairs is pretty good. Or, just for food, there's the *Marie Grazie* (℡081.808.1011) with its lovely shady beachside terrace at the far end of the beach, whose excellent *antipasti* really hit the spot at lunch; the spaghetti *alle zucchine* special is tasty too.

Sant'Agata sui Due Golfi

Immediately south of Sorrento, high up in the hills that form the backbone of the Sorrentine peninsula, **SANT'AGATA SUI DUE GOLFI** is an airy hill-town and provincial capital, so named for its spectacular view of both bays – though to be honest there are actually precious few places you can experience this view. It's a pleasant place, busy with tour buses going to and from the Amalfi Coast, but there's nothing much to keep you. The best place for views is the **Deserto** convent, a short walk – ten minutes or so – from the main square, where there's a belvedere (daily: April–Sept 5–8pm; Oct–March 3–4pm), perfectly sited for the purpose; if the belvedere's closed you can still enter the grounds, which afford good views of the Sorrento side. The church of **Sant'Agata** is worth a peek for its a mid-seventeenth-century polychrome altar of marble and mother-of-pearl.

If you want to **stay** in Sant'Agata – and it's delightfully peaceful and relatively tourist-free at night – then *Don Alfonso*, right in the centre of town at Corso Sant'Agata 11/13 (℡081.878.0561, ⓦwww.donalfonso.com), is the pick of the options – a Michelin-starred restaurant and hotel that is the town's pride and joy, serving *haute* Italian and Mediterranean cuisine, and offering overnight **stays** in one of eight individually furnished suites from around €400. A humbler option is *Villa Green Paradise*, Via Deserto 14/c (℡081.808.0152; doubles €70–90), two-minutes' walk from the square on the way to the Deserto convent, with plainly furnished but well-equipped rooms. It also has a nice garden, but only accepts bookings for a minimum of two nights in high season. More information can be had from the **tourist office** on the town's main square (daily 9am–1pm & 4–8.30pm; ℡081.533.0135).

Even if you can't afford *Don Alfonso*'s €130 menus (see above), Sant'Agata is a good place to stop for **lunch or dinner**: *Lo Stuzzichino*, just off the main square at Via Deserto 1/A (℡081.533.0010; closed Wed), has an attractive garden and serves well-priced local specialities – the usual seafood dishes, cannelloni and *scaloppine sorrentine* – and is relaxed and welcoming. Otherwise *Da Mimi*, Via Termine 3 (℡081.533.0585), just the other side of the main square, left off the main street, does decent pizzas.

The Amalfi Coast

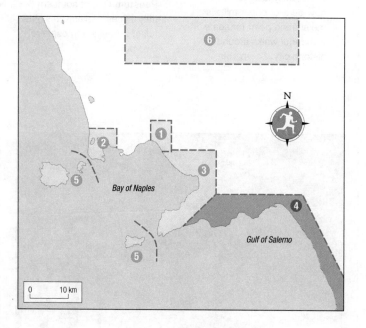

CHAPTER 4 # Highlights

✳ **Marina di Conca** Although reached by several hundred steps down from the road, this beach is one of the coast's best – and for much of the year is relatively uncrowded. See p.153

✳ **Valle dei Mulini, Amalfi** This wonderfully lush valley of now derelict paper mills is the starting point for some wonderful walks around the historic city. See p.158

✳ **Atrani** Amalfi's tiny neighbour is an often-overlooked gem on this coast. See p.160

✳ **Villa Cimbrone, Ravello** Lofty Ravello can make you feel on top of the world – and nowhere more so than on this fabled belvedere. See p.164

✳ **Paestum** One of southern Italy's finest Hellenistic sights, full of brooding atmosphere. See p.171

▲ The Temple of Ceres, Paestum

The Amalfi Coast

O ccupying the southern side of the Sorrentine peninsula, the **AMALFI COAST** (Costiera Amalfitana) can lay claim to being Europe's most beautiful coastline, its corniche road winding around towering cliffs that slip almost sheer into the sea. You've seen it all before, of course, in countless films and car adverts; but nothing quite prepares you for the reality: the rocky outcrops topped by Saracen towers; the impossibly balanced umbrella pines; the tunnels cut through the rock; the green-speckled peninsulas stretching out like lizards as far as you can see; and the sea shimmering invitingly far below. The settlements here are triumphs of faith over reason, and you can't even see a lot of the buildings from the road, due to the fact that most of the villas cling limpet-like to the cliffs, often only accessible by way of hidden steps down from the road.

By car or bus it's an incredible ride (though it can get mighty congested in summer), while getting there by sea – easy and affordable with a wealth of coastal ferries – is a gentler experience, but an equally special one, taking in the precarious houses, decked with flowers, along the serpentine coast road, and the river valleys that cut through the mountainous cliffs, opening out at almost inaccessible beaches. The coast as a whole is inevitably rather developed, and the villas atop its precipitous slopes are some of the country's most sought-after; it's also home to some of the most aesthetically lovely hotels in Italy, and budget travellers should be aware that you certainly get what you pay for here. But if there is anywhere in the country that you might be tempted to blow your budget, this, most definitely, is it.

Of the main coastal targets, high-profile **Positano** gets most of the plaudits – undeniably picturesque, but these days it's almost entirely the province of high-end mass tourism, and somewhat the worse for it. Smaller resorts like **Praiano**, which haven't been entirely overrun, make more appealing options, as does **Amalfi** itself – a less claustrophobic place than Positano, with a hint of a life beyond tourism, and a fascinating old whitewashed centre that stretches up the valley from the sea. Amalfi also provides easy access to the more low-key seaside village of **Atrani** – one of the nicest places to stay on the coast – as well as the fabled village of **Ravello**, whose mountain-top villas and gardens occupy a space that feels "closer to the sky than the sea", in the words of the French writer André Gide.

Getting around the Amalfi Coast is very straightforward, thanks to regular **buses** to all the major settlements and **ferries** to Naples and the islands; see p.148 for details.

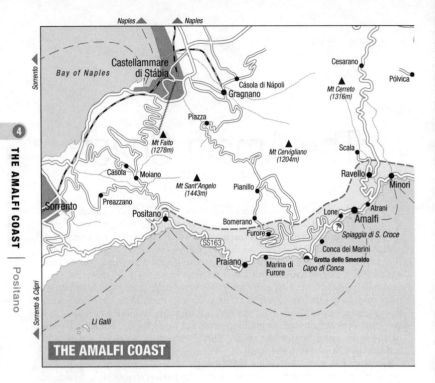

Naples ▲   ▲ Naples

Sorrento ◄

Bay of Naples   Castellammare di Stábia   Cesarano   Pólvica

Cásola di Nápoli   Mt Cerreto (1316m)
Gragnano

Piazza

Mt Faito (1278m)   Mt Cervigliano (1204m)   Scala

Casola   Moiano   Ravello   Minori

Mt Sant'Angelo (1443m)   Pianillo
Preazzano   Lone   Atrani
Sorrento   Positano   Amalfi
Bomerano   Spiaggia di S. Croce
Furore
SS163   Conca dei Marini

Praiano   Marina di Furore   Grotta dello Smeraldo
Capo di Conca

Sorrento & Cápri ◄

Li Galli

THE AMALFI COAST

Positano

The first place that can really call itself a town on the coast, **POSITANO** was in the Middle Ages a commercial rival to Amalfi. But it proved to have far less staying power than the city-state, and these days there's not much to show for its longevity; indeed it is so completely consumed by the tourist trade that it can be a hard place to like in summer. It has a couple of decent beaches and a great many boutiques – the town has long specialized in clothes made from linen, georgette and cotton, as well as handmade shoes. But it is the spectacular setting – a jumble of pastel-coloured houses heaped up in a pyramid high above the water – that has inspired a thousand postcards and helped to make it a moneyed resort that runs a close second to Cápri in the celebrity stakes. Since John Steinbeck wrote up the place in glowing terms back in 1953 – he called it "a dream place that isn't quite real when you are there and becomes beckoningly real after you have gone" – Positano has enjoyed a fame quite out of proportion to its tiny size. Franco Zefferelli is just one of many famous names who have villas nearby, and the crowds that pack the beach here consider themselves a cut above your average sun-worshipper.

Arrival and information

Buses stop at various points along the main coastal road, Via Marconi, which skirts the top of the old town of Positano; there's a stop on the Amalfi side of town, from where it's a steep walk or a short bus ride down to the little square at the bottom end of Via Cristoforo Colombo, five-minutes' walk from the

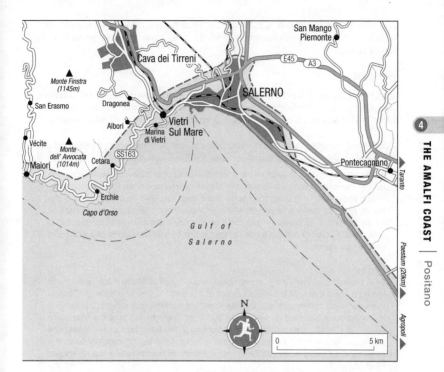

seafront; or you could get off on the other side of the centre, by the *Bar Inter-nazionale*, from where Viale Pasitea winds down to the Fornillo part of town. **Ferries** and **hydrofoils** from Cápri, Naples, Amalfi and Salerno pull in at the jetty just to the right of the main beach, where there are also plenty of ticket booths. Arriving by **car**, you'll shell out a lot on garage space as parking is very limited; reckon on at least €20 a day.

There's a busy **tourist office** just back from the beach by the church steps at Via del Saracino 4 (June–Oct Mon–Sat 8.30am–8pm; Nov–May Mon–Fri 8.30am–3pm; ☎089.875.067, ⓦ www.aziendaturismopositano.it).

Accommodation

Like everything else in town, **accommodation** in Positano tends to be pricey. If money is no object, you could easily blow your entire holiday budget on a few nights at the *San Pietro* (see p.149), Positano's most celebrated hotel, which is out of town, a couple of kilometres towards Praiano. Not surprisingly, it's cheaper to stay up in the newer neighbourhoods near the main road through town, or above Fornillo beach, than in the area closer to the Spiaggia Grande. There's one **hostel** in town, the *Brikette* at Via Marconi 358 (☎089.875.857, ⓦ www.brikette.com; dorms €22–25), a couple of minutes walk from the bus stop on the coast road. It's friendly and clean, with stunning views, bar and internet access, but the dorms are a bit spartan and airless.

Perhaps the most spectacular **self-catering** option is the *Torre Trasita* (☎978.453.7839, ⓦ www.tuscanestates.com/seaside_torre_trasita.php; €1500–2500), a fourteenth-century Saracen tower on the path between the main part of Positano and Fornillo beach, which has been turned into three pleasant one-bedroom apartments with amazing views; the largest has its own roof terrace on top of the tower.

Hotels

Maria Luisa Via Fornillo 42 ℡089.875.023, ⓦwww .pensionemarialuisa.com. Very friendly, and great value at almost half the price of the nearby *Vittoria* – though you don't have the luxury of a lift down to the beach, and the climb up can be a killer. Breakfast isn't included, but there's a coffee machine and

---

Getting around the Amalfi Coast

The dream, of course, is to **drive** the coast road in a convertible – an exhilarating ride by any standards. Just be aware that whatever car you're driving, the sheer concentration required to negotiate the bends in the road can limit your enjoyment of the views, and that parking when you reach your destination can leave you a frazzled wreck at the end of the day – and you'll usually pay a premium to keep your car at your hotel. For those without a car, navigating the Amalfi Coast on **public transport** couldn't be easier.

Buses

SITA **buses** travel frequently up and down, stopping off at all the major resorts and linking them in turn with the major centres of Sorrento, Naples and Salerno. Coming from Sorrento, buses normally join the coast road a little way west of Positano. If the coast road is closed, however, the bus from Sorrento will take the alternative route, via Castellammare and Agerola, right over the backbone of the Sorrentine peninsula, which is itself a journey worth making – the bus zigzagging down the other side in a crazy helter-skelter of hairpin bends to join the road a few kilometres west of Amalfi.

Ferries

In summer, the Metrò del Mare **ferries** (℡199.600.700, ⓦwww.metrodelmare.com) run from Naples and Sorrento to Positano, Amalfi, Minori and Salerno, with regular services supplementing the private operators that cover the Amalfi Coast; they also link the major towns with key points around the region as far north as Pozzuoli and as far south as the Cilento. The transport system is well integrated, with Unico-Costiera **tickets** allowing travel on both Metrò del Mare ferries and SITA buses for €6 for 24 hours, or €15 for three days; for more information, see ⓦwww.unicocampania .it. Among the private ferry operators, Alicost (℡089.227.979, ⓦwww.lauroweb.com) runs services from towns along the Amalfi coast to the islands and Salerno; Coop Sant'Andrea stops at towns all along the coast and also operates services from Minori and Maiori to Cápri (℡089.873.190, ⓦwww.coopsantandrea.com); Tra.Vel. Mar ferries (℡089.872.950, ⓦwww.travelmar.it) go to Positano, Amalfi and Salerno, as well as to Cápri from Positano. For specific timings, see the daily newspaper *Il Mattino*, check with the local tourist offices or look up schedules online.

Walks

The coast can also be enjoyably explored **on foot**. The mountains that sweep down to the sea are magnificent walking country, with some well-marked-out routes, and if you're up to scaling some pretty precipitous inclines, you get to see a different side to the coast, a world away from the often crowded places on the shore. We've noted some circular routes in this chapter, from Positano and Amalfi (see p.151 & p.160); the extensive bus routes make it easy to pick and choose your starting point. Chapter 3 also has details of a walk you can do from the north side of the Sorrentine peninsula to the coast (see p.132).

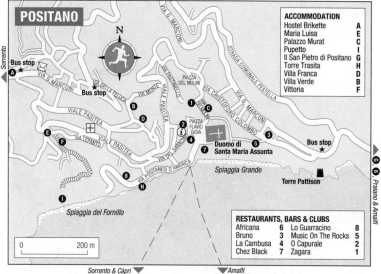

POSITANO

N

Sorrento

Bus stop Ⓐ ★

VIA G. MARCONI

VIA DELLA FELICA

VIA MONTE PASTINATO

VIALE PASITEA

PIAZZA
DEL MULINI

Bus stop

VIA CRISTOFORO COLOMBO

VIA G. MARCONI

STRADA COMUNALE PESTELLA

STRADA COMUNALE PESTELLA

Ⓑ

Ⓓ

Ⓒ

PIAZZA
FLAVIO
GIOIA

VIALE PASITEA

Ⓔ

Ⓕ

VIA LEPANTO

VIALE PASITEA

VIA DEL SARACINO

Ⓖ

Ⓗ

VIA POSITANESI D'AMERICA

Ⓘ

Duomo di
Santa Maria Assunta

Bus stop
★

Spiaggia Grande

Torre Pattison

Spiaggia del Fornillo

G, 6, Praiano & Amalfi

0   200 m

Sorrento & Cápri ▼   ▼Amalfi

ACCOMMODATION
Hostel Brikette	A
Maria Luisa	E
Palazzo Murat	C
Pupetto	I
Il San Pietro di Positano	G
Torre Trasita	H
Villa Franca	D
Villa Verde	B
Vittoria	F

RESTAURANTS, BARS & CLUBS
Africana	6	Lo Guarracino	8
Bruno	3	Music On The Rocks	5
La Cambusa	4	O Capurale	2
Chez Black	7	Zagara	1

fridges for keeping breakfast provisions, not to mention a lovely light breakfast room and terrace for consuming them. Doubles €80, with terraces and sea views, or €70 without. Closed Jan & Dec.

Palazzo Murat Via dei Mulini 23 ☏089.875.177, ⓦwww.palazzomurat.it. Perhaps the nicest place to stay if you want to be right in the heart of things, just 2min from the beach, and with good-sized rooms – though most of them are not in the old *palazzo* itself but in the newer extension. Around half have sea views, if a little obscured by the church, and all have satellite TV, a/c, large bathrooms and balconies. Internet access is free for the first 30min. Doubles €255–370.

Pupetto Via Fornillo 37 ☏089.875.087, ⓦwww .hotelpupetto.it. With its sister hotel, the *Vittoria*, to which it is connected by elevators, the *Pupetto* has pretty much colonized the Fornillo beach. It has rooms with sea views on the first and second floor for €170, and ground floor garden rooms for €150; all have TV and a/c, and are decently furnished. Prices include beach access, and there's a good, reasonably priced restaurant. Closed Jan–March.

Il San Pietro di Positano ☏089.875.455, ⓦwww.ilsanpietro.it. High on a promontory around 3km east of Positano proper, the *San Pietro* has a host of celebrity admirers, a range of individually designed rooms, beautiful public spaces that make

the most of the all-round views, and a private beach and waterfront bar to which you're whisked by elevator. All this, plus a tennis court, and a restaurant supplied by its own kitchen garden make this many people's idea of the ultimate five-star hotel. Doubles €420–550.

Villa Franca Viale Pasitea 318 ☏089.875.655, ⓦwww.villafrancahotel.it. The most upmarket choice along this stretch, with 38 rooms (though 10 are in the residence up the road), including a good selection overlooking the beach below. Prices range from €210 for a standard double (no terrace, partial sea views) to €390 for the deluxe alternative (terrace and sea views). There's a pool on the roof, a well-established restaurant, and parking – though this will cost you an extra €21 a day.

Villa Verde Viale Pasitea 338 ☏089.875.506, ⓦwww.pensionevillaverde .it. Just below the main road through town, this place is friendly and relaxed, and its 14 good-sized rooms have balconies overlooking central Positano from a wonderfully peaceful vantage point. Doubles €70–100, including parking. Excellent value.

Vittoria Via Fornillo 19 ☏089.875.049, ⓦwww .hotelvittoriapositano.com. Sister hotel to the *Puppetto* down below, to which it is connected by elevator, the simply furnished *Vittoria* makes a decent alternative, with doubles for €150–170 – all with sea views and balconies, a/c and TV.

▲ Positano

The Town

Positano's inordinately crowded centre is a mass of shops aimed at the tourist trade, and there's little in the way of sights apart from the church of **Santa Maria Assunta** (daily 8am–noon & 4–7pm), right in the heart of town, which harbours a thirteenth-century statue of the Madonna and Child. However, the **beaches** are nice enough and not overly busy most of the time – though watch out for the jellyfish, abundant in these waters. The main stretch, the **Spiaggia Grande** right in front of the town, is reasonable, although you'll be sunbathing among the fishing boats unless you want to pay over the odds for the nicer area on the far left. There's also another, larger stretch of beach, the **Spiaggia del Fornillo**, around the headland to the west, accessible in five minutes by a pretty path that winds around from above the hydrofoil jetty. It's a pleasant, wide strip of sand and shingle but is almost entirely covered in sun-loungers, with barely a spot to throw a towel down; the tiny shingle beach in the cove just before Fornillo is free.

Eating, drinking and nightlife

Positano's many **restaurants** can make a dent in your holiday budget; those listed below are the more reliable options. The bar-terrace of the *Puppetto* hotel (see p.149), on the Spiaggia del Fornillo, is a cheaper place to eat and drink than anywhere in Positano proper. For **picnics**, there's an *alimentari* by the steps up to the church, just back from the seafront, and the *Buca di Bacco* on the seafront does excellent **ice cream**.

Positano considers itself a truly sophisticated resort, which means that its **nightlife** is on the quiet side – the main thing to enjoy in the evening here is the fact that the day-trippers have gone home.

Restaurants

Bruno Via C. Colombo 157 ☎089.875.392. Some way from the more touristy places near the beach, both in distance and in price. The decor is dubious, and despite the lovely views over the water at night, you're basically sitting right on the main road. But the food is good, and well priced; main courses – heavily weighted towards fish and seafood – start at around €16.

La Cambusa Piazza Vespucci 4 ☎089.875.432. One of the fancier options near the seafront, and unashamedly a tourist hangout, just back from the Spiaggia Grande on the left. But its fish and seafood options are pretty good, and it's a fine place to watch the self-regarding Positano world go by. A full fish blowout here will set you back around €60 a head. Closed Tues.

Chez Black Spiaggia Grande ☎089.875.036. A long-established seafood restaurant, a bit over-branded these days, but the food is good, and along with the usual seafood options it does pizza too, from around €7. Closed Jan.

🏃 **Lo Guarracino** Via Positanesi d'America 12 ☎089.875.794. For a restaurant that has perhaps the best views in town – you eat on a bright, flower-fringed terrace overlooking the sea and Fornillo beach – this place is relatively reasonably priced, at least by Positano standards (pastas €10–16, mains €16–22), and does great food too. The *antipasti* and *primi* are great: try the *caponatina* – tuna, olives and cherry tomatoes on a slab of oily bread – or the *linguini ai ricci di mare* (with sea urchins). There's pizza too.

O Capurale Via Regina Giovanna 12 ☎081.811.188. Just around the corner from *La Cambusa*, this place has been around for over a century, and it shows. The largely touristy clientele choose from a really good seafood-dominated menu, and there's an attractive fish-themed ceiling too. Closed Nov–March.

Bars and clubs

Africana On the coast near Marina di Praia ☎089.874.042. This long-established club is probably the most spectacular place for a big night out hereabouts – housed in a grotto with a glass floor that looks down onto the rocks and sea below. June–Sept Thurs–Sun.

Music On The Rocks Via Grotte dell'Incanto 51, at the far end of the Spiaggia Grande ☎089.875.874. A club-restaurant with slick grotto-effect main room and dance floor, dazzling sea views and a glitzy clientele.

Zagara Via dei Mulini 8/10 ☎089.875.964. A late-night bar-cum-*pasticceria* with a leafy terrace and occasional live music.

Listings

Boat rental Try Lucibello, Via del Brigantino 9, Positano ☎089.875.032, ⊛www.lucibello.it; they also have a desk on the Spiaggia Grande. Lots of different boats, rentable without skipper, from €35 a day. There are also excursions to the nearby attractions, such as Cápri and the Grotta dello Smeraldo.
Luggage Positano Porter will transport luggage to and from your hotel for a fee (☎089.875.310, ⊛www.positanoporter.it).
Scooter rental Praia Costa in nearby Praiano (see p.152).
Walking tours Christine Omelas organizes tours of the town (☎338.869.1396, ⊛www.discoverpositano.it).

Walks from Positano

As with everywhere on this coast, Positano offers plenty of opportunities for **walks**, though most involve a steep uphill gradient to start off, unless you want to cheat and take the bus. One of the easiest circular walks from town is up to **Montepertuso** and along the cliff to the village of **Nocelle** for lunch, and then back down again – a walk that would take you 2–3 hours there and maybe half that coming back down, though any leg of the journey can be done by bus.

Walking up from the centre of Positano, take the path to Via Cristoforo Colombo and then the steps up to the coast road and continue east along here as far as the bus stop, opposite which there's a path off to the left that begins the ascent. For a more serious hike, you can take the path east from Nocelle along the so-called **Sentiero degli Dei** ("Path of the Gods"). From Nocelle follow the path to **Colle la Serra**, a two-hour hike, and from there to **Bomerano**, a relatively easy one-hour walk. From here you could pick up the Agerola–Amalfi bus which descends down through the Furore gorge to the coast – a spectacular ride.

Praiano and around

Some 5km east of Positano, **PRAIANO** is much smaller and very much quieter than its more renowned neighbour. The town consists of two tiny centres: **Véttica Maggiore**, which is Praiano proper, scattered along the main road from Positano high above the sea; and **Marina di Praia**, squeezed into a cleft in the rock down at shore level, a couple of kilometres further along towards Amalfi.

There's not much to either part of Praiano, but it does make a more peaceful and more authentic place to stay than Positano. Although lacking in sights, there are a few decent places to **swim**. The closest are the swimming spots off rocks immediately below the village, most notably the **Spiaggia Gavitella**, which you can reach from the main road by taking the path from the *San Gennaro* restaurant or from the *Smeraldo* hotel; there's also the small patch of shingly beach at Marina di Praia, surrounded by a couple of restaurants and places offering rooms to rent. Beyond Marina di Praia on the way to Amalfi you'll find some decent, properly sandy spots (see p.153). **Boat rental** is available from La Sibilla at Via Umberto 1 (℡089.874.365, www.lasibilla.org), and you can rent **scooters** from €45 a day from Praia Costa, Via Marconi 45 (℡089.813.082, www.praiacosta.com).

Accommodation

Casa Angelina Via Caprigilione 147 ℡089.813.1333, www.casangelina.com. This modern boutique hotel has a lobby full of contemporary art and a selection of rooms decorated with stark white minimalism, ranging from €320 for a room with a small balcony to upwards of €500 for one of the waterside suites. There's also a restaurant, a smallish pool, a fitness centre and a lift that takes you part-way down to the beach. It's excellently done, if a little too self-consciously cool for its own good – and families should be warned that they're not welcome at peak periods.

Continental Via Roma 21 ℡089.874.084, www.continental.praiano.it. By the bus stop on the main road above Marina di Praia, this converted old *palazzo* is run by three brothers who have extended the enterprise to include more rooms and even a campsite, *La Tranquillità* (℡089.874.084; May–Oct). Rooms in the old *palazzo* are simply furnished with faded frescoes and large balconies; those in the adjacent block are not quite as atmospheric, but also have large terraces. You can also swim off the rocks immediately below the hotel. €70–90.

Costa Diva Via Roma 12 ℡089.813.076, www.locandacostadiva.it. Above Marina di Praia, this hotel spills down a lovely, leafy series of terraces from the road – 15 rooms, all with sea views, TV, a/c, fridge and balcony for €110–130, parking included. There's a garden and a decent restaurant too, so in theory you never have to leave its shady confines except to take the steps down to the beach at Marina di Praia nearby.

Onda Verde Via Terramare 3 ℡089.874.143, www.ondaverde.it. Perched on the cliff edge at Marina di Praia, just 5min walk from the beach, and with lovely rooms for €170–190, in a series of cliff-side villas. The rooms are beautifully furnished and have all facilities, including satellite TV; there's also an excellent restaurant with great views over the sea.

Il Pino Via Caprigilione 13 ℡089.874.389, www.hotelpino.it. This hotel's neat, modern and well-equipped rooms are right on the main road in the centre of Praiano – a decent choice if you can't afford the delights of the nearby *Casa Angelina*, with doubles – all with balcony and sea views – for €113–140.

Eating and drinking

La Brace Via Caprigilione 146 ℡089.874.226. This restaurant on the main road is perhaps Praiano's best eating option, with pizzas straight from the wood-fired oven and excellent fresh fish from around €10, all of which you can enjoy on the covered terrace. Closed Tues Oct–March.

Trattoria San Gennaro Via Caprigilione 75 ℡089.874.293. Right next to the church, this is as central as you get in Véttica Maggiore, and serves huge portions of *antipasto di mare* and *primi* like *scialatielli con zucchine e gamberetti* (home-made pasta with courgettes and prawns) for €8. Closed Thurs.

Vivaro Via Capriliglione 156 ☎335.562.4805. Next door but one to *La Brace*, this is a comfortable wine bar open for lunch and dinner that does simple pasta dishes, cold cuts and cheese plates.

The coast between Praiano and Amalfi

Shortly after Praiano you pass the **Furore** gorge, which gashes into the mountainside just above the coast road. Just below the bridge that crosses the beginning of the gorge, **Marina di Furore** is a small beach accessible by way of steps down from the bridge, with just a handful of fishermen's houses and a disused paper mill where the gorge cuts into the mountain. Recently spruced up, the beach is nice enough, with a café-restaurant and even a local museum. Some of the steepest paths you'll encounter on the coast lead up from here to the scattered houses of the village of **FURORE** (600m) above – a two-hour walk. If this doesn't appeal, do the walk in reverse by taking the Agerola bus from Amalfi – you can get off in the upper part of the village and walk down. Down by the sea, the highlights along this stretch of coast are the **Grotta dello Smeraldo** and **Conca dei Marini**, both easily reached from Praiano.

The Grotta dello Smeraldo

About 4km out of Praiano, the **GROTTA DELLO SMERALDO** (daily: March–Oct 9am–5pm; Nov–Feb 10am–4pm; €5) is one of the most highly touted natural features locally. You can reach it by taxi boat from either Praiano or Amalfi for €10 return, plus the entrance fee, but there's also a bus stop and car parking nearby. Arriving by boat leaves you at grotto level, whereas by road you have to take the lift down to the grotto, which you then tour by boat.

Discovered by an Amalfi fisherman in 1932, the grotto is not unimpressive, but it's basically one huge chamber and it doesn't take long for the boatmen to exhaust their patter and whisk you around the main features – an underwater nativity scene and various statues that supposedly resemble famous people. The real draw, though, is the intense green of the water on one side, caused by the sun shining through the water to a depth of 16 metres, and the stalagmites and stalactites that drip from every surface.

Conca dei Marini and beyond

Just around the headland from the grotto, **CONCA DEI MARINI** has a slightly bigger stretch of beach than Praiano – **Marina di Conca**, accessible by way of 300 or so steps after the *Belvedere Hotel* – worth the trek as it's often relatively empty. The longer strip next door is the private preserve of the *Hotel Saraceno* up above (☎089.831.148, ⓦwww.saraceno.it) – one of the posher options along here, with palatial doubles from €235 and a great pool and terrace; it also has its own chapel, which makes it a popular spot for wedding parties. The house below the road past the next headland, a fairly modest white villa with green shutters and its own landing-stage, used to belong to Sophia Loren, and is within swimming distance of the **Spiaggia di Santa Croce** a little further along – also reached by around 400 steps from the roadside signpost. There's another small beach down below the hamlet of **Lone**, which is the last village you pass before the road starts to descend into the outskirts of Amalfi.

Amalfi

Set in a wide cleft in the cliffs, **AMALFI**, a mere 4km or so further east, is the largest town and perhaps the highlight of the coast, and a good place to base yourself. It has been an established seaside resort since Edwardian times, when the British upper classes found the town a pleasant spot to spend their winters, but Amalfi's credentials actually go back much further: it was an independent republic during Byzantine times and one of the great naval powers, with a population of some 70,000. The city's traders established outposts all over the Mediterranean, setting up the Order of the Knights of St John of Jerusalem in the eleventh century. Amalfi was finally vanquished by the Normans in 1131, and the town was devastated by an earthquake in 1343, but the odd remnant of its past glories remains, and there's a crumbly attractiveness to its whitewashed courtyards and alleys that makes it an appealing place for a wander.

Arrival and information

SITA **buses** from Positano, Ravello and Sorrento arrive at Piazza Flavio Gioia on the seafront. **Ferries** and **hydrofoils** from Salerno, Positano, Cápri and Ischia arrive at the landing stages in the tiny harbour, as do the smaller boats to the Grotta dello Smeraldo and other points along the coast. The **tourist office** is in a courtyard on the seafront Corso delle Repubbliche Marinare, next door to the post office (Mon–Fri 9am–1pm & 4–7pm, Sat 9am–noon; ☎089.871.107, ⓦwww.amalfitouristoffice.it), and is not overburdened with information, but it will provide you with a map of the town and answer basic questions.

Accommodation

Amalfi is a great place for a splurge, with few inexpensive options. If you're on a tight budget you could either stay in the adjacent village of **Atrani** (see p.160)

The Regatta of the Maritime Republics

Held since the 1950s, the **Regatta of the Maritime Republics** is a good time to be in town, although the event only takes place once every four years here. The regatta is a boat race with much at stake, as the modern-day descendants of the four maritime city-states of Venice, Genova, Pisa and Amalfi pit their wits and strength against each other to be the fastest rowing team. The race alternates from city to city each year (next held in Amalfi in 2009) – an event that excites huge local interest and a long build-up. Usually held on the first Sunday in June, it begins with a procession of 400 people dressed in historic costume and representing episodes in each city's history. This starts in Atrani about 4.30pm before heading to Amalfi, where the so-called "regatta of the galleons" takes place at 6pm.

The **rules** are pretty exacting: the crews are composed of eight rowers and a helmsman, all of whom must be local men; each team's boat has to be built in the same way and measure and weigh exactly the same as the others – eleven metres long and precisely 760kg. The boats are decked out in traditional colours – blue in Amalfi's case, with the symbol of a winged horse; Genova's boat sports the cross of St George; Pisa's a red eagle; and Venice's the lion of St Mark. The course is two kilometres long, starting opposite the Santa Croce beach a little way west of the city and finishing in front of the specially erected grandstands in Amalfi's harbour not long after. Revellers fill the streets late into the evening, and the day concludes with a fireworks display – whatever the result.

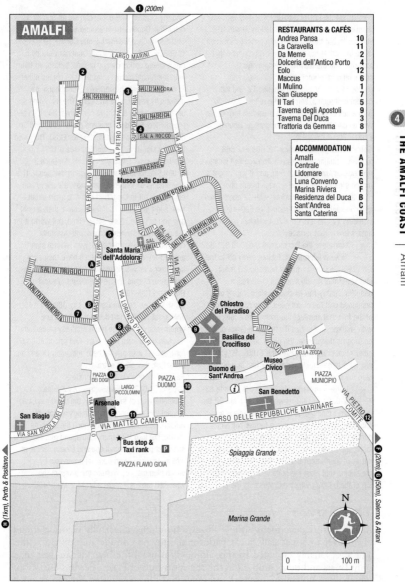

AMALFI

① (200m)

RESTAURANTS & CAFÉS
Andrea Pansa 10
La Caravella 11
Da Meme 2
Dolceria dell'Antico Porto 4
Eolo 12
Maccus 6
Il Mulino 1
San Giuseppe 7
Il Tari 5
Taverna degli Apostoli 9
Taverna Del Duca 3
Trattoria da Gemma 8

ACCOMMODATION
Amalfi A
Centrale D
Lidomare E
Luna Convento G
Marina Riviera F
Residenza del Duca B
Sant'Andrea C
Santa Caterina H

Museo della Carta

Santa Maria dell'Addolora

Chiostro del Paradiso

Basilica del Crocifisso

Duomo di Sant'Andrea

Museo Civico

San Benedetto

PIAZZA MUNICIPIO

PIAZZA DEI DOGI

LARGO PICCOLOMINI

PIAZZA DUOMO

Arsenale

San Biagio

Bus stop & Taxi rank

P

PIAZZA FLAVIO GIOIA

CORSO DELLE REPUBBLICHE MARINARE

Spiaggia Grande

Marina Grande

N

0   100 m

Salerno, Positano, Ischia & Cápri

or opt for the cosy **hostel** *Beata Solitudo*, located at Piazza Avitabile 4 in Agerola, 16km north of Amalfi (☎081.802.5048, Ⓦwww.beatasolitudo.it; dorm beds €11.50, 2–5-person bungalows €50–90, double rooms €80), which has attractive en-suite rooms, as well as a small **campsite** with a few **bungalows**. Regular buses run between Agerola and Amalfi.

Amalfi Via dei Pastai 3 ☎089.872.440, ⓦwww
.hamalfi.it. A relatively large hotel by Amalfi
standards, but tucked away in a peaceful location
off to the left of the main street. Its rooms either
look out onto the narrow passageways that
surround or the hotel garden; although well
equipped with TV, a/c and satellite TV, and with
decent bathrooms, some of the rooms could do
with a lick of paint. There's a breakfast terrace, as
well as parking at a next-door garage. Doubles
€100–170.

Centrale Largo Piccolomini 1☎089.872.608,
ⓦwww.amalfihotelcentrale.it. An excellent location,
overlooking Amalfi's main hub, and if you've got a
bit more money to spend a much better choice
than the dowdier *Sant'Andrea*, with 17 good-sized
and pleasantly furnished rooms for €90–100,
including TV and a/c. Breakfast is taken on the
hotel's lovely roof terrace.

🏃 **Lidomare** Via Piccolomini 9 ☎089.871.332,
ⓦwww.lidomare.it. Tucked away off to the
left of Piazza Duomo, this is perhaps the most
characterful of Amalfi's central cheapies, a
beautiful, family-run ex-ducal palace, nicely old-
fashioned and full of antiques. They're very proud
of the fact that some of the rooms are equipped
with jacuzzis, but in fact it's the sometimes grotty
bathrooms that can let the place down. In every
other respect it's well worth the €100–120 you
pay for a large double room, over half of which
face the sea.

🏃 **Luna Convento** Via Pantaleone Comite 33
☎089.871.002, ⓦwww.lunahotel.it. Off the
main road running east out of Amalfi, this is a
charming five-star housed in a former convent
dating from 1200, with some of the rooms
fashioned from cells. The rooms vary quite a bit –
not all of them merit the high prices – but some
are superb, not least the suite with terrace at the
top of the building which has views up the coast.

And the cloister, where you can sip an aperitif, is
delightful. Doubles from around €300.

Marina Riviera Via Pantaleone Comite 19
☎089.871.104, ⓦwww.hotelmarinariviera.com.
Not a cheap option by any means, but not up there
with the Amalfi's most stratospheric places either.
In a central location overlooking the beach, it's
beautifully kept, bright and light. The 39 rooms are
on the large side and have sea views, and it's very
friendly too. Standard doubles go for €210 and up,
deluxe doubles (with balconies) for €280. They also
host the stylish *Eolo* restaurant (see p.159).

Residenza del Duca Via Mastalo del Duca 3
☎089.873.6365, ⓦwww.residenzadelduca.it. This
tiny hotel is tucked away amongst the alleys and
courtyards off to the left of Amalfi's main street –
take a left just past *Trattoria Gemma,* then a right
and you're there. It's a steep climb, but worth it for
the most recently refurbished and tastefully
realized of Amalfi's *pensioni*, with several smart
antique-style rooms, 2 of which have their own
large terraces with loungers. All have bathrooms
with jacuzzi-style showers, satellite TVs and a/c.
Doubles €120–130.

Sant'Andrea Via San Camera 1 ☎089.871.145.
This small hotel, stuffed full of pictures and
ornaments, couldn't be more centrally placed, and
its plain but decent rooms are well priced at €80
for a double with private bath, including TV and a/c.
Breakfast, though, is extra.

Santa Caterina Via Maura Comite 9
☎089.871.012, ⓦwww.hotelsantacaterina.it. A
kilometre west of town right on the coast road, this
elegant villa with period furnishings is probably
Amalfi's best hotel, and very much the celebrity
choice, but also still family-owned and run. There's a
seawater pool and small spa and fitness centre, as
well as rocks to swim from, all accessible by a lift
which plummets down from the bougainvillea-
wreathed terrace. Rooms start at around €400.

The Town

Amalfi's immediate focus is the seafront, a humming, cheerfully vigorous strand
given over to street stalls, a car park for the town's considerable tourist traffic,
and a reasonably crowded **beach**, although as usual the best bits are pay areas
only. Boats and buses drop off at the transport hub of Piazza Flavio Gioia, from
which all sights can be reached within around fifteen minutes, closest of which
is the imposing **Duomo**, a short stroll north. Running alongside Piazza del
Duomo is the town's main drag, **Via Lorenzo d'Amalfi**, surrounded by a
maze of pretty lanes that are an invitation to explore.

The Duomo and its museum

Dominating the town's main piazza, just in from the seafront, is the **Duomo**
(daily: summer 9am–6.45pm; winter 10am–5pm; church free, cloister, museum
and crypt €2.50), at the top of a steep flight of steps, its tiered, almost gaudy

facade topped by a glazed-tiled cupola that's typical of the area. The church's bronze doors came from Constantinople and date from 1066, while the heavily restored interior is a mixture of Saracen and Romanesque styles, with a major relic in the body of St Andrew buried in its crypt. Off to the left, the cloister – the so-called **Chiostro del Paradiso** – is the most appealing part of the building, oddly Arabic in feel with its whitewashed arches and palms.

The adjacent **museum**, housed in the ancient, bare Basilica di Crocifissio which itself dates back to the sixth century, has various medieval and episcopal treasures, most intriguingly an eighteenth-century sedan chair from Macau, which was used by the bishop of Amalfi; a thirteenth-century mitre sewn with myriad seed pearls, gold panels and gems; and a lovely fourteenth-century bone and ebony inlaid box, made by the renowned Embriachi studio in Venice. Steps lead down from the museum to the heavily decorated **crypt**, where the remains of the apostle St Andrew lie under the altar, brought here (minus head) from Constaninople by the Knights of Malta in 1204. The altar is topped by a giant bronze statue of the saint, and flanked by statues of saints Stefano and Lorenzo by Pietro Bernini – father of the better-known Gianlorenzo. A small receptacle is placed on top of the saint's coffin to catch a miraculous fluid that has supposedly emanated from the saint since the fourteenth century.

The rest of the town

Turn left at the bottom of the cathedral steps and then left again up some steps just before the *Andrea Pansa* café, and a narrow, partly covered passage takes you through to Piazza Municipio. Up the stairs in the left wing of the Municipio itself, the **Museo Civico** (Mon & Fri 8.30am–1.30pm, Tues–Thurs 8.30am– 1.30pm & 4.30–6.30pm; free) is housed in the Morelli Salon – so called for the paintings of the twelve apostles and the *Apocalypse of St John* displayed here, painted by the nineteenth-century Neapolitan painter Domenico Morelli, and reproduced in mosaic on the facade of the cathedral. Also viewable up close are

▲ Amalfi's harbour

Amalfi paper

The **Monte Lattari** or "Mountains of Milk" that rise up behind the coast here are so named for the colour the local water took on when mixed with cotton to make **paper** – an industry that goes back to the twelfth century in Amalfi, when the merchants of the maritime republic brought back the secrets of paper-making techniques from the Arabs they did business with. With a ready supply of fast-running water, Amalfi's location was ideally suited to the manufacture of paper, and it gained such a reputation for both quality and quantity that it was soon patronized by the court at Naples, and then by the Vatican and an international clientele.

The industry thrived here for several hundred years, and only fell into decline in the late eighteenth century, when machinery began to replace the traditional techniques and made it hard for producers to remain competitive; by the mid-twentieth century very few mills remained. However, a few dedicated producers managed to stay in business, and nowadays a tiny industry in luxury and faux-antique paper survives; although inevitably focused on the tourist trade, it does provide an authentic connection with Amalfi's commercial past, as well as turning out exquisite notebooks, envelopes and writing paper of a quality you'd be hard pushed to find anywhere else.

the costumes worn by the great and the good of Amalfi for the Regatta of the Maritime Republics (see box, p.154), and the city banner, showing the emblems of Amalfi – the diagonal red strip and Maltese cross you see everywhere. In front of this is the museum's most valuable treasure, the **Tavoliere Amalfitana**, the laws of the maritime republic, which were formulated during the town's eleventh-century heyday and remained in force for 500 years.

From the Municipio you can cut through to the waterfront, a little way along which the old **Arsenale** is another reminder of the military might of the Amalfi republic; its ancient vaulted interior has been renovated and now hosts art exhibitions and the like. Cutting back into the centre of town, follow the main street of **Via Lorenzo d'Amalfi** back past the Duomo up through the heart of Amalfi. Off to the right and left are the vaulted passageways and alleys that make Amalfi such a joy to explore, and it's difficult to get lost as the steep walls of the valley that encloses the town ensure that you can't stray far.

At the top of Via Genova, a fifteen-minute walk from the main square, the **Museo della Carta** (daily 10am–6.30pm; €3.50; Ⓦwww.museodellacarta.it) is not an essential stop by any means, but it is the only dynamic remnant of the city's now virtually defunct high-quality paper industry, housed in a mill that dates back to 1350 and claiming to be the oldest in Europe. Tours take in the tools of the trade and the original paper-making process and equipment, including that in use when the mill shut down in 1969; there's also a shop selling paper products, calligraphy pens and other stationery.

The valley beyond the museum is still known as the **Valle dei Mulini** (Valley of Mills), from the fact that it was once the heart of Amalfi's paper industry, with around fifteen functioning mills. Only one survives, and it makes all of the high-spec paper you see on sale around town. If you're feeling energetic, you could do a **walk** from here that takes you right up into the heart of the valley, past some of the remains of the mills which sit by the river in charming dereliction (see box, p.160).

Eating and drinking

Inevitably, most of Amalfi's **restaurants** are aimed squarely at the tourist trade, but quality on the whole remains high. The town also boasts two great

pasticcerie that are well worth seeking out: *Andrea Pansa*, right on the main square at Piazza Duomo 40, is *the* place to sit and drink coffee, with an unrivalled selection of cakes and pastries – try the candied sweets made with fruit brought from the Pansa family's nearby farm, or the tasty *sfogliatelle*, chocolate-coated almond biscuits and home-made chocolates; *Dolceria dell'Antico Porto*, tucked away in the arcades off the main street at Supportivo Rua 10, is another fine cake and sweet shop. For picnic supplies, there's a tardis-like **supermarket** on Piazza del Dogi.

Restaurants

La Caravella Via Matteo Camera 12 ☎089.871.029. One of the town's posher options for a night out, or when you're tired of same old offerings everywhere else. They serve creative takes on traditional dishes, all put together with fresh local ingredients – a cut above the rest in price as well as tone. Closed Tues.

Da Meme Salita Marino Sebaste 8 ☎089.830.4549. Decent pasta dishes from €6, pizzas for €4 and even fish fairly cheaply priced at €8 upwards, and a great setting too: you can eat in the vaulted interior of this former monastery, or outside among the white vaulted passageways of old Amalfi.

Eolo Via Pantaleone Comite 3 ☎089.871.241. This restaurant aims to provide Amalfi's most refined dining experience, and with one room, overlooking the main beach, and a small outside terrace, it doesn't do badly – the ultimate romantic Amalfi night out, only spoilt by the schmaltzy background music. The seasonal menu is short, with 4–5 pasta dishes (around €20) and 4–5 *secondi* (around €30) such as salt-encrusted fish and Neapolitan fish stew – but usually with a couple of vegetarian options too.

Maccus Largo S. Maria Maggiore 13 ☎089.873.6385. This place serves good, reasonably priced food from a menu that's a touch different to the competition. All the usual fish and pasta dishes are here, and the *spaghetti alle vongole* is superb, with lots of chilli, but there are also good stand-bys like *pasta e fagioli* and simple steaks. It's nice enough inside, but get an outside table if possible, to get the most out of this atmospheric little square.

Il Mulino Via della Cartiere 36 ☎089.872.223. At the top of the main street, 10min walk from the Duomo, this is a cheery, family-run place that does good home-made pasta *alla pescatora* for around €8. Closed Mon.

San Giuseppe Via Ruggiero 4; no phone. Left off the main street by *Trattoria Gemma* and then right, this very simple restaurant puts a few tables out on a tiny courtyard and serves excellent pizzas and pretty much everything else at low prices – great value. Closed Thurs.

Il Tari Via P. Capuano 9/11 ☎089.871.832. Right in the heart of town on Amalfi's main drag, but not as touristy as you might think, this place is cheap and not at all bad, with all the pasta classics and pizzas too. Closed Tues.

Taverna degli Apostoli Supportivo Sant'Andrea 6 ☎089.872.991. Because of its location next to the cathedral steps, most people assume this is just another tourist joint. But its relatively small menu chalked on the blackboard outside is a good indication that it's not. Tasty food and a warm welcome.

Taverna del Duca Piazza Spirito Santo 26 ☎089.872.755. A cosy atmosphere, and its *felicelli allo scoglio con frutti di mare* (pasta with seafood) is well worth a try. Closed Thurs.

Trattoria da Gemma Via Frá Gerardo Sasso 11 ☎089.871.345. A stalwart of the Amalfi restaurant scene, and still one of the best and most appealing places to eat in town, with a small, carefully considered menu, strong on fish and seafood with mains at around €25, and a lovely terrace overlooking the main street. Closed Wed.

Listings

Boat rental There are quite a few places touting boats by the hour, half-day and day down in the far corner of the harbour; try Amalfi Boats (☎089.831.890, ⓦwww.amalfiboats.it).
Shopping Amalfi is the place for souvenir-shopping, with no end of shops selling *limoncello*, local ceramics and fine paper. Also look out for Domenico Colonnese at Via Lorenzo d'Amalfi 24

(☎089.873.362) – just the place if you're inspired by the maritime history of Amalfi, with lots of nautical merchandise, from sextants to compasses. The waterfront Scuderia del Duca at Largo Cesareo Console 8 (☎089.872.976, ⓦwww.carta-amalfi.it) sells classy paper products, along with prints, cards and books on old Amalfi.

A walk to the Torre dello Zio

Time 2 hours 30 minutes – 3 hours **Level** moderate

A relatively easy **walk** from Amalfi is up the Valle dei Mulini to the village of **Pontone**, perched on a clifftop high above Amalfi, and then back down to the town, taking in, if you have the energy, the paths that loop around the headland that divides Amalfi and Atrani to the ruins of the **Torre dello Ziro**.

To start, follow Amalfi's main street to the top and take a right opposite the paper museum, about 50m past the *Bar della Valle*, and then a sharp left up a moderately steep flight of steps which soon level out to become the path that proceeds gently up the valley. After 1.5km or so it leaves the town behind and becomes unpaved, following the bubbling river past several derelict paper mills. The river alternates between waterfalls and rock pools, some of them deep enough for at least a cooling paddle. At the fourth mill, signalled by a wide arch, the path leads right, climbing out of the valley and up towards Pontone – some 1.5km away at the top. You should arrive at Pontone around 1 hour 45 minutess after you set off from Amalfi's main square. Leave Pontone's main square through the arch and bear right to the main road; cross over and follow the path underneath the church, round to the beginning of the promontory, from where you can either fork right back to Amalfi – a steep, 30-minute descent (not to be attempted in reverse) – or left up some zigzagging flights of steps that lead to the paths that loop around the overgrown outcrop of rock to the ruins of the Torre dello Ziro, where there are some precipitous views (allow at least an additional 30min).

Atrani

A short walk around the headland (take the path off to the right just before the road tunnel and cut through the *Zaccaria* restaurant), **ATRANI** is to all extents and purposes an extension of Amalfi, and was indeed another part of the maritime republic, with a similarly styled church sporting another set of bronze doors from Constantinople, manufactured in 1086; it's here that the Regatta of the Maritime Republics (see box, p.154) begins every four years. It's a quiet place, with a pretty, almost entirely enclosed little square, Piazza Umberto, giving onto a gloriously peaceful (and free) patch of sandy beach – hard to believe the bustle of Amalfi is just around the corner.

Practicalities

As good a reason as any for coming to Atrani is the **hostel** and **hotel** ⚶ *A'Scalinatella* at Piazza Umberto 1 (☎089.871.492, ⓦ www.hostelscalinatella .com; dorms €21–€25, en-suite doubles around €80), one of the cheapest places to stay on the entire coast, a friendly, family-run establishment that offers excellent-value hostel beds and private rooms in various buildings around town, some of them overlooking the main square. There's an office on the square; if that's closed, walk up the street off to the left of the square and the main building is signposted on the right. An attractive alternative is ⚶ *Villa Rosa* at Via Civita (☎082.523.738 or 348.319.6669, ⓦ www.residencevillarosa.it), in a fantastic location up the jagged valley behind Atrani. These ten villas occupy a beautifully kept, flower-filled complex built around a pool, and the well-equipped apartments provide a cool retreat from the summer craziness next door. It's a five-minute hike down to Atrani's main square; the trudge back up the 300 or so steps will keep you fit after too much sun-lounging.

Theatrical Naples

Naples is the home of performance, with an innate exuberance and a flair for drama that stretches back for millennia. The city is perhaps best known for its opera, with a suitably ornate venue in the Teatro di San Carlo, but it doesn't stop there. From the slapstick of commedia dell'arte to the flamenco-style tarantella, the city's long tradition of boisterous entertainment is ingrained in its inhabitants, whose love of theatrics is one of their defining and most appealing characteristics.

Pulcinella on the stage ▲

Naples' Teatro Mercadante ▼

Commedia dell'arte

With its origins in Roman farce, commedia dell'arte has always enjoyed disproportionate popularity in Naples, which is why you see trinkets of one of its main characters, Pulcinella, for sale all over the city. It started as a form of street theatre in the sixteenth century, when masked troupes performed all over the city, with a set cast of characters who would play out a variety of plots on the fundamental themes of love, jealousy, revenge and death, but always with a strong anti-authoritarian streak. The equivalent to Britain's Mr Punch, Pulcinella is a hunchbacked, beak-nosed wifebeater and an outlaw, optimistic one minute and plunged into melancholy the next. He takes his place alongside the other popular figures: Arlechinno, or Harlequin, the forebear of the modern-day clown with his diamond-shaped costume; Colombina, Arlechinno's girlfriend; Il Dottore, an insufferable old bore; and Scaramuccia, a cowardly rogue, among others. Master puppeteer Bruno Leone keeps the tradition alive in Naples with performances involving the whole cast of characters; see Ⓦwww .guarattelle.it for details of shows.

Opera

Many of the stock characters that appear in commedia dell'arte were the inspiration for a peculiarly Neapolitan form of comic opera or opera buffa, a genre which burgeoned in the eighteenth century when Naples was one of Europe's cultural centres. Alessandro Scarlatti was one of its greatest exponents, whose works were distinguished both for their memorable music and their preposterous plots, often involving low-life characters and servants interacting with members of the aristocracy. The prestigious Teatro di San Carlo (see p.94) is the obvious place to catch an opera in the city; as well as staging the old favourites, they are also committed to reviving eighteenth-century comic operas by the likes of Domenico Cimarosa and Giovan Battista Pergolesi.

Neapolitan song

Further evidence of the locals' passion for music is the enduring popularity of the canzone napoletana, almost the archetypical Italian serenade, sung in Neapolitan dialect: one of the city's most cherished traditions. The genre grew out of an annual song-writing competition held for the Festival of Piedigrotta in the mid-nineteenth century, the first of which was won by Donizetti's *Te Voglio Bene Assaje* ("I love you lots"), an instant hit. You'd be surprised how many of these folksy tunes you recognize: *O Sole Mio* and *Funiculì Funiculà* are among the multitude of songs whose fame spread around the world as Neapolitans left their homeland to seek their fortunes abroad. The great tenor Caruso chose Neapolitan songs as encores; Luciano Pavarotti and Placido Domingo both recorded albums of Neapolitan favourites; and the local singer Roberto Murolo was one of the leading lights of the scene, devoting his life's work to the *canzone napoletana*, and recording new songs right up until his death in 2003. Even if you don't catch a performance at one of many venues around town (see p.94), you're unlikely to leave Naples without hearing a hearty rendition of one of the classics: buskers angling for small change belt out Neapolitan favourites all over the city.

▲ The stage at Villa Rufolo, Ravello

▼ A songbook of traditional Neapolitan songs

An early twentieth-century Neapolitan postcard ▲

A tarantella dancer in traditional costume, 1908 ▼

The tarantella

Another Neapolitan tradition with ancient roots is the gypsy-style tarantella, a 2000-year-old folk dance found in the Naples region and throughout southern Italy. Performances involve strident singing, as well as the driving, hypnotic keening of traditional musical **instruments**: the *putipù* (a kind of "burping" drum), the *triccaballacco* (a wooden clacker with small cymbals), the *siscariello* (whistle), and more.

The **origins** of the dance are much debated. One local legend has it that the muses taught it to the women of Cápri to enhance their allure and ability to compete with the Sirens; others believe it derives from the ancient Greek cult of Dionysus, imitating the frenzied ecstasies of the Bacchante – a cult that even the pleasure-seeking Romans banned for its excesses; while some ancient authorities claim it originated in Libya, as a fertility ritual mimicking the mating behaviour of the partridge, considered the most lascivious of all animals – making it the original "lemme see you shake your tail feather" dance. Perhaps the most widespread theory is that it was a hypnotic dance invented to cure a tarantula's bite; the writhing movements are in imitation of the delirium and contortions of the supposed victim.

The tarantella was brought to the Bourbon court in Naples between the seventeenth and eighteenth centuries, and became a more formalized courtship dance. In this version, dancers move alternately, growing ever closer to each other but not quite touching, and twisting their arms and wrists, flamenco-style. Today, the dance is best witnessed at one of the many local saints' days in the small towns north of Naples.

If you're just looking for somewhere for a snack or a coffee, the two principal **bars** on the main square, *Birecto* and *Risacca*, host quite a scene, vying for the custom of young travellers from the *Scalinatella* hostel. There's not much to choose between them, but our favourite is Luigi's *Birecto*, which has reasonably priced drinks, decent pizzas and other food, and free internet access. For a more formal meal, try the **restaurant** *A'Paranza*, on the road that leads inland from the main square, at Traversa Dragone 2 (℡089.811.840; closed Tues), a friendly seafood *trattoria* with fabulous home-made pasta and a speciality of *zuppa di pesce*. *Le Arcate* (℡089.871.367; closed Mon), right by the beach, hogs the best location in Atrani, and serves pizza and a seafood pasta dishes – try the pasta with shrimps and courgettes, or with garlic, chilli and anchovies.

Ravello

The loveliest views of the coast can be had inland from Amalfi in **RAVELLO**: another of the Amalfi Coast's renowned beauty spots. The town was also an independent republic for a while, and for a time an outpost of the Amalfi city-state. Now it's little more than a large village, but its unrivalled location, spread across the top of one of the coast's mountains, 335m up, makes it more than worth the thirty-minute bus ride through the steeply cultivated terraces up from Amalfi.

Like most of this coast, the charms of Ravello are no recent discovery. Wagner set part of *Parsifal*, one of his last operas, here; D.H. Lawrence wrote some of *Lady Chatterley's Lover* in the town; it was the location for John Huston's 1953 film *Beat the Devil* (a languid movie in which the setting easily outshines the plot); and Gore Vidal is just one of the many celebrities who used to spend at least part of the year here; his former home, La Rondinaia or "swallow's nest", is one of the most spectacular villas on the entire coast (see p.165).

Arrival, information and accommodation

SITA **buses** run up to Ravello from Amalfi roughly hourly from Piazza Flavio Gioia and drop off by the main Piazza Duomo. If you're driving, there's a useful **car park** that often has space just below the main square. **Taxis** stop just through the tunnel outside the *Garden* hotel at the top of Via della Repubblica – though be aware that taxis up here from Amalfi are ruinously expensive – around €30 one-way. The **tourist office** is two minutes from the main square, off Via Roma (Mon–Sat: May–Sept 9am–8pm; Oct–April 9am–7pm; ℡089.857.096, ⓦwww.ravello.it).

It's worth staying overnight to experience Ravello's more tranquil side, after the day-trippers have left. It also has some of southern Italy's finest – and priciest – **hotels** along Via San Giovanni del Toro, if you really want to push the boat out. But there are also some excellent budget options, and the tourist office has information on private **rooms**.

Hotels

Garden Via Boccaccio 4 ℡089.857.226, ⓦwww .hotelgardenravello.it. Just the other side of the tunnel from central Ravello, this small hotel and restaurant occupies a prime spot looking up the coast, and makes the most of it with its 10 rooms, all with sea views. The rooms aren't huge but they have small terraces and are well equipped. Doubles €125. Closed end Nov–Feb.

I Limoni Via Gradoni 14 ℡089.858.056, ⓦwww .bb-limoni.com. A bit of a hike, down a series of very steep flights of steps way below the centre of

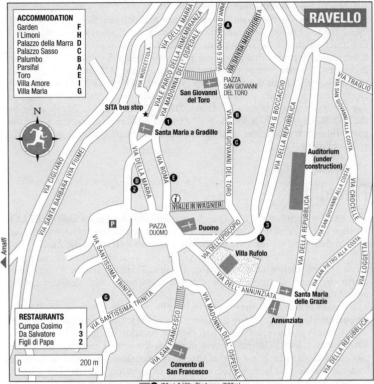

ACCOMMODATION
Garden	**F**
I Limoni	**H**
Palazzo della Marra	**D**
Palazzo Sasso	**C**
Palumbo	**B**
Parsifal	**A**
Toro	**E**
Villa Amore	**I**
Villa Maria	**G**

RESTAURANTS
Cumpa Cosimo	**1**
Da Salvatore	**3**
Figli di Papa	**2**

RAVELLO

▼ **①** (50m) & Villa Cimbrone (500m)

Ravello, but its wonderfully peaceful location, garden and two lovely rooms make this B&B worth considering for €90 a night.

Palazzo della Marra Via della Marra 3 ☏089.858.302, ⓦwww.palazzodellamarra.com. Very central, and with a nice restaurant (see p.165), this is perhaps the cheapest place to stay in central Ravello, with doubles for €90 a night. The 4 rooms are decent enough and you couldn't be more central, just off the main square.

Palazzo Sasso Via San Giovanni del Toro 28 ☏089.818.181, ⓦwww.palazzosasso.com. Housed in a converted medieval villa on the top ridge of Ravello, this is a contender for the best hotel in Italy, with elegant rooms and public areas and attention to detail and service that you don't often find – as well as a pool with about as breath-taking a view as you could imagine. Doubles range from €330 to €500 for a room with a sea view.

Palumbo Via San Giovanni del Toro 16 ☏089.857.244, ⓦwww.hotel-palumbo.it. A great opportunity to experience old-world luxury in a historic building incorporating columns from

Paestum and handsomely decorated with antiques and works of art, including a Guido Reni. Doubles start at €600.

Parsifal Viale G. d'Anna 5 ☏089.857.144, ⓦwww.hotelparsifal.com. This former convent, dating from 1288, is 5min walk from the centre of Ravello, and has 14 doubles, some with sea views, that go for around €135, though they prefer you to take half-board during summer. It's in a great location, and has a beautiful garden overlooking the sea, although some of the rooms are a little uninspiringly furnished.

Toro Via Roma 16 ☏089.857.211, ⓦwww .hoteltoro.it. In about as central a location as you can get, just off the main piazza, the 10 good-sized rooms here vary quite a bit in size and style – many are on the dark side – but they're tastefully furnished and make a cool and peaceful retreat from the touristy hubbub outside, and there's a pleasant garden to boot. Doubles go for €113, with TV but no a/c.

Villa Amore Via dei Fusco 5 ☏089.857.135, ⓦwww.villaamore.it. Down a short path off the main route between the centre of Ravello and the Villa Cimbrone, the rooms here are nothing special but some of them enjoy stunning views. There's also a restaurant that uses ingredients from the hotel's own small and peaceful garden. The drawback is that you have carry your luggage from the nearest car park a 10min walk away back on the main piazza – or pay €5 per piece for the hotel to do it for you. Doubles €95.

Villa Maria Via Santa Chiara 2
T 089.857.255, W www.villamaria.it.

A charming, old-fashioned hotel 5min from the centre of Ravello on the way to Villa Cimbrone. It's not especially cheap, but the price includes free parking and the use of the pool at the nearby co-owned *Giordano*. Doubles start at €225, many of which have large terraces and are in fact much nicer than the "superior" rooms which basically charge more for the views of the sea – not really worth it in a town where the views are hard to avoid anyway.

The Town

Ravello sprawls across quite a wide area, but its centre is indisputably Piazza Duomo, a large and rather featureless square edged by one or two cafés and focused on the **Duomo**. A few minutes south and east of the Duomo respectively, **Villa Rufolo** and **Villa Cimbrone** offer lush greenery and dazzling panoramas, their gardens making photogenic locations for the town's international music festival (see box below).

The Duomo and its museum

Ravello's **Duomo** (daily 9am–7pm; after noon, entrance via the museum) is a bright eleventh-century church, renovated in 1786, that's dedicated to St Pantaleone, a fourth-century saint with miraculous blood like that of Naples' San Gennaro (see p.56). A pair of twelfth-century bronze doors, cast with 54 scenes of the Passion, lead to a richly ornamented interior, with two monumental marble thirteenth-century pulpits, both wonderfully adorned with intricate and glittering mosaics. The more elaborate of the two, to the right of the altar, the Gospel pulpit, dated 1272, sports dragons and birds on spiral columns supported by six roaring lions, and the coat of arms and the vivacious profiles of the Rufolo family, the donors, above the door, while on the left, the Epistle pulpit depicts *Jonah and the Whale*. The chapel to the left of the main altar is dedicated to San Pantaleone and holds a vial of his blood – a murky liquid that is said to become translucent every July 27, the day of his martyrdom; a door gives access to a passage behind the altar if you want to get a closer look. Downstairs in the crypt, the **museum** (daily 9am–7pm; €2) holds the superb bust of Sigilgaita Rufolo and the embossed silver and wood reliquary of Saint Barbara, alongside a collection of highly decorative, fluid mosaic and marble reliefs from the thirteenth century.

Villa Rufolo and around

The Rufolos figure again on the other side of the square, where various leftovers of their **Villa Rufolo** (daily: June–Sept 9am–9pm; Oct–May 9am–6pm;

The Ravello Festival

Ravello's **arts festival** (W www.ravellofestival.com) has grown into quite an annual event, and these days it dominates the summer months, with performances all over town stretching from the end of June to the end of October. Concentrating on classical music, dance, film and the visual arts, it makes the most of the town's settings and attracts an increasingly high level of performers. It can only get better when the inauguration of Oscar Neimeyer's new **Auditorium** in 2009 will give it what it's been lacking: a venue of international stature.

€5) lie scattered among lush gardens overlooking the precipitous coastline; this is the spectacular main venue for the prestigious series of open-air chamber concerts held from March to October; though there are plans to build a viewless modern auditorium for the festival on the same site, which critics fear could prove a triumph of acoustics over aesthetics. The programme is widely advertised and tickets cost €20 (℡089.858.149, ⓦwww.ravelloarts .org). If the crowds – best avoided by coming early in the morning – put you off, turn left by the entrance and walk up the steps over the tunnel for the best (free) view over the shore, from where it's a pleasant stroll through the back end of Ravello to the main square.

Turn right outside Villa Rufolo and a tunnel takes you through to the other side of Ravello's central ridge. Or you can walk across the footbridge to the end of the town's upper level, where **Via San Giovanni del Toro** is home to some of Ravello's most prestigious hotels (see p.162), though sadly its municipal gardens are currently closed for restoration. Down below, the **Ravello Auditorium** is being built on Via della Repubblica, and it's an enormous undertaking, designed by the prolific Brazilian architect – 101 at the time of writing, no less – Oscar Niemeyer; it's supposed to be ready in time for the 2009 Ravello Festival (see box, p.163).

Villa Cimbrone
Turn left out of Villa Rufolo and walk in the opposite direction through some of Ravello's most characteristic and peaceful streets to reach the **Villa Cimbrone** (daily 9am–sunset; ⓦwww.villacimbrone.com; €6), ten minutes away, whose formal gardens spread across the furthest tip of Ravello's ridge. It's a unique and ravishing spot: if Ravello itself sometimes feels removed from the rest of the coast, then here you can feel one step removed from the rest of Ravello, such is the sense of isolation. Most of the original buildings are given

▲ View from Villa Rufolo, Ravello

La Rondinaia

The only place to rival the views from the Villa Cimbrone's belvederes is the former home of maverick US writer **Gore Vidal**, La Rondinaia or "swallow's nest", which was built by the former owner of the Villa Cimbrone for his second daughter in 1930 and juts out over the edge of the ocean in a spectacular location next door to the villa's gardens – as Vidal himself had it, "I don't live in Ravello, I live at La Rondinaia". A magnificent, six-floored property, only reachable on foot, Vidal bought the place in 1972 for around a quarter of a million dollars and sold it in 2006 for many times that amount when he became too infirm to negotiate its steps and balconies (he currently lives in Los Angeles). During the thirty or so years he lived here Vidal entertained guests as diverse as Sting and Tennessee Williams, Erica Jong, Andy Warhol and the Clintons, to name just a few. The villa was bought by a hotel developer, but was put on the market again shortly afterwards and its future is currently uncertain. With its unique cachet – not to mention its stratospheric price tag – it's likely that it will end up as a luxury hotel; with any luck, though, the developers will preserve the Vidal connection, as well as making it accessible to the public.

over to a smart hotel, but you can peep into the crumbly, flower-hung cloister as you go in, and the open crypt down the steps from here – perhaps the only crypt in the world with views over cliffs and open sea. But the **gardens** are entirely accessible, dotted with statues and leading down to what must be the most famous spot in Ravello – a belvedere, fittingly known as the "terrace of infinity" that looks down to Atrani and the sea. There's a pricey **café** serving salads, sandwiches and ice creams with tables set out on the grass, from which you can enjoy the views of the Dragone valley below. Elsewhere in the gardens there are any number of corners to explore, and you could spend a good few hours here if you're in no hurry. Take in the viewpoints on the western side at the little Tempietto di Bacco and Poggio di Mercurio, wander through the rose garden near the entrance, and consider stopping for lunch at the hotel's lovely restaurant. Better yet, stay at the hotel (ⓦ www.villacimbrone.com; doubles from €410) or visit Gore Vidal's former home, Villa Rondinaia (see box above), also set in the gardens, to really soak up the unique atmosphere.

Eating and drinking

Ravello isn't overloaded with restaurants, and most of its **restaurants** are attached to hotels. Not surprisingly, the cheaper places are those without views, but whatever the location, you won't eat badly anywhere.

Cumpa Cosimo Via Roma 48
ⓣ 089.857.988. This long-standing, unpretentious favourite serves great local food – homemade pasta, great fish *fritti misti* – at moderate prices. No views or outside seating.

Da Salvatore Via della Repubblica 2
ⓣ 089.857.227. In business for over fifty years, *Salvatore* has fantastic views from the restaurant and outside terrace, and an intriguing menu – tuna carbonara, gnocchi with cod, and rabbit doughnuts, to name just some of the more bizarre items. The food is excellent, and not all weird (you can order spaghetti *alle vongole* and

steak if you want). *Primi* from €12 and mains around €15; there's also a cheaper pizzeria downstairs, which does starters and pizzas only in the evenings.

Figli di Papa Via della Marra 7 ⓣ 089.858.302. Housed in the *Palazzo della Marra* hotel, the menu here is quite varied and well priced, with a reasonable selection of non-fish options like cannelloni, Italian sausage and escalopes, and good *antipasti* too. You can eat outside on the terrace – and for once you're not paying for the views. They also do a two-course tourist menu for €15. Closed Tues Nov–March.

The coast to Salerno

The coast between Amalfi and Salerno is quite different from that further west – not as busy and less obviously wealthy, its settlements a mixture of down-to-earth resorts like **Minori**, **Maiori** and **Vietri** and small, relatively undisturbed fishing villages like **Cetara** and **Erchie**. It's no less dramatic, though, the coast road only really straightening out as you come into Vietri, which signals the end of the Amalfi Coast.

Minori

There's not much to **MINORI**, a small town named after the Regina Minor river, which reaches the sea here – just a decent sandy beach fronting the main road, behind which there's a compact old centre and Minori's only real sight, right by the main road, the **Villa Romana** (daily 9am–6.30pm; free), where you can see the remains of an originally two-storey Roman villa, most notably a frescoed and mosaiced nymphaeum and pool. There are a couple of good family-owned places to **eat** nearby: *Il Giardiniello*, just two minutes back from the seafront at Corso Vittorio Emanuele 17 (℡089.877.050), whose covered garden is a nice place to escape the heat and sit down to a seafood feast; and ⅄ *La Botte*, down below road level at Via Santa Maria Vetrano 15 (℡089.877.893; closed Tues), around the corner from the Villa Romana, which is a little more basic but just as good, with excellent pasta, meat and fish – try the *orechiette* with seafood and broccoli – eaten either in the restaurant's vaulted interior or the covered patio outside.

Maiori

Around the next headland from Minori, **MAIORI** sits at the mouth of the larger tributary of the same river – the Regina Maior – and it's this that is responsible for the town's largely modern and slightly characterless appearance: it was almost entirely destroyed by floods in 1952. These days it's home to the coast's longest stretch of beach and is as good a place as any along here to rest up and enjoy the seaside. At the far end of Maiori's bay, the *Torre Normanna*, housed in the bulky sixteenth-century tower on the main road at Via Diego Tajani 4 (℡089.877.100), is the town's best place to eat, and certainly its easiest to find. It has a smart **restaurant** in the vaulted interior of the tower that serves good fish and great pizzas, as well as a relaxing **bar**, and even its own private beach down below.

Erchie

The coast from Maiori to Vietri is if anything more rugged, and more sparsely populated than in the other direction towards Positano, though the road doesn't have the same number of dizzyingly high hairpins either. Beyond Maiori the first settlement of any kind is **ERCHIE**, a small village nestled in a pretty cove that grew up originally in the shadow of a Benedictine monastery. It's little more than a cluster of buildings – two or three restaurants, a grocer's and *tabacchi* and a handful of **rooms** to let – but the **beach** is one of the coast's best. A reasonably wide stretch with fairly fine sand, it's more or less dominated by scruffy beachfront establishments that levy the usual charges for umbrellas and sun-loungers – but is nonetheless quite a gem.

Cetara

CETARA, just beyond, is a busy and – for the Amalfi coast – unpretentious and untouristed fishing village, straggling down its valley to a small port area and a slightly scrappy stone and shingle beach. The furthest eastern outpost of the Amalfi republic, its name is based on a old word for "tuna net", but in fact the fish they're known for landing here are anchovies, samples of which you can taste in its many restaurants – of which there are several located on and around the main drag. Try *Il Convento*, Piazza San Francesco 16 (℡089.261.039; closed Wed), a cavernous dining room up above the main street with a terrace outside to watch the evening *passeggiata*. Down by the harbour, *A Cianciola*, Piazza Cantone 13 (℡089.261.828; closed Mon), is also good, while *Acqua Pazza*, on the main street at Corso Garibaldi 38 (℡089.261.606; closed Mon), attempts to be the coolest restaurant in town, but it too serves decent food. If you want to **stay**, the *Hotel Cetus* (℡089.2611388; doubles €180–290), just outside Cetara, in the direction of Vietri, perched right by the road and with steps leading down to a tiny private beach, is a good choice. It has clean, modern rooms, as well as a restaurant and terrace with views round the bay to Salerno.

Vietri sul Mare

A few kilometres further down the coast from Cetara, **VIETRI SUL MARE** is a larger and more sprawling town than anywhere else along the Amalfi Coast, its eastern suburbs almost mingling with the port areas of Salerno, for which it is the closest major resort. Its wide sandy beaches are well used, but the town is mostly known as a centre of the ceramics industry, in particular the brightly coloured Mediterranean pottery that you will have seen in every town along the coast. Nonetheless the stuff they still make here is a cut above what you'll find elsewhere, as evidenced in the **Museo della Ceramica Vietrese**, housed in a tower of the Villa Guariglia in the Raito quarter of town (Mon–Sat 8.30am–3.30pm, Sun 8.30am–1pm; free), with displays of precious antique ceramics and other pieces by the colony of German artists and ceramicists who have been attracted here over the years – as well as a collection of fans, paintings and various pieces of silverware and weaponry in the main part of the villa. The **Ceramica Artistica Solimene**, at Via Madonna degli Angeli 7, is also worth a look: it's the longest-established and best manufacturer of the local pottery, in business for more than a century.

Salerno

Capital of Campania's southernmost province, and an alternative jumping-off point for the Amalfi Coast, the lively port of **SALERNO** is much less chaotic than Naples and is well off most travellers' itineraries, giving it a pleasant, relaxed air. It has a good supply of cheap accommodation, which makes it a reasonable base for some of the closer Amalfi resorts and for the ancient site of Paestum to the south. During medieval times the town's medical school was the most eminent in Europe; more recently, it was the site of the Allied landing of September 9, 1943 – which reduced much of the centre to rubble. The subsequent rebuilding has restored neither charm nor efficiency to the town centre, which is an odd mixture of wide, rather characterless boulevards and a medieval core full of intriguingly dark corners and alleys. It is, however, a lively place, with a busy seafront boulevard and plenty of nightlife and shops.

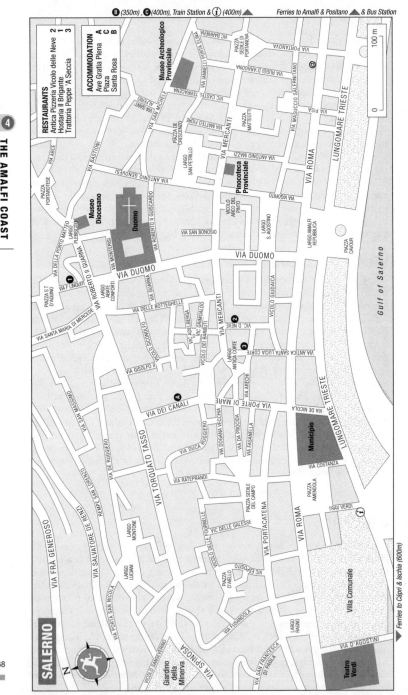

4

168

SALERNO

N

B (350m) , **C** (400m), Train Station & **i** (400m) ▲

RESTAURANTS

Antica Pizzeria Vicolo delle Neve 2
Hostaria Il Brigante 1
Trattoria Peppe 'A Seccia 3

ACCOMMODATION

Ave Gratia Plena A
Plaza C
Santa Rosa B

Museo Archeologico
Provinciale

PIAZZA
SEDILE DI
PORTANOVA

VIA BARRIERA

VIA IANNELLI PORTA ELINA

VIA CASTEL TERRACENA

VIA RUGGI D'ARAGONA

VIA PORTANOVA

VIA SANT'ALFIERO

VIA SAN MICHELE

VIA MATTEO FIORE

PIAZZA DE
DESCENZA

LARGO
SAN PETRILLO

VIA ANTONIO GENOVESI

VIA MERCANTI

PIAZZA
MATTEOTTI

VIA ANTONIO MAZZI

VIA MASUCCIO SALERNITANO

VIA PISA

VIA ROMA

LUNGOMARE TRIESTE

0   100 m

PIAZZA
PORTAROTESE

VIA ARCE

VIA BASTIONI

Museo
Diocesano

LARGO
PLEBISCITO

Duomo

VIA ROBERTO IL GUISCARDO

VIA SAN BONOSIO

Pinacoteca
Provinciale

VICOLO
ARCO DEL
PINTO

LARGO
S. AGOSTINO

VIA VIGHRITO

LARGO AMALFI
REPUBLICA

VIA DUOMO

VIA DUOMO

PIAZZA
CAVOUR

Gulf of Salerno

VIA DELLA PORTO MATTEO

LARGO
DEL PORTO MATTEO

VIA MONTERISI

VIA ROBERTO IL GUARNA

PIAZZA ST
D'AQUINO

VIA F LINGUITI

VIA SANTA MARIA DI MERCEDE

LARGO
ABATE
CONFORTI

VIA GUARNA

VIA DELLE BOTTEGHELLE

VIA ADELBERGA

VICOLO SICONOLFO

VIC GRIMOALDO

VICOLO DEI BARBUTI

VIA MERCANTI

VIC D NEVE

VIC ANTICA SANTA LUCIA CORTE

LARGO
ANTICA CORTE

VICOLO GIUDAICA

VIA DE NICOLA

LUNGOMARE TRIESTE

VIA GISOLFO II

VIA DEI CANALI

VIA TORQUATO TASSO

VIA SAN MASSIMO

VIA DE RUGGIERO

VIA PORTE DI MARE

VIA ARECHI

VIA DOGANA VECCHIA

VIA DA PROCIDA

VIA FASANELLA

Municipio

VIA COSTANZA

VIA DUCA RUGGIERO

VIA RATEPRANDI

PIAZZA AMENDOLA

VIA FRÀ GENEROSO

VIA SALVATORE DE RENZI

REMPE SAN LORENZO

LARGO
MONTONE

VIA PORTACATENA

VIA ROMA

TRAV VERDI

i

VIA PORTA SAN NICOLA

LARGO
LUCIANI

VICOLO DELLE FOURNELLE

VIC DELLE GALESSE

PIAZZA SEDILE
DEL CAMPO

PIAZZA
D'AIELLO

VIA FISANDOLA

VIC ESPOSITO

LARGO
RAGNO

Villa Comunale

VIA D'AGOSTINI

Giardino
della
Minerva

VICOLO SANS SEVERINO

VIA SPINOSA

VIA SAN FRANCESCA
DI PAOLA

Teatro
Verdi

▼ Ferries to Cápri & Ischia (600m)

Arrival, information and accommodation

Salerno's **train station** lies at the southeastern end of the town centre on Piazza Vittorio Veneto. City and local **buses** pull up here; those from Paestum and further south arrive and leave from Piazza della Concordia, down by the waterside nearby; buses from Naples use the SITA bus station at Corso Garibaldi 119. **Ferries** and **hydrofoils** from Amalfi, Cápri and Positano arrive in the harbour, five minutes' walk from the centre of town, and ten minutes from the train station.

There are two **tourist offices**: one right in front of the station on the corner of Piazza Vittorio Veneto and Corso Garibaldi (Mon–Fri 9am–2pm & 3–8pm, Sat 9am–1pm & 3.30–7.30pm; ☎089.230.411); and another, slightly more helpful one, on the seafront at Lungomare Trieste 7/9 (Mon–Fri 9am–2pm & 3–8pm, Sat & Sun 9am–noon; ☎089.224.744).

The town isn't chock-full of **hotels**: the comfortable *Plaza*, Piazza Vittorio Veneto 42 (☎089.224.477, ⓦwww.plazasalerno.it), is a decent choice and handy for transport and the town centre, with doubles for around €90; and, close by, the friendly if fairly basic *Santa Rosa* on the second floor at Corso Vittorio Emanuele 16 (☎089.225.346), provides a cheaper alternative, with doubles for €75. Alternatively, there's the *Ave Gratia Plena* official HI **youth hostel**, the other side of the centre on Via dei Canali (☎089.234.776, ⓦwww.ostellodisalerno.it), a clean and welcoming place with dorms (€15) and doubles (€45–60) in a former church and cloister complex – follow Via Mercanti to its end, continue under the arch onto Via Dogana and Via dei Canali is on the right.

The Town

Although low on sights, Salerno's vibrant centre is a pleasant place to wander through, especially the ramshackle old medieval quarter, which starts at the far end of the pedestrianized main shopping drag of **Corso Vittorio Emanuele**. The old quarter's main street, **Via Mercanti**, has been spruced up in recent years; part of the makeover is the **Pinacoteca Provinciale di Salerno**, housed in the seventeenth-century Palazzo Pinto at Via Mercanti 63 (Tues–Sun 9am–7.45pm; free) – half a dozen rooms, displaying some fairly missable paintings. There are a few highlights, however, including some fifteenth-century altarpieces and a couple of works by Carlo Rosa and other followers of the Neapolitan Baroque artists, but it's the small collection of modern paintings and drawings of local scenes – of Salerno, Vietri and Maiori – that is most enjoyable.

Off to the right of Via dei Mercanti, up Via Duomo, the **Duomo** (Mon–Sat 10am–6.30pm, Sun 1–6.30pm) is Salerno's highlight, an enormous church built in 1076 by Robert Guiscard and dedicated to St Matthew. Entrance is through a cool and shady courtyard, built with columns plundered from Paestum, and centring on a gently gurgling fountain set in an equally ancient bowl. In the heavily restored interior, the two elegant mosaic pulpits are the highlight, the one on the left dating from 1173, the other, with its matching paschal candlesticks, a century later. Immediately behind there's more sumptuous mosaic work in the screens of the choir, as well as the quietly expressive fifteenth-century tomb of Margaret of Anjou, wife of Charles III of Durazzo, in the left aisle. To the left of the tomb, steps lead down to the polychrome marble crypt, which holds the body of St Matthew, brought here in the tenth century.

From the cathedral, turn right at the bottom of the steps for the **Museo Diocesano** (daily 9.30am–12.30pm & 3–6.30pm; free), where the sole attraction is a large eleventh-century altar-front, embellished with ivory panels, 69 in all, depicting Biblical scenes, that claims to be the largest work of its kind in the world. If you turn left out of the church, left at the bottom of the steps, left again and then first right, 100m or so further on is the **Museo Archeologico Provinciale** (Tues–Sun 9am–7.45pm; free), which occupies two floors of a restored Romanesque palace. It's full of local archeological finds, and has an array of terracotta heads and votive figurines, jewellery, lamps and household objects, from Etruscan as well as Roman times, but its most alluring piece is a sensual *Head of Apollo* upstairs, a Roman bronze fished from the Gulf of Salerno in the 1930s.

However, after the cathedral, Salerno's best – and most unique – attraction is the **Giardino della Minerva** on Via Ferrante Sanseverino (summer Tues–Sun 9am–1pm & 5–9pm, winter Mon 3–6pm, Tues–Sun 9am–1.30pm; free), a medicinal garden that was restored a decade ago to something like it would have been in the time of Matteo Silvatico, court physician to the king of Naples in the fourteenth century. Set across a series of terraces, laid out according to medieval medical principles and traversed by channels of tinkling water, it's a gloriously fragrant place, its shady terraces a wonderful retreat in summer – and there's even a café serving herbal tea to ensure you leave healthier than you arrived.

Eating and drinking

Salerno is a sociable place, and while it's not geared towards tourists there are plenty of inviting places to **eat and drink**. The *Hostaria Il Brigante*, just above the cathedral at Via Fratelli Linguiti 4 (℡089.226.592; closed Mon) is a great, old-fashioned *osteria* near the Duomo with mains at around €10 – try the *zuppa dell'aglio* (garlic soup) and dishes made with *calamarata* (tubular pasta). The *Antica Pizzeria Vicolo della Neve* (℡089.225.705; closed Wed & lunch), a left turn off Via Mercanti about 50m past the Duomo, is an attractively

▲ The Giardino della Minerva

downbeat place serving pizzas and local specialities, with a particularly good *calzone*, while a block further on, *Trattoria Peppe 'A Seccia*, Via Antica Corte 5 (☎089.220.518; closed Mon), has tables outside on its small square and serves good fish and seafood, including *zuppa di cozze* (mussel soup), at reasonable prices.

Paestum

About an hour's bus ride south of Salerno, the ancient site of **PAESTUM** (daily 9am–1hr before sunset; site €4, site and museum €6.50) spreads across a large area at the bottom end of the **Piana del Sele** – a wide, flat plain grazed by the buffalo that produce a good quantity of southern Italy's mozzarella cheese. Paestum, or Poseidonia as it was known, was founded by Greeks from Sybaris in the sixth century BC, and later, in 273 BC, colonized by the Romans, who Latinized the name. But by the ninth century a combination of malaria and Saracen raids had decimated the population and left the buildings deserted and gradually overtaken by thick forest, and the site wasn't rediscovered until the eighteenth century during the building of a road through here.

The site and museum

Paestum is a dramatic, windswept place even now ("inexpressibly grand", Shelley called it), mostly unrecognizable ruin but with three golden-stoned **temples** that are among the best-preserved Doric temples in Europe. Of these, the Temple of Neptune, dating from about 450 BC, is the most complete, with only its roof and parts of the inner walls missing. The Basilica of Hera, built a century or so earlier, retains its double rows of columns, while the Temple of Ceres at the northern end of the site was used as a Christian church for a time. In between, the forum is little more than an open space, and the buildings around are mere foundations.

The splendid **museum** (daily 9am–7pm; closed first and third Mon every month; €4, or €6.50 including site), across the road, holds Greek and Roman finds from the site and around. Straight ahead of you as you enter are some stunning sixth-century bronze vases (*hydriae*), decorated with rams, lions and sphinxes; behind them lies more bronze – gleaming helmets, breastplates and greaves. Make a point of seeing the rare Greek tomb paintings, the best of which are from the Tomb of the Diver, graceful and expressively naturalistic pieces of work, including a diver in mid-plunge, said to represent the passage from life to death, and male lovers banqueting. Attractive fourth-century terracotta plates depict all sorts of comestibles – fruit, sweets and cheese – and a set of weathered, archaic-period Greek metopes from another temple at the mouth of the Sele River, a few kilometres north, shows scenes of fighting and hunting. On the first floor, which is devoted to Roman finds, highlights include a statue of an abstracted-looking Pan with his pipes, a third-century relief showing a baby in pointed hat with amulets, and a sarcophagus cover of a tenderly embracing couple.

Practicalities

It's perfectly feasible to see Paestum on a day-trip from Salerno. CSTP **bus** #34 runs here from Salerno train station, a journey of 55 minutes. The **tourist office**, tucked away on a side street to the left of the museum at Via Magna Grecia 887 (Mon–Sat 9am–1pm & 3–7pm, closes 5pm in winter, Sun 9am–1pm; ℡0828.811.016, Ⓦwww.infopaestum.it), has details of **accommodation**: there are plenty of hotels and campsites strewn along the sandy shore about a fifteen-minute walk beyond the site. Close to the site, to the left of where the main road hits the beach, is the *Calypso*, Via Mantegna 63 (℡0828.811.031, Ⓦwww .calypsohotel.com; doubles €70–110), one of the few hotels around that can cope with unusual dietary requests (with traditional food as well). The cheerful and very good-value *Baia del Sole*, Via Torre di Mare 48 (℡0828.811.119, Ⓦwww.baiadelsolepaestum.it; doubles around €50), does not require half board in high season and has a nice garden. If you prefer to be a little more secluded try *Villa Rita* at Via Nettuno 9 (℡0828.811.081, Ⓦwww.hotelvillarita.it; doubles €80–90), which is pleasantly situated in relaxing gardens with a pool, just south of the archeological site.

There's some excellent food in the area, with the locally produced buffalo mozzarella featuring heavily on menus of most **restaurants**. Try the excellent *Nettuno* on Via Principe di Piemonte (℡0828.811.028; lunch only), in an old building right by the temples, where the house speciality is crepes with mozzarella, or the more intimate and upmarket *Enoteca Tavernelle*, Via Tavernelle 14 (℡0828.722.440), about 1km out on the Salerno road.

The islands

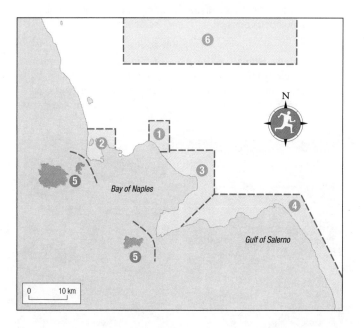

CHAPTER 5 # Highlights

✳ **Villa Jovis, Cápri** The ruins
of Tiberius' city-sized palace
overlook a stunning panorama
of the Amalfi Coast.
See p.184

✳ **Villa San Michele, Cápri** The
Swedish physician's house
and classical collections are
a marvellously poetic re-
creation of ancient splendours
in a tremendous position.
See p.188

✳ **La Mortella, Ischia** This
verdant garden paradise is
a labour of love by a noted
expat couple. See p.205

✳ **Chiaiolella Beach, Prócida**
The tiny island's most
appealing beach includes
a picturesque cove, a well-
appointed lido and views of
the Vivara nature reserve.
See p.206

✳ **Spiaggia dei Maronti, Ischia**
The island's broadest, longest
beach, on Ischia's tranquil
southern side. See p.209

✳ **Monte Epomeo, Ischia**
Approached from all sides,
the perfect cone of this
dormant volcano makes for
memorable hiking. See p.210

▲ La Mortella

The islands

Guarding each prong of the Bay of Naples, the alluring trio of **Cápri**, **Ischia** and **Prócida** make up the best-known group of Italian islands. Although radically different from each other in terms of landscape and culture, each has been the stuff of myth, anecdote and, in some instances, international scandal.

Cápri swarms with visitors but is so beautiful that a day or more here is by no means time squandered. The most dramatic and storied by far, it's a small place that has spurred imaginations and incited lavish, as well as lascivious, dreams for millennia. Home to the mythical Sirens of the ancient world, it has been much-eulogized as a playground of the super-rich in the years since – though it has now settled down to a lucrative existence as a target for day-trippers from the mainland.

The largest island of the three, low-key **Ischia**, absorbs tourists more readily and is a lively and attractive setting in which to while away an entire holiday. Its natural hot springs have always been a target for cure-seekers; these days, it mostly attracts package tourists (predominantly from Germany) and weekenders from Naples, but its size means that it never feels as crowded as Cápri, and the sandy beaches and green volcanic interior are further draws.

Pretty **Prócida** is notable for its unpretentious, non-touristy attitude. The smallest but most densely populated of the islands, it has least to offer in the way of sights, but is also arguably the most unspoiled. Life goes on here much as it has for generations, and happily, tourism is still an afterthought, making it probably the best venue for peaceful lazing since it's relatively untouched by the high-season swarm.

Doing all three of the islands any kind of justice reasonably requires at least a week. Prócida is easily covered on foot in a day or two; Cápri deserves at least an overnight stay to see what it's really like after the tidal wave of the curious has left; and to see multifaceted Ischia properly could certainly take up to a week all by itself. Travelling to and between the islands is a fairly simple matter, with conveniently scheduled **ferries** and hydrofoils (see box, p.171).

The islands on the web

Ⓦ**www.capri.net** An excellent site with a wealth of information on the island, from ferry schedules to helicopter rental.

Ⓦ**www.ischiaonline.it** Full of useful details on the island's main settlements, plus a hotel booking service and events calendar.

Ⓦ**www.procida.it** Ferry timetables, weather reports and much besides.

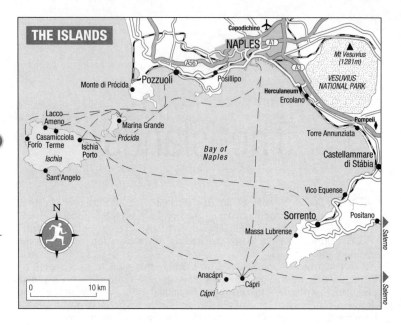

Cápri

The island of **CÁPRI** has long been the most sought-after destination in the Bay of Naples. No place is more glamorous than this tiny isle of immense, weatherworn crags, jutting out of the deep blue waters just off the Sorrentine peninsula. Composed primarily of softly gleaming white limestone, Cápri is a mostly perpendicular environment, presenting tall rock faces around much of its perimeter. Still, where vegetation does grow across the island's jagged surface, it is lush, dense and fragrant – nearly a thousand species of flowers and plants grow here – helped along by the agreeable climate.

Cápri tends to get a mixed press, the consensus being that while it's undoubtedly an attractive place, it's pretty much ruined by the crowds and the prices. And it *is* crowded, to the degree that in July and August, and on all summer weekends, it would be sensible to give it a miss. But reports that the island has been irreparably spoilt are overstated, and though it is expensive, prices aren't much higher than at other major Italian resorts; you can find reasonably priced and attractive accommodation in Anacápri, and even in Cápri town, if you know where to look.

High season brings day-trippers in their droves, most of whom come to see the **Blue Grotto**, the re-discovery of which in the early nineteenth century coincided with the rise of tourism. But most are gone by sundown, when the real Cápri comes out of hiding, offering leafy bowers and stunning views that few tourists ever get to see. Celebrities and their hangers-on have been flocking to these shores for decades, but these days they come to enjoy the island's secret retreats in peace and quiet, notwithstanding the island's petite size – a mere 6km long and 2.7km wide. Beyond its inevitably touristy core, the island retains an unspoiled charm that is well worth seeking out.

Some history

Cápri has been inhabited since Palaeolithic times, and Greek colonists from Cumae and, later, Neapolis are known to have used it as an outpost as early as the eighth century BC. The island's illustrious reputation dates back about 2000 years, to the days when it served as the private pleasure enclave of Roman emperors. It entered the history books in 29 BC when soon-to-be Emperor Augustus persuaded the local Greek rulers to trade him Cápri for Ischia, which belonged to Rome at the time. Then, most famously, in 27 AD the island was chosen by **Emperor Tiberius** as the spot where he wanted to live out the remainder of his days: in effect, making Cápri the empire's de facto capital for a time. Literary gossipmonger Suetonius, in his *Twelve Caesars*, claims that Tiberius got up to all sorts of debaucheries while ensconced here, including throwing hapless subjects off the island's sheer cliffs. Tiberius had some twelve sumptuous palaces built on the island, one dedicated to each of the Olympian gods – most notably **Villa Jovis**, the House of Jove (Jupiter), the vast ruins of which still dominate the eastern peak.

Following the fall of Rome, Cápri went about its modestly bucolic business for some fifteen hundred years, well out of the international limelight. Finally, in 1776, it was none other than the **Marquis de Sade** who visited the island and discovered its potential for personal freedom – and, judging from his letters, sex tourism. He was filled with admiration for the classical beauty of the Cápri natives of both sexes and wrote enthusiastically about their charms. That occasion served not only to carry forward the island's ancient libertine tradition, but also to set the dominant tone for over a century to come. Ancient tradition held the island to be the home of the cannibalistic Sirens, whose ravishing, maddening song lured men to their doom, and the island's powers of seduction were to attract a legion of modern-day pleasure-seekers. For more on the island's many devotees in recent history, see the box on p.185.

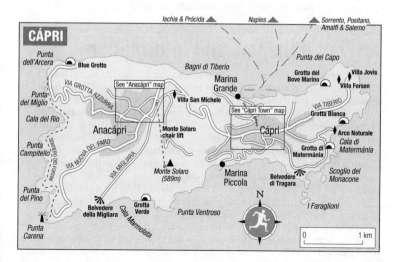

The easiest point of departure to the islands for most visitors is Naples' main port, the **Molo Beverello** at the bottom of Piazza Municipio, though the quayside at **Mergellina** is also handy enough, with the port of **Pozzuoli** a rather out-of-the-way option (providing transport to Prócida and Ischia only). If departing from the Amalfi Coast, take the ferry or hydrofoil from **Sorrento** to Cápri or Ischia. From April to October, there are also hydrofoils operated by Metrò del Mare, part of the public transport network, to Cápri, if not the other islands, from around the Bay and the Gulf of Salerno. There are also hydrofoils between Cápri and Ischia – though, curiously, these two major islands are not at all well connected at any time of year.

Whichever route you take, **day-trips** are quite feasible; usually the last connection delivers you back on the mainland in time for dinner. On foot, you can simply buy **tickets** when you turn up at the offices at the port; in general it's better to buy a single rather than a return ticket since it doesn't work out to be more expensive and you retain more flexibility on the time you come back. Having said that, on summer Sundays (especially on Cápri and Prócida, and especially by hydrofoil), it's a good idea to buy your return ticket as soon as you arrive, to avoid the risk of finding the last boat or hydrofoil fully booked. The state-run ferry Caremar is usually the cheapest; tickets start at €4.70 for a ferry and €10.50 for a hydrofoil. Note that you can't take a car to Cápri.

The following gives a rough idea of frequencies during the summer (they're greatly reduced off-season). For specific timings you can look in the daily newspaper *Il Mattino*, check with the local tourist offices or look up schedules online: Caremar (☏892.123, ⓦwww.caremar.it); Alilauro (☏081.497.2238, ⓦwww.alilauro.it); SNAV (☏081.428.5555, ⓦwww.snav.it); NLG (☏081.552.0763, ⓦwww.navlib.it); Med Mar (☏081.333.4411, ⓦwww.medmargroup.it); Prócida Lines (☏081.896.0328); and Metrò del Mare (☏199.600.700, ⓦwww.metrodelmare.com).

Hydrofoils and fast ferries
Naples (Molo Beverello)–Cápri (20 daily; 45–50min)
Naples (Molo Beverello)–Casamícciola, Ischia (6 daily; 1hr)
Naples (Molo Beverello)–Forío, Ischia (6 daily; 50min)
Naples (Molo Beverello)–Ischia Porto, Ischia (20 daily; 45–60min)

Arrival, transport and information

All **hydrofoils** and **ferries** arrive at Marina Grande, roughly in the middle of Cápri's northern coast, with the island's main town perched up the hill. If you've booked a hotel, you can arrange for a porter to meet you at the pier. Otherwise, you can generally bypass the hubbub of the port and take the **funicular** (April–Sept 6.30am–midnight, Oct–March 6.30am–10pm; €1.40 one-way; wait in line at the ticket window to get tickets) directly up to Cápri town. Or take a **bus** (no need to queue at the ticket windows); the service runs from end to end and from side to side of the island, connecting all the main centres – Marina Grande, Cápri town, Marina Piccola, Anacápri – every fifteen minutes. Buses also run regularly down to the Blue Grotto from Anacápri, and also to Punta Carena. Tickets cost €1.40 for a single trip, €2.20 for an hour and €6.90 for a day, and they're available from ticket booths, newsstands and *tabacchi*, as well as upon boarding.

Cars are not allowed to embark or disembark ferries to Cápri and you can't hire a car here. Although roads are narrow and often very steep, **scooters** are a possibility (see p.195 for rental details), but plan on doing as much on foot as

Naples (Molo Beverello)–Prócida (9 daily; 35–40min)
Naples (Mergellina)–Cápri (6 daily; 35min)
Naples (Mergellina)–Casamícciola, Ischia (6 daily; 45min)
Naples (Mergellina)–Forío (via Ischia Porto: 3 daily; 1hr)
Naples (Mergellina)– Ischia Porto, Ischia (10 daily; 40min)
Naples (Mergellina)–Prócida (2 daily; 20min)
Casamícciola, Ischia–Prócida (6 daily; 20min)
Ischia Porto, Ischia–Prócida (3 daily; 15min)
Ischia Porto, Ischia–Cápri (1 daily; 50min)
Prócida–Ischia Porto, Ischia (3 daily; 20min)
Salerno–Cápri (2 daily; 1hr)
Sorrento–Ischia Porto, Ischia (1 daily direct, and 1 daily via Cápri; 1hr)
Sorrento–Cápri (16 daily; 20–25min)

Ferries

Naples (Molo Beverello)–Cápri (3 daily; 1hr 20min)
Naples (Molo Beverello)–Casamícciola, Ischia (4 daily; 2hr)
Naples (Molo Beverello)–Ischia Porto, Ischia (8 daily; 1hr 30min)
Naples (Molo Beverello)–Prócida (6 daily; 1hr)
Pozzuoli–Ischia Porto, Ischia (7 daily; 1hr)
Pozzuoli–Casamícciola, Ischia (6 daily; 1hr 30min)
Pozzuoli–Prócida (6 daily; 35min)
Ischia Porto, Ischia–Prócida (6 daily; 25min)
Sorrento–Cápri (2 daily; 50min)
Salerno–Cápri (2 daily; 2hr 10min)
Salerno–Ischia Porto, Ischia (1 daily; 2hr 30min)

Besides ferries and hydrofoils for getting to Cápri, pricier options for the well-heeled include **water taxis**, departing from Naples Beverello (℡081.837.8781, ⓦwww .capriseaservice.com; €600 for the 50min one-way ride, carrying up to six people), as well as private **helicopters** (℡0828.354.155 or 800.915.012, ⓦwww.capri-helicopters .com), taking up to four passengers on the Naples-to-Cápri trip of about seventeen minutes for a cool €1650 one-way.

you have time for. The island's stylish convertible **taxis** are an alternative – but very expensive – option; there's a taxi rank out of the port and up to the right (℡081.837.0543). Finally, you can simply **walk** up the steep hill to Cápri town: go to the fountain at the centre of Marina Grande's semicircular port and turn right. The steps start on the left a few metres up, and are clearly marked. They number about 300 in all and take from 20 to 45 minutes to climb, depending on your stamina and/or your urges to stop and admire the views.

There isn't much to hold you in Marina Grande itself, just a strip of waterside shops, cafés and restaurants hawking overpriced tourist tat and mediocre food. However, it is here that you will find the first of the island's three **tourist offices** (April–Oct Mon–Sat 9am–1pm & 3.30–6.45pm, Sun 9am–1pm; Nov–March Mon–Sat 9am–3pm; ℡081.837.0634, ⓦwww.capritourism.com), just on the left at the beginning of the quay. They sell a handy map (€1) and offer free promotional materials. Once up in Cápri town, there is also an office in the famed "Piazzetta" at Piazza Umberto I (April–Oct Mon–Sat 8.30am–8.30pm, Sun 9am–3pm; Nov–March Mon–Sat 9am–1pm & 3.30–6.45pm; ℡081.837.0686), offering the same services. The third office is in Anacápri, at Via G. Orlandi 59 (Mon–Sat 9am–3pm; ℡081.837.1524).

Accommodation

Given its world-class cachet, Cápri **accommodation** prices are uniformly inflated. Still, there are relative bargains in the midst of some very high-end properties – and if you can afford to splurge, the luxury options are well worth it. Around Cápri town the hotels have always tended to be the island's priciest, while just up from Marina Grande there are a few budget options, as well as in Marina Piccola and Anacápri, though the latter is also home to two of the island's chicest hotels. In any case, real bargains are just about impossible to find, so book very early if you want to snag a moderately priced room.

Cápri town and around

The hotels below are marked on the **map** on p.182.

'A Paziella Via Fuorlovado 36 ☎081.837.0044, ⊛www.apaziella.com. Cool and breezy even on the hottest day, the interplay of gardens and arcades at this hotel evokes a sense of quiet luxury and serenity, even though it's located in the middle of town, just seconds from the action. Closed mid-Oct to March. Doubles €220–300.

Belvedere & Tre Re Via Marina Grande 264 ☎081.837.0345, ⊛www.belvedere-tre-re.com. The attractions here are the extensive terrace and fine views, as well as easy private access to the beach just below, and the port. The recently spruced-up rooms are fresh and clean, some with balconies, and many have sea views. Closed Jan & Feb. Doubles €110–140.

Bristol Via Marina Grande 217 ☎081.837.6144, ⊛www.hotelbristolcapri.com. Built on a panoramic site near where Emperor Tiberius had one of his villas, just a few hundred metres from the beach, this hotel stands out brilliantly due to its rich Pompeian-red decor. It's a fairly luxurious option, with light, airy rooms and a pool. Closed Jan to mid-March. Doubles €120–160.

Da Giorgio Via Roma 34 ☎081.837.5777, ⊛www.dagiorgiocapri.com. With gracious rooms affording views of the bay, this modest little hotel is an excellent choice, not least because it also boasts one of the island's most appealing restaurants (see p.193); full board in high season is an additional €50 per person. Closed Jan & Feb. Doubles €110–140.

Italia Via Marina Grande 204 ☎081.837.0602, ⊛www.hotelitaliacapri.com. This charming, elegant old mansion is surrounded by flower-filled gardens and occupies its own corner on the road up to Cápri town. All rooms have private balconies and half of them sea views; the others look out over the gardens. Breakfast €10 extra. Doubles €120–130.

Quattro Stagioni Via Marina Piccola 1 ☎081.837.0041, ⊛www.hotel4stagionicapri.com. In a pretty location, a little way out of Cápri town at the fork of the roads to Marina Piccola and Anacápri, this place has friendly staff, and offers a ten-percent discount to carriers of this book from mid-March to Oct. Doubles €70–125.

Quisisana Via Camerelle 2 ☎081.837.0788, ⊛www.quisi.com. Historic, chic, grand and elegant, the *Quisisana* started out as a health spa but quickly became the top choice for visiting dignitaries and celebrities – and it has the distinction of having refused service to Oscar Wilde. Guests enjoy a selection of gardens, pools and restaurants, the rooms are tranquil, and there's a spa too. Closed Nov–Easter. Doubles from €320.

Villa Krupp Viale Matteotti 12 ☎081.837.0362, ⊛www.villakrupp.it. You'd never guess that this sophisticated villa with great views was once home to Russian revolutionary Maxim Gorky – and his house guest for a time, Lenin. Before that, it was planned as the Krupp estate, though Herr Krupp left the island under a cloud of scandal before he got to enjoy it (see p.184). The style is a nice blend of Italian and Moorish touches, with lots of light and soft colours. Closed Nov–March. Doubles €130–170.

Villa Sarah Via Tiberio 3a ☎081.837.7817, ⊛www.villasarahcapri.com. A bit of a walk from Cápri town, this historic villa with magnificent views has been lovingly restored to retain much of its old-world flavour – such as an ancient stone well gracing the terrace – without skimping on modern comforts. Gracious gardens complete the quintessential Cápri experience. Closed Nov–March. Doubles €130–205.

Weber Ambassador Via Marina Piccola ☎081.837.0141, ⊛www.hotelweber.com. This quiet, comfortable choice offers great views from its multi-levelled terraces, particularly of the iconic Faraglioni rocks. The decor is cosy and elegant, with warm terracotta accents, and steps lead directly down to the Marina Piccola beach. Doubles €105–178.

Anacápri and around

The hotels below are marked on the **map** on p.188.

Alla Bussola di Hermes Traversa La Vigna 14 ☎081.838.2010, ⓦwww.bussolahermes.com. A rags-to-riches success story: what was once little more than a dorm for backpackers has been reincarnated as a really rather luxurious boutique hotel. Lots of marble accents and other classical touches contribute to an oasis of light-filled comfort in a garden setting. Closed Nov–Feb. Doubles €140.

Bellavista Via G. Orlandi 10 ☎081.837.1463, ⓦwww.bellavistacapri.com. Gardens and spectacular views greet the eye as you arrive: this hotel boasts one of the island's most photogenic trellised walkways and terraces framing the main building, while the rooms are spacious and comfortable. The panoramic restaurant is excellent too; half and full board €25 and €50 respectively. Closed Nov–Easter. Doubles €75–115.

La Bougainville Viale Tommaso De Tommaso 6 ☎081.837.3641, ⓦwww.hlb.it. Featuring a mix of modern and classically Cápri touches, such as marble floors and white columns, the hotel is set in a lush flower garden, which some rooms overlook, and is on the main bus line from Anacápri to the rest of the island. Amenities include a good restaurant, a solarium and guest pick-up/drop-off at Marina Grande. Closed mid-Nov to mid-March. Doubles €135–180.

Caesar Augustus Via G. Orlandi 4 ☎081.837.3395, ⓦwww.caesar-augustus .com. Its terrace has always been a major attraction, touted as the having the most beautiful panorama in the world. In one sweeping vista, it takes in the entire Bay of Naples, overlooked by a statue of the Emperor Augustus. The place offers a truly imperial experience, from the refurbished rooms to the infinity pool – which seems to merge with the distant sea – to the manicured gardens. Closed Nov–Mar. Doubles from €430.

Da Gelsomina Via Migliara 72 ☎081.837.1499, ⓦwww.dagelsomina.com. The location is stunning, but getting there with luggage may dampen your enthusiasm: it's a good 20min walk from Piazza Vittoria along a paved, pedestrian-only path. However, it does offer a pool, an excellent restaurant and a stupendous setting, with plenty of hiking trails nearby. Rooms are simple but fresh, and each has its own terrace. Always full in high season. Doubles €120–150.

Mediterraneo Via Caposcuro 12 ☎081.837.2907, ⓦwww.mediterraneo-capri.com. Down the curving staircase from the pedestrian-only lane is a garden courtyard decorated with classical statuary and terracotta pots. The airy, fresh feel is maintained throughout, and the rooms evoke understated elegance. Very friendly service. Closed mid-Nov to March. Doubles €95–135.

Villa Eva Via La Fabbrica 8 ☎081.837.1549, ⓦwww.villaeva.com. *Villa Eva* has long been Cápri's cult budget option: with buildings like some *Arabian Nights* fantasy and gardens that evoke Eden, this amazing place is nestled in the forest on the way down to the Blue Grotto. There's a wide choice of rooms, as well as a grand-piano-shaped pool. Closed Nov–March. Doubles €90–120.

▲ Marina Piccola, Cápri

The island

There are two towns on the island, Cápri and Anacápri. Passenger craft arrive at Marina Grande on the north shore, from which there is a funicular up the hill to **Cápri town**, a spot known for its upscale designer boutiques. It's also ideal for leisurely strolling, being mostly off-limits to cars. Northwest of the town centre, the best known imperial villa, the **Villa Jovis**, rises above the sea, offering astoundingly beautiful views from all sides. The island's western coast is punctuated by grottoes, most only accessible from the sea, and a hike along the ridge above is the best way to take in the island's natural beauty. Following the coast to the south, you encounter a number of small islands, collectively known as **I Faraglioni**, where the European jet set park their yachts and sailboats in the summer months. Nearby **Marina Piccola** has the island's only extensive beach facilities. From here, it's a short bus ride back up to the centre of town.

   Anacápri, perched above Cápri town on a mountainous slope, has long been described as the more rustic and down-to-earth of the two towns – although these days the differences are less obvious. Anacápri's restaurants and hotels still tend to offer better value, but it has its fair share of boutiques too. The town is also the starting point for some worthwhile excursions: the island's highest peak, **Monte Solaro**, a short chair-lift ride or stiff hike uphill, has an awe-inspiring panorama, and there's a good **hike** along the island's

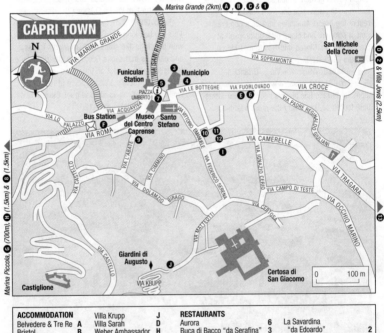

ACCOMMODATION		Villa Krupp	J	RESTAURANTS		La Savardina	
Belvedere & Tre Re	A	Villa Sarah	D	Aurora	6	"da Edoardo"	2
Bristol	B	Weber Ambassador	H	Buca di Bacco "da Serafina"	3	Villa Verde	10
Da Giorgio	F			Canzone del Mare	8		
Italia	C	CAFÉS & GELATERIE		La Capannina	4		
'A Paziella	E	Bar Caso	5	Da Gemma	9	BARS & CLUBS	
Quattro Stagioni	G	Il Gelato al Limone	1	Da Giorgio	F	Anema e Core	11
Quisisana	I	Bar Tiberio	7	Le Grottelle	13	Numbertwo	12

western perimeter; known as the **Sentiero dei Fortini**, the path is littered with fortress remains built to defend the island throughout its millennial history, and ends at the **Blue Grotto**, Cápri's most iconic attraction, on the island's north coast.

Cápri town and around

CÁPRI is the main town of the island, nestled between two mountains. Once peopled by fishermen and farmers, it has long since been given over entirely to the pursuit of pricey pleasure. Its winding alleyways are lined with whitewashed houses and clustered with cafés, hotels and shops, all with an air of polished Mediterranean grace, and many of the town's beautiful villas are adorned with handmade tiles announcing their names on vine-trellised entrances. There aren't many sights as such, but it's the atmosphere that provides the allure: it's rich with history and fascination, but unassumingly so.

The community centres on the dinky main square of **Piazza Umberto I**, known to all as **La Piazzetta**, crowded with café tables and in the evenings lit by twinkling fairy lights. Most new arrivals take the funicular up from Marina Grande and head straight for this bustling little square; its little domed bell tower in one corner makes a modest landmark, but La Piazzetta is really nothing more than a cluster of cafés, surrounded by quaint arcades. But the square has a powerful allure that transcends its diminutive dimensions: to this day, it still evokes the glamour that makes Cápri unique, fizzing with gossip and preening glitterati – at least when the day-trippers have gone home.

On one side of the square, steps lead up to a series of covered walkways, and to the domed seventeenth-century parish church of **Santo Stefano** (daily 9am–7pm), worth a look for its marble floor originally from the ancient Villa Jovis and the ruins of other Tiberian villas. Directly across from the church, the

Beaches

Sandy **beaches** aren't what Cápri is known for: the shore is almost all pebbly. The island nevertheless offers plenty of opportunities for a swim and for watersports (see box, p.187), being encircled by some of the deepest waters in the Bay of Naples. The following are the most promising spots for a dip.

Blue Grotto Great flat sections carved out of the living rock, with concrete platforms and metal ladders. From the Blue Grotto bus stop, head left past the restaurants, and walk all the way to the end.

Marina Grande Walk out of the port area and past the ticket windows, up to the bus terminal; from here, go down the steps of the beachside restaurant and out onto the sand. The beach itself is free, but you can pay for the usual facilities if you prefer, and the water is as clean and clear here as anywhere else around the island.

Marina Piccola Small, pebbly strands across the south side of the island, with a full complement of seaside services. This is also one of the most kid-friendly beaches in the area, since there's a shallow, calm lagoon and plenty of cheap beach toys for sale.

Punta Carena A similar setup to the Blue Grotto area. The beach is down to the right, below the lighthouse.

Via Krupp More daring souls can try their luck down beyond the lowest point of this precipitous road, where a rough trail cuts off and down to the left. At the bottom, there are huge, flat stones lying right along the shore, facing I Faraglioni. Bring water and snacks, and a pair of plastic slip-on shoes is a good idea, or you risk scraped feet from the sharp rocks, and possibly sea-urchin spines too.

modest **Museo del Centro Caprense "Ignazio Cerio"** at Piazzetta Cerio 5 (Tues, Wed, Fri & Sat 10am–1pm, Thurs 3–7pm; €2.60) was founded in honour of the Cerio family, who were hugely influential in Cápri in the nineteenth and early twentieth centuries. It houses archeological remains, artefacts of the island's prehistory, and various zoological and botanical finds, the product of Ignazio Cerio's studious efforts upon his arrival here in the mid-nineteenth century.

The Certosa San Giacomo

Through elegant, shop-lined lanes and on across to the far side of town, the terrain suddenly turns bucolic. Here you'll soon spy the recently restored **Certosa San Giacomo** on Viale Certosa 11 (Museum Diefenbach and monastery Tues–Sat 9am–2pm, Sun 9am–1pm; park 9am–1hr before sunset; free; ☎081.837.6218), a fourteenth-century monastery recognizable by its signature Moroccan-style vaults forming a series of little domes. Inside, the **Museum Diefenbach** has a handful of metaphysical paintings, rather quirky visionary works by the nineteenth-century German Symbolist painter Wilhelm Diefenbach, who once lived here. A couple of shapeless Roman statues dredged up from the deep, the Prior's apartments, a frescoed chapel (closed for restoration at the time of writing) and two cloisters complete the visit. At one time, the monks here owned the grazing and hunting rights to most of the island. In later periods, the monastery was used as a prison and then a military hospital.

South of Cápri town

Past the monastery, taking Via Matteotti to the far side of the island, the **Giardini di Augusto** (daily dawn to dusk) afford astonishing panoramas of the rocky coast below and the towering jagged cliffs above. These lushly green terraced gardens are dotted with benches, flowers and marble statuary, making it a very pleasant place to while away an hour or two. They were once part of the estate of German industrialist **Alfred Krupp**, one of the most notorious of the island's nineteenth-century freedom-seekers, but he was eventually forced to leave Cápri under a cloud of shame due to his sexual liaisons with local fishermen and other young men. He was obliged to return to Germany, where he shortly afterwards committed suicide. Krupp also bequeathed to the island the dramatic, zigzagging pathway down, still known as **Via Krupp**, which you can see from the gardens. It was reopened in 2008 after being closed for 32 years due to the danger of falling rocks. The way to its entry passes under a high archway and from there you can take the picturesque switchbacks down, either all the way to the bottom and beyond to a beach of large flat rocks, or around to the right to **Marina Piccola** (see p.186).

Villa Jovis and Villa Lysis

Taking a different direction out of Cápri town, along Via Castello, which starts at Via Roma, a pleasant fifteen-minute walk leads you to the **Belvedere del Cannone**, which offers marvellous views, especially overlooking **I Faraglioni** rockstacks to the left and Marina Piccola to the right.

Further out of town, there's a more demanding walk to the eastern summit of the island, where you can visit the ruins of Emperor Tiberius's villa, **Villa Jovis** (daily 9am–1hr before sunset; €2) – a steep forty-minute hike from La Piazzetta, following Via Botteghe out of the square, then Via Tiberio up the hill and all the way to its end. It was here that Tiberius retired in 27 AD, to the grandest of his twelve imperial Cápri villas, dedicated to the king of the gods.

According to Suetonius and Tacitus, he came to lead a life of vice and debauchery and to take revenge on his enemies, many of whom he apparently had thrown off the overhanging cliff-face, known infamously as *Il Salto di Tiberio* (Tiberius' Leap).

You can see why he chose the site: it's dazzling, among Cápri's most exhilarating, with incredible **views** of the Sorrentine Peninsula, including the Amalfi Coast, and the bay; on a clear day you can even see to Salerno and beyond. There's not much left of the **villa** – which was almost a town in itself, covering some 7000 square metres – but you can get a good sense of the shape and design of its various parts. Arched halls and narrow passageways survive, though to the untrained eye much of it remains inscrutable. From 27 AD, when Tiberius first set foot on the island, until his death ten years later, the emperor never returned

Cápri's thrill-seekers

It was the Marquis de Sade who "discovered" Cápri, but the divine madness only really got underway about a century after his time, when more and more northern Europeans of a nonconformist stripe discovered that they could let it all hang out, at least more easily, in this southern, sunlit Arcadia. From the late 1800s until World War II, Cápri was awash with all sorts of exiles, almost all of them seeking the sexual emancipation denied to them in their starchier home countries.

The very long list of mostly wealthy and/or aristocratic Cápri visitors and residents includes **Oscar Wilde** and his partner Lord Alfred Douglas, who visited Cápri in 1897, to the outraged consternation of some of those present, not long after he was released from Reading Gaol. **W. Somerset Maugham** knew Cápri well, too, even setting one of his most famous short stories, *The Lotus Eater*, on the island. Among the international writers who resided for a time on Cápri was **D.H. Lawrence** – who called the isle "a gossipy, villa-stricken, two-humped chunk of limestone, a microcosm that does heaven much credit, but mankind none at all" – as well as **Henry James**, **George Bernard Shaw** and **Joseph Conrad**.

But Cápri's allure drew devotees of all professions, including British entertainer **Gracie Fields**, who bought a villa here in 1933, in which she died forty-six years later. In her memoirs she recalled, "I knew that if only one small blade of grass of this gentle, wonderful place could belong to me, I would be happy." Even radical politicos in exile found their way here, including **Maxim Gorky** and no less a revolutionary force than Vladimir Illich **Lenin**, who visited in 1910 and is said to have observed that "Cápri makes you forget everything."

The end of World War II and the rise of Hollywood's international status brought a new breed of star to Cápri, marked most notably by the disembarkation of movie-goddess **Rita Hayworth** in 1949. Perhaps the biggest single cultural contribution the island made at the outset of this era was designer Emilio Pucci's creation of pencil-thin "Capri pants" that same year. Suddenly Cápri was the place to be, a sure sign that you had arrived, and were part of the glamorous elite. Now everyone who was anyone was showing up here to be photographed strolling the quaint, whitewashed lanes: film stars, royalty, anyone rich and famous enough and who wanted to make their mark. **Aristotle Onassis**' floating palace, the *Christina*, was often seen, first bearing opera diva **Maria Callas** and later **Jacqueline Kennedy** and her entourage; and **Princess Grace of Monaco** put in an appearance most years, too. Pozzuoli was the home town of **Sophia Loren**, and in 1960, after achieving international stardom, she shot a romantic comedy on Cápri, *It Started in Naples*, co-starring the King of Hollywood himself, **Clark Gable** – his penultimate film. The island had become a powerful symbol of style, to the extent that just being seen here could gain even the most illustrious stars extra charisma points in the eyes of the public.

to Rome, in effect making Cápri the de facto capital of the empire. Some of the artistic treasures that were unearthed here are now part of the collection in Villa San Michele in Anacápri (see p.188).

Just down from this site, there's another villa, the much more recent **Villa Lysis**, known to locals as Villa Fersen, on Via Lo Capo (April–Oct Mon–Sat 9am–1.30pm & 2.30–6.30pm; closed Nov–March; free): a Neoclassical pastiche and home of one **Count Fersen-Adelsward**, a French millionaire poet who built the house in the early 1900s to entertain his young Italian boyfriends, as well as indulging his drug habit. The building is interesting from the outside, especially for the view, but there's nothing left of the original outlandish furnishings inside. It's the scandalous story that's interesting, a monument to one man's dream of ideal love, evoked by the Latin inscription over the portico: *Amori et dolorum sacrum* ("A Shrine to Love and Sorrow"). The count finally succumbed to his preferred drug concoction, an apparent suicide.

The Arco Naturale and the Grotta di Matermánia

Another, more leisurely walk is to the **Arco Naturale**, an impressive natural rock formation at the end of a high, verdant valley, a 25-minute stroll from Cápri town, again following Via Botteghe out of the square but branching off up Via Matermánia after ten minutes or so; just follow the signs. Towards the end of the trail, a series of rustic stairways offers some precipitous panoramas. Finally you reach the arch itself, where the plummeting views can only be described as vertiginous: a huge arc of limestone amidst lush greenery, with the glittering sea far below. Specially constructed viewing platforms allow you to get quite close.

Alternatively, just before the path begins to descend, past the restaurant *Le Grottelle* and towards the Arco Naturale, steps lead down to the right to the **Grotta di Matermánia**, a ten-minute trek down steep steps and through a rocky overhang. The cave is a dusty cutaway out of the rock that was converted to house a shrine to the goddess Cybele ("Magna Mater" means the Great Mother) by the Romans. Looking at it now, it is difficult to imagine Cybele's frenzied priests, who would ritualistically castrate themselves in an ecstasy of devotion. Since then it has also occasionally been used for neo-Pagan rites of dubious nature, according to island gossip and legend.

From the grotto, steps continue on down through the trees, before flattening into a fine path that you can follow all the way round to the **Belvedere di Tragara**, comprising some of the island's best views. From here, follow the panoramic **Via Tragara** back to Cápri town – reachable in about half an hour from the belvedere. Along the way, take time to admire **I Faraglioni**, the picturesque rock stacks just off the island, as well as the **Villa Malaparte** nearby (not open to visitors), built for the eponymous eccentric Italian writer in 1937. Like a giant red anvil plonked unceremoniously down on one of the island's most scenic promontories, it's an extreme piece of minimalist architecture, and seems utterly incongruous here.

Marina Piccola

Directly across the lowest central point in the island's "saddle", **MARINA PICCOLA** is a small harbour on the seaward side – a modest group of houses, restaurants and shops clustered round an even more modest pebble beach. It's reasonably uncrowded out of season, though in July or August you'd be advised to steer well clear. **Buses** from Cápri town drop off here – certainly an appealing prospect for the return trip back up the hill. The best

Watersports at Marina Piccola

Taking a **kayak** around the island is a memorable experience. You can rent single and double kayaks (about €15 per hr) at Marina Piccola; make sure you take water and something to eat, though also be aware that there's not room for carrying very much. Count on about five hours to make the circuit, including stops for ducking into the many grottoes and for pulling up on beaches for a swim. You could also consider disembarking on **I Faraglioni**, where a unique species of lizard lives, brilliantly cobalt blue in imitation of the surrounding sea; the middle rock stack is pierced by a 60m-long tunnel, wide enough for small boats to pass through.

Windsurfers can also rent gear at Marina Piccola at about the same rate, though the water, facing the open sea, can get too choppy for smooth sailing.

way to get here, however, is to **walk**, but not on the switchback road. Take the steps down from the island's main roundabout at the beginning of Via Roma to find a walkway and a series of staircases – it's a twenty-minute walk down Via Mulo.

Once at the **beach**, you can pay for the usual facilities or just lay your towel on the arc of pebbles – not all that comfortable, but the swimming is good and there's diving from the small rock stacks just offshore, in the middle of the lagoon. This is also the one spot on the island where you can rent **kayaks**: the best way to explore the island's coastline, or even to go for a complete circum-navigation (see box above).

Anacápri and around

The island's other main settlement, **ANACÁPRI**, is more sprawling than Cápri town and less obviously picturesque, though quieter and greener. The prefix *ana* is Greek, indicating "an elevated place", and it's certainly true that getting to the island's second town is a rather hair-raising ride up a lofty and sheer cliff, to a point some 300 metres higher than Cápri town. The minuscule switchback road, the only way to get there, seems hardly wide enough for two of the island's diminutive buses to pass, and when two do encounter each other, passengers on the seaward side stifle gasps of awe and horror at the sight of the rocky seashore below.

Anacápri's main square, **Piazza Vittoria**, is pleasant enough, ascending in broad terraces with flowers, and larger than Cápri's La Piazzetta. It's flanked by souvenir shops, nondescript fashion boutiques and restaurants decked with multilingual tourist menus – Cápri without the chic, but without the chichi, too. A short walk away, down shop-lined Via G. Orlandi and to the right, you'll find the church of **San Michele** in Piazza San Nicola (daily: April–Oct 9am–7pm; Nov–March 9.30am–3pm; €2), one of Anacápri's star attractions. The entire floor consists of thousands of tiles painted with a delightful depiction of the *Earthly Paradise*, completed in 1761 by Leonardo Chiaiese, a tile-maker from the Abruzzo region. To view the work, you climb a narrow, rickety staircase to an upstairs balcony, in order to take in the entire image in all its richness and detail. Taken from a drawing by the prolific Baroque Neapolitan painter Solimena, it's executed in clear blues and honey yellows, portraying cats, unicorns and other creatures, enjoying their jungle-like world in Surrealistic harmony with Adam and Eve, though with the serpent at the centre of the scene. The fallen pair, displaying repentance at their crime, are no longer nude, though animal hides rather than fig leaves preserve their modesty. A smug Archangel Michael straddles a cottony cloud, sword raised,

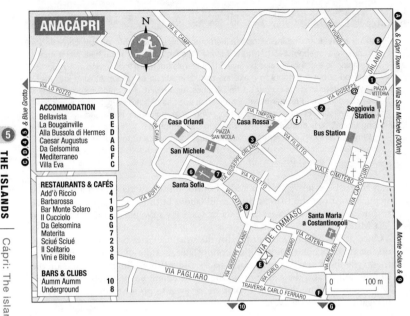

ANACÁPRI

N

Ⓐ & Cápri Town

Ⓑ

ORLANDI

VIA IL CAMPI

VIA VIGNOLA

① PIAZZA VITTORIA

Villa San Michele (300m)

VIA LO POZZO

④ & Blue Grotto

VIA GIUSEPPE

VIA TIMPONE

②

Seggiovia Station

ACCOMMODATION
Bellavista   B
La Bougainville   E
Alla Bussola di Hermes   D
Caesar Augustus   A
Da Gelsomina   G
Mediterraneo   F
Villa Eva   C

Casa Orlandi

Casa Rossa

ⓘ

Bus Station

PIAZZA SAN NICOLA

San Michele

VIA CAVA

VIA FILIETTO

VIALE CIMITERO

③

Villa San Michele (300m)

RESTAURANTS & CAFÉS
Add'ò Riccio   4
Barbarossa   1
Bar Monte Solaro   9
Il Cucciolo   5
Da Gelsomina   G
Materita   7
Sciué Sciué   2
Il Solitario   3
Vini e Bibite   6

Santa Sofia

⑥ ⑦

VIA GIUSEPPE ORLANDI

VIA FILIETTO

VIA CATENA

VIA CAPOSCURO

Monte Solaro & ⑨

VIA BOFFE

⑧

VIA DE TOMMASO

Santa Maria a Costantinopoli

VIA CATENA

VIA MIGLIERA

BARS & CLUBS
Aumm Aumm   10
Underground   8

VIA PAGLIARO

VIA GIUSEPPE ORLANDI

Ⓔ

VIA CARLO FERRARO

Ⓕ

0   100 m

TRAVERSA CARLO FERRARO

▼⑩   ▼Ⓖ

pointing the transgressors to the nearest exit. The animals – who presumably get to stay – indifferently watch them go.

Monte Solaro

Off Piazza Vittoria, to the right of the upper terrace, there's a **chair lift** (*seggiovia*) station (daily: March–Oct 9.30am–6.30pm; Nov–Feb 10.30am–3pm; €6 single, €8 return), operating regular services up to **Monte Solaro**, the island's highest point (596m). The twelve-minute ride seems precarious, but the whole experience is well managed, and once you're up and away, swinging out into space, pulled by cables from tower to tower, it's a surprisingly restful and serene experience. The views of the sea on the way up are dazzling, and the 360-degree panorama you get from the top is perhaps the bay's best. From certain overlooks, the minute boats in the coves directly below seem miles away, and on a clear day you can easily see the entire Sorrentine peninsula and Vesuvius. Pause before going down to check out the ruined castle and the photogenic classical statuary, bask in the sun and have a drink at the bar. Instead of taking the chair lift back, many prefer to take the pleasant and well-marked path that winds through the vegetation and old stone walls down to the main piazza. The downhill trip takes about an hour (allow an hour and a half for the hike up to Monte Solaro).

Villa San Michele

At the top of Piazza Vittoria, turn left at the swish *Capri Palace Hotel* and continue on past a gauntlet of souvenir boutiques and stalls to the **Villa San Michele** (daily: March 9am–4.30pm; April & Oct 9am–5pm; May–Sept 9am–6pm; Nov–Feb 9am–3.30pm; ⓦwww.villasanmichele.eu; €5), a ten-minute walk. This rambling, nineteenth-century Neoclassically Mediterranean villa, built by Swedish physician, pioneer psychiatrist, philanthropist, naturalist and writer **Axel Munthe** (1857–1949), has been a popular tourist draw ever since he published his international bestseller *The Story of San Michele* in 1929.

Munthe first climbed up the long, steep Scala Fenicia staircase from Cápri town – 800-odd steps carved from the rock – in 1874 and was immediately and permanently captivated by Anacápri's serene charms. Fifteen years later, after making his fortune as a society physician in Paris, he was able to build his dream home, on the site of one of Tiberius's villas (and a later monastery). It's a light, airy dwelling with luxuriant and fragrant gardens and splendidly plunging panoramas – one of the real highlights of the island. About his beloved creation, Munthe said, "My house must be open to the sun, to the wind, to the light of the sea, like a Greek temple, with light, light, light everywhere!" He lived here for a number of years, until, ironically, it was the light that became too overwhelming for his failing eyesight. He was finally obliged for health reasons to leave the island forever in 1943 and return to Sweden.

The interior

The legacy Munthe bequeathed to Anacápri, managed by the Swedish government, boasts a wonderful **interior** full of his furniture and knick-knacks, as well as Roman artefacts and columns plundered from ruined villas on the island, including that of Tiberius over which it is built. It's an appealing hotchpotch of ancient Etruscan, Roman, Egyptian, Romanesque, Renaissance and Moorish styles, some of the pieces being imitations dating from the seventeenth to the nineteenth centuries. Notable objects include the much-photographed granite sphinx looking out over the isle at the far end, a head of Medusa, and a marble bust of Tiberius himself. Elsewhere, Corinthian capitals serve as coffee tables, surfaces are formed of intricate medieval Cosmati mosaic-work, and bronzes on marble plinths adorn every arcaded breezeway.

The gardens and bird sanctuary

The terraced **gardens** with their pergolas and balconies are magnificent, and give wonderful views over Marina Grande and Cápri town. One bronze statue of a boyish resting Hermes (a copy of the original from the Villa dei Papyri at Herculaneum) was given to Munthe by the city of Naples in gratitude for his healing work during the devastating cholera epidemic of 1884. The villa's belvederes are especially lovely, affording some of the best views on the island, and the arboured gardens also hold an attractive natural history exhibition, which fills you in on local flora and fauna, to the (recorded) accompaniment of the golden oriole and the nightingale.

Munthe's famous book – more an autobiography than anything – has been translated into dozens of languages and is well worth a read. It encompasses all of his interests, passions and projects, including that of establishing an island bird sanctuary in the ruins of the **Castello Barbarossa**, a fortress on the mountain peak above the villa that dates at least to the eleventh century, perhaps all the way back to Tiberius. Guided **tours** take in the fortress on Thursday afternoons from April to October; call ☏081.837.1401 to book.

The Blue Grotto

Most famous of all the island's sights, of course, is the **Blue Grotto**, or Grotta Azzurra (daily 9am–1hr before sunset, but closed in bad weather; boat from Marina Grande €11, rowing boat into the grotto €6, plus admission €4; or take a rowing boat from Anacápri for €6, saving the price of the trip from Marina Grande). Its renown means that it's also the island's most exploitative sight, the boatmen whisking visitors onto boats and in and out of the grotto in about

Cápri walks

Once you get away from the tourist centres, Cápri abounds in easy-to-mildly-challenging **hikes**. The walks below take in most of the major panoramas and form complete circuits. See also the walk to the **Arco Naturale**, p.186.

Anacápri
Time about 2 hours **Level** moderate

From Anacápri's Piazza Vittoria, walk down Via Tommaso, in the opposite direction to Cápri town until you get to the bus terminus. Turn left here and take the short walkway, Viale Cimitero, up to the town **cemetery**, which is worth a visit for its serene atmosphere and delicately carved marble monuments. Turn right onto the paved pathway, called both Via Caposcuro and Via Migliara. Walk along this pleasant ridge with sea views to the right for about twenty minutes until you come to the *Gelsomina* hotel and restaurant, which enjoys a panoramic perch. If the timing is right, this makes a good spot for lunch.

Directly across from the *Gelsomina* is the **Parco Filosofico** (daily sunrise−sunset), the brainchild of a Swedish economics professor and part-time resident of the island. It's basically a patch of untamed vegetation, crisscrossed with rudimentary pathways and set about with benches, meant to provide a place of contemplation and meditation. The significant feature here are the tiles placed all around, hand-painted with pithy quotes by important Western thinkers ("Know thyself" and "I think, therefore I am" among them) to get your ruminations going.

Continuing on a bit you soon reach the end of the walkway, at the **Belvedere di Migliara**, an elevated spot from which you can take in one of the island's most astounding views, of wild crags and pinnacles of wind-sculpted limestone, and of the turquoise sea below. From here, stone steps lead down to the right into a pine forest, with a path that continues along the ridge for about a quarter of an hour, eventually coming to some buildings and then leading out onto the paved road. At the road, turn left and go down the hill about a hundred metres. Look for a sign marked "Punta Carena" (viewable only coming up the hill, in the opposite direction, so keep looking back), indicating concrete steps going down. Take the series of stairways all the way down the steep hillside until you get to **Punta Carena** and the **Faro** (lighthouse).

five minutes flat. The entrance is a good 45-minute hike from Anacápri, starting off down Via Lo Pozzo, or reachable by bus every twenty minutes from Piazza Vittoria.

In use since Roman times – it was Tiberius' own personal nymphaeum, decorated then with marble statues of gods and goddesses – it has been the island's most celebrated attraction since its legendary rediscovery sometime in the eighteenth century by a poor fisherman named Zoccolone (roughly translated as "big clog"). Others claim, however, that islanders always knew of its existence but that it was German writer August Kopish who created the first international buzz in 1826, putting Cápri firmly on the tourist map.

Perhaps surprisingly, despite the hype and brevity of the experience, the grotto manages to live up to its reputation well enough. It isn't by any means the only sea-grotto of the sort – there are more around the island and along the Amalfi Coast too – but it is certainly the largest, and seeing it does give you an undeniable thrill. Part of the fun is the system of boats and oarsmen, all bobbing chaotically about the tiny entrance. People enter in twos; when the boatman instructs you to duck, in order to enter the low opening, one person will need to lean back into the other one's lap to make it through and avoid scraped heads. Instantly, all is a uniquely glowing blue; the radiance and

Here you'll find swimming facilities and all services, as well as the beginnings of the **Sentiero dei Fortini**, a much longer nature walk (4–5hr) past old forts, which eventually arrives at the Blue Grotto. From Punta Carena, there are buses to take you back to Anacápri.

Sentiero dei Fortini: Punta Carena to the Blue Grotto
Time 4–5 hours **Level** moderate
The Sentiero dei Fortini path begins at **Punta Carena** and the **Faro** (see above) and meanders along Cápri's west coast to **Punta dell'Arcera** and the **Blue Grotto**, passing a series of *fortini*, blockhouses built by the British to defend against French invasion in 1806. The path covers a distance of 4.5km and can be done in reverse.

Beginning at Punta Carena, follow Via Nuova del Faro for around 500 metres until a fork in the road curves left towards the **Cala del Tombosiello**. From here, there is a steep concrete path that leads past the first of three *fortini*, the **Forte del Pino**, a circular building 60 metres in diameter clinging to the cliff 40 metres above sea level. Before the fort, a dirt path leads to a worthwhile detour, a belvedere with breathtaking views over the **Cala di Limmo** and the Faro. This area was once a military outpost where cannons defended against Napoleon's fleet. Back on the Sentiero dei Fortini, and past the Forte del Pino, follow the marked path along the steep cliffs trimmed with artemisia and juniper bushes. Around 600 metres on, stone steps lead to an unsightly wood-and-iron bridge built to traverse the **Cala di Mezzo**. After another 600 metres, head off the main trail to the right to reach the **Fortino di Mesola**, a circular structure, on the wild **Punta Campetiello**. Return to the main trail and continue up towards the valley to cross the Rio Cesa and Rio Chiuso, then walk up along the cliff. After a few hundred metres, head downhill, pass a side path, and continue to the final fort, the semicircular **Fortino Orrico**. It was here, on the **Punta del Miglio**, that French troops disembarked in October 1808, breaching the British fortifications to take the island. Back on the Sentiero, the path continues for around 500 metres until you reach Via Grotta Azzura, the curving road that hugs the Punta dell'Arcera before descending to the **Blue Grotto**.

intensity is caused by sunlight entering the cave from beneath, up through the water. Technically, you're allowed to swim into the cave – it's not the exclusive preserve of the boatmen, though they'll try to persuade you otherwise – but the route through is so hectic that unless you're a very strong swimmer it's only advisable to try at the end of the day after the tours have finished.

Eating, drinking and nightlife

The island is overloaded with places to **eat**, but only a few of them are anywhere near good value, so you can always knock yourself up a **picnic** if you prefer: Cápri town has a supermarket and bakery a little way down Via le Botteghe, off La Piazzetta, and a well-stocked *salumeria* at Via Roma nos. 13 and 30; the local cheeses are especially good. Tucked away just a few metres back down towards Marina Grande from the island's little roundabout, there's also a sizeable, well-stocked supermarket. After dark, Cápri comes into its own, with La Piazzetta a lively hub, and a number of decent **clubs** dotted around the island (see p.194).

All places listed below are marked on the **maps** on p.182 and p.188.

Cafés & gelaterie

No visitor can really get the full taste of Cápri without taking a ringside seat at one of its cafés or *gelaterie*, sampling the wares and eyeing up the ebb and flow of holidaymakers and locals.

Bar Caso Piazza Umberto I 4, Cápri town. Of the quartet of bars on La Piazzetta, this one is traditionally the gay favourite. In any case, on offer is the same smart service, refreshing treats, and extortionate prices as anywhere else in this glitzy spot.

Bar Onda d'Oro Marina Piccola. A well-sited beach bar for taking a break from the sea and sun and cooling down in the shade, with I Faraglioni as part of your panoramic view.

Bar Tiberio Piazza Umberto I 18, Cápri town. This is supposedly where Neapolitans go when they want to while away an hour or two, while Cápri natives are said to favour the rival *Piccolo Bar* on the same square. Which one you choose depends on whether you prefer to people-watch in the direction of the new arrivals up from the marina, or to keep an eye on who's wending their way along from the chic hotels.

Bar Monte Solaro Monte Solaro, Anacápri. Probably the island's ultimate café experience, good for cooling drinks and tasty snacks while you catch some sun, ogle the international clientele and take in the stupendous views.

Il Gelato al Limone Piazzetta Fontana 63, Marina Grande. Whether arriving or waiting for a ferry, this is a good place to indulge in some Caprese *limoncello* ice cream. Lemons are harvested at the foot of the Scala Fenicia and all other ingredients are of the highest quality. Sweets and cakes for sale as well.

Restaurants and pizzerias

Dining on Cápri can mean anything from indifferent tourist rations to a true gourmet experience. The island is known, of course, for its signature dish, **insalata caprese**: fresh tomatoes and whole basil leaves just plucked from the volcanic soil, which gives them an unparalleled rich flavour, and *mozzarella di bufala*, made from local buffalo milk, known for its complex, pleasantly sour taste and juicy texture, topped off with pungent extra-virgin olive oil. The quality is generally high – especially the succulent, wood-fired-oven **pizza** – so it's difficult to go wrong. Still, when things get too busy here, standards do sometimes slip below the acceptable; the places below offer consistently tasty food and good value, within the parameters of the island's high prices.

▲ Eating out in Anacápri

Cápri town and around

Aurora Via Fuorlovado 18–22 ☎ 081.837.0181.
This attractive place is the longest-established
restaurant on the island, with tables outside and a
crunchy speciality called pizza *all'acqua* (€6–10
depending on topping). Full meals are much pricier,
easily €35 a head. Closed Nov–March.

Buca di Bacco "da Serafina" Via Longano 25
☎ 081.837.0723. This old favourite is rated by
locals and visitors alike as one of the best; try the
spaghetti *alla pescatora* for €15, or fresh fish
mains from around €10. It's located just behind La
Piazzetta; look for the whitewashed interior with
coral-coloured tablecloths. Some tables have sea
views. Closed Mon & Jan.

Canzone del Mare Via Marina Piccola 93
☎ 081.837.0104. The top choice on the island's
southern side, with the freshest fish, great views
and real linen. Meals generally come to at least
€30 a head. Open for lunch and dinner Easter to
mid-Oct, dinner only mid-Oct to Easter.

La Capannina Via Le Botteghe 12bis
☎ 081.837.0732. Up to the left from La Piazzetta,
this place is considered by many to be the island's
top restaurant; fish mains such as *pezzogna* (red
snapper) go for around €28. Closed Wed & Nov to
mid-March.

Da Gemma Via Madre Serafina 6 ☎ 081.837.0461.
This one-time hangout of Graham Greene has
found its way onto many people's list of Cápri
favourites. The buffet spread is generally good,
featuring local savouries and salads, and there's
pizza too. Come for lunch to take in the views
through the picture windows. Expect to pay
upwards of €30 a head for dinner. Closed Nov–April
& Thurs May, June & Oct.

Da Giorgio Via Roma 34 ☎ 081.837.0898. This
popular local hangout is surprisingly inexpensive
(for Cápri) and yet in a picturesque location off the
street, with views. Try the *linguine ai frutti di mare*
at €12. The restaurant also offers good-value hotel
rooms (see p.180). Closed Tues & Jan–Feb.

Le Grottelle Via Arco Naturale 13 ☎ 081.837.5719.
Almost all the way down to the Arco Naturale, the
appeal of this family-run place is its stunning
position, set amidst lush greenery and with precipitous views down to the sea. The traditional cookery
is generally good and the service amiable, though
both have suffered of late, perhaps from too much
tourism. Prices have also been jacked up – at least
€35 per person – but it's still worth a visit. June &
Sept closed Thurs; Apr & Oct closed dinner &
Thurs; closed Nov–March.

🏃 **La Savardina "da Edoardo"** Via Lo Capo
8 ☎ 081.837.6300. Coordinate lunch or
dinner here with your hike up to Villa Jovis and
you're onto a winner. The location is gorgeous,
thick with orange and lemon groves, flowers and
arbours, with nice views. The food is excellent, too,
the best of traditional country garden cooking, and
it's run by a welcoming family. About €30 for a
meal. Closed Nov–Feb and Tues March–May, Sept
& Oct.

🏃 **Villa Verde** Vico Sella Orta 6a
☎ 081.837.7024. Great *antipasti* and
vegetable soup are among the culinary delights
here, as well as excellent focaccia. The soothing
garden setting, complete with grotto and fountain,
feels intimate, but everything is within easy reach.
The Calabrian red wine is superb. Dinner will set
you back about €50. Closed Tues & Nov–Feb.

Anacápri and around

Add'ò Riccio Via Grotta Azzurra 11
☎ 081.837.1380. A Cápri institution for decades,
serving up heaps of freshly caught seafood, and it's
a standout choice for those who want to indulge and
don't mind paying the price, starting at about €35 a
person. Mid-March to Oct open daily for lunch &
Fri–Sun also dinner; closed Nov to mid-March.

Barbarossa Piazza Vittoria 1 ☎ 081.837.1483.
Right by the bus stop, with a nice terrace
overlooking the square, this is a modest place, but
very good value. The pizzas are excellent, and the
pastas and salads are tempting too. There's
always something seasonal on offer, such as
artichokes or stuffed courgette blossoms. From
about €20 a head.

Il Cucciolo Via La Fabbrica 52 & Traversa Veterino
50 ☎ 081.837.1917. This rather pricey choice has
a terrace overlooking the sea and distant Ischia. If
you're a *Villa Eva* guest, ask for the special menu
and pay much less. Phone for someone to come
and pick you up from your hotel or anywhere on
the island, and take you back again. Closed Wed
April, May & Oct, Mon–Thurs Nov–March.

🏃 **Da Gelsomina** Via Migliara 72
☎ 081.837.1499. This excellent restaurant
makes a wonderful lunch option, with lovely views.
The food is traditional Cápri fare and consistently
delicious, with lunch going for about €35 per
person. Try the spicy, "hunter-style" rabbit with
tomatoes (*coniglio alla cacciatora*). The attached
hotel is equally good (see p.181). Closed Jan, Feb
& Tues; lunch only Oct–April.

Materita Via G. Orlandi 140/Piazza Diaz
☎ 081.837.3375. Attractive and well located, with
cosy indoor seating and terrace tables, too. The
signature dish is the Neapolitan-style pizza (€6 for
a margherita), served both lunch and dinner, but
there's also a full menu. Closed Tues & Nov to
mid-Dec.

Sciué Sciué Via G. Orlandi 73 ☎081.837.2068. Hardly more than a hole in the wall, this friendly joint turns out delicious pizza by the slice and other traditional snacks, for when time is short and you need nourishment on the hoof.

🏃 **Il Solitario** Via G. Orlandi 96 ☎081.837.1382. Take the little walkway back from the street and discover an arboured garden patio decorated with appealingly kitsch painted statues and coloured fairy lights. The food is excellent, the prices moderate, and the service very friendly. Closed Tues, Nov & 2 weeks in Feb.

Vini e Bibite Piazza Diaz ☎081.837.3320. Tucked to the left side of this square's little church, this *tavola calda* (with dishes already prepared and kept warm) is probably the island's most economical option and not at all bad. You eat on throwaway plates, but you can have a full and satisfying meal for about €10. Closed Tues.

Nightlife

Cápri's main square, La Piazzetta, is always bustling, but after dark is when it begins to show its true colours. Everyone, sooner or later, will pass through, on their way back from dinner, or out for a night on the tiles.

Anema e Core Via Stella Orta 39e, Cápri town ☎081.837.6461. The "Soul and Heart" was and still tries to be the epitome of the *Dolce Vita* lifestyle. Ideally located right in the poshest of the posh areas – across from the sumptuous *Hotel Quisisana* – this club is frequented by a self-consciously fashionable set. Live Neapolitan and Italian music and some Latin American acoustic sets. Admission from €25, includes 1 drink.

Aumm Aumm Via Caprile 18, Anacápri ☎081.837.2061. This good-sized bar doubles as a pizzeria and, with its huge screen, as a sports bar whenever there's a big game on. Locals love it, and it's open till late.

Numbertwo Via Camerelle 1, Cápri town ☎081.837.7078. Depending on the whims of the in-crowd, *Numbertwo* has been known to take the number one slot. The dressier the better, and never show up before 2am. Admission €25–50, includes 1 drink.

Underground Via G. Orlandi 259, Anacápri ☎081.837.2523. Cosy and inviting, this bar-club offers exotic cocktails and a mix of pop sounds and a video wall, making summer nights a virtual beach disco. There's occasional live music, and cabaret on Sat nights.

Shopping

Cápri is known for its sun-kissed local produce, above all the prized *limoncello*, but there are handmade crafts of all sorts, too, some of them following very ancient traditions. Cápri town's famous **boutiques** are, of course, on the pricey side, including a fair sprinkling of international designer labels. Below are a few of the more artisanal enterprises, most of them in more economical Anacápri.

L'Arte del Sandalo Caprese Via G. Orlandi 75, Anacápri. Getting sandals made to fit is a Cápri tradition. Unless you choose one of the most elaborate models, chances are Antonio Viva will have your made-to-order pair ready within a matter of hours.

CapriNatura Via Veruotto 5, Cápri town. Located just down from the island's roundabout, off Via Marina Grande, this micro-producer of Mediterranean digestive liqueurs also sells them from their gourmet boutique. Flavours include lemon, mandarin, laurel and basil, as well as the island's wild *cedro*, a lemon-like fruit as big as a grapefruit.

La Conchiglia Via Le Botteghe 12 & Via Camerelle 18, Cápri town; Via G. Orlandi 205, Anacápri. This fascinating bookshop specializes in Cápri literature, including writings in several languages about the island, and the rather bizarre assortment of people who have frequented it. There's also a selection of reproductions of antiques, as well as original paintings and prints.

🏃 **Corallium** Via G. Orlandi 163–5, Anacápri. This boutique is the family-run outlet for a coral and cameo factory in Torre del Greco, a seaside town near Vesuvius, where the craft has roots in antiquity. The shop stocks everything from strands of coral branches to the finest hand-carved pieces set in gold, and prices are reasonable. All items come with a guarantee of authenticity.

Eureka Via G. Orlandi 55–7, Anacápri. Cápri has its own take on traditional Mediterranean pottery – softly colourful and cheerful. You'll find a wide range of styles and shapes here by local artisans, and you can also order exactly what you want, from a set of dishes to a personalized plaque.

L'Iris Piazza Vittoria 5, Anacápri. Of all the souvenir shops that crowd round the main piazza, this one offers items of real quality. Lots of nautical-themed items, as well as good copies of Roman bronzes and other handicrafts.

Il Sandalo Caprese di Attilio Via Sopramonte 9a, Cápri town. Doing a brisk business in keeping the chic shod for decades, Attilio even made shoes once upon a time for the likes of Jackie Onassis. You can choose the simplest and sturdiest of designs, or go for the baroque and jewel-encrusted numbers – there are plenty of styles to choose from for women, men and children.

Listings

Boat rental and watersports Leomar ☎081.837.7181. Located to the right of Marina Grande, near the beach bar *Da Zio Ciccio*, you can rent boats for a minimum of 3hr (10am–6pm; closed Nov–March). Kayak rental is available at Lo Scoglio delle Sirene, Via Mulo 63, Marina Piccola (☎081.837.0221); other watersports equipment too.

Festivals Two main events commemorate the island's patron saints: San Costanzo on May 14 in Cápri town, and Sant'Antonio on June 13 in Anacápri. The Settembrata Anacaprese in the first week of Sept celebrates the grape harvest in Anacápri, while Sept 8 sees a costumed procession up Monte Solaro. On Jan 1 and 6, New Year and

Epiphany celebrations include the famous *tarantella* dance in La Piazzetta.

First aid ☎081.838.1205; nights and holidays ☎081.837.5019; emergency at sea ☎1530.

Hospital Via Provinciale Anacápri 5, Cápri town ☎081.838.1205.

Internet Piazza Vittoria 13, Anacápri (☎081.837.3283; €4 per hr).

Post office Branches at Via Marina Grande 152; Via Roma 50; Via De Tommaso 8.

Scooter rental Via Marina Grande 280 (☎081.837.7941), just up from the port to the right; Piazza Barile 26, Anacápri (☎081.837.7941).

Taxis Cápri ☎081.837.0543; Anacápri ☎081.837.1175.

Ischia

Largest of the islands in the Bay of Naples, **ISCHIA** rises out of the sea in a series of pointy green hummocks. Its perfect cone shape is the giveaway to its geological roots: the island is essentially a long-inactive volcano (last known eruption 1301), although in this notoriously seismic area, perpetual slumber is no certainty. The main port is defined by the nearly perfect rim of an extinct crater, opened up to the sea only in 1855, when part of the ring was ordered to be cut away by Ferdinand II.

A sure sign that all has far from cooled off underground is the plentiful **hot springs**, which are part of the island's long-standing allure, offering everything from luxury spas to moonlit skinny-dipping in coves with natural steam-heated rockpools. The island's thermal spas, some of them radioactive, claim cures for almost anything that ails you, be it "gout, retarded sexual development, or chronic rheumatism", to quote one old brochure.

Sometimes called the Emerald Island, Ischia is studded with pine groves and surrounded by sparkling waters that lap its long sandy beaches. German, Scandinavian and British tourists, in particular, flock to its good-value beach resorts in droves during peak season. The island's reputation has always been poorer than

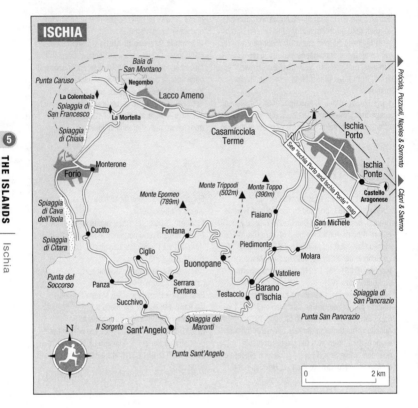

ISCHIA

Baia di San Montano
Punta Caruso
Negombo
La Colombaia
Spiaggia di San Francesco
La Mortella
Lacco Ameno
Spiaggia di Chiaia
Casamicciola Terme
Ischia Porto
Monterone
Forio
Ischia Ponte
Castello Aragonese
Monte Trippodi (502m)
Monte Toppo (390m)
Monte Epomeo (789m)
Spiaggia di Cava dell'Isola
Fiaiano
San Michele
Cuotto
Fontana
Piedimonte
Spiaggia di Citara
Ciglio
Buonopane
Molara
Vatoliere
Punta del Soccorso
Panza
Serrara Fontana
Barano d'Ischia
Spiaggia di San Pancrazio
Succhivo
Testaccio
Punta San Pancrazio
Spiaggia dei Maronti
Il Sorgeto
Sant'Angelo
Punta Sant'Angelo
N
0   2 km

See Ischia Porto and Ischia Ponte " map

Prócida, Pozzuoli, Naples & Sorrento   Cápri & Salerno

Cápri's, and it is perhaps not so dramatically beautiful. But you can at least be sure of being alone in exploring many parts of the mountainous interior, which rises to the peak of **Monte Epomeo** (793m) at its centre. As for sights, **La Mortella**, the exotic garden cultivated by the British composer William Walton and his widow Susana, is an unmissable attraction, as is the **Castello Aragonese**, the island's most historic landmark.

Some history

The island's history is probably the area's most ancient, having known habitation since about 2000 BC. From the eighth to the fifth centuries BC, this area became an important part of **Magna Graecia** (Greater Greece) when colonists from Greek city-states in Euboea came here to set up trading posts and new cities. The first ones established themselves on Ischia, which they called Pithek-oussai (in reference to the abundance of potting clay, *pithos*), but the eruption of Montagnone (now extinct) shortly thereafter led them to settle Cumae on the mainland. The Greeks evolved a myth to explain their uneasy relationship with the island's volcanic nature: it was said that Zeus had imprisoned beneath the island the monstrous giant Typhon, creator of volcanoes. The hot springs and steam were believed to be his tears of frustration and huffs of rage. Archeological evidence shows that there was a significant disturbance in the second century BC, too, which again drove island inhabitants away. The last time Typhon grumbled was in 1883, causing an earthquake.

The island's present name is thought to be the result of the slow distortion of the Latin word *insula*, which simply means "island". During most of the Roman period, the island was of oddly little importance, the archeological record showing mostly humble peasant activity – probably due to the pronounced seismic activity during that epoch. Following the fall of the Roman Empire, the island was little more than a political football for many centuries.

In the Middle Ages, a combination of natural catastrophes and attacks by Saracen corsairs plagued the island's serenity. The high point of Ischia's cultural heritage was the early 1500s, when Renaissance Humanist Vittoria Colonna resided in the Castello Aragonese. Much later, the island (like Cápri) attracted its share of artistic and just plain disgraceful foreign residents: the Norwegian playwright Henrik Ibsen penned *Peer Gynt* here in the nineteenth century, and later the locals of Forío were honoured, puzzled and scandalized, in equal measure, by the antics of gay English poet W.H. Auden and his circle – giving the island a reputation for attracting outsiders that was eclipsed only by its more famous neighbour.

Arrival, transport and information

Ferries and **hydrofoils** from various points around the bay (see box, pp. 178–179) arrive at three points: the main port, **Ischia Porto** (from Naples, Cápri, Prócida and Pozzuoli, and seasonally from the Amalfi Coast as well): at **Casamícciola Terme** (from Naples, Prócida and Pozzuoli); and on the western end of the island at **Forío** (from Naples). If you arrive at the main port of Ischia Porto, you will need to walk up to the main road to find the **bus terminal**, where there is a kiosk for purchasing tickets before boarding. If you arrive at another port town, you'll find bus stops at several points along the main ring road – the stops are easy to spot as you leave the quay. The island is fairly large and has some two dozen towns, villages and hamlets, spread around in a ring, with the cone of the dormant volcano in the centre, and the more reasonable order for a visit is anticlockwise, given the way the towns are clustered.

Unless you bring or rent a **car** or **scooter** (see "Listings", p.212), you can rely on the efficient **bus** system to get to all of the major towns and some of the other popular spots, such as Maronti Beach and the various points of departure for hikes. The main buses, #CS (clockwise) and #CD (anticlockwise), circle the entire island at thirty-minute intervals, while some sixteen lesser lines gain access to various byways and smaller settlements; the tourist office can provide you with timetables. **Tickets** cost €1.20 and are valid for 90 minutes; day tickets are available for €4, two-day tickets for €6.

Ischia Porto's helpful **tourist office** is right by the quayside ferry ticket offices in the old Terme Comunali building (Mon–Sat 9am–2pm & 3–8pm; ☏081.507.4231, ⓦwww.infoischiaprocida.it). It's a branch of the main office at Via Sogliuzzo 72, halfway between Ischia Porto and Ischia Ponte (Mon–Fri 9am–2pm; ☏081.507.4211).

Ischia Porto and Ischia Ponte

Ischia's main town, **ISCHIA PORTO**, or simply Ischia, is the arrival point for most hydrofoils and ferries, inside the protective ring of the uniquely circular little port. It's an appealing enough stretch of hotels, wannabe ritzy boutiques, and beach shops along lanes planted with lemon trees and Indian

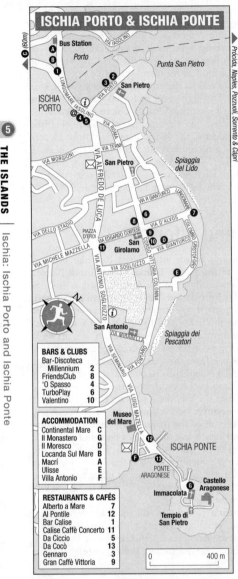

ISCHIA PORTO & ISCHIA PONTE

(600m)

Bus Station

Porto

San Pietro

Punta San Pietro

ISCHIA
PORTO

Pozzuoli, Sorrento & Capri

Pròcida, Naples,

VIA JASOLINO

LUNGOMARE JASOLINO

VIA PORTO

VIA ROMA

VIA TERME

VIA MORGIONI

VIA ALFREDO DE LUCA

San Pietro

Spiaggia
del Lido

VIA R GIANTURCO

LUNGOMARE

COLOMBO CRISTOFORO

VIA DELLO STADIO

PIAZZA
D'EROI

VIA EDGARDO CORTESE

San
Girolamo

VIA D'ALVOS

CORSO VITTORIA COLONNA

VIA GIANTURCO

VIA MICHELE MAZZELLA

VIA ANTONIO SOGLIUZZO

VIA SOGLIUZZO

San Antonio

VIA MIRABELLA

Spiaggia dei
Pescatori

N

VIA SEMINARIO

VIA PONTANO

BARS & CLUBS

Bar-Discoteca	
Millennium	2
FriendsClub	8
'O Spasso	4
TurboPlay	6
Valentino	10

ACCOMMODATION

Continental Mare	C
Il Monastero	G
Il Moresco	D
Locanda Sul Mare	B
Macrí	A
Ulisse	E
Villa Antonio	F

Museo
del Mare

VIA LUIGI MAZELLA

ISCHIA PONTE

PONTE
ARAGONESE

Castello
Aragonese

Immacolata

Tempio di
San Pietro

RESTAURANTS & CAFÉS

Alberto a Mare	7
Al Pontile	12
Bar Calise	1
Calise Caffè Concerto	11
Da Ciccio	5
Da Cocò	13
Gennaro	3
Gran Caffè Vittoria	9

0   400 m

figs. Beyond a few churches, Ischia Porto has no special sights, and amounts to pretty much what first meets the eye – a stretch of low-key resort commercialism and hotels, some of them lavish, with plenty of gardens and greenery. The best way to occupy your time here is to window-shop, slurp a *gelato* and stroll along the mostly pedestrianized Corso Vittoria Colonna and parallel lanes.

But Ischia Porto is really just the snootier, parvenu half of a two-part urbanized spread. Follow Corso Colonna past the Baroque extravaganza of the colourful tile-domed church that goes by two names, **San Pietro** and **Santa Maria delle Grazie**, alongside the shaded plantings of the Villa Nenzi Bozzi (daily sunrise–sunset) and then on past the impressive park of umbrella pines. This is the woodsy line of demarcation between Ischia Porto and **ISCHIA PONTE** (3km away from the port at its furthest tip; also reachable by bus #7) – the quieter, centuries older and generally less touristy half of the island's main settlement. Despite signs of gentrification, such as one or two elegant antiques shops and several art galleries, things are just a bit more run-down here, a bit earthier – home to the less crowded **Spiaggia dei Pescatori** ("Fishermen's Beach"), as well as the island's major landmark, the **Castello Aragonese**.

Accommodation

There's no lack of **accommodation** in Ischia Ponte and Porto, though many places close from November to Easter, opening only for a short time between Christmas and New Year. Ischia Porto makes a livelier base, but Ponte is decidedly more charming, and preferable for long-term stays. The most convenient **campsite**, *Eurocamping dei Pini* at Via delle Ginestre 28, Porto (☎081.982.069, ⓦwww.ischia.it/camping), also has bungalows from €60, and is a short walk from the port. To get there, follow Via Mazzella away from the sea and turn right several roads after the football pitches.

Continental Mare Via B. Cossa 25, Porto ☏ 081.982.577, ⊛ www.continentalmare.it. This breezily elegant hotel west of the port enjoys a splendid location above the sea, a pool and spa, as well as its own stretch of private beach. Rooms are spacious and briskly contemporary in style, the best ones enjoying balconies with sea views. Half and full board available. Doubles from €120.

Locanda Sul Mare Via Jasolino 80, Porto ☏ 081.981.470, ⊛ www.locandasulmare.it. Near the port, this tiny, idiosyncratically decorated and very pleasant hotel is a bargain, and has a decent restaurant too. Doubles €70–125.

Macrì Via Jasolino 96, Porto ☏ &℻ 081.992.603. Just steps from the arrival docks of Ischia Porto, this prettily furnished and simple place has its own bar, parking and garden, and is handy for a night out in lively Porto. Breakfast is an additional €6 per person. Doubles €75.

🏃 **Il Monastero** Castello Aragonese, Ponte ☏ 081.992.435, ⊛ www.albergoilmonastero .it. On the upper floors of the Castello Aragonese, with twenty rooms, former nuns' cells, that are coolly comfortable, accented with interesting contemporary art and carefully chosen *objets*. The hotel has a sunny terrace overlooking the sea and a picturesque café-restaurant, with sweeping views. The grounds host occasional art exhibitions and concerts. Doubles €160.

Il Moresco Via E. Gianturco 16, Porto ☏ 081.981.335, ⊛ www.ilmoresco.it. This plush and luxurious hotel is housed in a quirky 1950s villa in the heart of Ischia Porto, but still manages to feel secluded thanks to its high walls and lush garden. There are grottoes, thermal pools and a spa, as well as a private beach. The spacious rooms and suites feature traditional tiles and botanical prints, some with private balconies and terraces. Doubles €350.

Ulisse Via Champault 9, Porto ☏ 081.991.737, ⊛ www.hotelulisse.com. A laid-back choice at the eastern end of Porto's centre with two swimming pools and extensive gardens. Locally crafted tiles give the spacious rooms a homespun touch, and some have balconies with views of the sea and the Castello. Half-board is obligatory and there is a three-night minimum stay. Closed Nov–March. Doubles €176.

🏃 **Villa Antonio** Via S. Giuseppe della Croce 77, Ponte ☏ 081.982.660, ⊛ www .villantonio.it. Spectacularly perched on the promontory overlooking the Castello, with appealingly unfussy rooms, most with balconies. But the main draw is the abundance of artwork: original paintings adorn the walls, and the broad terrace facing the Castello is a whimsical sculpture garden. This romantic hideaway also has access to the sea, with a private bathing platform hewn from the rock. Doubles €100.

The Castello Aragonese

The dominant focus of Ischia Ponte is indubitably the island's emblem, the regal **Castello Aragonese** (daily 9am–1hr before sunset; €10; allow at least an hour for a visit). The Castello crowns an offshore volcanic outcrop about 113m high – affording stupendous views – accessible by Ischia Ponte's causeway of 220m, built by Alfonso of Aragon in the fifteenth century. The hulking structure's distinctive pyramid shape acted as a backdrop in the film *The Talented Mr Ripley* and serves almost daily as the picturesque setting for wedding photos, usually complete with classic car in the foreground.

A fort of some sort has crowned this rock since at least the fifth century BC, and it's belonged to the Greeks, the Romans, the Goths, the Arabs and others, though its most famous occupant was the Renaissance poet **Vittoria Colonna** (see box, p.200). The citadel itself where she lived is a mere shell now, part of so much that was destroyed by British bombardment in the early nineteenth century. At one time the entire mount was covered with buildings, forming a sizeable town boasting a population of some eight thousand souls. Now the only extant structures lie landward from the abandoned citadel, constituting a ramble of buildings. You arrive by elevator in the midst of these, and you can stroll freely around.

Vittoria Colonna, the Renaissance poet, Humanist luminary and close friend of Michelangelo, lived out much of her life in the Castello Aragonese, banished here following the seizure by Pope Alexander VI of her family's land in and around Rome. In 1509, she was married in the castle's cathedral to the scion of the d'Avalos family, Ischia being one of their feudal fiefdoms. Vittoria created a brilliant court here – one of the most renowned of a sparkling era – while her husband Ferrante was away fighting wars. After his death in the Battle of Pavia in 1525, she continued to maintain her intellectual circle and life of spiritual retreat here until 1536. Her close friendship with Michelangelo was a lifelong Platonic affair — including dedications of works of art and mutual exchanges of high-flown poems — ending with her death in 1547, in Rome.

To the right, you'll find the graceful sixteenth-century **Tempio di San Pietro**, like a mini-Pantheon, and further up, the remains of the fourteenth-century *carcere* that once held political prisoners during the upheavals of Italian Unification. To the left is the weird open shell of the ruined **cathedral**, built in 1301 but reworked in the eighteenth century in Baroque style; the largely intact crypt holds Giotto-inspired frescoes painted in the fourteenth century. Close by is the fairly undamaged eighteenth-century **Immacolata** church, noted for its imposing dome. You can also explore the grim remains of the **convent of the Poor Clares**, many of whose inmates were not here by choice, but were sent by their families. A couple of dark rooms ringed with a set of commode-like seats used to serve as a macabre open cemetery for the dead sisters – propped up here to putrefy and eventually mummify in full view of the living members of the community, a practice that continued until the early nineteenth century; the rest of the convent has been turned into a hotel (see p.199).

The beaches and the Museo del Mare

Ischia Porto has some good **beaches**, once you get past the buildings hugging the shoreline. The **Spiaggia San Pietro** and **Spiaggia del Lido** are to the right of the port – follow Via Buonocore off Via Roma – while the **Spiaggia degli Inglesi**, its name hailing back to the brief British hegemony in the early nineteenth century, is on the other side of the port; take the narrow path that leads over the headland from the end of Via Jasolino.

Not only does Ischia Ponte claim the proletariat, dark-sand "**Fishermen's Beach**", it is also home to the island's **Museo del Mare** in Palazzo Orologio at Via Giovanni Da Procida 3 (Museum of the Sea; daily: April–June, Sept & Oct 10.30am–12.30pm & 3–7pm; July & Aug 10.30am–12.30pm & 6.30–10pm; Nov–Jan & March 10.30am–12.30pm; €3), tracing the community's seafaring roots. Housed in a historic building of modest local Baroque style, the fascinating displays explore Ischia's maritime connections over the millennia. They include ancient, barnacle-encrusted pottery retrieved from the sea and exhibits of marine fauna, as well as navigation instruments from sextants to sonar, along with displays of nautical and fishing gear. Perhaps most appealing are the meticulously detailed models of typically Ischian sailing vessels, though the colourful collection of sea-themed stamps is also eye-catching and includes some blocks depicting amphibious dinosaurs and other monstrous denizens that plied these waters aeons ago.

From the Museo del Mare, Via Mazzella leads to the elegant **Ponte Aragonese** bridge, built in 1438, which connects the town to the Castello Aragonese (see p.199).

Eating, drinking and nightlife

Ischia Porto is full of **cafés** catering to tourists just off the ferry and dense with tourist traps serving mediocre food at inflated prices. There are a few exceptions, however: *Bar Calise* at the exit of the ferry terminal is a pleasant place to stop for a coffee, pastry or drink, while nearby at Piazza Antica Reggia 5, the ice cream at *Da Ciccio* is considered to be among the best on the island. Heading towards Ponte at Via V. Colonna 110, *Gran Caffè Vittoria* serves delicious pastries and biscuits as well as savoury snacks. There are a handful of decent **restaurants** near the port, though Ischia Ponte is a better bet for a moderately priced, authentic meal.

For **nightlife**, head for the lively run of late-night bars and cafés along Via Porto. More laid-back entertainment is provided in the gardens of *Calise Caffè Concerto* (see below), where there's live music after dark until 4am in summer.

The places listed below are marked on the **map** on p.198.

Restaurants and cafés

Alberto a Mare Viale C. Colombo 8, Porto ☏081.981259. Right on the seafront, this upmarket restaurant on stilts over the sea has immaculate service and beautifully presented seafood. The *marinata mista* (fish carpaccio marinated in lemon, orange and balsamic vinegar) is a wonderful starter, and *linguine con cozze* (with mussels) is the pasta speciality. Meals from €55 without wine. Closed Nov to mid-March.

Al Pontile Via Luigi Mazzella 15 & Lungomare Aragonese 6, Ponte ☏081.983.492. On the waterfront directly opposite the Castello, this café and unassuming little restaurant with an outdoor terrace serves anything from just drinks and snacks to pasta and salads. The bruschetta is particularly delicious, garnished with sweet ripe tomatoes from the island's volcanic slopes.

Calise Caffè Concerto Piazza degli Eroi 69, Porto ☏081.991.270. Set in the midst of a veritable jungle of greenery, with sleek rooms and garden terraces. An all-purpose gastronomic venue, you'll find everything from excellent *gelato* to scrumptious cakes to meals (from €20). After hours, *Calise* turns into a lounge bar and music venue, open until 4am in summer. Closed Wed Nov–March.

Da Cocò Piazzale Aragonese, Ponte ☏081.981.823. In an enviable position just below the Castello Aragonese, this bar-restaurant has lovely sea views and serves up great seafood, such

as *seppie in umido* (stewed cuttlefish) and *frittura di paranza* (small fried gulf fish), each for around €10. Closed Wed Sept–April.

Gennaro Via Porto 59, Porto ☏081.992.917. Established in 1965, this seafood specialist in the harbour serves traditional Ischian fare like *zuppa di cozze* (mussels in broth), spaghetti *alle vongole* (with clams), and grilled fish and seafood. Wash it down with the local Ischia DOC wine made with white *biancolella* grapes. Meals from €40. Closed Nov to mid-March.

Bars and clubs

Bar-Discoteca Millennium Via Porto 86. The island's best club also serves as a café by day with internet access (2pm till late).

FriendsClub Corso Vittoria Colonna 123. A piano bar, cocktail lounge and club all in one, with vaulted ceilings and low lighting creating an intimate atmosphere.

'O Spasso Via E. Cortese on the corner of Piazza degli Eroi. One of the newest nightspots, more sophisticated than most, with low lighting and exotic touches.

TurboPlay Corso Vittoria Colonna 147. Combines a late-night (till 3am) internet café with video games and a trendy bar.

Valentino Corso Vittoria Colonna 97. A popular and fun-loving club for all ages, with pricey admission and mainly house and dance music.

The rest of the island

The island is at its most developed along its northern and western shores. Heading west from Ischia Porto, **Casamícciola Terme** and **Lacco Ameno** are spa centres known for their restorative radioactive waters, while in the island's northwestern corner, the lush greenery of the gardens of **La Mortella** have a quite different appeal. On the island's eastern flank, workaday **Forío** has plenty to offer in the way of beaches, but Ischia is most pleasant on its southern side, comprising areas generally referred to as the **Serrara Fontana** (west) and **Barano d'Ischia** (east). The landscape here is steeper and greener, making it ideal hiking territory, and there's a picturesque hub in the form of **Sant'Angelo**, a former fishing village that's now one of the island's most appealing places to rest up for a few days.

Casamícciola Terme

The first village you reach heading west from Ischia Porto, **CASAMÍCCIOLA TERME**, is a spa centre with an array of hotels and a crowded beach. The village's claim to fame is that Ibsen spent a summer here, writing *Peer Gynt*, but most people stop off here for its spa waters, which are said to be full of iodine (reputedly beneficial for the skin and the nervous system).

For **spa treatments**, the *Terme Belliazzi* in Piazza Bagni (℡081.994.580, Ⓦwww.termebelliazzi.it; mid-April to Oct) is a bathing complex built above a hot spring prized by the Romans. Dedicated to medicinal cures – the radioactive waters are thought to help respiratory disorders – it also offers the usual pampering treatments. You can soak in pools beneath ancient brick arches (€25) or opt for a massage or mud treatment (from €30). The sea can be quite rough here, but if you must take a dip, there's a **beach** with facilities around the Spiaggia dei Bagnitelli, on the road heading east torwards Ischia Porto.

One other feature that may tweak your interest is the 500-year-old **ceramic factory** and shop Ceramiche Mennella on the main road, 800m back towards Ischia from the port at Via S. Girardi 47 (summer daily 9am–1pm & 3.30–8pm, winter Mon–Sat 9am–1pm & 3.30–8pm), which is in effect a living museum dedicated to the traditions of Ischian pottery. Historic pieces are on display, along with current fabrications: colourful tiles, classical-style terracotta sculptures and a host of more conventional faience creations such as vases and hand-painted plates.

Practicalities

If you decide to make Casamícciola your base, you'll have over sixty **hotels** to choose from, from sumptuous five-star palaces to simple *pensioni*, but the best options take advantage of the thermal springs and panoramic views. The *Terme Elisabetta* at Corso Garibaldi 97 (℡081.994.355, Ⓦwww.hoteltermeelisabetta.it; Easter–Oct; doubles €64–106) is good value: a sparkling white structure with a large thermal pool, spa facilities and handsome rooms with balcony views of the sea or the gardens. Another good choice is the *Ape Regina* at Via Cretaio 59 (℡081.994.813, Ⓦwww.hotelaperegina.it; doubles €64–96; a/c an extra €6 per day), a pleasant villa nestled in greenery, with a thermal pool, inspiring views and an excellent restaurant; having your own car is recommended, as it's about 2km up from the port.

As for the question of where to **eat**, the stylish complex just up from the port, above Piazza Marina, is a handily placed option. Another branch of the island-wide institution *Calise* (see p.201), you'll find all the same sweets and snacks here, along with pizzas and full meals, starting at about €12 a head. There's also a pleasant piano bar, with terrace seating. To sample the wares at Casamícciola's most celebrated restaurant – if you have your own transport, or don't mind taking a taxi – make your way up to Via Cretajo al Crocefisso 3, where *Il Focolare* (℡081.902.944; June–Oct open daily for lunch and dinner; Nov–May Mon, Tues, Thurs & Fri dinner only, Sat & Sun lunch and dinner) offers traditional home-made pastas like tagliatelle with porcini mushrooms, and earthy forest fare such as *lumache in umido* (snails in broth) and *coniglio all'ischitana* (rabbit with tomatoes and herbs), an island classic not to be missed. Expect to pay about €30 per person.

Lacco Ameno

Less than 3km further west is **LACCO AMENO**, a brighter, altogether more stylish little town, with a beach and spa waters that are reputedly the most radioactive in Italy, a property that is said to ease a host of ailments. A 10m-tall tufa rock sprouting out of the sea is the town's most distinctive landmark: affectionately nicknamed **Il Fungo**, it vaguely resembles a mushroom and is volcanic in origin, likely to have been spewed from the erupting cone of Mount Epomeo millennia ago. Nowadays Lacco Ameno is simply an attractive place to pass some time, its earthy elegance comparable to Cápri at its best. Its considerable appeal is preserved thanks to a curve in the main road just before it reaches the town centre, leaving the area along the waterfront pedestrian-only, with gurgling fountains in piazzas, low-key shops and waterside cafés.

The Town

Lacco Ameno is a resort above all, but the town also has a strong sense of place and a colourful history. Legend holds that the martyred body of fourth-century Tunisian virgin **Santa Restituta** was borne to this spot by lilies, and there's a sugary pink-and-white confection of a church in Piazza Santa Restituta decorated with a nineteenth-century painting cycle remembering those events. Archeological excavations have revealed that it's built on top of a fourth-century paleo-Christian basilica, a second-century BC Roman town, and even more ancient remains – such as a pottery kiln – of what was once the Greek colony of Pithecusa. Artefacts exhibited in the **Area Archeologica di Santa Restituta**, under the church (Mon–Sat: March–May 9.30am–12.30pm; June–Oct 9.30am–12.30pm & 5–7pm; €3), include votive amphorae, some very large, and *ex voto* objects accumulated over many centuries, as well as Byzantine, Roman and Greek ceramics, coins, toys and statuettes dating as far back as the fifth century BC.

Museo Archeologico di Pithecusa

Above the main square on Corso Rizzoli, in a panoramic spot across from where the ancient Greek acropolis once stood, the eighteenth-century Villa Arbusto houses the **Museo Archeologico di Pithecusa** (Tues–Sun: May–Oct 9.30am–1pm & 4–8pm, Nov–April 9.30am–1pm & 3–7pm; €5), consisting of well-displayed finds from the acropolis of Monte di Vico, in continuous use from the eighth to the first centuries BC. Pithecusa (modern Ischia) was the first and northernmost Greek settlement in the West, a thriving and vital staging post at the western end of routes from the Aegean and the Levant; in addition to local artefacts, the museum preserves locally excavated burial paraphernalia imported from Syria, Egypt and Etruria.

The most celebrated piece is the so-called **Coppa di Nestore** (Nestor's Cup; display case XX), a typical eighth-century BC pottery drinking cup (*kotyle* in Greek) in the so-called late geometric style, probably made on the island of Rhodes. There's a famously puzzling three-line verse incised on the humble vessel (scratched in, actually, at some point well after its fabrication), which reads something like "I am Nestor's cup, good to drink from. Whoever drinks from this cup, straightaway desire for beautiful-crowned Aphrodite will seize him."

Scholars disagree on exactly what the poem signifies, though some say it was most likely the consequence of a drinking game, while at least one authority claims it's meant to be a humorously ironic comparison to the splendour of the legendary golden cup of Nestor described in Homer's *Illiad*. In any case, the inscription is one of the earliest known examples of writing in the Greek alphabet. Elsewhere in the collection, a catastrophic shipwreck scene whimsically depicted on a locally made pot (*krater*, display case XVI, also dating to the eighth century BC) is judged to be the oldest example of figurative painting in Italy.

Spas and beaches

The town and its immediate vicinity have their share of excellent spas, including one of the island's very best. Walk on through town, up and over the hill and follow the signs (for about 20min) to **Negombo** on the Baia di San Montano (℡081.986.152, ⓦwww.negombo.it; May to mid-Oct 8.30am–sunset; €28 for a day pass, €30 in Aug, €24 for an afternoon pass, €25 in Aug), whose namesake is a renowned bay in Sri Lanka. Billing itself as a "thermal garden", the spa covers nine hectares and is home to some five hundred species of flowers and plants. Amenities consist of a variety of mineral bathing pools – hot, cold, cascading, wading and more – laid out amidst lush vegetation on a hillside overlooking a private beach and an unspoiled bay. For the price of admission you get the use of all facilities, including changing rooms, swimming pools, and a jacuzzi and Turkish bath; there are restaurants on site too.

Lacco Ameno boasts one of the island's best sandy **beaches**, Lido San Montano on the crystalline bay of the same name. Most of the crescent shore is dominated by Negombo's spa and beach club, but there is a small public beach at the bay's western end. To get there, either follow signs for Negombo (a steep 20min hike) or take the #CD, #CS, #1 or #2 bus to Via San Lorenzo and walk the last 250 metres downhill along Via San Montano. Alternatively, you can take a dip at one of the paid beach clubs along Corso Rizzoli next to the Marina.

Practicalities

Lacco Ameno's **accommodation** focuses on quality rather than quantity, with fewer than twenty hotel options. A good choice near the sea is the *Villa Svizzera*, Via Litoranea 1 (℡081.994.263, ⓦwww.villasvizzera.it; closed Nov–Feb; doubles €170), offering spa services, a seawater pool, extensive gardens and terraces, private parking and a swimming platform on the bay. Rooms are simple, Mediterranean-style, and the panoramic restaurant (half and full board available) offers an eclectic menu. ⚇ *Villa Angelica*, Via IV Novembre 28 (℡081.994.524, ⓦwww.villaangelica.it; closed mid-Nov to mid-March; 3-day minimum; half-board also available; doubles €140) stands in whitewashed modesty just above the little harbour and offers lush gardens and a thermal rockpool, along with spa services. The rooms have terracotta floors and some have balconies with views.

The town has no shortage of **cafés** and **restaurants** at all price levels. For just a drink, choose one of the seaside establishments, the ⚇ *Caffetteria del Corso*, Corso Rizzoli 47, being the classiest; look for the handsome green awning and the red doors facing the main street, but get a seat on the waterside terrace. Otherwise *La Battigia* at no. 5b provides snacks and views with the best of them. For something a little more formal, up Corso Rizzoli to no. 106, *Delfino* (℡081.900.252; closed Wed & Nov to mid-March) serves up succulent seafood dishes such as spaghetti *allo scoglio* or risotto *alla pescatora*, both with mixed seafood, for about €10.

La Mortella

Nestled in the hills halfway between Forío and Lacco Ameno is one of Ischia's highlights: the ravishingly beautiful gardens of **La Mortella** (Via F. Calise 39 Easter–Nov Tues, Thurs, Sat & Sun 9am–7pm; €10, or €15 with concert; ask the bus driver to drop you off; free parking at upper entrance; ℡081.986.220, Ⓦwww.lamortella.org), whose name derives from the Neapolitan dialect and translates as "The Place of the Myrtles", the flower sacred to Aphrodite, goddess of love, and worn by brides in ancient Greece. The gardens are the creation of the English composer Sir William Walton and his Argentinian widow Susana, who still lives here. The Waltons moved to Ischia, then sparsely populated and little known to tourists, in 1949, forerunners of a coterie of writers and artists, including W.H. Auden and Terence Rattigan. With the help of garden designer Russell Page they created La Mortella from an unpromising volcanic stone quarry, the first phase of landscaping alone taking seven years to complete.

Walkways wind up through the profusely luxuriant site, home to hundreds of species of rare and exotic plants, most of them clustered around the fountain and the large rockpool up to the left from the main entrance. The emphasis in the lower garden, known as the Valley, is on water plants, and further still to the left is a glasshouse, the Victoria House, sheltering the world's largest waterlily, *Victoria amazonica*, a gender-bending giant that flowers as a female with white petals, imprisons beetles for pollination purposes, and reopens later in the day with male organs and deep crimson petals. Above the glasshouse sits a charming terraced tearoom, where the strains of Walton's music can be heard, and an enclosure with bright hummingbirds flitting about. Paths loop through prolific foliage to the pyramid-shaped rock that holds Walton's ashes; a cascade guarded by a sculpted crocodile; and a pretty Thai pavilion, surrounded by heavy-headed purple agapanthus and serene pink lotus. At the garden's summit, the upper area known as the Hill, a belvedere provides superb views across the island.

Devotees of Walton's music shouldn't miss the prettily theatrical **museum** above the tearoom, which shows a video about the composer and features portraits by Cecil Beaton, a bust by Elizabeth Frink, paintings and set-designs by John Piper and even an Italian puppet theatre by Luzzati. It's also well worth combining your visit to the garden with a **concert** (see the website for timings), held in the adjoining recital hall and featuring mostly classical standards, usually by soloists and small ensembles of gifted young musicians.

La Colombaia

If you're visiting La Mortella, another sight worth a stop, especially for cinema buffs, is **La Colombaia** (Via F. Calise 130; ℡081.333.2147; April–Sept Mon–Sat 10am–2pm & 3–7pm; Oct Mon–Sat 10am–1pm & 3.30–6pm; at other times phone for an appointment; €6), the summer retreat of the Italian film and theatre director **Luchino Visconti**, whose stylishly epic films included *The Leopard*, *Death in Venice* and *The Twilight of the Gods*. The striking house dates to the late nineteenth and early twentieth centuries and is a whitewashed, neo-Moorish pseudo-castle with exotic Art Nouveau flourishes, ensconced in thick forest and gardens and affording splendid views. It was here that Visconti entertained his lovers of both sexes, threw legendary parties, and consoled his close friend and opera diva Maria Callas when Greek tycoon Ari Onassis ditched her to marry Jackie Kennedy. The building is now a public trust and houses not only a foundation dedicated to promoting Visconti and his legacy but also a **museum** bringing together photographs and multimedia images, costumes and an array of memorabilia relating to the director's exceptional life.

In the summer, performances are sometimes also held in the Greek-style theatre at the centre of the gardens.

Forío

At the opposite side of the island from Ischia Porto, on the west coast, the island's most populous town, **FORÍO**, possesses none of the polish found elsewhere in Ischia but is definitely not without its charms. A bustling, down-to-earth port town, it sprawls around the bay, with a seafront of bars, pizzerias and cheerful chaos, focusing on the attractive, pedestrianized Corso Umberto.

Arrival and accommodation

Buses stop right in the centre of Forío as well as on the main road just outside, and there are lots of **hotels** within easy walking distance.

Accommodation

Poggio del Sole Via Baiola 193 ☎081.987.756, ⊛www.hotelpoggiodelsole.it. Above the town proper, towards the foot of Monte Epomeo, the *Poggio del Sole* offers views over this entire stretch of the island, where the sunsets are especially spectacular. The bright, light-filled rooms with balconies are set in greenery and there's a pool too. It's run by a very friendly family, who also have one of the area's best restaurants on the same property (see p.207). Closed mid-Nov to mid-April; doubles €160–220.

Punta del Sole Piazza Maltese ☎081.989.156, ⊛www.casthotels.com. The charming and central hotel has balconied rooms set in a beautiful garden close to sandy beaches; plus it offers full health and beauty services in its own recently created spa. Doubles €90–170.

Residence La Rotonda sul Mare Via Aiemita 29 ☎081.987.546, ⊛www.larotondasulmare.com. At the start of the Spiaggia di San Francesco, about a 20min stroll from the centre of Forío, this is a rental property offering comfortable holiday-let apartments that sleep up to six. It's a bit isolated from the shops, but there are restaurants and cafés handy, plus it's in an ideal position for catching sunsets – and has its own swimming platform. Closed Dec to mid-March. Apartments €60–100.

Ring Hostel Via G. Morgera 72 ☎081.987.546, ⊛http://ringhostels.com. In the centre of Forío is the fun-loving hostel, run by three outgoing local brothers who speak English, provide shuttle services free of charge and are full of ideas for making everyone's stay better. It's just a short walk from the beaches and other facilities. Dorm beds €18, private doubles from €50.

La Scogliera Via Aiemita 27 ☎081.987.651, ⊛www.hotellascogliera.it. To the north, on the Spiaggia di San Francesco, this hotel offers gardens, three swimming pools, and softly lit comfort in public rooms and guestrooms, which all have either sea or mountain views from private balconies or terraces. The buffet breakfast is fresh and tempting, and the sea is only a short walk away. Doubles €140–210 half board; a/c €8 per day; minimum 7 nights stay; closed Nov to mid-April.

Il Vitigno Via Bocca 31 ☎081.998.307, ⊛www .ilvitigno.com. About 1.5km south of town and 0.5km inland is this wonderfully rustic *agriturismo* with grape-arboured terraces, bucolic views and a pristine rockpool, plus delicious meals prepared from proprietor Giuseppina's own home-grown produce. Dinner is served at a communal table for €15. Doubles €90–100.

The town and beaches

Forío's main landmark is the late fifteenth-century **Torrione**, the gnarly stone cylinder that dominates the town's modest skyline, one of sixteen watchtowers built around the coast to keep a fearful eye out for invading Saracen corsairs. Inside the tower, the former jail houses the **Museo Civico** (Easter–Oct Tues–Sun 10am–1pm; €2), which preserves accomplished if rather dull portraits and busts by the local late nineteenth-century Realist sculptor, painter and poet Giovanni Maltese. Much more interesting are his scenes of everyday Ischian life and his true-to-life, if rather sentimentalized, sculptures of island dwellers.

There's not much else to see in Forío, but the twisting medieval alleyways of its old town are worth a wander, full of little votary niches with colourfully painted tiles of the Virgin, with the odd bunch of flowers offered in an old jam jar. Make your way out to the point on the far side of the old centre (turn right at the far end of Corso Umberto) to the simple **Chiesa Soccorso**, a bold, whitewashed landmark that looks more Spanish that it does Italian. It's worth the short walk to stand on the majolica balustrade, from which there's a good view back towards the town.

There are good **beaches** either side of Forío: the **Spiaggia di Chiaia**, a short walk to the north, followed immediately by the **Spiaggia di San Francesco**; to the south, **Cava dell'Isola**, popular with a younger crowd; and the **Spiaggia di Citara**, a somewhat longer walk south along Via G. Mazzella. Here you'll find the venerable **Giardini Poseidon** (April–Oct daily 9am–7pm; €28 per day, €23 for a half-day, beginning at 1pm; prices increase in Aug; ⓣ081.908.7111, ⓦwww.giardiniposeidonterme.com), an extensive garden complex of relaxing thermal and mud baths, jacuzzis and saunas – twenty-one pools in all – on its own white-sand beach. It's pricier than most, and besides admission there are surcharges for extras, such as towels, which cost €4 per day and require a €6 deposit. There are three places to eat on site: a self-service restaurant; a garden café by the sea, which also has a piano bar; and a so-called wine grotto, which has outdoor picnic tables with tiki-style umbrellas.

Eating, drinking and nightlife

Forío has some good **restaurants**, but be warned that the overwhelming northern-European presence means that many places have given up altogether serving Italian food. In the town centre, along Via Marina on the port, there are several good-value places that specialize in fish. The port is also where you'll find a modest concentration of **bars**.

Restaurants, cafés and bars

Atlantic Via Marina 30. A pub and piano bar that draws people of all ages.
La Bussola Via Marina 36 ⓣ081.997.645. One of the best of the fish restaurants along this stretch, *La Bussola* also serves wood-fired pizzas for both lunch and dinner, starting at just €2.40 for the classic Neapolitan version. Pasta dishes start at about €5, fresh fish at about €10, and there's ample terrace seating for people-watching.
Le Cantine Pietratorcia nell'Antica Libreria Mattera Via Marina, behind the San Gaetano church just up from the port ⓣ081.333.2037. A kind of literary wine bar of considerable charm, specializing in fine Ischian wines and traditional canapés; it's open till late. Closed Wed mid-Sept to mid-June.
Il Fortino Via Fortino 37 ⓣ081.507.8003. One spot whose menu can be relied upon to feature all-Italian fare is *Il Fortino*, at the beginning of the Spiaggia di San Francesco, about a 20min

promenade north along the *lungomare* from the centre of town. It's a café, bar and restaurant with a pleasant grotto-like feel and its own covered terrace right on the sea. Closed Oct–Easter.
Poggio del Sole see p.206. Above the town, in the foothills of Monte Epomeo, this small hotel has a large garden restaurant where Mamma Tina turns out dish after dish of superbly inventive yet deeply authentic Ischian cookery (full meals start at about €20 per person): home-made pizza, courgette flowers stuffed with mozzarella, and fresh mussels in wine sauce, among other dishes. Since it's rather far from the centre, just call and someone will give you a lift up and back.
Umberto a Mare Via Soccorso 2 ⓣ081.997.171. The delightful *Umberto a Mare* is tucked under the Chiesa Soccorso; its pretty whitewashed interior looks out onto the sea and it offers seasonal cuisine with lots of elegantly presented seafood, at around €65 for a full meal. Closed lunch & Jan–March.

Sant'Angelo and around

Ischia's restful southern side, divided into the Serrara Fontana (west) and Barano d'Ischia (east) is quieter and greener. The area also boasts one of the island's longest, finest beaches, the **Spiaggia dei Maronti**, 1km east of **SANT'ANGELO**,

▲ Sant'Angelo

which in turn is probably Ischia's most attractive coastal settlement. It's a tiny former fishing village, clustered evocatively around a narrow isthmus linking with the humpy islet that gives the place its name, topped with the ruins of a watchtower. Inevitably, the clutch of mostly white cubic buildings has been developed since the access road was first built in 1948: centring on the harbour and a square crowded with café tables and surrounded by pricey boutiques, it has a gentrified feel. But if all you want to do is laze next to the sea on a white-washed terrace or beach, it's perhaps the island's most appealing spot to do it.

Arrival and accommodation

Sant'Angelo is out of bounds to **buses**, which drop you just outside, from where it's a five-minute walk down to the village. There are several dozen places to **stay** in and around the village, including a **campsite**, the *Mirage*, at Via Maronti 37, Lido Maronti, Barano (℡081.990.551, Ⓦwww.campingmirage.it; take bus #5 from Ischia Porto and get off at the last or penultimate stop), a friendly beachside spot in a eucalyptus grove. It has its own restaurant serving up good pastas, such as their speciality *tubettoni cozze e pecorino* (with mussels and ewe's milk cheese) and *vermicelli ai frutti di mare* (with seafood).

Accommodation

Casa Giuseppina Via Gaetano D'Iorio 11 ℡081.907.771, Ⓦwww.casagiuseppina.it. Up in Succhivo, 10min walk back in the direction of Forío (the bus passes right by), this family-run, pleasantly rustic garden villa has a swimming pool and hot tub, and organizes mountain-bike excursions through the surrounding countryside. April–Oct; minimum stay 3 nights at weekends. Doubles €90–120 half board.

La Conchiglia Via Chiaia delle Rose 1 ℡081.999.270, Ⓦwww.conchigliahotel.com. The very central *La Conchiglia* is primarily a good family-run restaurant, its terrace with a good view of the port (see p.209). However, upstairs it has rooms to rent as well, which though simple are great for the price, many with views of their own. April–Oct. Doubles €90; breakfast €3.

Conte Via Nazario Sauro 42 ℡081.999.214, Ⓦwww.ischialberghi.it. Out on the rocky headland facing the town and the long arc of Maronti Beach, the *Conte* is excellent value: a homely setting practically on the water, with simple, well-appointed rooms, some with balconies, and terrace dining. Look for the pink-and-white scalloped trim at the foot of the rock. April–Oct; seven-day minimum stay. Doubles €118–198.

La Palma Via Conte Maddalena 15 ☎ 081.999.215, ⓦ www.lapalmatropical.it. Well placed in the centre of town, this recently renovated Moorish-style villa offers great views of Sant'Angelo and the bay and has plushly furnished rooms with tasteful decor, some with balcony, and an inviting garden terrace restaurant, too. Admission to their thermal complex included in half-board price. Mid-March to Oct. Doubles €140–240 half board.

Punta Chiarito Via Sorgeto 51, Panza ☎ 081.908.102, ⓦ www.puntachiarito.it. To the west towards the Sorgeto, set on a dramatic promontory some forty metres above the sea is this memorable hotel, where gardens and groves add to the lush feel, and there's a thermal spring just for guests. Rooms are handsomely furnished and many have their own terraces with views. Feb–Oct. Doubles €120–240.

Villa Casa Bianca towards the eastern end of Maronti Beach ☎ 081.905.212, ⓦ www .casabiancaischia.it. Right on the beach, this is one of the area's best bargains: a gleaming Mediterranean villa with a sweeping terrace that affords views of Cápri. Services include a swimming pool and sauna, plus beach facilities, and all rooms have either a balcony or terrace. March–Oct. Doubles €100–130 half board; weekly rates available.

Beaches and spas

There's a reasonable **beach** lining one side of the isthmus that connects Sant'Angelo to its islet, and plentiful taxi boats to **Spiaggia dei Maronti** (around €5), or it's accessible on foot in about 25 minutes, taking the steep path to the right from the top of the village. The broadest sands lie at the eastern end of Maronti, but taxi boats will drop you at one of a number of specific sites. One, the **Fumarole**, at the Sant'Angelo end, is a kind of outdoor sauna, where steam emerges from under the rocks, and is popular on moonlit nights. Further along, near a couple of hotels, a path cuts inland through a mini-gorge to the **Terme Cavascura**, one of the most historic hot springs on the island, used since Greek times (mid-April to Oct daily 9.30am–6pm; €10 swim and sauna; €8–45 treatments; ⓦ www.cavascura.it). Its waters are reported to be particularly effective in treating conditions related to joints, lungs and skin, as well as gynaecological problems. Treatments offered include thermal soaks, mud packs, massage and more, but don't expect the luxury and comfort of the larger establishments: facilities are all-natural, simple and basic. Still further along the beach and about 1km inland, there's another ancient spa, the **Fonte delle Ninfe Nitrodi** at Via Pendio Nitrodi, Barano (daily 9am–7pm; ☎ 081.990.335, ⓦ www.fonteninfenitrodi.com; €7), a humble little place these days but once sacred to the Greeks, as attested by the many carved votive images unearthed here, now in the Museo Nazionale Archeologico in Naples. Nitrodi is legendary for its warm sulphate mineral waters, officially recognized as therapeutic by the Italian Ministry of Health.

On the other side of Sant'Angelo, about 1500m back down the road and then down several flights of steps, **Il Sorgeto** is a small but dramatic cove, near the hamlet of Panza, where a natural rockpool thermal bath, located in the eastern corner of the cove, draws midnight skinny-dippers.

Eating and drinking

Eating out in Sant'Angelo can be pricey, but it's certainly an atmospheric spot for a meal; some of the most appealing and beautiful places are built out over the sea just to the west of town.

La Conchiglia see p.208. In the heart of the old village, this hotel restaurant offers panoramic dining and a menu of fresh seafood and Italian standards for as little as €20 a head. Closed Nov–March.

Da Pasquale Via Sant'Angelo 79 ☎ 081.904.208. Restaurants in Sant'Angelo don't come cheap, but you could do worse than stoke up on the fine pizzas (from €5) they serve at the unpretentious

Da Pasquale, up in the old centre of the village. Closed mid-Nov to mid-March.

La Floreana ℡081.999.570. On the road back to Forío, about 1km along just before it curves inland, this friendly, family-run restaurant is perched high above the sea on the Belvedere di Serrara Fontana and has incredible views, plus the food is good – drinks, snacks, pizzas and more. Closed mid-Nov to March.

Neptunus Via Chiaia di Rose 1 ℡081.999.702. One of the most alluring places west of town, built on descending terraces and offering postcard-perfect views of Sant'Angelo by day, or of its glittering constellation of lights by night. The food is delicious, with an emphasis on fresh seafood – the *linguine allo scoglio* is superb. Expect to pay about €35 per head for dinner. Closed Jan to mid-March.

Tavernetta Il Pirata ℡081.999.098. If you just want a café to hang out in – possibly into the small hours – which offers simple snacks or full meals, this is the spot, located right next to the classy marina. Indoors and outdoors, it's delightfully decorated with a veritable hanging garden of vibrantly coloured pottery made on site, as well as baskets brimming with flowers. Closed Jan & Wed in Oct, Nov & Feb.

The southeast corner

The coastal areas east of the Spiaggia dei Maronti present almost all unscalable cliffs until just before Ischia Ponte. The **Spiaggia di San Pancrazio** is a tiny pebble beach accessible only by boat, and further around the curve of coast, the **Spiaggia di Cartaromana** is easily reached on foot from Ischia Ponte, although bus #C12 from Ischia Porto can get you pretty close. It's a pleasant sandy beach with thermal springs, as well as submerged ancient ruins, which make it a draw for snorkelling archeologists. Beaches aside, this quadrant of the island is pretty much without interest for the average tourist, with only one sight of note: snaking through the hamlets and villages of the Barano valley are **I Pilastri**, the beautiful stone double-arches of an aqueduct (take bus #5 or #6 from Ischia Porto) – not Roman, but dating back to the sixteenth century when it was built to transport mountain spring water from the Buceto source down to Ischia Ponte.

Monte Epomeo

There are plenty of opportunities for **walks and hikes** in the pastoral wilderness of southern Ischia (see box opposite), the least frequented part of the island, though perhaps the best of the hikes is towards the centre of the island, to the craggy summit of Ischia's now dormant volcano, **Monte Epomeo**. Buses #CD and #CS regularly stop at the small village of **Fontana**, the usual departure point for hikes to the top, and it's a superb ride up, with wonderful views back over the coast. To climb up to the summit of the volcano from here, follow the signposted road off to the left from the centre of Fontana; after about five minutes it joins a larger road. After another ten to fifteen minutes take the left fork, a stony track off the road, and follow this up to the summit – when in doubt, always fork left and you can't go wrong. It's a steep hour or so's climb, especially at the end when the path becomes no more than a channel cut out of the soft rock. At the summit, there are two terraces. One holds a little **church** dedicated to San Nicola di Bari, built in 1459, with an attractive majolica floor; a governor of the island fled here in the eighteenth century, eschewing politics for a hermit's existence. On the other terrace, there's a scenically placed **café**, *La Grotta* (March–Oct; lunch only), serving freshly prepared and reasonably priced food.

Bear in mind, too, that you can drive to within twenty minutes' walk of the summit, leaving your vehicle by the signs for the military exclusion zone. Also reachable by car is the **restaurant** *Il Grotto di Mezza Via*, on Via Cortodomo (℡081.904.319; summer only) halfway to the top, which serves excellent *bruschette*, as well as good Ischian wines, and there are great views from the terrace.

There's almost no limit to the number of **walks and hikes** you can take on Ischia, of varying degrees of difficulty. The populated areas are generally clustered along the coast, and most of the island is still wild and rocky terrain, broad areas of it swathed in dense forest. The two hikes below are just a sample of the possibilities, and they both make complete circuits. Along both recommended trails, routes are **colour coded**, with one colour arrow indicating the main route, and one-way detours in another colour.

Monte Toppo, the Sorgente di Buceto and II Fondo Ferraro
Time 2hr 15min **Level** moderate

Take bus #6 from Ischia Porto to Fiaiano and ask to get off at *Bar Nik*, well before the bus heads down a steep gradient to the end of the line. The route is very well marked all the way; follow the directions indicated by the lizard and arrow on red. From the *Bar Nik*, where there is a helpful sign, head up the road, follow the signs up the rustic stairs and then onto the trail proper. You'll walk into thick forest, mostly chestnut trees, with several clearly marked side trails that lead to viewpoints. At several places along the way, the canopy of oak trees opens up and you can take in splendid panoramas of the Castello, the sea and Prócida. The top of the hike skirts the base of **Monte Toppo** (390m), and then the trail proceeds on to the **Sorgente di Buceto**, finally descending into the leafy extinct crater – the island's largest – known as **Il Fondo Ferraro**. Eventually you wind up back on paved road, passing old stone houses as you walk back down to the starting point.

The crater of Vatoliere and the sanctuary of Montevergine
Time 2hr **Level** moderate to difficult

Take bus #5 (make sure it's marked "via Vatoliere") to Vatoliere. The trail begins at the scruffy and overgrown old volcanic crater that is now home to the hamlet of **Vatoliere**; throughout, follow the directions indicated by the lizard and arrow on violet. This is an altogether rougher and rockier hike than the one above, little forested and so open to the sun, with vineyards and chestnut copses as nearly the only significant vegetation except for grasses and cacti. You'll do a bit of trudging and even scrambling up and along dusty ridges, with steep drop-offs to one side, and you should keep an eye out for troglodytic dwellings cut into the rock here and there. The trail follows the coast for a while, affording great views out to the south, until you arrive at the splendid white-washed **sanctuary of Montevergine**, an island pilgrimage site in a superb position, at nearly 230m. From here, the trail continues north through similar terrain until it rejoins the road for a while, winding down again to Vatoliere.

La Falanga, above Forío
Time 4hr **Level** moderate

Begin the hike at the *La Floreana* restaurant, Via Giglio 4, in Serrara Fontana (℡081.999.570), reachable by bus #CD or #CS. Follow a stony ridge to the left for about an hour, taking in stupendous coastal views down to the left and massive rock formations all the way along, and then enter the leafy canopy of the forest of **La Falanga** – a dense chestnut grove concealing many so-called troglodyte dwellings – actually hollowed-out tufa boulders, some of them enormous, that served as clandestine hideouts for the islanders when the Saracens struck their coastal settlements. Along with grottoes, complete with rudimentary kitchens, there were also cisterns to catch rainwater incorporated into the design of most of the houses. The boulder dwellings are difficult to spot at first, being camouflaged with layers of moss and lichen, but look out for them after the end of a long dry-stone wall on the right. There are also large stone carvings of Modigliani-esque faces and other images dotted around. When you've had your fill of this gnomic world, turn around and make your way back to the starting point.

Listings

Boat rental Ischia Porto: Nautica De Angelis (Via
Iasolino 100; ☎081.981.500). Forío: Noleggio
Barche Monti (next to the docks; ☎339.751.4876
or 338.226.8720). Craft with skipper also available,
for fishing trips or excursions.
Car and scooter rental Ischia Porto: Autonoleggio
Ischia (Via Iasolino 27; ☎081.992.444). Forío: In
Scooter (Via Consortile 20, just up from the port to
the right; ☎081.998.513).
Festivals The island has a lively festival calendar,
with a number of saints' days throughout the year
celebrated with processions, concerts and
fireworks, including the following: Jan 22 (San
Sebastiano; Barano); March 4 & 5 (San Giovan
Giuseppe della Croce; Ischia Ponte); month of
March (Madonna Addolorata; Forío); May 3 (San
Francesco di Paolo; Forío); May 16–18 (Santa
Restituta; Lacco Ameno); June 13 (Sant'Antonio;
Porto and Ponte); June 14–16 (San Vito; Forío); July
21–24 (Santa Maria Maddalena; Casamícciola
Terme); July 26 (Sant'Anna; Ischia Ponte); Aug 16
(San Rocco; Barano); Sept 8 (Santa Maria del

Monte; from Ischia and Forío to Monte Epomeo);
Sept 29 (San Michele Archangelo; Sant'Angelo).
There's also a jazz festival in the first week of Sept.
Hospital Ospedale Anna Rizzoli (Via Fundera 2,
Lacco Ameno; ☎081.507.9111). Emergency at sea
☎1530.
Internet Pointel Store (Piazza Trieste e Trento 9,
Ischia Porto; ☎081.333.4711), as well as the bars
mentioned on p.201.
Post office Ischia Porto: Via Alfredo de Luca; Ischia
Ponte: Via Mazzella, Piazza dell'Orologio; Forío: Via
Matteo Verde. Mon–Fri 8am–1.30pm, Sat
8am–12.30pm.
Taxis Ischia Porto: ☎081.984.998, ☎081.992.550
or 081.993.720; Forío: ☎081.997.482.
Sant'Angelo: ☎081.999.899.
Watersports The major beaches are geared up for
windsurfing and paddle-boating, as well as to sell
equipment for skin-diving and snorkelling. For
more serious divers, Diving Nettuno, at Via Marina
70, Forío (☎081.998.588; closed Oct–April), offers
equipment rental and lessons.

Prócida

A serrated hunk comprising the remnants of at least four volcanoes – part of
the same volcanic archipelago as Ischia – **PRÓCIDA** is the bay's smallest island,
barely 4km long and scarcely half that wide. It's also the most densely inhabited
of the islands – in fact, with over 10,000 residents it's the most densely
populated of any island in the Mediterranean. However, it has so far managed
to fend off the tourist onslaughts that have flooded Cápri and Ischia, remaining
unassumingly immune to mass tourism, except during the height of summer. It
may lack the spectacle or variety of the other islands in the trio, but it more
than compensates with its easy accessibility and laid-back pace, and retains an
authentic feel too – something that's obvious on the evening ferry back to
Pozzuoli, when it is thronged with working-class commuters who still make
their living as fishermen. No wonder that this spot, the closest island to Naples
itself, was chosen as a true-to-life backdrop for the films *Il Postino* (1994) and
The Talented Mr Ripley (1999).

Some history

The island's name is said to derive from the Greek word *prochyta*, meaning
"stretched out" and by implication "flat" – which it certainly is, the several
promontories notwithstanding. Apart from a period as a royal hunting
preserve in the eighteenth century under the Bourbons, it has had a mostly
humble, peasant and proletarian history, its doggedly self-reliant populace
given over to cultivating the rich volcanic soil or to mastering the sea. An old

Graziella

Prócida's home-grown literary legend – which accounts for the names of bars and businesses across the island, as well as an annual beauty pageant – derives from the largely autobiographical mid-nineteenth-century novel **Graziella** ("Little Grace") by French poet and statesman Alphonse de Lamartine. Fascinated by the smouldering beauty of Neapolitan girls, many Northern European men who travelled here in the nineteenth century found themselves smitten. Lamartine was no exception, and some say his great love was either a cigarette girl or the daughter of a humble Prócidan fisherman. His potboiler recounts the girl's tragic end when her lover turns out to be a love rat, and returns home to marry a more suitable match. Graziella dies of a broken heart and enters the panoply of island iconography. Each summer, as part of the **Festival of the Sea**, young beauties put their charms on show, bedecked in traditional costumes.

saying goes that every seaport in the world has at least one Prócidan sailor working in it, and it is true that the great majority of ferry skippers on the Bay of Naples are Prócidans as well. Prócida's maritime and ship-building reputation has been well-founded for centuries, but especially in the eighteenth century when the island boasted one of the wealthiest fleets in the Mediterranean and the population reached 16,000. Attracting greater attention in the late twentieth century – sparked in 1957 by Elsa Morante's prizewinning epic novel *L'isola di Arturo* (Arturo's Island) and the subsequent film – Prócida nevertheless remains today a quiescent afterthought, worlds away from the drama of Cápri.

Arrival, information and accommodation

Ferries and **hydrofoils** from Naples and Ischia (see pp.178–179) arrive in the port of Marina Grande. **Buses** #L1 and #L2 (€1.10 single, tickets sold in *tabacchi* and newsstands and on board) coincide with all arrivals and connect Marina Grande with Chiaiolella roughly every twenty minutes. Given the island's tiny size and good transport links, not to mention its challenging traffic, using a **car** here is not recommended. Traffic is anyway very restricted: cars and motorbikes are strictly forbidden on Sundays and holidays from 11am to 1pm and from 5pm to 8pm, extended until midnight in the summer months.

The friendly **tourist office** (daily 9.30am–1pm & 3–6pm; ☎081.810.1968, ⓦ www.procida.it) is in the port at Via V. Emanuele 72; the office at Via Sogliuzzo 72 in Ischia Porto is the provincial office for Prócida as well. Travel agency Graziella Travel (Via Roma 117, Marina Grande; ☎081.896.9594, ⓦ www.isoladiprocida.it) is also a good source of information about the island, its services and facilities.

There's not much choice if you want to stay on the island, and advance booking is essential. An excellent **self-catering** option is the imposing *Le Grand Bleu* at Via F. Gioia 37 (☎081.896.9594, ⓦ www.isoladiprocida.it; from €550 per week, rates go up in August), just off the main road, about halfway between Corricella and Chiaiolella. The apartments are smartly contemporary and each has its own terrace with exceptional views over the island and beyond. Chiaia Beach is not far away, and there's a bus stop just in front. There are five **campsites** on the island, most within easy walking distance of the sea; your best bet is *Vivara* at Via IV Novembre 2 (☎081.896.9242; mid-June to mid-Sept),

30m from the sea, with caravans for rent and a bar. To get there, take the Marina Grande–Chiaiolella bus #L1 and get off at Piazza Olmo.

Hotels

La Conchiglia Via Pizzaco 10, Spiaggia Chiaia
☏081.896.7602, ⊛www.laconchigliaristorante
.com. This restaurant (see p.218) also has four
simple apartments with sea views to rent near the
beach. Closed Nov–Feb.

La Corricella Via Marina Corricella 88
☏081.896.7575, ⊛www.hotelcorricella.it.
Spacious rooms, tastefully decorated, in a lovely
position at the heart of this colourful little fishermen's community, with an exotic and almost
African beauty. When you get to the port and face
the water, look for the pink building up at the left
end. It also has its own restaurant, *La Lampara*,
offering terrace dining high above the sea. Closed
Nov–Easter. Doubles €120.

Crescenzo Via Marina Chiaiolella 33
☏081.896.7255, ⊛www.hotelcrescenzo.it.
Painted a beautiful sky-blue with white trim, this

hotel with on-site restaurant-pizzeria near a sandy
beach is a family-run, friendly place with plenty of
repeat guests. Some of the ten rooms overlook
Chiaiolella harbour and others have a small
balcony, while there are also quieter choices, set
behind the harbour. Doubles €120; half and full
board also available.

La Casa sul Mare Via Salita Castello 13, Terra
Murata, on the way to San Michele
☏081.896.8799, ⊛www.lacasasulmare.it.
One of the top choices, consisting of ten bright,
elegant guestrooms with private balcony and
views, in a pale pink seventeenth-century villa with
gardens and terraces. Free shuttle to beaches.
Doubles €168.

La Tonnara Via Marina Chiaiolella 51
☏081.810.1052, ⊛www.latonnarahotel.it.
This handsome building on the marina – which
once housed nets used to catch tuna – has

fourteen luxury guestrooms, all with panoramic sea views. Colours are cheerfully kaleidoscopic in the public spaces and there's an excellent restaurant (half and full board available; half board obligatory in Aug). Doubles €150.

Riviera Via Giovanni da Procida 36 ☎081.810.1812 & 081.896.7197, ⓦwww .hotelrivieraprocida.it. A bit out-of-the-way, amidst lemon and bougainvillea at the highest point overlooking Chiaiolella, this hotel is a comfortable choice. All of its twenty-five rooms have views and some have balconies. Half and full board also available. Closed Oct–March. Doubles €110.

Savoia Via Lavadera 32 ☎081.896.7616, ⓦwww .mediturhotels.it. In the middle of the island, this handsome old building offers sixteen appealing rooms, all with a/c, and some with small balconies. It isn't close to the beaches, but there are fine views and there's a swimming pool in the garden. It also has its own restaurant, specializing in fish dishes. Doubles €130; obligatory half board second half of Aug.

The island

The pleasures of minuscule Prócida are reliably low-key: visitors arrive at the diminutive main town of **Marina Grande**, which offers warrens of gritty streetlife behind its pastel facades, as well as a surprisingly menacing castle. The next cove over, **Corricella**, is the classic Neapolitan fishermen's enclave, while elsewhere lovely beaches await, the best being around the picturesque little bay at **Chiaiolella**.

Marina Grande

The island's main town is **Sancio Cattolico**, commonly called simply **MARINA GRANDE**, a lived-in, unpretentious place where all ferries dock, and whose gently dilapidated state only adds to its allure. As you approach the island from the sea, you'll immediately notice the houses' confetti-like colours. Look closer and you'll also spot the unique elements of the local architecture: arched boat-storage shelters are built into the bottom of many of the tall fishermen's houses, with long external staircases adding to the delicate appeal of this vernacular design.

Among the picture-perfect conglomeration of pastel houses lining the port, the twelfth-century **Palazzo Merlato** (or Palazzo Montefusco; no visitors) dominates the right end, its broad, pink flatness topped with arches and Venetian-looking finials.

Terra Murata

At the end of the port, beginning at Via Principe Umberto just before the marina, multi-hued cubic houses rise from the waterfront to a network of steep streets winding up to the island's fortified acropolis – the so-called **Terra Murata** (91m). It's a wonderful walk up, especially for the slice-of-life glimpse it gives of the town, but also to see the abbey complex of **San Michele** at Via Terra Murata 89 (Mon–Sat 9.45am–12.45pm & 3–6pm, Sun 9.45am–12.45pm; €2 donation expected), which dates to the eleventh century. The ceilings and domes are decorated with paintings by Baroque master Luca Giordano and others, including several stirring scenes of the archangel Michael beating back the Turkish saracens from Prócida's shore. The museum also contains fascinating votive offerings, including cataclysmic depictions of storms at sea donated by sailors who made it back home alive; a wonderfully detailed eighteenth-century nativity scene; and a spooky maze of catacombs, ending in a hidden chapel.

Outside, from the nearby belvedere, the panorama is among the region's best, taking in the whole of the Bay of Naples, from Capo Miseno right in front of you all the way around to the end of the Sorrentine peninsula and Cápri on the far right. Part of this summit is the site of a rather forbidding prison-fortress, the **Castello d'Avalos**, only abandoned in 1988. The best view of it is on the promontory's far side, where it looms over Corricella beach.

Corricella

The most characteristic spot on Prócida and its oldest village, **CORRICELLA** is also known as the "Borgo di Pescatori" because it remains very much a working port for local fishermen. You may recognize it as the quaintly pictur-esque place that featured so prominently in the Oscar-winning film *Il Postino*. The restaurants here are disarmingly no-nonsense, and provide the island's best bargains, specializing in the freshest catch of the day. Stay a while to take in the view from here back towards the overweening ruined citadel; it's one of Prócida's most evocative sights, especially given the stark contrast between the stronghold's sprawling grimness and the gentle whimsy of typical Prócidan dwellings.

Chiaiolella and the beaches

Prócida's appeal for most visitors lies in its fine opportunities to laze on one of its half-dozen **beaches** in relative peace. There are two beaches near Marina Grande itself, one of which is to the right as you enter the dock, just on the far side of the jetty (take Via Roma). This is **Spiaggia della Silurenza** – lovely (when it's clean), fairly large and sandy, and offering all facilities, as well as rocks for diving off. In the opposite direction, beyond the marina on the way to Punta Lingua, lies the much smaller **Spiaggia Lingua**, a pebbly beach that boasts especially limpid waters. There are no facilities on this beach, but a small restaurant is within walking distance. Further away but theoretically walkable – at least at low tide – continuing along the coast and around the point is the small rocky beach made famous by Elsa Morante's novel, *L'isola di Arturo*: the **Spiaggia dell'Asino**, below the looming Terra Murata fortress. Beyond

The Vivara nature reserve

Just beyond Chiaiolella beach, the island nature preserve of **Vivara**, a pronounced hump at the extreme western end of the island, is officially closed, and has been for some time. But locals sometimes make their way over there, and there's nothing stopping you doing the same – although you very much do so at your own risk as the bridge is badly in need of repair. Not surprisingly, the island is very peaceful and verdant, and a stroll here will make it clear why *coniglio* features so commonly on island menus – the place is teeming with wild rabbits. The islet was inhabited at least as early as the sixteenth century BC, and archeological finds here include Neolithic and Mycenaean artefacts left by eighth-century BC Greeks (now in the archeological museum on Ischia). Much later, in the eighteenth century, it was a royal hunting preserve, and several buildings in the centre of the island remain from that era, most recently used by environmentalists to monitor the hundreds of species of migratory birds that flock here. Dating from the nineteenth century, when the place was given over to the cultivation of grape and olive, there are also farmhouses and cottages to be explored. In addition to the main walkway, the land is criss-crossed by numerous woodland paths.

Other relatively wild and beautiful areas are the **Pizzaco** and the **Solchiaro** penin-sulas, both on the southeastern coast and ending in promontories affording excellent views. The former is accessible from Piazza dell'Olmo, the latter from either Chiaiolella or the hamlet of Centane.

▲ Good Friday procession to the Terra Murata, Prócida

Corricella is **Spiaggia Chiaia**, an arching strip of grey volcanic sand that wraps around the Cala di Sant'Antonio's serene waters. **Buses** #L1, #L2 and #C1 stop nearby at Piazza dell'Olmo, or you can walk from Marina Grande – uphill then down again – in about half an hour. Follow Via Vittorio Emanuele and head down the flight of nearly 200 steps from near the Church of Sant'Antonio Abate; once on the beach, you'll find facilities enough to make a day of it.

On the whole, if you want to swim you're better off making the fifteen-minute bus journey (#L1 or #L2), or the 40-minute walk, from Marina Grande to **CHIAIOLELLA**, where there's a handful of bars, restaurants and hotels around a pleasant, almost circular bay and two long stretches of good sandy beach along the entire western (right-hand) shore, divided by the so-called **Faraglione di Prócida**, a large pyramid-shaped rock. The closest of these beaches is **Ciraciello**, also called Chiaiolella or simply the Lido, with full facilities right next to Chiaiolella Marina. Afternoon winds make it a perfect spot for windsurfing. The beach further back to the right as you face the sea, **Ciraccio** (reached by bus #C1) is the island's longest, with facilities and situated near several campsites. Finally, there's the **Spiaggia del Pozzo Vecchio** in a cove at the northwest corner of the island (also accessible by bus #C1), located down a cliff from the island's cemetery. Its sand is grainy, but the swimming is excellent due to the sheltered waters. It's sometimes referred to as the Postino Beach, as it was one of the picturesque locations featured in the famous film.

Eating, drinking and nightlife

Eating well on Prócida is generally easier and somewhat cheaper than on the other islands. In addition to those in the hotels on p.214, **restaurants** line the waterfront along Via Roma in Marina Grande. A number of **café-bars** in Marina Grande serve drinks and ice cream – try *Capriccio* at Via Roma 99 (closed Thurs). Start the evening with *aperitivi* here or at the *GM Wine Bar*, Via Roma 117, before heading for the tiny *Number Two*, Prócida's main **club**, at Via Libertà 64 (℡338.996.1391), off Via Roma and round to the right, parallel to the port.

Restaurants

La Conchiglia Via Pizzaco 10, Spiaggia Chiaia ℡081.896.7602. Perched above Chiaia beach and its enchanting bay, this restaurant is an ideal spot for lunch after basking in the sun, and is where locals come to tuck into excellent pasta dishes like *stracci cozze e broccoli* (strips of pasta with mussels and broccoli) and fish grilled to perfection. Closed Nov–Feb.

Il Galeone Via Marina Chiaiolella, Chiaiolella ℡081.896.9622. An unpretentious, attractive restaurant right by the bus terminus between the bay and the beach, offering pizzas from €3 and a tasting menu of fish specialities based on the day's freshest catch for only €15. Closed Wed; dinner only Nov–April.

La Medusa Via Roma 116, Marina Grande ℡081.896.7481. Opposite the ferry terminal and well positioned for an evening *passeggiata*, *La Medusa* offers a house speciality of *pepata di cozze* (mussels in a peppered broth) for €8 and

spaghetti *ai ricci di mare* (with sea urchins) for €12. The rest of the menu also draws on the day's catch. Closed Tues.

Mimante Via V. Emanuele 227 ℡081.896.9385. About halfway along the main road from Marina Grande to Chiaiolella, this café-pizzeria-restaurant is also known as the *Giardini di Elsa* because it was this pleasant spot that the author Elsa Morante chose as her base while she lived on the island. The gardens are extensive and the villa and its decor nostalgically atmospheric. Closed Mon & Jan–March.

La Taverna del Postino Via Marina Corricella 45, Corricella ℡081.810.1887. Set in the fishermen's cove of Corricella, with outside tables under big umbrellas and a charmingly shabby handwritten sign. Their delicious fish soup is prepared in the local way, with bread, and goes for about €10. The interior commemorates the eponymous hit film, with pictures of its beloved star, the late Neapolitan actor Massimo Troisi. Closed Tues & mid-Nov to mid-Jan.

Listings

Boat rental Blue Dream Sailing Charter (Via Ottimo 3, Marina Grande ℡081.896.0579; ⓦwww .bluedreamcharter.com); Barcheggiando (Pontile Meditour, Marina di Chiaiolella ℡081.810.1934).
Festivals Easter events, including Procession of the Hooded Apostles on Maundy Thursday, and Procession of the Mysteries and of the Dead Christ at Terra Murata on Good Friday. The Sagra del Mare (usually last weekend in July) is a beauty contest in honour of Graziella (see p.213). In Sept the Elsa Morante Literary Prize is celebrated, with a week of

cultural events, while the Sagra del Vino (wine festival) in the first week of Nov has wine-tasting, street performers and live music.
First aid ℡081.819.0510; emergency at sea ℡1530 or 081.553.6017.
Hospital Via SS. Annunziata 1 ℡081.896.9058.
Internet Capriccio at Via Roma 99, Marina Grande (closed Thurs; €3.50 per hr).
Post office Via Libertà 34, Marina Grande (Mon–Fri 8am–1.30pm, Sat 8am–12.30pm).
Taxis Marina Grande ℡081.896.8785.

North of Naples

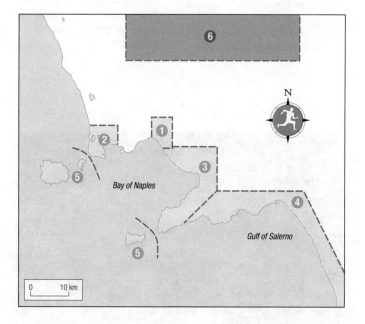

Bay of Naples

Gulf of Salerno

N

0   10 km

CHAPTER 6

Highlights

✳ **Reggia di Caserta** A vast royal palace with the most mind-bogglingly long water-garden imaginable. See p.223

✳ **Casertavecchia** One of the southern Italy's most intact medieval towns. See p.225

✳ **Cápua** The so-called "Gateway to the South" has a matchless collection of Madri Dei statuettes in its excellent archeological museum. See p.229

✳ **Sant'Agata dei Goti** An extraordinary little hill-town, built on a massive table of tufa. See p.230

✳ **Benevento** This ancient town was one of the most important in the Roman world, and has a superbly preserved triumphal arch to prove it. See p.232

▲ The gardens of the Reggia di Caserta

6

North of Naples

T here are not a great many attractions to draw you to the territory **north of Naples**, and certainly most visitors find plenty to occupy their time along the coast; only the most dedicated take the extra time and effort to venture inland. For one thing, to get here you will have to face the depressing reality of the towns just outside the city. Casoria, Afragola and Acerra are collectively known as the "Triangle of Death", due to their status as Camorra strongholds, and they make up a bleak conurbation of blighted housing, industrial mess and general squalor. Further out, the towns of Aversa, Villa Literno and Casal di Principe, among others, are also firmly in the grip of the mob – a control that extends as far as Caserta. Roberto Saviano, author of the Mafia-denouncing novel *Gomorrah*, writes of his home town:"compared to Casal di Principe, Corleone is like Disneyland … Since time immemorial this area has borne the weight of the Camorra."

Thankfully, no tourist is likely to come into contact with the mafia, and there are places of interest in these parts. **Caserta** itself doesn't have much in the way of charm, but it does have the remarkable royal palace and gardens to draw you here, and the adjoining towns of **Santa Maria Cápua Vétere** and **Cápua** boast some significant ancient sights. Once past Cápua, the countryside at last begins to assert itself, and you can push on to the lovely hill-town of **Sant'Agata dei Goti** and the pleasant market town of **Benevento**. Out here, you couldn't feel further from the coast, the Camorra, or Naples. And that, in a way, is precisely the appeal.

Caserta and around

Further inland, but just barely, from the really nasty Neapolitan suburbs, **CASERTA** is overwhelmingly the most popular destination in this part of Campania. It's a short train or bus ride direct from Naples' Piazza Garibaldi, at the end of an unsightly sprawl of industrial complexes and warehouses that stretches all the way back to Naples. The town is known as the "Versailles of Naples" for its vast eighteenth-century **Palazzo Reale**, generally known simply as **La Reggia**, which is said to have been the largest building constructed in that century – although one waggish historian noted that it was "a colossal monument to minuscule glory", since the kingdom of Naples was at that time far from a major power, and moreover in precipitous decline. Still, the royal structure is the only reason people are drawn to this otherwise completely nondescript modern town – a town that owes its existence, in fact, solely to the palace – and most tend to make a beeline for La Reggia and turn right around

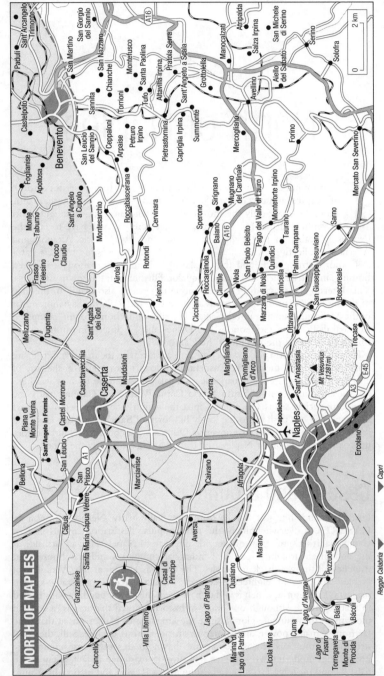

0   2 km

N

Montdragone ▲

Reggio Calabria ▲   *Capri* ▲

again. But if you do come this way, it's worth making time too for the medieval town of **Casertavecchia** and the remarkable factory town of **San Léucio**, both of which are just a short bus ride away.

La Reggia

Begun in 1752 for the Bourbon King Charles III to plans drawn up by Luigi Vanvitelli, and finally completed by his son Carlo nearly thirty years later, the **Reggia di Caserta** is an awesome behemoth, built around four cavernous courtyards, with a facade 247m long. It's an amazing building in its way, and if size and ostentation were everything, it would be perhaps the greatest European palace of all. In fact, it's a rather dull building, devoid of much inspiration, and only the majestic triple staircase up to the **royal apartments** manages to hit exactly the right note (Mon & Wed–Sun 8.30am–7.30pm; €4.20, or €6 for apartments and gardens combined), although the apartments themselves – a bombastic parade of heavy-handed gilt, frescoed and stuccoed rooms, sparsely furnished in Italian Rococo and French Empire style, some with great, overbearing Neoclassical statues – are strangely impressive in their own way, if only for their brazen display of wealth. Be sure to take in the smug portraits of the Bourbon dynasty and the House of Farnese (the family of the king's mother, Elisabetta, who was the last of her line), especially the one of podgy Francis I with his brat-like children, along with a sumptuous cradle with in-built guardian angel of gold, an ancient Roman-style basin of solid granite serving as the royal bathtub, and a very elaborate *presepe* or Neapolitan nativity scene.

More than its lavish contents, it's the icy-cold feel of this regal monstrosity and its pitiless overstatement that provides the real, morbid fascination. Five storeys high and larger than either Versailles or the Bourbon palace in Madrid, it has a total of 1200 rooms, including, besides the royal apartments, a vast, golden throne-room, a church-sized chapel, a private theatre in imitation of Naples' Teatro San Carlo, and a self-glorifying museum – some of which may or not be open when you show up, as the building is mostly used these days by the Italian military. The palace's recent history is also quite compelling: it was requisitioned as the centre of operations for the Allied forces in 1943, and it was on this spot that the Germans formally surrendered in 1945. More recently still, you might recognise it as the backdrop of the giant Naboo palace in the *Star Wars* films.

The gardens

Behind the palace, the **gardens** (Mon & Wed–Sun: Jan, Feb, Nov & Dec 8.30am–2.30pm, March 8.30am–4pm, April 8.30am–5pm, May & Sept 8.30am–5.30pm, June–Aug 8.30am–6pm, Oct 8.30am–4.30pm; €2) are if anything on an even more insanely grandiose and formal scale, stretching behind the palace along a central axis that's a full three kilometres in length, punctuated by huge yet perfunctory mythic-inspired fountains fed by a purpose-built, three-tiered aqueduct nearly 100m high. (The latter is an awesome sight, spanning the verdant Maddaloni Valley just 4km to the east, transporting water from mountain sources 40km away.) The fountains include waterfalls, as well as rapids and cascades of various heights, some, such as the Fountain of Aeolus, sporting numerous grottoes.

The main promenade is longer than it looks from the palace (a good half an hour's walk), and it climbs to an elevation of 204m, where a grotto spills over to form a 78-metre series of cascades. Regular shuttle buses make the circuit, dropping you off at intervals along the way and turning round by the main cascade at the top. Completed in 1779, this depicts Diana turning Actaeon into a stag while her nymphs gaze quizzically on. To the left side of the *Grande Cascata* as you face back towards the palace is the large **English Garden** (closes 1hr before the rest of the park) – a very pleasant spot for a picnic. The last part of the park to be completed, it's styled according to the principles of English landscape architect Capability Brown and has refreshingly non-rectilinear pathways winding through groves and meadows decorated with would-be ancient ruins, some of them adorned with copies of statuary from Pompeii. Have a wander further down and you'll discover a picturesque pond with swans and a mock Roman temple adorning a grassy islet at its centre.

Practicalities

Since Caserta is almost exclusively geared up for visits to the palace (it claims to be the fifth most visited site in Italy), **arrival** by public transport is easy, with buses every 20 minutes from Naples (journey time 1 hour) stopping just two blocks away at the town's train station, on Piazza Garibaldi. If you drive, finding the palace can be a little confusing – the signage being inadequate – but once there, you can park in the new car park under the restored formal gardens of Piazza Carlo III in front of the building. Caserta has two **tourist offices**: one inside the palace itself (daily 8am–3.45pm; ℡0823.550.011, Ⓦwww.casertaturismo.it) and another – the more helpful of the two – just a block away along Viale Douhet at the corner of Piazza Dante, to the right as you face the palace (Mon–Fri 9.30am–1.30pm & 2–4.50pm, Sat 10am–1pm; ℡0823.321.137).

Hotels cluster near the train station along Via Verdi, the cheapest decent choice being the two-star *Limone* at no. 50 (℡0823.443.504; doubles around €60), its eleven modern rooms basic but not too spartan. You could also consider staying in the much more appealing village of Casertavecchia, just 10km away (see opposite). As for **restaurants**, *Soletti* at Largo San Sebastiano 1 (℡0823.328.022), just up Via Mazzini to the left from Piazza Dante, is an excellent choice, where authentic pasta

Food festivals

In this expanse of rural Campania, every little town and village honours its patron saint with a procession or festival of some sort, in addition to those for **Carnevale** (especially in Cápua and Telese) and all other major religious holidays. However, since this is also one of the most fertile farming areas anywhere, abundant **harvest festivals** are also very much in evidence, with all sorts of bounty from the earth, including game. Keep an eye out for signs announcing such festivals, or *sagre*, from the word for "sacred": there are *sagre di funghi porcini* (porcini mushrooms), *cinghiale* (wild boar), gnocchi, *maiale* (pork), *maialetto* (suckling pig), *fichi* (figs), *fico d'India* (prickly pear), *castagna* (chestnut), *melanzana* (aubergine), *fagiolo* (bean), *carciofo* (artichoke), *'nfrennula* (a kind of biscuit made in Sant'Agata dei Goti, celebrated the second week of Sept) and many more, including, of course, wine and olive oil.

One of the most original agricultural products here is the **mela annurca** apple, fascinating due to the age-old method used to ripen the fruit. They're picked green and then carefully laid out row upon row for kilometres on *melari*, or ripening beds of straw, which are then covered with netting. Every apple is turned daily until it turns purply-red and is ready to eat. These apple beds line the country roads, and in the autumn you can see dozens of women on their hands and knees, lovingly rotating the precious *mele*. Italians consider the *annurca* the "Queen of Apples", and its *sagra* is held November 7–10 in the Valle di Maddaloni, between Caserta and Sant'Agata dei Goti. Besides savouring the fruit's firm and juicy white pulp, prepared in countless ways — to make cider, sauces and sweets — the festivities involve elaborate mosaics created using only the prized apples.

dishes go for about €6, and a tender *filetto al pepe verde* is €11. If you're only after a sandwich or light **snack**, head for the elegant *Antica Caffetteria La Reggia*, between the tourist office and the palace, at Corso Trieste 7–9, where they also whip up superb *pannacotta* and other desserts, along with a superior *cappuccino*.

Casertavecchia

Regular buses run from Caserta to **CASERTAVECCHIA**, the original "Caserta" before La Reggia was built: a medieval town perched on a precipitous hill just 10km away. Officially founded in the ninth century by the Longobards, "Casa Hirta" (Steep House), as it was then called, actually had a history stretching all the way back to the ninth century BC, when it was Etruscan and went by the name of Galatea or Galizia. Later, Samnite tribes held sway until the Romans finally beat them once and for all, at first calling the town Saticula. The settlement was completely abandoned with the construction of La Reggia, partly because all hands were needed to carry out the mammoth project, but also because there were ambitious plans to build a model city adjacent to the palace (a dream that was clearly not realized, given the disarray of Caserta today). As a happy result, the old hill-town was marvellously preserved and now stands as one of the most important examples of a medieval settlement in Italy, with narrow stone alleyways that are a delight to wander.

Having climbed to the top, the first monument you come to is the massive, thirty-metre-high, thirteenth-century **keep** (*mastio* in local dialect) of the now mostly vanished castle. This was the place of refuge in times of danger, and there's a persistent legend concerning a hoard of gold stashed somewhere beneath the tower's broad, sixteen-sided base. Turning right up into the centre of the village, you immediately catch a glimpse of the hamlet's other imposing structure, the great octagonal ciborium of the twelfth-century **cathedral** (daily 9am–1pm & 3.30–8pm; winter closes 6pm). The present edifice was constructed over an earlier church and is built in a very refined Romanesque style with sculpted white marble portals and the four animals representing the Evangelists, as well as striking Sicilian-Moorish elements, such as the intertwined blind arches adorning the facade's pediment and banding around the drum-like dome. The thirteenth-century campanile, to the right, continues the motifs, its base gracefully spanning the street with a broad Gothic arch. Inside, the delicate, irregularly-sized grey-white columns and their capitals are recycled from ancient temples, though they've now been given a setting with an almost Moorish feel, particularly the almost horseshoe-shaped arches they support. Also, don't overlook the exquisite Cosmatesque multicoloured marble floor mosaics, the unusual Gothic baptismal chapel, or the fourteenth-century Sienese fresco of the *Madonna and Child*, the only remnant of what was probably a complete fresco cycle embellishing most of the interior.

The town's only other sight is another church, the small, mostly Gothic-style **Santissima Annuziata**, down to the right from the cathedral. It has a lovely marble portal, and the whitewashed interior is now used for art exhibitions and other cultural events.

Practicalities

Buses (ACMS #110) make the twenty-minute hop from Caserta's Piazza Garibaldi, in front of the train station, roughly hourly. If you want to stay, you'll find **accommodation** down the hill at the *Hotel Caserta Antica* (☎0823.371.158, Ⓦ www.hotelcaserta-antica.it; doubles €75), just 100m past the café on Via Tiglio, a modern hotel with a swimming pool in the garden and free parking.

The rooms are handsome and simple, the setting quietly rural; ask for a view overlooking the valley.

When the time comes for lunch, there are some excellent **restaurants** with panoramic views of the entire valley, all the way to the sea on clear days. The best is the friendly ⚔ *Da Teresa* at Via Torre 6 (☏ 0823.371.270; closed Wed in winter), where a large, tempting buffet – with an amazing dessert table – is laid out in front of picture windows with magnificent views. There are also tables in the spacious, flower-arboured garden, which has the same view. Main courses, featuring mountain game and other regional highlights, average about €10; the set menus, including wine, go for €15–20.

San Léucio

In the opposite direction, just 3km outside Caserta on Via Atrio Superiore (and accessible by way of hourly buses from the train station) lies one of Europe's largest and most important eighteenth-century royal textile factories, complete with living quarters for both the king and his privileged workforce – and still in operation. It's commonly referred to simply as the **Belvedere**, though officially entitled the **Complesso Monumentale di San Léucio** (Mon & Wed–Sun 9.30am–6.30pm, winter 9am–6pm; by appointment only; ☏ 0823.301.817, ⓔ belvedere@comune.caserta.it; gardens open weekends only), and it is firmly linked in both spirit and epoch to La Reggia. Besides the commanding hilltop views, the draw here is the **Real Fabbrica della Seta** (the Royal Silk Factory) and its dependent buildings: a converted Royal Hunting Lodge (Casino Reale), the Belvedere itself, and houses (Il Borgo) for the employees of the factory. The complex has recently been meticulously restored, and the marvellous cherry-wood contraptions for working the silk reveal the cutting edge of late eighteenth-century technology – though destined only to provide the endless reams of fine fabric for the insatiable decorating demands of La Reggia.

Perhaps the most interesting aspect of the place, however, is that it was a self-conscious experiment in utopian socialism, the product of the egalitarian Enlightenment philosophy to which the era's Bourbon kings were at least in theory committed. The whole undertaking was the brainchild of Ferdinand IV, who handed down the community's very liberal charter in 1789. Admittedly, the venture was shamelessly paternalistic, with the king's colossal effigy, tricked out as a law-giving Roman emperor, dominating the central courtyard; and the royal apartments are no less self-indulgent than those in La Reggia, especially the queen's salon-size walk-in bathtub. But the row of workers' houses – away down the hill from the royal digs, of course – are comfortable, spacious and even beautiful, evincing a certain awareness of and respect for the co-equal nature of any successful enterprise. The scheme had just barely got off the ground, when the French Revolution sent the House of Bourbon into serious disarray. But modern-day San Léucio still turns out some of the finest silk in Europe, and you can watch the process at close hand in the factory itself. The complex also has a small café serving drinks and snacks.

Santa Maria Cápua Vétere

Regular buses make the fifteen-minute trip from Caserta, either from the train station or from the stop just to the left as you exit the palace, to **SANTA MARIA CÁPUA VÉTERE**, a not especially pleasant journey past petrol stations and run-down housing, to a not especially pleasant destination. Still, it's worth the trip to explore the historic town's profusion of Roman remains. In ancient times, when it was known simply as Cápua, the town was one of the most important cities on the Appian Way, Rome's all-important artery to the conquered lands of the South, and was, in its heyday, Italy's second city. The hub of the rich and powerful region of Campania, it was famous for its bronze and its production of rose perfume. Above all, perhaps, it was notorious for the hedonistic lifestyle of its citizens, becoming synonymous with sybaritic decadence, and, historians say, for being the source of the rather obscene line-up of ribald characters from the Neapolitan commedia dell'arte – including the city's alter ego, rascally and raspy-voiced Pulcinella. Legend has it, in fact, that Rome finally defeated Hannibal's army in the third century BC only because the pleasure-loving Cápuans invited the Carthaginian soldiers to winter there, after which sojourn they were simply too dissipated to put up much of a fight.

The amphitheatre

Cápua grew to be a city of great consequence in the Roman world, as confirmed by its first-century AD **amphitheatre** (Tues–Sun 9am–sunset; combined ticket with Mithraeum and Museo Archeologico €2.50), the largest in Italy after the Colosseum and located on the northwest edge of the present-day town, along the ancient Via Appia (now the SS7 for most of its length); take a right turn shortly after the central Piazza San Francesco d'Assisi. Unfortunately only a few, very minimal segments of it remain, the site having been pillaged as a ready-made rock quarry over the years, and it is much less well preserved than the one in Pozzuoli (see p.105), being bereft of almost all of its marble and surrounding tiers, with many of those remaining having been concreted over. However, the network of tunnels underneath survives reasonably intact and is partly accessible. Adjacent to the amphitheatre was a highly regarded Roman gladiator school, along with its barracks, the site of the slaves' and gladiators' revolt, led by Spartacus, in 73 BC – a massive rebellion that was only suppressed after two years of fighting and four lost battles. Amidst the heaps

▲ The amphitheatre at Santa Maria Cápua Vétere

of rubble and a handful of artefacts dotted around the area, look for a large fragment of mosaic – the floor of a *terme* (baths complex) – showing sea deities and delightful creatures, some of them mythical. Most of the other treasures that once decorated the baths are now in the Museo Provinciale in nearby modern-day Cápua (see below), while the very best are at the archeological museum in Naples (see p.72). However, there is an annexe in the amphitheatre grounds, the **Museo dei Gladiatori**, which also displays some finds.

The rest of the town

Oddly, the museum across the street from the amphitheatre houses archeological remains unearthed mostly at other sites around the area. The **Museo Archeologico dell'Antica Cápua** at Via Roberto D'Angiò 48 (Tues–Sun 9am–7pm; same ticket; to get here from the amphitheatre, cross the road, head left, then take the first right) exhibits its collections in chronological order, starting with Bronze Age artefacts, then Etruscan, and finally Greek and Roman. Highlights include painted terracotta heads with intense eyes, of both Greek and Etruscan origin; from the Samnites, beautiful funerary articles and painted tombs, which survived World War II bombing; and terracotta pots, jars and votive figurines from the ancient Temple of Diana Tifatina nearby (now incarnated as Sant'Angelo in Formis; see below).

Perhaps the most significant of the array of ancient sights to be found here is the **Mithraeum** (Tues–Sun 9am–2pm; same ticket), some 1800 years old and one of the most perfectly intact you can see. It's located about twenty minutes away on foot (ask at the museum about access), along Via Anfiteatro and then left, hidden away down and just off Via Morelli – you may need to ask directions from passers-by. This subterranean temple to the primordial Indo-Persian god Mithras was discovered only in 1922, and it is much more interesting and unusual than anything else here. The place is profoundly mysterious and redolent of the inscrutable, blood-letting rites that accompanied the secretive cult of Mithraism. There were once many thousands of such places of worship throughout the ancient world, from Britain to Asia Minor, all of which were relatively small, accommodating no more than thirty to forty men. This one boasts the best-preserved extant fresco of Mithras himself in action, slaying the sacred bull. Other frescoes along the sides, less well preserved, reveal esoteric details of the various stages of initiation, making this visual record of a once-dominant religion among the most complete known.

Along Via Caserta, which follows the ancient Via Appia, heading back down towards Caserta, are two well-preserved Roman tomb monuments which are worth a look. The misnamed **Carceri Vecchie** (old prisons) is a large, stepped cylindrical mausoleum, while further along, the **Conocchia** is a tomb in the form of a thickset tower, restored by Ferdinand IV.

Cápua and around

Hourly trains from Naples and regular buses from Caserta and Santa Maria Cápua Vétere arrive at the "new" **CÁPUA**, some 4km up Via Appia north of Santa Maria Cápua Vétere, situated on the broad curve of the Volturno River and a considerably more attractive place than its Roman counterpart. Originally called Casilinum, it became Cápua in the ninth century AD, when the Cápuans resettled here after Saracen invaders razed their city. While here, you should also take time to see the nearby basilica of **Sant'Angelo in Formis**, one of the finest Byzantine sights in southern Italy.

The Town

Most of the finds from ancient Cápua are now deposited in the excellent **Museo Provinciale Campano di Cápua** at Via Roma 68 (Tues–Sat 9am–1.30pm, Sun 9am–1pm; €5), housed in the fifteenth-century Palazzo Antignano, which sports a flamboyant Catalonian portal of dark volcanic rock. They include a series of some two hundred Madri Dei – vigorously carved tufa votive figures of earth mothers cradling tightly bundled babies in their arms, dating to the sixth to first centuries BC. Some seem so positively modern that they might have been early works of Henry Moore. These unique effigies, along with countless other decorative and architectural elements in terracotta, were unearthed in 1845 at a nearby ancient shrine to the Mater Matuta, a primordial Italic fertility divinity. Early versions hold two or three *bambini*, while later Roman-era statues are freighted with twelve, deemed by the Romans to be the ideal number. Opinion is divided about the exact purpose of the formidably hieratic statues: whether to ask for children, to give thanks for them, to honour departed parents or simply to glorify the Great Mother. The museum also contains remnants of statuary from the original Porta Federiciana di Cápua, the "Gateway to the South", constructed in 1234 during the reign of Federico II, of which two bulky tower-bases still loom outside the town. Fragments from the Porta include a headless statue of Federico on his throne and a bust of the emperor's advisor, Pier della Vigna, as well as a colossal head of Jupiter, dubbed the *Testa di Cápua Fidelis*. Unfortunately, due to chronic staff shortage, many of the forty rooms of exhibits are sporadically closed.

Among the many historic structures dotted around town are the fairly intact (destroyed in World War II and rebuilt) **Roman Bridge** taking the Via Appia across the Volturno River; the sixteenth-century **Palazzo Municipale**, adorned with seven heads of Roman deities removed from the Cápuan amphitheatre; the handsome sixteenth-century **Porta Napoli** gate; and the **Duomo**, which, although completely reconstructed after bombs reduced it to rubble in 1943, preserves notable works, especially the powerfully moving eighteenth-century sculpture of the *Dead Christ* by Bottigliero.

Sant'Angelo in Formis

Some 4km from Cápua and reached by daily buses from Caserta and Santa Maria Cápua Vétere, the tenth-century Basilica of San Michele Arcangelo, better known as **Sant'Angelo in Formis** (daily 9.30am–12.30pm & 3–6pm), is considered by some experts to be one of the best-preserved Byzantine churches in Italy. You pass through the tiny village, then through the gate known as the Arco di Diana, which leads to a large open space offering a splendid panoramic view of Vesuvius. The church was built on the ruins of a reputedly magnificent temple of Diana, the mismatched columns inside and out and other elements doubtlessly recycled from that ancient place of worship, including those in the hulking bell tower to the right. The portico is worth a closer look, with its squat Corinthian columns, its mix of Romanesque and Moorish arches, and, in the four lower lunettes, elegantly stylized twelfth-century frescoes relating the touching mystical bond between St Anthony Abbot and St Paul the Hermit – two Egyptian religious ascetics of the third and fourth centuries who were considered the founders of Christian monasticism.

Inside, nearly every inch is frescoed, even the undersides of arches, and the paintings are very well preserved. Scholars can date the paintings very closely because the Abbot Desiderius, who became Pope Victor III in 1084 and died in 1087, is pictured in the lower left of the apse, his halo square rather than round, indicating that the depiction was executed during his lifetime. Desiderius is shown offering a model of the church itself. Above him are the archangels, and above them Christ Pantocrator enthroned, the quintessential Byzantine icon. On the wall opposite, the Last Judgement is laid out, with sinners plunging into demon-infested Hell on the bottom right. The narrative cycle begins at the upper right-hand corner of the nave and reads like a book, all around the walls and then back again to begin at the next line down. The three levels relate significant stories from the Bible, including Old Testament myths, such as Noah and the Ark and Cain and Abel, as well as New Testament depictions of the life, teachings and passion of Christ; elsewhere Prophets and Sibyls, Virgins and Saints populate niches and pendentives. All in all, the decoration amounts to one of the earliest proto-types of such monumental cycles epitomized by the Sistine Chapel. Finally, don't overlook the intricate fragments of original mosaic flooring from the ancient temple to Diana, or the altar, pulpit and fonts, all refashioned from salvaged ancient materials.

Beyond Cápua

Once you've tired of the urban sprawl of the Caserta area, it's worth knowing that the nearby coastal settlements of **Mondragone** and **Castel Volturno**, along the ancient Via Domiziana, are pleasant enough places, and offer some decent possibilities for resting up by the beach. The most central **accommodation** here is the large and comfortable *International Hotel Siciliani*, Località le Vagnole, Mondragone (℡0823.772.144, Ⓦwww.internationalhs.it; doubles €60–100), actually a full resort with gardens, pool, tennis courts, bars and restaurants, sauna and hydromassage and a private beach. Inland, along the old Via Appia and Via Latina, towns such as **Sessa Aurunca** boast ancient ruins and early churches, and further inland, the pristine **Parco del Matese** offers dozens of hiking and trekking itineraries around its lake (Ⓦwww.parcodelmatese.com). If you want to explore this virtually untouched part of Campania, an excellent base of operations is the ⚑ *Villa de Pertis* in the tiny medieval village of **Dragoni** at Via Ponti 30 (℡0823.866.619, Ⓦwww.villadepertis.it; open March–Nov; doubles around €75): an aristocratic old house that's been converted into a cosy B&B with an excellent, good-value restaurant.

Sant'Agata dei Goti

Between Caserta and Benevento is an area frequently referred to as the **Sannio** (Samnium): the province of the ancient Samnites. Mostly mountainous and forested, it stretches all the way across the peninsula to border the region of Puglia. By far the most charming of the towns here is **SANT'AGATA DEI GOTI**, set in the Taburno Regional Park, with the Apennines as a distant backdrop – a richly endowed hill-town, boasting an important papal and feudal past, built on a large, flat table of tufa, dropping off on its sides into deep gorges. The town's Romanesque, medieval and Renaissance treasures suffered great damage in the 1980 earthquake but have now been mostly restored, and there are good reasons for an overnight visit if you can manage it.

Arrival, information and accommodation

Three daily buses make the hour's journey here from Naples' Piazza Garibaldi, or by car it's equidistant from Caserta and Benevento, just 15km north of the town of Apaia, which lies on the Via Appia. Sant'Agata's **tourist office** is the Pro Loco in Largo Torricella (Mon & Thurs 8am–2pm & 4–7pm, Tues, Wed & Fri 8am–2pm; ☎0823.717.159), offering guided tours as well as information. You should consider staying in Sant'Agata – it's magical after dark, and there's a perfect **accommodation** choice in ⚜*Agriturismo Mustilli* at Piazza Trento 4 (☎0823.718.142, ⓦwww.mustilli.com; doubles around €80). Set in a fine seventeenth-century palace, Palazzo Rainone, right in the heart of town, it features a beautiful garden courtyard, a series of aristocratic rooms on the *piano nobile*, and spacious, traditional and comfortable guestrooms graced with family antiques. The proprietors are very welcoming and Signora Marilì Mustilli, a noted chef, also puts on international cooking courses.

The Town

Most people arrive in the fairly conventional new part of town, where the first thing to do is stroll over the bridge spanning the Martorano River to take in the **view** – a much-photographed sweep of colourful domes above narrow stone houses on the edge of a cliff, which plunges into a lushly verdant ravine. What you're looking at is the **old town**, 1km in length and around 200m in width, its cobblestones shiny with centuries of foot traffic. You can spend a happy few hours just wandering around, but there are a few sights worth building your stroll around.

On the main piazza across the bridge is the **Castello**, which is currently being used as the offices of a law firm, but whose grand rooms you can peek into if you're discreet. Go up the broad stone staircase to take in the entrance hall of the *piano nobile*, frescoed from floor to ceiling mostly with images in imitation of works found at Pompeii, including cornucopias, gardens, Pan and his nymphs, and a scene of Diana being discovered at her bath by the ill-fated Actaeon. Across the square, the church of **San Menna** has an intricately sculpted Romanesque portal, blithely mismatched recycled columns of every type and colour, and the spectacular Cosmatesque mosaic floor, large sections of it still intact.

Nearby, the **Duomo**, on Piazza Sant'Alfonso, is notable for its handsome portico of ancient columns, the walls inset with imperial epigraphs, among other Roman artefacts – although its main draw is the crypt, all that remains of the original twelfth-century Romanesque structure. Its harmonious multi-vaulted ceilings are supported by a curious mix of slender recycled columns and an even odder assortment of capitals, some of them wedge-shaped and carved with fetching mermaids and randy little flute-playing fauns. The fourteenth-century frescoes, though badly faded, are also worth a look for their Giotto-esque naturalism.

Finally, another church of note, **Santissima Annunziata** has been de-Baroqued and returned to its thirteenth-century Gothic elegance. A fine topiary garden and a graceful Renaissance portal greet the faithful, but the interior's fourteenth- and fifteenth-century frescoes are the main event. The *Last Judgement* is depicted on the entrance wall, the elect popping up perkily out of their tombs on Christ's right and the damned opposite, suffering graphically appropriate indignities, including a fornicator being hanged from a tree by his genitals and various bureaucratic types being roasted alive at their desks – each sinner explicitly labelled. In the apse, look for the archetypal story of

St Nicholas the gift-giver, who is seen tossing a bag of money in through a window so that the three impoverished sisters lying in bed won't be constrained to take up a life of prostitution.

Eating and drinking

Regional cuisine is well represented in two central **restaurants**. *La Bottega di Zi' Paoluccio*, Via Roma 22 (℡329.989.1855; closed Mon), is a warmly earthy wine bar, serving aromatic local goat's and sheep's cheeses, pork sausages, *mostarde* (similar to chutney), and vegetables preserved in oil. A few of these country delicacies, plus some flavourful bread and potent local wine, easily make a full meal, all for about €20 a head. Another excellent choice is *L'Antro di Alarico*, Vico Gioelli 7–13 (℡389.993.9883; closed Mon), right beside the Duomo: a large, upbeat pizzeria-restaurant and wine-tasting establishment with a vast cellar carved out of the solid tufa rock on which the town sits – an ancient space they will be proud to show you. They serve up unique *mela annurca* (see p.224), *pizzelle* and *frittelle*, as well as legendary *antipasti* and pasta with truffles and wild herbs. Expect to spend about €25 for a full meal.

Benevento and around

The appealing and ancient city of **BENEVENTO**, further inland towards the mountains, is reachable in about an hour and a half from Naples by bus or train (the private FBN train line is quickest). Another important Roman settlement, it was a key point on the Via Appia between Rome and Brindisi, and as such a thriving trading town. Founded in 278 BC, it marked the furthest point from Rome to be colonized, and even now it has a remote air about it, circled by green hills, with the Apennines just in the distance. Its climate also ranks among southern Italy's most extreme; the Romans originally called it Maleventum, in fact, for its notoriously bitter winter winds – an anomaly in this balmy region – but changed the name to Beneventum after a victorious battle here in 275 BC, when they decided it wasn't really such a bad place after all. The city centre was (pointlessly) bombed to smithereens in World War II, but it's been beautifully restored, and has emerged a brighter, more liveable place as a result.

The Town

Benevento's main square, **Piazza IV Novembre**, centred on a fountain with an Egyptian obelisk, is dominated by the **Rocca de' Rettori**, a fourteenth-century papal stronghold, now used as government offices (though its grounds stretch out behind as a lovely park, the **Villa Comunale**). Most of the town's sights are within a ten-minute stroll of here.

Along Corso Garibaldi

A little way down Benevento's main street, **Corso Garibaldi**, stands a tower, engraved with maps showing the ancient independent states of which the city was once the capital. This is the erstwhile bell tower of the eighth-century church of **Santa Sofia**, just off the piazza, worth a look for its recycled columns and other ancient remnants, as well as its six-pointed star floor-plan, reputed to reflect the esoteric harmonics of medieval spiritual alchemy. You have to pass through Santa Sofia's handsome cloister, whose Romanesque capitals are carved with energetic scenes of animals, humans and beasts hunting, riding and attacking, to reach the excellent **Museo Sannio** (Tues–Sun 9am–1pm; €4). This displays a first-rate selection of local Roman finds, including exquisitely beautiful bas-reliefs, torsos, heads and other major fragments. The rarest pieces – in fact the largest such find in Europe – are the Egyptian artefacts from a nearby temple of Isis, the Egyptian goddess whose cult was much followed in the late empire. Objects include various sphinxes, falcons, bulls, an effigy of Emperor Domitian as Pharaoh, two headless statues of priests of Isis, and the granite head of the goddess herself. There are also very fine terracotta votive figurines from the fifth century BC, and a sizeable collection of Greek vases. The museum's upper rooms house a modest array of sixteenth- to nineteenth-century paintings and furniture.

Further along Corso Garibaldi, off to the right, the **Arch of Trajan** is one of Italy's most important remnants from the Roman era, a marvellously preserved triumphal arch of glimmering Parian marble embellished with far more distinct images than Rome's arches; most of the refined carving is still very crisp, and you can get close enough to study its intricate bas-reliefs. Built to herald the entrance to Benevento from the Via Appia and to mark the start of the Via Traiana, which stretched all the way to Brindisi, it's as obvious a piece of self-glorification as there ever was, showing the Emperor Trajan in various scenes of triumph, power and largesse. One frieze shows him being received into heaven by the gods themselves, and his adopted son and successor Hadrian being welcomed by the goddess Roma. Further down the main street, the city's star-crossed **Duomo** is an almost total reconstruction of the thirteenth-century Romanesque original, with just a few cobbled-together fragments of the original structure now forming the hotchpotch facade. The celebrated Byzantine bronze doors – bombed to bits in 1943 – are now being restored inside, and the interior is not currently open to visitors, with no date foreseen for it to reopen. Nevertheless, be sure to take a look at the bell tower, with its line-up of Roman busts scavenged from local funerary stelae.

The rest of the town

There are more Roman bits and pieces scattered around town. The **Bue Apis**, at the far end of Corso Dante, is a first-century BC Egyptian sculpture of a bull, another relic from the temple of Isis, and the rather shabby but picturesque medieval quarter, the **Triggio**, reached by following Via Carlo Torre down off to the left of Corso Garibaldi beyond the cathedral, has another Roman arch, terribly reduced, and the substantial but indifferently maintained remains of the **Teatro Romano** (daily 9am–sunset; €2), though this was closed at the time of writing. Built during the reign of Hadrian, it seated 20,000 people in its heyday, and it's still an atmospheric sight, with views over the rolling green countryside of the province. There's also a fragment of Roman bridge here – known as the **Ponte Leproso** after a medieval leper colony in the vicinity – that once brought the Via Appia across the River Sabato ("sabbath") and into town. Legends recount that a thousand years ago Benevento was seething with witches, who would conduct their rites on the river's bank near this spot, gyrating under a hoary old walnut tree. The witchy tradition persists in the form of the spellbinding yellow liqueur made here called Strega ("witch"), as well as in the city's Carnevale celebrations, which are famously *stregati* (bewitched).

One intriguing modern sight bears mentioning: the **Hortus Conclusus** (Mon–Sat 9.30am–1pm & 3–7.45pm, Sun 9.30am–1pm; free), in the enclosed garden-courtyard of the convent of San Domenico in Piazza Guerrazzi, off Via Pellegrini, which offers a fantastically unexpected and witty sculptural installation by local artist Mimmo Paladino.

Practicalities

Six daily **buses** make the ninety-minute trip from Naples, dropping off in a car park below Benevento's centre, where you can also park if you're driving. Most **trains** from Naples change at Caserta; the station is about a half-hour walk from the sights, but frequent buses run from the station to the centre. The **tourist office** is here too, on the corner of Via Sandro Bertini (daily 9am–1pm & 3.30–7.30pm; ℡0824.28.180). Benevento is emphatically not a tourist town, so finding **accommodation** can be a problem. There are only a handful of hotels, but at least even the very best choices are not very expensive. First choice is the handily located *Villa Traiano*, Viale dei Rettori 9 (℡0824.326.241, ⓦ www.hotelvillatraiano.it; doubles €150), a charming *belle époque* building that offers plush guestrooms with marble bathrooms, a tranquil terrace garden and a bar. At the other end of the scale, the *Osteria 'A Capannell'*, near the Duomo down quiet and quaint Via Pietro de Caro at no. 15 (℡0824.25.681), rents small **self-catering units** for €40 and serves up great pizza in a very friendly atmosphere. Also worth seeking out, between the museum and the main piazza, is ⴕ *Il Tricorno* at Via Capitano Pasquale De Juliis 13, on the corner of Via Mario La Vipera (℡0824.21.568; closed Sun), a **trattoria** which serves wonderful wood-fired pizzas from just €4 and has a superb *antipasto* buffet, in a convivial space painted Pompeian red.

Around Benevento

There are no compelling sights or towns near Benevento, but the countryside is glorious, and one or two places repay a visit if you want to have a poke around. **Morcone**, about 30km to the north, is a beautiful place, its white houses spilling down a picturesque slope, while **Telese Terme**, the same distance west, is an old spa town with a small lake and the nearby Roman ruins of Telesia. A few kilometres north of here lie the famous majolica centres of **Cerreto Sannita** and **San Lorenzello**, which continue the eighteenth-century tradition of the famed Giustiniani family of ceramists, and host an antiques fair on the last weekend of each month. On the way, the imposing castle at **Castelvenere** is a worthwhile stop. If you want time to explore the area, the *Grand Hotel Telese*, Via Cerreto 1, Telese Terme (℡0824.940.500, ⓦ www.grandhoteltelese.it; doubles €160), is a truly luxurious turn-of-the-century hotel with full spa facilities.

Of particular appeal to children is the **Paleo-Lab** (Sat & Sun 10am–7pm; ℡0824.29.919; €4) at Pietraroja, 15km north of Telese, where you can see the first dinosaur fossil ever discovered in Italy: a very young member of a species dubbed Scipionyx samniticus, a miniature version of a Tyrannosaurus rex that would only have reached a length of 2m as an adult. Good-quality exhibits include multimedia presentations revealing how the creature might have lived and other scientific marvels.

Further afield, the untamed limestone foothills of the Apennines afford excellent opportunities for **hiking**. Just 9km away from Pietraroja, the spectacular little hill-town of **Cusano Mutri** is the point of departure for a number of walks and treks into the **Parco del Matese** (see p.230). One of the most popular is a moderate trek, three hours there and back, to the 28-metre waterfall known as the **Salto dell'Orso**, the "Bear's Leap", where one of the rewards is a swim in the pristine natural rock-pool.

Contexts

Contexts

History

A comprehensive history of the Campania region would consist of a collection of more or less independent histories, as each of the major settlements has a complex story to tell. Instead, within a broad account of the evolution of the region, we have concentrated on the city that emerged as the dominant force – Naples – while background on the other major towns is given in the appropriate sections of the Guide. Naples' rich and varied history is ever-present on any tour of the city – in the street plan, the buildings, the art, and in the Neapolitans themselves, whose natural anti-authoritarian streak and in-built fatalism is perhaps a natural consequence of centuries of outside influence and misrule.

The Greeks and Etruscans

The oldest settlement in the Bay of Naples, inhabited since about 2000 BC, is Ischia – then known as Pithekoussai. From the eighth to the fifth centuries BC, this area became an important part of Magna Graecia (Greater Greece), when a contingent of Greeks travelled here from Euboea to set up trading posts. In the eighth century, Ischia's rumbling volcanoes led them to found **Cumae** on the mainland, and it soon became the region's major city: a prosperous commercial centre whose legendary oracle, the Sibyl, was thought to be the mouthpiece of Apollo.

The Greeks dominated the region for centuries, and gradually spread out around the bay, in the seventh century BC building a city they called Parthenope on the hill of Monte Echia. As the Greeks cemented their power, the powerful **Etruscans** began to have designs on the settlements around the Bay of Naples, moving from their homeland in Tuscany to claim Cápua as their southern capital in around 600 BC. The Etruscans twice invaded Cumae – in 524 and 474 – but were defeated on both occasions. Following the second attack, the Greeks created a colony called **Neapolis** or "New Town" on the lower ground below Partheope to strengthen their hold in the region. The conflicts had served to sap the rivals' strength and resources, however, leaving them an easy target for the approaching Samnite hill tribes, who seized Cápua in 424 BC and Cumae in 421 BC.

The Romans

The Samnites were soon usurped by the most powerful group to the north, the **Romans**, who moved into the area in the mid-fourth century BC, eventually taking Neapolis in 326 BC after a two-year battle. They quickly turned it into a colony of Rome, albeit one which remained at heart a Hellenistic city, highly regarded as a place of refinement and culture by the Romans. The city was attacked by – and resisted – Hannibal and his Carthaginian forces during the Second Punic War (218–201 BC), and during the Roman Civil War (88–82 BC) Sulla occupied the city on his way to take Rome from his rival Marius. Cápua, too, became notorious as the centre of the slave revolt led by the renegade Spartacus in 73 BC.

Above all, though, Naples and its bay during this period were regarded as a pleasure resort for wealthy Romans, who flocked here to build villas and palaces by the sea for their leisure time and retirement. Virgil wrote much of his poetry in Naples, Pliny lived in a house on the bay, and Julius Caesar's father-in-law resided in the refined Villa dei Papiri. Stabiae, Baiae and Herculaneum became popular holiday resorts, while Tiberius famously relocated his administration to Cápri in 26 AD until his death eleven years later. The largest town in the region, **Pompeii**, was a prosperous place, but was already in decline in 79 AD when Vesuvius erupted and buried it and the surrounding towns in volcanic ash.

The Byzantines and Normans

With the decline of the Roman Empire, the city was preyed upon by a myriad of invaders, first of which were the Ostrogoths who took the city in the mid-sixth century AD. They were, however, quickly dislodged by Byzantine forces under the general Belisarius, and the city changed hands several times until the Byzantines finally conquered the city in 553 after years of conflict. The following year it became a duchy ruled from Ravenna, during which time it prospered, its power increasing while that of Cápua waned. It was only a matter of time until the city came under attack again, however; this time its aggressors were the Lombards from the north, and Saracens from the east. Shifting its allegiances between Rome and Constaninople, the city somehow managed to remain independent of all these marauding powers, maintaining a quasi-independence for around four hundred years.

To the south, Amalfi and the coast west as far as Positano (as well as Cápri) and east as far as Cetara split from Naples in the ninth century and grew into a thriving commercial state in its own right, with its own currency and set of maritime laws, the **Tavola Amalfitana**. It continued to thrive into the tenth century, developing a rivalry with other mercantile city-states such as Pisa, Genoa and Venice, and vying for trade with the Byzantine empire to the east. However, in 1073 it fell prey to the **Normans**, who had already taken Cápua eleven years earlier, and went on to take Naples in 1139. The Normans controlled a considerable swathe of the surrounding area, and the Norman Roger II proclaimed himself king of both Sicily and Naples in 1140. He ruled his subjects from Palermo, keeping them sweet by presiding over an economic boom and offering the restless barons and landowners land and privileges in return for cooperation.

The Hohenstaufen and Angevins

Despite the peace and prosperity of much of their rule, the Normans didn't remain in Naples for long, and like the rest of the region the city came under the rule of the **Hohenstaufen** dynasty in 1194, who stayed rather half-heartedly until 1269, when their last monarch, Conradin, just fourteen years old, was beheaded in what is now Piazza del Mercato by the **Angevin** king, Charles I of Anjou.

Such was the unpopularity of the Hohenstaufen that the city welcomed its new ruler with open arms. Charles moved the capital of his Italian realm from

Palermo to Naples, forming the **Kingdom of Naples** and establishing it as one of the great cities of Europe, a centre of culture and diplomacy. He also made his mark on the cityscape, building the Castel Nuovo in 1279, redeveloping the surrounding area and expanding the port. In spite of this, the reign of the Angevin kings was not entirely harmonious, and they took much more from the city than they gave back. Furthermore, Charles was distracted by the loss of Sicily to the Aragonese from Spain; his subsequent struggle to win it back led to a fierce naval battle just outside the city during which his son and heir, also called Charles, was taken prisoner. He was eventually released and a truce with the Aragonese agreed, after which a long period of peace was overseen by the Angevins' most enlightened ruler, Robert the Wise, who ascended to the throne in 1310 and made the city a fitting capital for the dynasty, building impressive monuments – Santa Chiara, San Lorenzo and the Duomo and Castel Sant'Elmo among them – and attracting artists and craftsmen from all over Europe.

The Aragonese

The Angevins ruled Naples for the best part of two hundred years, while Sicily remained under Aragonese control, until 1422 when the **Aragonese** king Alfonso I took Naples and briefly unified the two kingdoms for the first time since the Normans. He handed over the reins to his son Ferdinand I, or Ferrante, on his death in 1458, who then passed them on to Alfonso II. In 1493, Charles VIII of France invaded but was soon forced out again by Ferdinand's grandson, Ferdinand II, or Ferrantino. After his premature death in 1496, the people wanted Ferdinand's widow Joan to take the crown, but his uncle Frederick was appointed instead – a move which angered both French and Spanish and led to the Franco-Spanish invasion of 1501. Faced with the loathing of his subjects, Frederick renounced the throne to King Ferdinand of Spain, who consolidated the Spanish hold on the city – a hold which would last for around three hundred years.

The Spanish didn't particularly have the interests of Naples at heart, and King Ferdinand III appointed a series of viceroys to run the city, which they did with increasing brutality and punitive taxation, not to mention an upsurge in corruption among the ruling classes. In spite of this, it was a settled time during the city's history, and by the beginning of the seventeenth century Naples was the second largest city in Europe, with a population of around 300,000. Many of the city's residents were living in squalid conditions, however, and the swelling population meant that parts of the city had become dangerously overcrowded; in an attempt to raise standards of living, viceroy Don Pedro redeveloped the city on a grand scale, creating a new quarter, the Quartieri Spagnoli, to house the masses.

Sporadic uprisings against Spanish misrule culminated in the so-called **Masaniello revolt** of July 1647, when a popular insurrection against taxes on basic necessities such as fruit and vegetables broke out in Palermo and was quickly emulated in Naples, with riots and assassinations of major political and aristocratic figures that lasted for several days. The ringleader of the rebellion was a Neapolitan fisherman called Tommaso Aniello ("Masaniello"), who after a week was invited by the Spanish to sign a truce in return for a prominent position in the governance of the city. Shortly after refusing the offer, he was assassinated while giving a speech, though his influence continued to be felt when later the same year a Neapolitan Republic was declared under the protection of the

Art and architecture: Naples' Golden Age

The greatest age of Neapolitan art and architecture were the **seventeenth and eighteenth centuries**, when the counter-reformation under the pious Spanish viceroys really took hold in the city, and as in Rome was expressed in a fervent flowering of the Baroque style. It was Naples' defining era, when it basked in its status as one of Europe's largest, most elegant and most prosperous cities.

Art

The most famous artist to work in Naples, **Caravaggio** (1571–1610), fled here from Rome in 1606 and quickly became the city's most celebrated painter and a major influence on a generation of Neapolitan artists. One of these was **Giuseppe Ribera** (1591–1652), actually a Spaniard from Valencia (he was known as *Lo Spagnoletto* or "Little Spaniard"), and perhaps the best-known artist from the early part of the Neapolitan Baroque period. Not surprisingly, he was popular with the Spanish in the city, who made sure he landed the plum commissions, and his style is typical of the period, heavily influenced by Caravaggio in its use of chiaroscuro, and tending to dramatic themes rendered in a deliberately theatrical style. Ribera was said to be the head of a group of painters who sometimes used violent means to eliminate their competitors, although this didn't do him much good as he died in poverty, despite the fact that his daughter married a prominent Spanish nobleman. A member of the same group, Giovanni Battista or **Battistello Caracciolo** (1578–1637) was unlike Ribera a native of Naples, but he was also heavily influenced by Caravaggio and painted in a dark and histrionic style that was the epitome of Neapolitan Baroque. His pupil, **Mattia Preti** (1613–99) also worked in Naples for a period, and a number of his works remain.

The most prolific painter of the era, however, was unquestionably **Luca Giordano** (1632–1705), known as *Luca fa presto*, or "Luca does it quickly" for the speed with which he could churn out works – a skill which was useful for the number of commissions it attracted, but which also meant he was not always taken seriously by his patrons. In fact, he was a great artist, and his paintings are dotted all over Naples, although arguably his greatest works were done elsewhere (in the Escorial in Spain, for example).

Among other Baroque artists who left their mark all over the city was **Massimo Stanzione** (1585–1656), another follower of Caravaggio, though with a style that was a little more refined than that of Giordano and Ribera, earning him the tag of the Neapolitan Guido Reni (1575–1642), whose smooth and elegant paintings are similar.

French. In spite of this, the Spanish were back by mid-1648, quickly restoring the city to order. Naples began to enjoy some degree of calm – at least until the devastating plague of 1656, which wiped out over half the urban population.

The Bourbons

Following the War of the Spanish Succession (1701–14), Naples was briefly ceded to the Austrians, before being taken, to general rejoicing, by **Charles of Bourbon** in 1734. Charles was a cultivated and judicious monarch and he added greatly to the city's infrastructure, building the Teatro San Carlo, the Reggia at Caserta, the Palazzo Reale di Capidomonte and the Albergo dei Poveri, as well as renovating the Palazzo Reale and setting up the Biblioteca Nazionale. However, he abdicated to become king of Spain in 1759, and his

The works of **Giovanni Lanfranco** (1582–1647), a native of Parma, can be seen in the Duomo and the church of Santi Apostoli, which he decorated in a dramatic, Mannerist style that influenced the local painters almost as much as Caravaggio. One of Stanzione's pupils was **Bernardo Cavallino** (1616–56), who died during the Neapolitan plague and left behind precious little work, but was arguably the better painter, as can be seen by a couple of works in the Capodimonte museum. His contemporary, **Andrea Vaccaro** (1600–70), the son of a family of painters, lived longer and left a lot more behind, most notably in the Certosa di San Martino, Capodimonte and in a number of churches, again mostly in Caravaggesque style.

The painter who really closes the Neapolitan Baroque era is **Francesco Solimena** (1657–1747) – immensely prolific, and extremely successful too, much in demand in the court of Naples. He had a large studio, and many pupils, among them **Francesco de Mura** (1696–1784), who painted a series of frescoes in the Nunziatella, **Giuseppe Bonito** (1707–89) and **Sebastiano Conca** (1680–1764), who were the two main artists of the Neapolitan Rococo period; perhaps the best-known artist of this period, however, was the landscapist **Gaspar van Wittel** (1653–1736), a Dutchman who spent his last years in Naples, where his son – the future architect Luigi Vanvitelli, was born (see below).

Architecture

As for **architecture**, Naples produced a number of names during the same era that crop up time and again on any tour of the city. **Cosimo Fanzago** (1591–1678) was one of most prominent architects of the period, known for his work in the Certosa di San Martino as well as a number of public spires and fountains, most notably the Guglia di San Gennaro. The most celebrated is **Ferdinando Sanfelice** (1675–1748), who was well known for his ingenious staircases, two examples of which can be seen in La Sanità. **Ferdinando Fuga** (1699–1781) continued in the same, late Baroque style, and was prolific in Rome, although he arrived in Naples towards the end of his career and built the huge Albergo dei Poveri and the Girolamini church. His successor as the city's principal architect, **Luigi Vanvitelli** (1700–73) was probably the foremost eighteenth-century Italian architect. The son of the Dutch landscape painter Gaspar van Wittel (see above), he's best known for the royal palace at Caserta – the last great building of the Baroque/Rococo era. After this, he tended to favour a blander, more classical style, as evidenced by his design for Piazza Dante and the church of the Annunziata – a style which was continued by his son Carlo.

eight-year-old son Ferdinand took over, assisted at first by his trusted lawyer, Bernardo Tannucci, and later by his scheming queen, **Maria Carolina of Austria**. With an intellect far greater than that of her dim-witted husband, on the birth of her first son in 1777 Maria Carolina entered the Council of State – a clause in her marriage contract – and was able to take control. She swiftly orchestrated the downfall of Tannucci and replaced him with an English-born, anti-French aristocrat, John Acton – a disastrous alliance that led eventually to them abandoning Naples to the republican French and Napoleon in 1798.

The following year the French set up the so-called **Parthenopean Republic** – a semi-autonomous state within the Kingdom of Sicily – under the charge of Napoleon's brother Joseph. He was replaced two years later by Napoleon's sister Caroline and his brother-in-law Joachim Murat, who ruled precariously until 1815, when they were deposed by the British and the Austrians. The Bourbon Ferdinand IV was immediately restored to the throne as monarch of both Naples and Sicily, the newly founded **Kingdom of the Two Sicilies** – the first time the two kingdoms had been united for several hundred years.

The British in particular dealt out vicious reprisals against the republican rebels under Admiral Nelson, who was famously having an affair with Lady Hamilton, the wife of the British ambassador to Naples. Under continuing Bourbon rule, the city became one of the most densely populated in Europe, and one of the most iniquitous, with a reputation for poverty, violence and corruption. In spite of this, for the rest of Europe, Naples was the requisite final stop on the **Grand Tour**, a position it enjoyed not so much for its proximity to the major classical sites as for the ready availability of sex. The city was for a long time the prostitution capital of the Continent, and its reputation drew people from far and wide, giving rise to the phrase – in the days when syphilis was rife – "see Naples and die".

Italian Unification

By the mid-nineteenth century Naples was a bastion of royalism in an increasingly republican world, and with the growing popularity of the Unification movement which was sweeping across the rest of Italy, it was only a matter of time before the Neapolitan monarchs were deposed. Alarmed by the capture of Sicily by Unification forces in May 1860, Ferdinand II's son Francesco II agreed to a constitution, but it was too late. **Giuseppe Garibaldi** entered the city on September 7, receiving a hero's welcome, and on October 21, the people voted in overwhelming numbers to become part of a united Italy under the Savoy king **Vittorio Emanuele II**. It was the first time for centuries that the city had effectively governed itself, but it also signalled that Naples' glory days as a great European capital were over, as Rome grew in importance. The city entered a period of decline, culminating in a cholera epidemic in 1884 that devastated much of Naples. In an attempt to clean up the city – now in a ruinous state – the worst of the slums were demolished, Corso Umberto I was bulldozed through the city centre, and a new residential district, Vómero, was constructed.

The twentieth century

The city continued its recovery during the early twentieth century: an airport was constructed in 1936, and infrastructure was improved with a network of railway and metro lines and funiculars. Naples was finding its place as a vital port in the new Italian kingdom, though this proved to be a disadvantage with the outbreak of **World War II**, during which the city was bombed more heavily than anywhere else in the country, leaving 20,000 people dead. Fortunately, most of its architectural treasures escaped undamaged, although the church of Santa Chiara was destroyed by Allied bombs in 1943. During the so-called *Quattro Giornate di Napoli* ("Four Days of Naples") from September 27 to 30, 1943, fierce street battles led by local residents routed the Germans and paved the way for the Allied troops. When the Anglo-American forces entered the city, they found a population close to starvation and much of the city in ruins – a period brilliantly documented by Norman Lewis in his war memoir, *Naples '44* (see p.246).

There was little real improvement in the living standards of the average Neapolitan during the **postwar years**, with a very high percentage unemployed, and a disgraceful number still inhabiting the typically Neapolitan one-room *bassi* – little more than slums, letting in no light and housing many people in extremely overcrowded conditions, particularly in the Quartieri Spagnoli area, widely held to be the most dangerous part of town. Although money poured into the city to rebuild its war-shattered infrastructure, the same period saw a rise in the power and influence of **organized crime**, with the Camorra creaming off a lot of the funds intended for reconstruction and diverting them into their own businesses. At the same time the Sicilian-American gangster, Lucky Luciano, arrived in Naples, having been deported from the US after helping with wartime intelligence operations in Italy.

The latter part of the century was no less bleak: in the late 1970s there was a cholera outbreak in part of the city, and in November 1980 the region suffered a massive **earthquake**, based in Irpinia but causing devastation across the whole area, leaving nearly 3000 dead and around 100,000 homeless. There was a huge relief effort, and a considerable amount of money was pledged to the recovery operation, not only by the Italian government but also from around the world. However, this proved just another business opportunity for the region's criminal gangs, and of around $40 billion donated it's thought that less than half went on genuine projects, while the rest went straight to the Camorra or into the hands of politicians in bribes. Naples and its surrounding area was also the recipient of much of the money that poured into the south under the national government's **Cassa per il Mezzogiorno** scheme to revive the Italian South, but again it's estimated that around a third of this was squandered due to corruption, with little benefit felt by local people.

The present day

Naples experienced a long-awaited upturn in its fortunes with the appointment of **Antonio Bassolino**, charismatic left-wing mayor of the city from 1993 until 2000 and president of Campania at the time of writing, who made it his business to turn things around, fighting the corruption that was endemic in the city, and making his administration more transparent. Bassolino was confident that supporting Naples' cultural strengths would boost local pride, and scores of neglected churches, museums and palaces were restored and are now regularly open; initiatives such as May's Maggio dei Monumenti festival, which sees buildings usually out of bounds to the public open their doors, are a further example of his influence. The city has also enjoyed a burst of creative activity from local film-makers, songwriters, artists and playwrights. One of the prime movers in this aspect of Naples' resurgence is **Giuseppe Morra**, whose Fondazione Morra promotes all aspects of the arts in the city, such as its funding of the challenging new Museo Nitsch and the annual Independent Film Show at the Palazzo delle Arti.

Bassolino's finest hour was perhaps the 1994 G7 summit, when world leaders met in a newly scrubbed Naples, at the request of Italian President Carlo Azeglio Ciampi. However, his efforts have been overshadowed by the fact that the real power in the area is still in the hands of organized crime: much of the coastline west of the city – to Bagnoli – was built with Camorra money, and, although it's not at all publicized, little that matters happens here without the nod of the larger families, who have consolidated their power bases around the city during the same period. Indeed it's clear that whatever Bassolino achieved – and it is undoubtedly a great deal – the Camorra is no

The Camorra

Most people associate the mafia with Sicily, but Cosa Nostra is just one of a number of southern Italian criminal organizations, and whereas the power of the Sicilian mafia has declined in recent years, so the influence and prosperity of its sister network in Naples, the **Camorra**, has risen hugely.

The Camorra is different to the Sicilian mafia in its **structure**: rather than one umbrella group that maintains control over numerous families and sectarian interests, it is less centralized and more parochial, with families and wider clans controlling their own tight-knit districts all over the region. Today's Camorra, and the parts of the city that it controls, is an ugly, brutal phenomenon that craves power at any cost, and even innocent bystanders are at risk when clan violence erupts, as it has frequently over the last decade. In recent years there have been some spectacularly indiscriminate territorial battles, and casual violence that's almost medieval in its brutality; the so-called Secondligiano war of 2004 resulted in over 100 deaths, and in 2006, a fight between prominent clans led to a dozen deaths in as many days. It's perhaps no coincidence that Campania has the highest murder rate in Italy by some way, and one of the highest in the world.

Some history

Organized crime in Naples is nothing new. The Camorra was at its height during the **nineteenth century**, until the Unification of Italy forced many of its members to flee to the US. The system then – and indeed right up until the 1980s – was mostly based on "*pizzo*" or the payment of protection money by businesses, and the illicit diversion of goods from Naples' port (even today less than half of the goods that come through the port of Naples pass through customs). The city centre was once the power base of the major families, and the main criminal activity was the black cigarette trade, which you could see on every street corner. This, however, has almost disappeared, and if there ever was an honourable tradition among Naples' thieves, it has pretty much evaporated.

The Camorra today

Estimates vary, but some reckon there are over 5000 *camorristi* living in Naples, divided between a hundred or so families, and their activities are so much part of life here that the network of organized criminal gangs is known collectively as *il sistema* or "the system". They have long been active in the poorer quarters of the

closer to being eradicated than it ever was. If anything, it's more powerful than ever, having developed into Italy's most notorious and vicious organized crime network, ahead even of Sicily's Cosa Nostra.

The well-publicized rubbish crisis of 2008 and Roberto Saviano's book and film **Gomorrah** (and his well-publicized exile from Naples), not to mention a fresh civic corruption scandal that emerged at the end of 2008, have only served city centre – Forcella, the Quartieri Spagnoli and La Sanità. But it's in the blighted **suburbs** mainly north of the city – Scampia, Secondigliano, Miano, Marigliano, and, further inland, around Caserta and Casal di Principe – that their newer power bases lie. With a third of the population officially unemployed, the local youth almost looks to the local *camorristi* as their careers advisors, and recent years have seen a rise in the Camorra's influence, and the bloodshed that goes with it. A handful of families lie at the centre of the network, and it's in these quarters that their presence is really felt. There's an unwelcoming air to these areas, and you'd be advised to stay away.

The Chinese too have begun to join forces with *il sistema*: most of Europe's vast Chinese imports enter Europe through the port of Naples, including a massive haul of illegal textiles which find their way into the garment business. Today the Camorra's main **commercial activities** are in high-quality designerwear, fake and otherwise; construction – they own the cement works and through contacts in local councils manage to land all the most lucrative contracts; drugs, which have brought the mob massive returns in recent years – Naples has Europe's highest ratio of drug dealers to inhabitants; arms dealing – Camorra clans supplied the Basque terrorist organization ETA at its height, and Serb irregulars during the Yugoslav wars of the 1990s; and, perhaps most notoriously, waste disposal: the city was in the grip of a rubbish crisis in the summer of 2008 which only now is beginning to get resolved. Most recently, there have been reports of the mob infiltrating the profitable bakery industry – worth €600 million a year across the province – by selling cut-price bread, baked in toxic ovens, from underground bakeries.

Ex-Prime Minister Romano Prodi threatened to send in troops to bring the mob to heel, and his inability to get to grips with the problem was to a large extent responsible for his downfall in 2007. Berlusconi has vowed to sort it out once and for all, sending 500 troops to Campania at the end of 2008, but so far has made little progress. Like most instances of racketeering in Italy, there's a widespread suspicion that the main Naples families have friends in very high places, but it's just possible that a determined national government with a clear mandate might be able to root out the key figures, as they have with the Cosa Nostra in Sicily – *if* they had local support. However, for the moment the Camorra march on regardless – still untouchable in a city that is naturally predisposed to mistrust the government, as well as too terrified of the potential consequences to revolt.

to emphasize the city's plight in recent years; where Naples goes from here is anybody's guess. The city is unique, certainly, but it can never join Europe's mainstream as long as the Camorra hold sway. For visitors, it's a vexed question: Naples could be so much better than it is: it has the location, the history, the culture, to compete with anywhere in Europe. But who, even amongst its inhabitants and fiercest critics, would want to change it?

Books and film

L isted below are a number of **books** on Naples and the Amalfi Coast region, and on Italy in general, that we think may enhance your trip; most should be readily available in bookshops or online (⦿www .amazon.com). We've added 🏃 to indicate books that make especially good reading; titles currently out of print are marked o/p.

See p.248 for our recommended **films**.

Travel and memoirs

Thekla Clark *Wystan and Chester.* Written with ease and affection, this memoir of the author's postwar friendship with W.H. Auden and partner Chester Kallman is extremely readable, and paints a vivid picture of Ischia, and in particular Forío, in the 1950s.

Shirley Hazzard and Francis Steegmuller *The Ancient Shore.* A slim collection of reflections on a lifetime of visits to Naples by this literary American couple. Some good old black and white photos help to illustrate a lyrical and nostalgic text.

🏃 **Dan Hofstadter** *Falling Palace.* Hofstadter's memoir of his time as a young man in Naples is a story of his love both for a local woman and also for the city, the peculiarities of which he documents with an intrepid and poetic fascination. One of the best and most revealing contemporary travelogues on the city in print.

🏃 **Norman Lewis** *Naples '44.* Lewis was among the first of the Allied troops to move into Naples following the Italian surrender in World War II, and this is his diary of his experiences there. Part travelogue, part journalism, this is without question one of the finest accounts available both on the region and the war in Italy.

H.V. Morton *A Traveller in Southern Italy.* This charming memoir, written by an intrepid traveller and Italophile, is worth a look for its evocative descriptions of Naples circa 1969, as well as fascinating background on sites such as Paestum and Cumae, and entertaining insights into the Neapolitan persona.

🏃 **Axel Munthe** *The Story of San Michele.* The oddly selective autobiography of a Swedish doctor to the rich and famous, documenting his discovery and conversion of the famous Anacápri villa he moved into in 1887 and the part he played in the Naples cholera epidemic of the 1880s. A great and very personal book, written with insight and humour.

Amanda Tabberer *My Amalfi Coast.* Above all, this is a sumptuous book of Amalfi Coast photographs, but it's also a guide and a memoir, with a personal perspective that really brings the region to life.

Robert Zweig *Return to Naples.* A recently published memoir of an American-Italian Jew who holidayed in Naples as a boy, and who returns to the city in middle age to dig up the truth about his family and the war. A personal history with lots of local colour.

History and current affairs

Luigi Barzini *The Italians* (o/p). Long out of print but worth getting hold of as it's still a highly readable and relevant work on the Italian nation.

Tom Behan *See Naples and Die.* The definitive and most up-to-date work on the Camorra until Saviano came along, and still well worth reading if you're after some really comprehensive history and background.

Alex Butterworth and Ray Laurence *Pompeii: the Living City.* A dramatic and successful re-creation of the last generation of Pompeii, imagined from actual sources by a historian and dramatist, and as such a marvellously readable social history of imperial-era Rome.

Christopher Duggan *The Force of Destiny.* This history of Italy since Unification exposes the flaws in the notion of a unified Italy, particularly with regard to the political crises of the last twenty years.

Jordan Lancaster *In the Shadow of Vesuvius.* Subtitled "a cultural history of Naples", this is a treat for anyone who wants to dig a little deeper, and is an accessible and revealing portrait of the city from the Greeks to the present day.

Valerio Lintner *A Traveller's History of Italy.* A brief history of the country, from the Etruscans right up to the present day. Well written and concise, and just the thing for the dilettante historian of the country.

Giuliano Procacci *History of the Italian People.* A comprehensive history of the peninsula, charting the development of Italy as a nation-state.

🏃 **Roberto Saviano** *Gomorrah.* Saviano's exposé of the Neapolitan Camorra is the first to have dished the dirt on the most violent grouping of Italy's various organized criminal gangs, and he is currently in hiding because of it. At its heart, the book is a passionate protest against a problem which only seems to get worse, and it has also been made into a highly regarded film (see p.248).

Food and wine

Carlo Capalbo *The Food and Wine Guide to Naples and Campania.* About as detailed a guide to the food, wine and produce of the region as anyone could ever want. Written with enthusiasm and authority, with details on producers, shops, restaurants and vineyards.

Marcella Hazan *The Classic Italian Cookbook.* A step-by-step guide that never compromises the spirit or authenticity of the recipes, Hazan draws her recipes from all over the peninsula, emphasizing the intrinsically regional nature of Italian food. The best Italian cookbook for novices.

Arturo Iengo *Cucina Napoletana.* A rare cookbook in English focusing on the food of Naples and Campania, and a great introduction to the recipes and ingredients of the region.

Various *The Silver Spoon.* The most successful cookbook sold in Italy, and now available in translation, this is the biggest collection of authentic Italian recipes anywhere.

Naples' golden age of cinema is generally considered to be the postwar **neorealist** years, its most celebrated exponent the director **Vittorio De Sica**, who put a comic spin on the traditionally gritty genre. His *L'Oro di Napoli* ("The Gold of Naples"; 1954) is an appealing tribute to a city De Sica knew well. The director turned his attention to Naples again in the comedy *Ieri, Oggi, Domani* ("Yesterday, Today, Tomorrow"; 1963), in which Sophia Loren plays a dealer in black-market cigarettes who uses pregnancy as a means to keep out of jail.

Also in a comic vein, the films of the actor **Totò** (1898–1967), born in La Sanità, are some of Italy's most loved. His favourite role was that of a hustler, getting by on nothing but his wits – which may explain his iconic status in Naples. Totò's modern-day successor in many ways, **Massimo Troisi**, was another gifted comic actor, known for his jittery, melancholic screen persona. His most famous movie, *Il Postino* (1994), set in Prócida, was sadly his last; he died just after completing filming, at the age of just 41.

Film has played a crucial role in Naples' much-heralded modern-day renaissance, with directors such as **Antonio Capuano**, **Pappi Corsicato** and **Paolo Sorrentino** focusing on the less salubrious aspects of Neapolitan life; in 2008, the international release of Roberto Saviano's bestselling book *Gomorrah*, directed by **Matteo Garrone**, put Naples firmly in the spotlight, marking a return to neorealism – but without the comedy plots of old to sweeten the pill.

Top ten films

Beat the Devil John Huston, 1953. An all-star cast star in this comedy-thriller shot on location in Ravello and Atrani. Great performances form Humphrey Bogart, Gina Lollobrigida and Robert Morley work wonders with its somewhat creaky plot (written, incidentally, on a daily basis while on set), and turn it into a truly atmospheric movie.

Gomorrah Matteo Garrone, 2008. Based on Roberto Saviano's ground-breaking bestseller (see p.247), this is as admirably candid and non-glamorous as the book. It portrays a Naples you're not likely to see on any visit – it's shot in the housing projects and wastelands north of the city and even uses locals as actors.

It Started in Naples Melville Shavelson, 1960. Clark Gable and local girl Sophia Loren star in this romantic comedy, which does indeed start in Naples but takes place mainly on Cápri. Well acted and fun, with great shots of Cápri especially.

The Life Aquatic Wes Anderson, 2004. This strangely deadpan and quirky comedy stars Bill Murray as a Cousteau-like underwater filmmaker having a midlife crisis against a backdrop of Naples and parts of the Amalfi Coast. Great shots of the theatre and main staircase of the Palazzo Reale, among other places.

Le Mani sulla Città Francesco Rosi, 1963. A political drama of corruption and property scams in Naples, starring Rod Steiger – perhaps the ultimate Naples movie. The opening in partricular has some impressive overhead shots of the city.

L'Oro di Napoli Vittorio de Sica, 1954. Local stars Sophia Loren and Totò star in this collection of six stories set in Naples, with memorable performances.

Il Postino Michael Radford, 1994. Procida's Chiaia beach, main waterfront and the post office were all used as locations in this life-enhancing movie about the friendship between the Chilean poet Pablo Neruda and a simple Italian postman.

Star Wars 1: the Phantom Menace George Lucas, 1999. The royal palace at Caserta is a ready-made, larger-than-life setting for Queen Amidala's palace on Naboo in this *Star Wars* prequel. It also doubled as the Vatican in *Mission Impossible III*.

The Talented Mr Ripley Anthony Minghella, 1999. Many of the Italian locations in this movie are in and around, most recognizably Naples' San Carlo opera house and the Castello Aragonese in Ischia.

Voyage to Italy Roberto Rossellini, 1954. An American couple travel to Naples for the first time and are pulled apart by the city's extremes. Lots of shots of Cápri, Pompeii and Naples itself.

Fiction

Luciano de Crescenzo *Thus Spake Bellavista* (o/p). One of the few books by this Naples-focused author to be translated into English, this is a marvellous exploration of all the things that make the city unique.

Michael Dibdin *Cosi Fan Tutti*. The late author's Aurelio Zen is a classically eccentric loner detective, and his novels take place in an array of Italian locations – this is his Naples yarn.

Norman Douglas *South Wind*. This gloriously camp and largely autobiographical classic, published in 1917, follows the fortunes of the expat crowd on a thinly disguised Cápri, where Douglas himself lived in exile following a prosecution for sexual molestation in the UK. An arch soap opera of disreputable sexual manners.

Neil Griffiths *Betrayal in Naples*. An assured debut novel, this tightly wrought thriller follows its hopelessly out-of-his-depth hero through a city swathed in a corruption he doesn't remotely understand. A convincing take on Naples and a great holiday read.

Robert Harris *Pompeii*. The days leading up to the eruption of Vesuvius and the destruction of Pompeii, Herculaneum and the surrounding area are skillfully recreated in Harris' dramatic novel. Told from the perspective of Pliny and a number of other characters, it does a good job of evoking the period in the Bay of Naples.

Patricia Highsmith *The Talented Mr Ripley*. This novel follows the fortunes of the eponymous hero through Italy, including Naples and Ischia, as he exchanges his own identity for that of the man he has murdered. Made into a stylish and evocative film in the 1990s.

John Horne Burns *The Gallery*. This novel captures brilliantly the devastation of Naples after the Allied liberation of 1944, telling the stories of a number of different characters in the wartime city whose lives converge in the bombed-out Galleria Umberto I. A mixture of fiction and reportage, it pulls no punches, but is beautifully written and stands as a classic of postwar fiction about the city, by a little-known American writer who died tragically young.

Language

Language

Italian

t's relatively easy to master some of the basics of **Italian**. Speaking at least a little of the language, however tentatively, can mark you out from the masses in a country used to hordes of tourists, and your efforts will be rewarded by smiles and genuine surprise. If you already have a smattering of French or Spanish, which are extremely similar to Italian grammatically, you should have no trouble in picking up the basics of Italian. *The Rough Guide to Italian* phrasebook can help set you on the right road.

Italian pronunciation

Pronunciation is straightforward: all Italian words are stressed on the penultimate syllable unless an accent (´ or `) denotes otherwise, and words are usually enunciated with exaggerated, open-mouthed clarity.

The only difficulties you're likely to encounter are the few consonants that are different from English:

c before e or i is pronounced as in church, while ch before the same vowels is hard, as in cat.

sci or sce are pronounced as in sheet and shelter respectively.

The same goes with g – soft before e or i, as in geranium; hard before h, as in garlic.

gn has the ni sound of onion.

gl in Italian is softened to something like li in English, as in stallion.

h is not aspirated, as in honour.

When **speaking** to strangers, the third person is the polite form (ie lei instead of tu for "you"). It's also worth remembering that Italians don't use "please" and "thank you" half as much as we do: it's all implied in the tone, though, if in doubt, err on the polite side.

Neapolitan dialect

Even fluent Italian speakers are taken aback when they arrive in Naples. Although everyone here speaks Italian, the local dialect sounds quite different to Italian. In fact, **Neapolitan** – *napoletano* in Italian, *nnapulitano* in dialect – was officially granted the status of minority language in 2008, and variations of it are spoken across much of the Italian South, particularly in Calabria and Sicily. Although similar to Italian in many ways, with its roots in Latin, it has been influenced by the fact that until the eighth century Naples was a Hellenistic city in which everyone spoke Greek; and of course by the South's numerous foreign colonists. When spoken, it sounds like a more guttural, slightly harsher version of Italian. If you see the language written down, you'll notice the predominance of the letters "u" and "j" in many words, and the doubling of consonants. The masculine and feminine definite articles are "o" and "a" rather than "il" and "la"; plurals are "e" for both genders rather than "i" and "le"; Naples is Napule in dialect, Napoli in Italian.

Words and phrases

Basics

good morning	buongiorno	I'm sorry	mi dispiace
good afternoon/ evening	buonasera	What's your name?	Come ti chiami/si chiama? (informal/ formal)
goodnight	buonanotte		
hello/goodbye	ciao (informal)	I'm here on holiday	Sono qui in vacanza
goodbye	arrivederci	I'm English/Irish/ Welsh/Scottish/ American	Sono inglese/irlandese gallese/scozzese Americano/a (m/f)
yes	si		
no	no		
please	per favore	Australian	Australiano/a (m/f)
thank you (very much)	(molte/mille) grázie	Canadian	Canadese
		a New Zealander	Neozelandese
you're welcome	prego	wait a minute!	aspetta!
all right/that's ok	va bene	let's go!	andiamo!
how are you?	come stai/sta? (informal/formal)	here/there	qui/là
		good/bad	buono/cattivo
I'm fine	bene	big/small	grande/píccolo
do you speak English?	parla Inglese?	cheap/expensive	economico/caro
		early/late	presto/tardi
I don't understand	non ho capito	hot/cold	caldo/freddo
I don't know	non lo so	near/far	vicino/lontano
excuse me	mi scusi	quickly/slowly	velocemente/ lentamente
excuse me (in a crowd)	permesso		

Questions

where?	dove?	why?	perché?
where is/are ...?	dov'è/dove sono ...?	is it/is there ...?	c'è ...?
when?	quando?	What time does it open/close?	A che ora apre/chiude?
what?	cosa?		
what is it?	cos'è?	What's it called in Italian?	Come si chiama in Italiano?
how much/many?	quanto/quanti?		

Travel and directions

Where is ...?	Dov'è ...?	hydrofoil	l'aliscafo
How do I get to ...?	Per arrivare a ...?	train	il treno
Turn left/right	giri a sinistra/destra	How long does it take?	Quanto ci vuole?
Go straight on	vai sempre diritto		
How far is it to ...?	Quant'è lontano a ...?	Can you tell me when to get off?	Mi può dire dove scendere?
What time does the ... arrive/ leave?	A che ora arriva/ parte ...?		
		I'd like a ticket to ...	Vorrei un biglietto per ...
bus	l'autobus	one-way	solo andata
ferry	il traghetto	return	andata e ritorno

Signs

entrance/exit	entrata/uscita	closed for restoration	chiuso per restauro
arrivals/departures	arrivi/partenze		
free entrance	ingresso líbero	closed for holidays	chiuso per ferie
gentlemen/ladies	signori/signore	pull/push	tirare/spingere
wc	gabinetto/bagno	cash desk	cassa
vacant/engaged	libero/occupato	out of order	guasto
no smoking	vietato fumare	ring the bell	suonare il campanello
open/closed	aperto/chiuso		

Restaurants

I'd like to reserve a table (for two)	Vorrei riservare una tavola (per due)	It's good	È buono
		The bill, please	Il conto, per favore
Can we sit outside?	Possiamo sederci fuori?	Is service included?	Il servizio è incluso?
		(set) menu	menù (fisso)
Can I order?	Posso ordinare?	waiter/waitress	cameriere/a
I'm a vegetarian	Sono vegetariano/a (m/f)	knife	coltello
		fork	forchetta
Does it contain meat?	C'è carne dentro?	spoon	cucchiaio
		plate	piatto

Shopping and services

I'd like to buy ...	Vorrei comprare ...	bank	banca
How much does it cost/do they cost?	Quanto costa/cóstano?	money exchange	cambio
		post office	posta
It's too expensive	È troppo caro	tourist office	ufficio di turismo
with/without	con/senza	shop	negozio
more/less	più/meno	supermarket	supermercato
enough, no more	basta	market	mercato
I'll take it	Lo/la prendo (m/f)	ATM	Bancomat
Do you take credit cards?	Accettate carte di credito?		

Days, times and months

What time is it?	Che ore sono?	Monday	Lunedì
It's (four) o'clock	Sono (le quattro)	Tuesday	Martedì
today	oggi	Wednesday	Mercoledì
tomorrow	domani	Thursday	Giovedì
day after tomorrow	dopodomani	Friday	Venerdì
yesterday	ieri	Saturday	Sabato
now	adesso	Sunday	Domenica
later	più tardi	January	Gennaio
in the morning	di mattina	February	Febbraio
in the afternoon	nel pomeriggio	March	Marzo
in the evening	di sera	April	Aprile

255

May	Maggio	September	Settembre
June	Giugno	October	Ottobre
July	Luglio	November	Novembre
August	Agosto	December	Dicembre

Numbers

1	uno	19	diciannove
2	due	20	venti, vinte
3	tre	21	ventuno
4	quattro	22	ventidue
5	cinque	30	trenta
6	sei	40	quaranta
7	sette	50	cinquanta
8	otto	60	sessanta
9	nove	70	settanta
10	dieci	80	ottanta
11	undici	90	novanta
12	dodici	100	cento
13	tredici	101	centuno
14	quattordici	110	centodieci
15	quindici	200	duecento
16	sedici	500	cinquecento
17	diciassette	1000	mille
18	diciotto	5000	cinquemila

Italian menu reader

Basics and snacks

aceto	vinegar	olive	olives
aglio	garlic	pane	bread
biscotti	biscuits	pepe	pepper
burro	butter	riso	rice
caramelle	sweets	sale	salt
cioccolato	chocolate	uova	eggs
formaggio	cheese	yogurt	yoghurt
frittata	omelette	zucchero	sugar
marmellata	jam	zuppa	soup
olio	oil		

Pasta

bucatini	thick, hollow spaghetti-type pasta common in Rome and Lazio	cannelloni	thick pasta tubes usually filled with veal
		capellini	thin noodles of pasta, thicker than *capelli d'angeli*

conchiglie	seashell-shaped pasta shapes, good for capturing thick sauces
farfalle	literally "butterflies", or bow ties
fettuccine	flat, ribbon-like egg noodles
fusilli	tight spirals of pasta
gnocchi	potato and pasta dumplings, often served "*alla sorrentina*", or with tomato and basil sauce
lasagne	big squares of egg noodles, most commonly baked in the oven with white sauce and beef *ragù*
linguini	thin, flat noodles, often served with seafood
macaroni	small tubes of pasta
maltagliati	flat triangles of pasta, often used in soup
orecchiette	small ear-shaped pieces of pasta
paccheri	large tubes of pasta, common in the Naples region
pappardelle	thick flat egg noodles
pasta al forno	baked pasta, usually with minced meat, tomato and cheese
pasta e fagioli	soup with pasta and beans
penne	the most common tubes of pasta
ravioli	flat, square parcels of filled pasta
rigatoni	large, curved and ridged tubes of pasta – larger than *penne* but smaller than *paccheri*
scialetelli	thick, twisted ribbons of spaghetti-like pasta, common in southern Italy

spaghetti	the most common pasta shape of all – long, thin, non-egg noodles
strozzapreti	twisted pasta tubes – literally "priest-stranglers"
tagliatelle	flat ribbon egg noodles, slightly thinner than *fettuccine*
tonnarelli	another name for *bucatini*
tortellini/tortolloni	small and big rectangular parcels of filled pasta
tortiglioni	narrow *rigatoni*

Pasta sauce (salsa)

amatriciana	cubed bacon and tomato
arrabbiata	("angry") spicy tomato with chillies
bolognese	meat
burro	butter
carbonara	cream, ham and beaten egg
funghi	mushroom
genovese	chunks of slow-cooked meat and onions
panna	cream
parmigiano	parmesan cheese
peperoncino	olive oil, garlic and fresh chillies
pesto	ground basil, garlic and pine nuts
pomodoro	tomato
puttanesca	("whorish") tomato, anchovy, olive oil and oregano
ragù	meat
vongole	clams

Meat (carne)

agnello	lamb
bistecca	steak
carpaccio	slices of raw beef
cervello	brain, usually calves'
cinghiale	wild boar

coniglio	rabbit	aragosta	lobster
costolette	cutlet, chop	baccalà	dried salted cod
fegato	liver	calamari	squid
maiale	pork	cefalo	grey mullet
manzo	beef	cozze	mussels
ossobuco	shin of veal	dentice	sea bream
pancetta	bacon	gamberetti	shrimps
pollo	chicken	gamberi	prawns
polpette	meatballs	granchio	crab
rognoni	kidneys	merluzzo	cod
salsiccia	sausage	ostriche	oysters
saltimbocca	veal with ham	pesce spada	swordfish
spezzatino	stew	polpo	octopus
trippa	tripe	rospo	monkfish
vitello	veal	sampiero	john dory
		sarde	sardines

Fish (pesce) and shellfish (crostacei)

		sogliola	sole
		tonno	tuna
acciughe	anchovies	trota	trout
anguilla	eel	vongole	clams

Vegetables (contorni) and salad (insalata)

asparagi	asparagus	insalata verde/mista	green salad/ mixed salad
carciofi	artichokes	lenticchie	lentils
carciofini	artichoke hearts	melanzane	aubergine
cavolfiori	cauliflower	patate	potatoes
cavolo	cabbage	peperoni	peppers
cipolla	onion	piselli	peas
erbe aromatiche	herbs	pomodori	tomatoes
fagioli	beans	radicchio	red salad leaves
fagiolini	green beans	spinaci	spinach
finocchio	fennel		
funghi	mushrooms		

Cooking terms

al dente	firm, not overcooked	ben cotto	well done
al ferri	grilled without oil	bollito/lesso	boiled
al forno	baked	cotto	cooked
al sangue	rare	crudo	raw
alla brace	barbecued	fritto	fried
alla griglia	grilled	in umido	stewed
alla milanese	fried in egg and breadcrumbs	pizzaiola	cooked with tomato sauce
allo spiedo	on the spit	ripieno	stuffed
arrosto	roast	stracotto	braised, stewed

Cheese (formaggio)

burrata	soft, fresh cheese made from mozzarella and cream	pecorino	strong, hard sheep's cheese
dolcelatte	creamy blue cheese	provola/provolone	smooth, round mild cheese, made from buffalo or sheep's milk; sometimes smoked
fontina	northern italian cheese, often used in cooking		
gorgonzola	soft, strong, blue-veined cheese	ricotta	soft, white sheep's cheese
mozzarella	soft white cheese, traditionally made from buffalo's milk		

Desserts (dolci), fruit (frutta) and nuts (noci)

amaretti	macaroons	macedonia	fruit salad
ananas	pineapple	mandorle	almonds
anguria/coccomero	watermelon	mele	apples
arachidi	peanuts	melone	melon
arance	oranges	pere	pears
banane	bananas	pesche	peaches
cacchi	persimmons	pinoli	pine nuts
ciliegie	cherries	pistacchio	pistachio nut
crostata	pastry tart with jam or chocolate topping	sorbetto	sorbet
		torta	cake, tart
fichi	figs	uva	grapes
fichi d'india	prickly pears	zabaglione	dessert made with eggs, sugar and marsala wine
frágole	strawberries		
gelato	ice cream		
limone	lemon	zuppa inglese	trifle

Drinks

acqua minerale	mineral water	succo	concentrated fruit juice with sugar
aranciata	orangeade		
bicchiere	glass	tè	tea
birra	beer	tonica	tonic water
bottiglia	bottle	vino	wine
caffè	coffee	rosso	red
caraffa	carafe	bianco	white
cioccolato caldo	hot chocolate	rosato	rosé
ghiaccio	ice	secco	dry
granita	iced drink with coffee or fruit	dolce	sweet
		litro	litre
latte	milk	mezzo	half
limonata	lemonade	quarto	quarter
spremuta	fresh fruit juice	salute!	cheers!
spumante	sparkling wine		

Glossary of artistic and architectural terms

agora square or marketplace in an ancient Greek city

ambo a kind of simple pulpit, popular in italian medieval churches

apse semicircular recess at the altar (usually eastern) end of a church

architrave the lowest part of the entablature

atrium inner courtyard

baldachino a canopy on columns, usually placed over the altar in a church

basilica originally a Roman administrative building, adapted for early churches; distinguished by lack of transepts

belvedere a terrace or lookout point

caldarium the steam room of a Roman bath

campanile belltower, sometimes detached, usually of a church

capital top of a column

cella sanctuary of a temple

chancel part of a church containing the altar

chiaroscuro the balance of light and shade in a painting, and the skill of the artist in depicting the contrast between the two

ciborium another word for baldachino, see above

cipollino an Italian marble with alternating white and green streaks

cornice the top section of a classical facade

cortile galleried courtyard or cloisters

cosmati work decorative mosaic work on marble, usually highly coloured, found in early Christian Italian churches, especially in Rome; derives from the name Cosma, a common name among families of marble workers at the time

cryptoporticus underground passageway

Decumanus Superior the main street of a Roman town – the second cross-street was known as the Decumanus Inferior

entablature the section above the capital on a classical building, below the cornice

ex voto artefact designed in thanksgiving to a saint

fresco wall-painting technique in which the artist applies paint to wet plaster for a more permanent finish

lararium a shrine for holding the *lares* (images of the household gods) and similar relics in the houses of ancient Rome

loggia roofed gallery or balcony

metope a panel on the frieze of a Greek temple

Mithraism pre-Christian cult associated with the Persian god of light, who slew a bull and fertilized the world with its blood

nave central space in a church, usually flanked by aisles

palestra a public place in ancient Greece or Rome devoted to the training of wrestlers and other athletes

pantocrator usually refers to an image of christ, portrayed with outstretched arms

peristyle a colonnade enclosing a court or building

piano nobile main floor of a *palazzo*, usually the first

polyptych painting on several joined wooden panels

portico covered entrance to a building, or porch

presepio/presepe Christmas crib

putti cherubs

reliquary receptacle for a saint's relics, usually bones; often highly decorated

sgraffito decorative technique whereby one layer of plaster is scratched to form a pattern

stucco plaster made from water, lime, sand and powdered marble, used for decorative work

thermae baths, usually elaborate buildings in Roman villas

triptych painting on three joined wooden panels

trompe l'oeil work of art that deceives the viewer by means of tricks with perspective

Small print and
Index

A Rough Guide to Rough Guides

Published in 1982, the first Rough Guide – to Greece – was a student scheme that became a publishing phenomenon. Mark Ellingham, a recent graduate in English from Bristol University, had been travelling in Greece the previous summer and couldn't find the right guidebook. With a small group of friends he wrote his own guide, combining a highly contemporary, journalistic style with a thoroughly practical approach to travellers' needs.

The immediate success of the book spawned a series that rapidly covered dozens of destinations. And, in addition to impecunious backpackers, Rough Guides soon acquired a much broader and older readership that relished the guides' wit and inquisitiveness as much as their enthusiastic, critical approach and value-for-money ethos.

These days, Rough Guides include recommendations from shoestring to luxury and cover more than 200 destinations around the globe, including almost every country in the Americas and Europe, more than half of Africa and most of Asia and Australasia. Our ever-growing team of authors and photographers is spread all over the world, particularly in Europe, the USA and Australia.

In the early 1990s, Rough Guides branched out of travel, with the publication of Rough Guides to World Music, Classical Music and the Internet. All three have become benchmark titles in their fields, spearheading the publication of a wide range of books under the Rough Guide name.

Including the travel series, Rough Guides now number more than 350 titles, covering: phrasebooks, waterproof maps, music guides from Opera to Heavy Metal, reference works as diverse as Conspiracy Theories and Shakespeare, and popular culture books from iPods to Poker. Rough Guides also produce a series of more than 120 World Music CDs in partnership with World Music Network.

Visit www.roughguides.com to see our latest publications.

Rough Guide travel images are available for commercial licensing at www.roughguidespictures.com

Rough Guide credits

Text editor: Natasha Foges & Ruth Blackmore
Layout: Umesh Aggarwal
Cartography: Katie Lloyd-Jones, Miles Irving, Karobi Gogoi & Rajesh Chhibber
Picture editor: Scott Stickland
Production: Rebecca Short
Proofreader: Amanda Jones
Cover design: Chloë Roberts
Photographer: Karen Trist
Editorial: Andy Turner, Keith Drew, Edward Aves, Alice Park, Lucy White, Jo Kirby, James Smart, Róisín Cameron, Emma Traynor, Emma Gibbs, Kathryn Lane, Christina Valhouli, Monica Woods, Mani Ramaswamy, Harry Wilson, Lucy Cowie, Helen Ochyra, Alison Roberts, Joe Staines, Peter Buckley, Matthew Milton, Tracy Hopkins, Ruth Tidball; **Delhi** Madhavi Singh, Karen D'Souza, Lubna Shaheen
Design & Pictures: **London** Dan May, Diana Jarvis, Mark Thomas, Nicole Newman, Sarah Cummins, Emily Taylor; **Delhi** Ajay Verma, Jessica Subramanian, Ankur Guha, Pradeep Thapliyal, Sachin Tanwar, Anita Singh, Nikhil Agarwal
Production: Vicky Baldwin

Cartography: **London** Maxine Repath, Ed Wright; **Delhi** Ashutosh Bharti, Rajesh Mishra, Animesh Pathak, Jasbir Sandhu, Alakananda Bhattacharya, Swati Handoo, Deshpal Dabas
Online: **London** George Atwell, Faye Hellon, Jeanette Angell, Fergus Day, Justine Bright, Clare Bryson, Aine Fearon, Adrian Low, Ezgi Celebi, Amber Bloomfield; **Delhi** Amit Verma, Rahul Kumar, Narender Kumar, Ravi Yadav, Debojit Borah, Rakesh Kumar, Ganesh Sharma, Shisir Basumatari
Marketing & Publicity: **London** Liz Statham, Niki Hanmer, Louise Maher, Jess Carter, Vanessa Godden, Vivienne Watton, Anna Paynton, Rachel Sprackett, Libby Jellie, Laura Vipond, Vanessa McDonald; **New York** Katy Ball, Judi Powers, Nancy Lambert; **Delhi** Ragini Govind
Manager India: Punita Singh
Reference Director: Andrew Lockett
Operations Manager: Helen Phillips
PA to Publishing Director: Nicola Henderson
Publishing Director: Martin Dunford
Commercial Manager: Gino Magnotta
Managing Director: John Duhigg

Publishing information

This first edition published May 2009 by
Rough Guides Ltd,
80 Strand, London WC2R 0RL
14 Local Shopping Centre, Panchsheel Park, New Delhi 110017, India
Distributed by the Penguin Group
Penguin Books Ltd,
80 Strand, London WC2R 0RL
Penguin Group (USA)
375 Hudson Street, NY 10014, USA
Penguin Group (Australia)
250 Camberwell Road, Camberwell, Victoria 3124, Australia
Penguin Group (Canada)
195 Harry Walker Parkway N, Newmarket, ON, L3Y 7B3 Canada
Penguin Group (NZ)
67 Apollo Drive, Mairangi Bay, Auckland 1310, New Zealand
Cover concept by Peter Dyer.

Typeset in Bembo and Helvetica to an original design by Henry Iles.
Printed in Italy by L.E.G.O. S.p.A, Lavis (TN)
© Martin Dunford, 2009
No part of this book may be reproduced in any form without permission from the publisher except for the quotation of brief passages in reviews.
272pp includes index
A catalogue record for this book is available from the British Library
ISBN: 978-1-84353-714-4
The publishers and authors have done their best to ensure the accuracy and currency of all the information in **The Rough Guide to Naples & the Amalfi Coast**, however, they can accept no responsibility for any loss, injury, or inconvenience sustained by any traveller as a result of information or advice contained in the guide.

1 3 5 7 9 8 6 4 2

Help us update

We've gone to a lot of effort to ensure that the first edition of **The Rough Guide to Naples & the Amalfi Coast** is accurate and up-to-date. However, things change – places get "discovered", opening hours are notoriously fickle, restaurants and rooms raise prices or lower standards. If you feel we've got it wrong or left something out, we'd like to know, and if you can remember the address, the price, the hours, the phone number, so much the better.

Please send your comments with the subject line "**Rough Guide Naples & the Amalfi Coast Update**" to ®mail@roughguides.com. We'll credit all contributions and send a copy of the next edition (or any other Rough Guide if you prefer) for the very best emails.

Have your questions answered and tell others about your trip at ®community.roughguides.com

Acknowledgements

Martin would like to thank: Natasha for her patience, calm editing and inspired interventions, which made the book much better than it would have otherwise been; Katie Lloyd-Jones for some great last-minute maps; Katie and Jeffrey for outstanding contributions; and most of all Caroline, Daisy and Lucy for input on the road as well as putting up with my absences and late nights and early mornings. **Katie** thanks Fiorella Squillante. **Jeffrey** would like to thank Jean-François Martin, the Cefalo Family, the Colella Family, Alfonso della Ratta, the Mustilli Family, Dott. Giuseppe Affaitati, Dott. Francesco Melisi, Christine Salerno, Laura Mori, Principe Giovanni del Drago, Conte Adriano Matarazzo, Terri Howell, Clare Merlo, Kate McBride, Lee O'Hara, Susanna Carpenter, Margaret Hunting, Stephen Jones, Roseanne Ullman, Helen Davis, Phyllis Butler, Debbie Jarvis, the Golding Family, Anna Torsoli, Hanja Kochansky, Virginia Case and the Igliori Family. Thanks also to Angelo Caratunti of Circumvesuviana.

SMALL PRINT

Photo credits

All photos © Rough Guides except the following:

Title page
Largo del Corpo di Nilo statue, Naples © Mario Matassa/Alamy

Things not to miss
02 Cable car to summit of Monte Faito © Brenda Kean/Alamy
03 Museo di Capodimonte, Naples © CuboImages srl/Alamy
06 Making pizza, Naples © Vittorio Sciosia /Alamy
11 Walkers on the crater of Mount Vesuvius © Stan Kujawa/Alamy
13 The Solfatara © CuboImages srl/Alamy
14 Amalfi © Fuste Raga/PhotoLibrary
15 Head of the veiled Christ, Cappella Sansevero, Naples © Mimmo Jodice/Corbis

Cucina napoletana colour section
Preparation of pizza *marinara*, Naples © CuboImages srl/Alamy
Scamorza cheese on a market stall © Ian Stuart/Alamy
Scarola greens © CuboImages srl/Alamy
Spaghetti *alle vongole* © Bon Appetit/Alamy
Pizza *marinara*, Naples © CuboImages srl/Alamy
Mushroom *arancini* © Rawdon Wyatt/Alamy
Cakes and pastries in Spaccanapoli, Naples © Peter Forsberg/Alamy
Sfogliatelle © Conde Nast Archive/Corbis

Theatrical Naples colour section
Illustration of Pulcinella from the book *Masks and Clowns* © Imagno/Getty Images
Pulcinella on the stage, Teatro Mercadante © courtesy of the Teatro Mercadante
Teatro Mercadante, Naples © courtesy of the Teatro Mercadante
Score cover of *Canta Napoli*, a collection of Neapolitan songs. Illustration by Gino Boccasile © Lebrecht Music & Arts
Tarantella dancers in traditional costume © Lebrecht Music & Arts
The tarantella © Mary Evans Picture Library/Alamy

Black and whites
p.144 The Temple of Ceres, Paestum © Richard Broadwell/Alamy
p.170 Giardino della Minerva, Salerno © Platinum Gpics/Alamy
p.192 Restaurant in Anacápri © Atlantide Phototravel/Corbis
p.217 Good Friday procession to the Terra Murata, Prócida © CuboImages srl/Alamy
p.227 Remains of the amphitheatre at Santa Maria Cápua Vétere © Adam Eastland/Alamy

Index

Map entries are in colour.

I

N
D
E
X

O

Map symbols

maps are listed in the full index using coloured text

– – –	Chapter boundary	ⵟ	Lighthouse
	Motorway	⌂	Campground
	Major road	◉	Accommodation
	Minor road	⊠	Gate/entrance
	Steps	ⓘ	Tourist office
	Pedestrianized street	⊠	Post office
- - - -	Path	@	Internet access
— —	Ferry route	★	Transport stop
	Railway	✈	Airport
—Ⓜ—	Metro line	🅿	Parking
	Funicular	⊞	Hospital
•----•	Chair lift	⊙	Statue
	Waterway	⸸	Church (regional maps)
	Wall		Church (town maps)
✦	Point of interest		Building
▲	Mountain peak		Cemetery
⌂	Cave		Park
▮	Tower		Beach
⭭	Viewpoint		

We're covered. Are you?